Davenport Sampson

1866: Salem City Directory

Davenport Sampson

1866: Salem City Directory

ISBN/EAN: 9783743624252

Printed in Europe, USA, Canada, Australia, Japan

Cover: Foto ©Andreas Hilbeck / pixelio.de

Manufactured and distributed by brebook publishing software (www.brebook.com)

Davenport Sampson

1866: Salem City Directory

THE

SALEM DIRECTORY,

1866,

CONTAINING THE

CITY RECORD,

THE

NAMES OF THE CITIZENS,

AND

A BUSINESS DIRECTORY,

WITH OTHER USEFUL INFORMATION.

By SAMPSON, DAVENPORT, & CO.,

(FORMERLY ADAMS, SAMPSON, & CO.)

PUBLISHERS OF THE BOSTON DIRECTORY, MASSACHUSETTS REGISTER, NEW ENGLAND BUSINESS DIRECTORY, NEW YORK STATE BUSINESS DIRECTORY, ETC.

OFFICE, 47 CONGRESS STREET, BOSTON.

—————

SALEM:

GEO. M. WHIPPLE & A. A. SMITH, No. 243 ESSEX STREET.

PRICE, ONE DOLLAR.

—————

DAKIN AND METCALF, PRINTERS, CAMBRIDGE.

Beside the main topic, this book also treats of

CHANGES IN THE SALEM DIRECTORY.

Names in Directory of 1864, ... 6,796
Names erased in preparing Directory of 1866, ... 1,484

5,312
Names added in preparing Directory of 1866, . . . 1,874
Names in Directory of 1866, ... 7,186

CENSUS OF SALEM.

WARD.	Churches.	School-houses.	Houses.	Families.	Ratable Polls.	Legal Voters.	Naturalized Voters.	1865. Inhabitants.	1860. Inhabitants.
				1865.					
1,	4	5	542	912	942	579	103	3,988	4,339
2,	6	4	581	861	969	876	56	3,753	3,777
3,	5	8	514	750	796	580	84	3,252	3,645
4,	5	4	570	811	629	582	79	3,680	4,102
5,	1	2	454	727	892	430	144	3,655	3,529
6,	0	3	413	632	725	454	83	2,869	2,872
	21	21	3,074	4,703	5,153	3,501	549	21,197	22,252

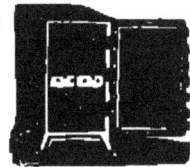

1866 ‖ ALMANAC. ‖ 1866

JANUARY.

Su	Mo	Tu	W	Th	Fr	Sa
–	1	2	3	4	5	6
7	8	9	10	11	12	13
14	15	16	17	18	19	20
21	22	23	24	25	26	27
28	29	30	31	–	–	–
–	–	–	–	–	–	–

FEBRUARY.

Su	Mo	Tu	W	Th	Fr	Sa
–	–	–	–	1	2	3
4	5	6	7	8	9	10
11	12	13	14	15	16	17
18	19	20	21	22	23	24
25	26	27	28	–	–	–
–	–	–	–	–	–	–

MARCH.

Su	Mo	Tu	W	Th	Fr	Sa
–	–	–	–	1	2	3
4	5	6	7	8	9	10
11	12	13	14	15	16	17
18	19	20	21	22	23	24
25	26	27	28	29	30	31
–	–	–	–	–	–	–

APRIL.

Su	Mo	Tu	W	Th	Fr	Sa
1	2	3	4	5	6	7
8	9	10	11	12	13	14
15	16	17	18	19	20	21
22	23	24	25	26	27	28
29	30	–	–	–	–	–
–	–	–	–	–	–	–

MAY.

Su	Mo	Tu	W	Th	Fr	Sa
–	–	1	2	3	4	5
6	7	8	9	10	11	12
13	14	15	16	17	18	19
20	21	22	23	24	25	26
27	28	29	30	31	–	–
–	–	–	–	–	–	–

JUNE.

Su	Mo	Tu	W	Th	Fr	Sa
–	–	–	–	–	1	2
3	4	5	6	7	8	9
10	11	12	13	14	15	16
17	18	19	20	21	22	23
24	25	26	27	28	29	30
–	–	–	–	–	–	–

JULY.

Su	Mo	Tu	W	Th	Fr	Sa
1	2	3	4	5	6	7
8	9	10	11	12	13	14
15	16	17	18	19	20	21
22	23	24	25	26	27	28
29	30	31	–	–	–	–
–	–	–	–	–	–	–

AUGUST.

Su	Mo	Tu	W	Th	Fr	Sa
–	–	–	1	2	3	4
5	6	7	8	9	10	11
12	13	14	15	16	17	18
19	20	21	22	23	24	25
26	27	28	29	30	31	–
–	–	–	–	–	–	–

SEPTEMBER.

Su	Mo	Tu	W	Th	Fr	Sa
–	–	–	–	–	–	1
2	3	4	5	6	7	8
9	10	11	12	13	14	15
16	17	18	19	20	21	22
23	24	25	26	27	28	29
30	–	–	–	–	–	–

OCTOBER.

Su	Mo	Tu	W	Th	Fr	Sa
–	1	2	3	4	5	6
7	8	9	10	11	12	13
14	15	16	17	18	19	20
21	22	23	24	25	26	27
28	29	30	31	–	–	–
–	–	–	–	–	–	–

NOVEMBER.

Su	Mo	Tu	W	Th	Fr	Sa
–	–	–	–	1	2	3
4	5	6	7	8	9	10
11	12	13	14	15	16	17
18	19	20	21	22	23	24
25	26	27	28	29	30	–
–	–	–	–	–	–	–

DECEMBER.

Su	Mo	Tu	W	Th	Fr	Sa
–	–	–	–	–	–	1
2	3	4	5	6	7	8
9	10	11	12	13	14	15
16	17	18	19	20	21	22
23	24	25	26	27	28	29
30	31	–	–	–	–	–

SYMPTOMS OF CATARRH

BY

A. P. LIGHTHILL, M.D.

The first sensation is usually a feeling of dryness and heat in the nose, and a frequent inclination to sneezing. There is an inability to breathe freely, as the nose becomes stopped up, sometimes on one side, sometimes on the other.

Soon a clear, watery, acrid discharge makes its appearance, excoriating the nostrils and edges of the lips, which become red and somewhat swollen. After a few days, the discharge becomes thick, yellowish, extremely frequent, and continues to be a marked feature of the disease, and a source of much danger and the greatest annoyance. After more or less time, it becomes purulent, highly offensive, and assumes an extremely fetid odor. It is usually so profuse as to require, when confined to the nose, the frequent application of the handkerchief; or, if it drops into the throat, which is more particularly the case while the body is in a horizontal position, constant expectoration, and sometimes both.

Sleep is frequently disturbed by a sensation of choking, caused by the presence of the discharge in the throat. Owing to the heat in the head, the watery portion of the discharge often evaporates, and, assuming a condition of solidity, is deposited upon the membrane of the nose and upper part of the throat in the shape of crusts or hardened lumps. The accumulation of these incrustations produces a feeling of discomfort, and narrows the nasal passages so as to embarrass respiration. Therefore frequent efforts have to be made to remove them, either by forcibly blowing the nose, or by persistent hawking, a practice as disagreeable to the one affected as it is to those around him. After the removal, that side of the incrustation which adhered to the mucous membrane will sometimes be found bloody, a fact which explains the force required for its dislodgement. During sleep these incrustations accumulate more rapidly, and the feeling is therefore most uncomfortable in the morning. Sometimes, all efforts to clear the throat are futile until after breakfast, or after something warm is swallowed. Some patients state that they are not successful until they have swallowed some whiskey or brandy. The discharge, which is at first without smell, assumes in the progress of the complaint an excessively fetid odor; the breath participates in this, and becomes occasionally so revoltingly offensive as to render the patient an object of disgust to himself as well as to others. Ulceration of the mucous membrane of the nose takes place frequently, sometimes even attacking the bones, when small particles of that substance will occasionally be found mixed with the discharge. The accumulation of the discharge, together with the thickened condition of the mucous membrane, renders respiration through the nasal passages very difficult, and oftentimes impossible, necessitating respiration principally through the mouth, a method very deleterious to the general health, but more particularly so to the lungs, as will be shown hereafter. The unpleasant noise produced during sleep, known as snoring, originates from the same cause. The voice loses its musical quality, and assumes a discordant, harsh, and nasal character; the sense of smell becomes much impaired or entirely lost, and the same effect, though less frequent, is produced on the sense of taste. Occasionally, while blowing the nose, a crackling or babbling sound will be heard in the ear, and hearing will be found thick and stopped up, but returns suddenly with something like a snapping sound. This phenomenon is usually repeated until at one time hearing does not return, and remains permanently injured. Noises in the head, of every conceivable description, will make their appearance, and add to the distress of the sufferer, and hearing may be lost so gradually that a considerable degree of deafness may exist before the person is really aware of the fact. The eyes are apt to become weak, irritable, and disposed to water on exposure to cold and wind, or after the slightest exertion. A pain, more or less acute, or a distressing feeling of pressure, is experienced over the eyes, and sometimes on the top or back of the head, and also pain in the face, closely resembling neuralgia, for which it is very often mistaken. The distress in the head weakens the memory, and produces irritability and moroseness of disposition. The stomach generally suffers more or less, is weak and irritable; the appetite is capricious, and is nearly always bad in the morning. In severe cases the system becomes feeble and prostrated, and there is an aversion or inability to either physical or mental exertion. Not unfrequently Catarrh proves fatal, either by debilitating the system and wearing out the patient, or by travelling downward and producing throat affection, bronchitis, and, finally, CONSUMPTION. It may be safely asserted, that, after hereditary predisposition, Catarrh is the most frequent and important cause of this fatal complaint.

The symptoms of Catarrh vary considerably in different individuals, and the degree of their severity depends upon constitutional idiosyncrasies and various external influences. With some the complaint continues for a number of years in a mild form and without causing any of the injurious results above described, while with others all the worst effects are produced in a very short space of time, and cases, apparently most harmless, may, through imprudent exposure, additional cold, or unfavorable changes of weather, suddenly exhibit all the violence and malignity which characterizes the severest ones.

With certain individuals the disease assumes periodicity, attacking them regularly each year at certain seasons, as in the early part of spring, when the roses are in bloom, and hence the name, Rose Catarrh; or in midsummer, during haying time, when it is known as Hay Catarrh. Some can tell the exact day, and even the hour, of attack. They usually claim to be entirely relieved of the difficulty in the intervals; but we have reason to suppose that symptoms of the complaint are constantly present in some mild form or other, which are roused into activity by the odor peculiar to roses or new mown hay, with which the atmosphere is impregnated during the seasons just mentioned. The comparative quiet enjoyed in the intervals no doubt leads to the belief that the complaint has ceased entirely.

DR. LIGHTHILL treats Catarrh, Deafness, &c., and Diseases of the Eye, Ear, Throat, and Nose, at No. 20 Boylston Street, Boston, between the hours of 9, A.M., and 3, P.M.

ALPHABETICAL INDEX OF ADVERTISERS.

WE take pleasure in referring all who consult the Directory, to the following names of our most prominent and enterprising business people. Every class of business is represented by them, and we predict that they will be prepared at all times to serve those who may favor them with their patronage, in the most satisfactory manner.

The figures opposite the names refer to the page in the Advertising Department on which their business card may be found.

Foley Edward, painter . . 51
Follette L. B. hoop skirts . . . 10
Foote & Horton, printers . . 58
Foster Isaac P. grocer . . 84
Foster & Roby, copper and brass work and ship fastenings . 64
Fowler Geo. & Co. slaters . . 58
Fuller Enoch P. carpenter . 46
Gayle & Co. com. merchants . 22
Goldthwaite Willard, carpets . 11
Goodhue Wm. P. ship chandlery 25
Goss F. P. plumber . . . 19
Grant J. C. pattern maker . 42
Grant Joshua B. curriers' tools . 35
Griffin James & Co. plasterers' hair 60
Griswold B. L. sewing machines [front cover
Gwinn Thomas W. West India goods 28
Hale Henry, hardware . . 4
Hamond Wm. C. carpenter . 52
Hanson Lizzie Mrs. music teacher 8
Hart Wm. H. plumber . . 53
Hartigan Patrick, horseshoer . 48
Hatch L. B. coal, &c. . . 54
Hobard B. F. combination oil . 68
Helms H. billiard table . . 64
Henderson & Thurston, furniture 38
Henderson & Co., boot and shoe stock 18
Henderson D. painter . . 51
Henderson Wm. C. paper boxes 18
Hodgkins Geo. L. grocer . . 33
Holbrook J. oysters . . . 29
Holbrook J. M. Miss, milliner . 9
Holyoke Mut. Fire Ins. Co. . 208
Howard Charles D. printer . 235
Howe & Stevens, family dye colors [front colored
Hubon H. G. undertaker . . 40
Hunt, Lyon, & Co. belting, back col'd
Institution for the Blind, bedding, mattresses, &c. . . 62
John Hancock Mut. Life Ins. Co. 62
Jones J. S. & Co. com. merchants 22
Jewett D. H. lumber, &c. . . 64
Kimball Geo. printer . . 55
Langmald J. P. lumber . . 52
Lations Jonathan P. painter . 44
Leavitt J. S. hotel   back colored
Leavitt Wm. teacher of navigation 8
Lighthill A. P. physician . . 6
Lombard & Co. grindstones [back colored
Lord & Fuller, architects . . 47
Lord A. &. D. marbleworkers . 41
Low Aaron T. boots and shoes . 19
Lyon N. U. patent medicines . 68
Mackenzie Roderick A. tailor . 3
Manning R. C. & Co. coal, &c. . 55
Mansfield B. S. painter . . 47
Mansfield Ira, mason . . 50
Martin & Cunningham, boots and shoes 17
Maynard & Noyes, writing ink [front colored
Millett Joseph Henry, groceries . 24
Mills Wm. plumber   back colored
Moore H. W. carriage painter 45

Moore Samuel, button hole machines 6
Morris, restaurant . . . 80
Moulton J H. express   front cover
Nelles A. C. baker . . . 87
Nelson J. S. grain and fruit . 24
Newcomb George L. machinist . 42
Nichols David A. grocer . . 83
Nichols John, shipsmith . . 42
Nichols John H. insurance agent 209
Noyes E. K. & Co. groceries . 23
O'Connell T. boots and shoes 15
Osborn, hatter 4
Osborn Henry M. grocer . 283
Palmer Theron, boots and shoes 17
Palmer Wm. H. clothing . 4
Peabody E. C. Jr. & Co. groceries 26
Peabody Geo. H. & Co. grocers 236
Peabody John P. millinery goods, &c. [back colored
Pease George W. printer . 59
Pepper Geo. W. confectioner . 212
Perkins & Morrill, shoe stiffenings 238
Peirce N. broker   back colored
Perkins Wm. A. patternmaker . 48
Perley J. bookbinder . . 7
Phillips A. Mrs. periodicals . 9
Phillips Willard P. coal, &c. [back colored
Porter M. A. skirtmaker . 12
Pousland George A. painter . 50
Pray John H. Sons & Co. carpeting 61
Price C. H. & J. apothecaries [front colored
Pulsifer D. & Co. painters . 48
Raddin Alonzo, boots and shoes 239
Reith & Co. millinery goods [back colored
Reynolds M. C. & Co. grocers . 28
Robbins Thomas A. stables . 21
Roberts E. F. & J. W. fruits . 28
Robertson S. W. soap . . 27
Rogers S. F. dining saloon . . 37
Roies Samuel Jr. dyehouse . 11
Ropes Charles A. flour and grain 26
Ropes John T. stoves, &c. . 2
Rowell Benjamin, painter . 48
Rowell Edward, kegs . . 85
Rowell Frederick, Jr. cigars . 28
Salem Boot and Shoe Co. . . 16
Salem Gazette . . . 58
Salem Leg Co. artificial limbs [back cover
Salem Marine Ins. Co. . . 207
Salem Mutual Ins. Co. . . 208
Sampson, Davenport, & Co. directories . . . 67
Savory & Co. express .   back cover
Sanders Robert J. veterinary surg. 86
Sawyer & Tilton, provisions . 81
Shaw & Winson, crockery, &c. . 1
Shepard J. B. & S. D. dry goods 11
Shoules Charles J. carriage smith 44
Sibley Geo. boots and shoes . 17
Sibley Moses H. tailor . . 8
Simon Stephen A. confectioner 18
Simonds Charles, stable . . 282
Simonds S. C. & E. A. crockery, hardware, &c. . . . 25

Simonds Washington, hotel . 232
Skerry H. F. jeweller back colored
Small William F. gas fixtures . 20
Smith & Chamberlain, jewellers 3
Smith James A. carpenter . . 48
Smith Jesse, watchmaker front col'd
Smith J. R. machinist . . 42
Smith Sterry, iron founder . 48
South & Howard, boots and shoes 15
Staten E. H. gasfitter front colored
Stetson S. A. & Co. gas fixtures,
  lamps, &c. 61
Stone Henry N. pumps, ship fix-
  tures, &c. 63
Stratton T. W. collector . . 66
Story Joseph, penrhyn marble 65
Straw Benjamin, mouldings . 46
Sumner & Carter, teamsters . 29
Symonds J. W. & Co. boots and
  shoes 15
Symonds Pauline Miss, milliner 18
Tabour William, cigars . . 24
Thyng & Babbidge, printers . 56

Tibbetts Russell S. dining saloon 36
Townes Samuel, fish packer . 29
Trask Thomas auctioneer . 235
Tucker Henry G. lobsters . 30
Walker Geo. S. tailor back cover
Wallis Joseph, furniture . . 39
Walton Timothy, bones . . 23
Ward J. O. provisions . . 81
Washburn B. D. roofing . 66
Webb Wm. jr. apothecary front col'd
Webber I. J. groceries . . . 27
Welch Wm. E. provisions . 81
Weston John W. machinist . 42
Wheeler Benjamin S. provisions 83
Whidden Henry L. painter . . 234
Whipple G. M. & A. A. Smith,
  booksellers . . front colored
Whipple Henry, charts,&c. back cover
White Benjamin R. mason . . 46
Wiggin & Clark, coal, wood, &c. 52
Wiggin & Munroe, provisions . 32
Williston S. S. cutler . . 30
Winn S. B. mineral water . 9

CENSUS OF 1865 — CITIES OF MASSACHUSETTS.

CITIES.	Churches.	School houses	Dwelling Houses.	Families.	Population.	Ratable Polls.	Legal Voters.	Naturalized Voters.
Boston, . .	115	80	20,649	38,021	192,324	51,111	33,890	7,952
Cambridge, .	24	19	4,679	5,852	29,114	7,264	5,152	1,148
Charlestown, .	11	20	3,679	5,456	26,398	6,442	5,596	1,008
Chelsea, . .	11	13	2,535	3,034	14,409	3,685	2,502	427
Fall River, .	16	32	2,265	3,489	17,525	4,455	3,204	915
Lawrence, .	14	15	2,482	3,753	21,733	5,085	2,668	656
Lowell, . .	22	45	5,324	6,400	31,004	7,774	5,150	1,121
Lynn, . . .	21	20	3,267	4,434	20,800	5,301	4,212	269
New Bedford, .	29	22	3,265	4,487	20,863	5,600	4,545	351
Newburyport,	16	20	2,410	2,964	12,980	3,300	2,636	189
Roxbury, . .	11	25	3,746	5,634	28,426	6,442	4,483	1,565
Salem, . . .	21	21	3,074	4,703	21,197	5,153	3,501	549
Springfield, .	14	35	3,556	5,059	22,036	6,155	4,238	441
Taunton, .	17	32	2,507	3,234	16,005	4,154	3,086	443
Worcester, .	19	27	3,797	6,048	30,058	8,478	5,880	769

POPULATION OF MASSACHUSETTS, 1865.

Total . . . . 1,267,320.

BARNSTABLE COUNTY.

Barnstable	4,913
Brewster	1,459
Chatham	2,637
Dennis	3,512
Eastham	757
Falmouth	2,294
Harwich	3,540
Orleans	1,580
Provincetown	3,475
Sandwich	4,105
Truro	1,448
Wellfleet	2,298
Yarmouth	2,466
	34,489

BERKSHIRE COUNTY.

Adams	8,298
Alford	461
Becket	1,395
Cheshire	1,650
Clarksburg	530
Dalton	1,187
Egremont	928
Florida	1,173
Great Barrington	3,920
Hancock	967
Hinsdale	1,517
Lanesborough	1,295
Lee	4,084
Lenox	1,667
Monterey	737
Mount Washington	233
New Ashford	178
New Marlborough	1,649
Otis	962
Peru	494
Pittsfield	9,679
Richmond	913
Sandisfield	1,411
Savoy	866
Sheffield	2,461
Stockbridge	1,907
Tyringham	650
Washington	859
West Stockbridge	1,621
Williamstown	2,563
Windsor	758
	56,966

BRISTOL COUNTY.

Acushnet	1,251
Attleborough	6,200
Berkley	888
Dartmouth	3,434
Dighton	1,515
Easton	3,064
Fairhaven	2,548
Fall River	17,525
Freetown	1,484
Mansfield	2,131
New Bedford	20,868
Norton	1,709
Raynham	1,868
Rehoboth	1,834
Seekonk	929
Somerset	1,791
Swanzey	1,385
Taunton	16,005
Westport	2,802
	88,505

DUKES COUNTY.

Chilmark	547
Edgartown	1,846
Gosnold	108
Tisbury	1,699
	4,200

ESSEX COUNTY.

Amesbury	4,210
Andover	5,809
Beverly	5,944
Boxford	868
Bradford	1,567
Danvers	5,144
Essex	1,630
Georgetown	1,928
Gloucester	11,038
Groveland	1,620
Hamilton	800
Haverhill	10,660
Ipswich	3,911
Lawrence	21,733
Lynn	20,800
Lynnfield	725
Manchester	1,843
Marblehead	7,330
Methuen	2,576
Middleton	922
Nahant	313
Newbury	1,868
Newburyport	12,980
North Andover	2,622
Rockport	3,807
Rowley	1,106
Salem	21,197
Salisbury	3,600
Saugus	2,006
South Danvers	6,050
Swampscott	1,619
Topsfield	1,212
Wenham	915
West Newbury	2,088
	171,192

FRANKLIN COUNTY.

Ashfield	1,221
Bernardston	902
Buckland	1,922
Charlemont	904
Coleraine	1,726
Conway	1,538
Deerfield	3,040
Erving	576
Gill	685
Greenfield	3,211
Hawley	687
Heath	642
Leverett	914
Leyden	592
Monroe	192
Montague	1,575
New Salem	1,115
Northfield..	1,660
Orange	1,909
Rowe	568
Shelburne	1,503
Shutesbury	788
Sunderland	861
Warwick	902
Wendell	602
Whately	1,012
	31,342

HAMPDEN COUNTY.

Agawam	1,665
Blandford	1,087
Brimfield	1,316
Chester	1,286
Chicopee	7,681
Granville	1,363
Holland	368
Holyoke	5,648
Longmeadow	1,480
Ludlow	1,233
Monson	3,132
Montgomery	354
Palmer	3,081
Russell	619
Southwick	1,155
Springfield	22,038
Tolland	511
Wales	606
Westfield	6,634
West Springfield	2,100
Wilbraham	2,111
	64,438

HAMPSHIRE COUNTY.

Amherst	3,413
Belchertown	2,680
Chesterfield	802
Cummington	980
Easthampton	2,869
Enfield	999
Goshen	412
Granby	908
Greenwich	847
Hadley	2,246
Hatfield	1,405
Huntington	1,163
Middlefield	728
Northampton	7,927
Pelham	739
Plainfield	579
Prescott	506
South Hadley	2,008

POPULATION OF MASSACHUSETTS.

Southampton	1,216	Canton	3,318	Clinton	4,021
Ware	3,307	Cohasset	2,048	Dana	789
Westhampton	637	Dedham	7,108	Douglas	2,157
Williamsburg	1,972	Dorchester	10,729	Dudley	2,077
Worthington	925	Dover	610	Fitchburg	8,119
		Foxborough	2,776	Gardner	2,553
	39,199	Franklin	2,510	Grafton	3,902
MIDDLESEX COUNTY.		Medfield	1,011	Hardwick	1,968
Acton	1,660	Medway	3,228	Harvard	1,353
Ashby	1,060	Milton	2,769	Holden	1,846
Ashland	1,702	Needham	2,793	Hubbardston	1,646
Bedford	820	Quincy	6,718	Lancaster	1,707
Belmont	1,278	Randolph	5,734	Leicester	2,528
Billerica	1,808	Roxbury	28,426	Leominster	3,818
Boxborough	454	Sharon	1,394	Lunenburg	1,167
Brighton	3,859	Stoughton	4,859	Mendon	1,207
Burlington	594	Walpole	2,018	Milford	9,102
Cambridge	29,114	West Roxbury	6,912	Milbury	3,780
Carlisle	629	Weymouth	7,981	New Braintree	752
Charlestown	26,398	Wrentham	3,072	Northborough	1,623
Chelmsford	2,296			Northbridge	2,042
Concord	2,281		116,334	North Brookfield	2,514
Dracut	1,905	**PLYMOUTH COUNTY.**		Oakham	925
Dunstable	533	Abington	3,576	Oxford	2,713
Framingham	4,681	Bridgewater	4,106	Paxton	626
Groton	8,176	Carver	1,059	Petersham	1,866
Holliston	3,126	Duxbury	2,877	Phillipston	726
Hopkinton	4,140	East Bridgewater	2,977	Princeton	1,238
Lexington	2,223	Halifax	739	Royalston	1,441
Lincoln	710	Hanover	1,545	Rutland	1,011
Littleton	967	Hanson	1,195	Shrewsbury	1,571
Lowell	31,004	Hingham	4,176	Southborough	1,750
Malden	6,871	Hull	260	Southbridge	4,131
Marlborough	7,200	Kingston	1,628	Spencer	3,026
Medford	4,860	Lakeville	1,110	Sterling	1,688
Melrose	2,866	Marion	960	Sturbridge	1,993
Natick	5,220	Marshfield	1,810	Sutton	2,803
Newton	8,978	Mattapoisett	1,451	Templeton	2,390
North Reading	991	Middleborough	4,525	Upton	2,017
Pepperell	1,709	North Bridgewater	6,335	Uxbridge	2,836
Reading	2,436	Pembroke	1,486	Warren	2,205
Sherborn	1,049	Plymouth	6,075	Webster	3,608
Shirley	1,217	Plympton	924	Westborough	3,141
Somerville	9,306	Rochester	1,156	West Boylston	2,293
South Reading	8,245	Scituate	2,269	West Brookfield	1,548
Stoneham	3,299	South Scituate	1,578	Westminster	1,639
Stowe	1,537	Wareham	2,842	Winchendon	2,602
Sudbury	1,703	West Bridgewater	1,825	Worcester	30,055
Tewksbury	1,801				
Townsend	2,056		63,074		162,923
Tyngsborough	624	**SUFFOLK COUNTY.**		**RECAPITULATION.**	
Waltham	6,897	Boston	192,324	*By Counties.*	
Watertown	3,779	Chelsea	14,403	Barnstable	34,489
Wayland	1,138	North Chelsea	858	Berkshire	56,066
West Cambridge	2,760	Winthrop	634	Bristol	89,505
Westford	1,506			Dukes	4,200
Weston	1,231		208,219	Essex	171,192
Wilmington	850	**WORCESTER COUNTY.**		Franklin	31,342
Winchester	1,969	Ashburnham	2,163	Hampden	64,438
Woburn	7,002	Athol	2,813	Hampshire	39,199
		Auburn	959	Middlesex	220,018
	220,616	Barre	2,858	Nantucket	4,830
NANTUCKET COUNTY.		Berlin	1,062	Norfolk	110,334
Nantucket	4,830	Blackstone	4,857	Plymouth	63,074
NORFOLK COUNTY.		Bolton	1,504	Suffolk	208,219
Bellingham	1,240	Boylston	702	Worcester	162,923
Braintree	3,725	Brookfield	2,100		
Brookline	5,262	Charlton	1,925		1,267,329

INDEX TO BOSTON ADVERTISEMENTS

IN

SALEM DIRECTORY.

STREETS, COURTS, AND PLACES.

Aborn, from 161 Boston to S. Danvers line
Adams, from opposite 65 Mason
Albion, from South end of Prospect
Allen, from 17 English to Webb
Andover, from 24 Beckford to 8 Lynn
Andrew, from 18 Pleasant to Webb
Arabella, from 77 Bridge
Ash, from 14 Federal to 155 Bridge
Barr, from 20 Mason
Barton from 63 Bridge to Collins's Cove
Barton square, from 15 Washington to 255 Essex
Beach, from 75 Mason to North River
Beaver, from Grove to 150 Boston
Becket, from 23 Essex to 44 Derby
Becket ave. from 25 Becket to 38 Derby
Beckford, from 346 Essex to River st.
Bentley, from 51 Essex to 84 Derby
Blaney, from 47 Derby to Webb's wharf
Boston, from 410 Essex to S. Danvers line
Bott's court, from 343 Essex to 18 Chestnut
Bow, from 9 Aborn
Bridge, from Beverly bridge to North
Briggs, from 15 Pleasant to Webb
Broad, from 42 Summer
Brown, from 20 Pleasant to St. Peter
Bryant, from 123 North to 48 Buffum
Buffum, from 12 Mason
Cabot, from Cedar to Hancock
Cambridge, from 321 Essex to 10 Broad
Carlton, from 33 Essex to 52 Derby
Carpenter, from 134 Federal
Cedar, from 58 Lafayette to Mill Pond
Cedar court, from 24 Cedar
Central, from 185 Essex to Front
2

Charter, from 23 Central to 150 Derby
Cherry, from Porter to Cedar
Chestnut, from 34 Summer to Flint
Church, from 23 St. Peter to 62 Washington
Churchill, from Myrtle, 2d above Mason
Collins, from Webb to Barton
Conant, from 56 Bridge
Congress, from 44 Harbor
Creek, from 16 Mill to 35 Summer
Crombie, from 281 Essex to 26 Norman
Cross, from Lemon to Conant
Cross street court, from Cross
Curtis, from 89 Essex to 116 Derby
Daniels, from 59 Essex to the water
Dean, from 388 Essex to North River
Dearborn, from 90 North to the river
Derby, from the Neck to Central
Derby sq. from 215 Essex to Front
Dodge, from 12 Walter to Southwick
Dodge's court, from 18 Lafayette
Dow, from 47 Lafayette to 14 Salem
Downing, from 13 Margin to Prescott
East Webb, east from 9 Webb
Elm, from 121 Essex to 162 Derby
Endicott, from 36 Mill to 15 Winthrop
English, from 13 Essex to 28 Derby
Essex, from Webb to Salem Turnpike
Everett, from 55 Lafayette to Salem
Federal, from 23 St. Peter to 36 Boston
Federal court, from 89 Federal
Felt, from Dearborn to Orne
Flint, from 389 Essex to Broad
Forrester, from 20 Essex to 14 Newbury
Fowler, from 18 Boston
Foye's court, from Webb
Franklin, from 46 North
Friend, from 89 Mason to North River
Front, from 22 Central to 12 Washington
Gardner, from 74 Lafayette to E. R. R.
Gardner court, from 14 March
Gardner st. (East), from 70 Harbor

Gedney court, from 47 Summer to 20 High
Gerrish place, from 15 Essex
Goodhue, from 60 Boston to Frye's Mills
Grafton from 11 Hanson
Grove, fr. 96 Boston to junct'n School & Tremont
Hamilton, from 353 Essex to 22 Chestnut
Hancock, from 82 Lafayette
Hanson, from 93 Boston
Harbor, from 69 Mill to the water
Harbor street court, from 20 Harbor
Hardy, from 45 Essex to the water
Harmony, from 27 Buffum to Barr
Harrod, from Tremont to Harmony Grove
Harrison ave. from 6 Everett to Lagrange
Hathorne, from 31 Broad to the water
Herbert, from 99 Essex to 128 Derby
Higginson sq. from 277 Essex to Derby sq.
High, from 26 Mill to 51 Summer
High street court, from 13 High
Hodges court, from 95 Essex
Hollingsworth Hill, on the Neck
Holly, from 98 Lafayette
Howard, from 20 Brown to 131 Bridge
Irving, from Grove to Harrod   [Laboratory
Ives, from 32 Dearborn to the river, rear of the
Ives court, from 24 Brown to 38 St. Peter
Japonica, Mason Hill   .
Jeffrey court, opens 54 Washington
Laboratory, fr. 68 North to Laboratory buildings
Lafayette, from Front opp. Central to Marblehead
Lagrange, from 69 Lafayette
Laurel, from 112 Lafayette to Linden
Lawrence place, cor. Washington and Front
Leach, from 107 Lafayette street east
Ledge Hill, from Grove, near the cemetery
Lemon, from 96 Bridge street
Lemon court, from 20 Lemon
Liberty, from 137 Essex to Derby
Liberty Hill, near North and Nursery streets
Liberty Hill Road, from 128 North
Linden, from Holly to Laurel

Lummus court, (see Tuttle's court)
Lynde, from 51 Washington to 16 North
Lynn, from 124 Federal to 20 River
Mall, from 8 Brown to Bridge
Maple, from Aborn near S. Danvers line
March, from 30 Bridge
Margin, from Summer to Winthrop
Market court, from 225 Essex south
Mason, from 55 North to Grove
Mason court, from 9 Liberty
Mason Hill, on Adams, rear Mason
May, from 11 Boston to 416 Essex
May street court, from 10 May street
Meade court, from 89 North
Mechanic, from 72 North to Walter
Melcher court, from 79 North
Milk, from 18 Pickman to Andrew
Mill, from 3 Norman to Lafayette
Mill street court, rear 36 Mill
Monroe, from 366 Essex to 125 Federal
Mount Vernon, from 64 Summer to 9 Winthrop
Myrtle, formerly Adams
Neck, eastern section of the city
Newbury, from 124 Essex to 12 Brown
Nichols, from 103 Boston
Norman, from 1 Washington to 29 Summer
North court, from 149 Bridge
North Pine, from 400 Essex to Fowler
North, from 308 Essex to S. Danvers line
Northey, from 104 Bridge
Nursery, from opposite 149 North
Oak, from 81 Mason to North River
Odell square, from 30 North to 58 Federal
Oliver, from 6 Brown to Bridge
Orange, from 85 Essex to 114 Derby
Ord, from 3 Aborn
Orne, from 108 North to Orne's Point
Osgood, from 31 Bridge
Palfrey court, from 100 Derby
Park, from 30 Harbor
Parker's court, from 35 Pleasant

Peabody, from 25 Lafayette to 55 Harbor
Pearl, from 64 Bridge to the river
Perkins, from 57 Harbor
Phelps court, from 51 Broad to the water
Phillips, from Grove to S. Danvers line
Pickering, from 25 Chestnut to Broad
Pickman, from 17 Winter to Webb
Pickman place, from 169 Essex
Pine, from 401 Essex to Warren
Pingree, from 64 Harbor
Pleasant, from 68 Essex to 85 Bridge
Pleasant st. ave. from 23 Pleasant to Winter
Pond, from 58 Mill to Mill Pond
Pope's court, from 49 Boston
Porter, from 48 Lafayette to Mill Pond
Porter court, from 8 Porter
Pratt, from 18 High to 30 Endicott
Pratt street court, from 4 Pratt
Prescott, from 23 Winthrop to Margin
Prince, from 34 Harbor
Proctor court, from 61 Boston
Prospect, from Nichols to Ord
Putnam, from Hanson to Proctor court
Randall, from 83 North to 26 Buffum
River, from 29 Beckford to 13 Lynn
Ropes, from 70 Mill
Roslyn, from Lafayette above Hancock
Rust, from 18 Federal to Bridge
Salem, from 24 Harbor to Lagrange
Salem turnpike, from 428 Essex to Lynn line
Saunders, from 78 Bridge to R. R.
School, from 105 North to Grove
Sewall, from 284 Essex to 17 Lynde
Shillaber, from Aborn near S. Danvers line
Silver, from 30 Beaver to 44 Beaver
Skerry, from Bridge to North River
South Prospect, from Congress to East Gardner
Southwick, from opposite 31 Dearborn to Dodge
Spring, from 28 Pleasant to Webb
St. Peter, from 170 Essex to Bridge
St. Peter court, from 4 St. Peter

Summer, from 384 Essex to Mill Pond
Summit, from Prospect Hill
Sutton, from Aborn to Salem turnpike
Sylvan, from Myrtle 1st above Mason
Thorndike, from Bridge, near Beverly Bridge
Tremont, from junction of Grove and School
Turner, from 39 Essex to Salem harbor
Tuttle court, from 183 Federal
Union, from 105 Essex to S. Salem
Union place, from 102 North
Upham, from 9 Dearborn to Orne
Varney, from Nichols to Putnam
Vale from 10 Phelps court
Walnut, from 111 Essex to 20 Charter
Walter, from Laboratory to Orne
Ward, from 29 Lafayette to Peabody
Warner, from Barton to Arabella
Warren, from Pickering to Turnpike
Warren court, rear 57 Warren .
Washington, from E. R. R. Depot to Bridge
Watson, from 134 Boston to 37 Beaver
Webb, from 1 Derby to 85 Bridge
Webster, from 32 Pleasant to Webb
West place, rear 186 Essex to 11 Church
Whittemore, from 11 Mechanic to 10 Dearborn
Williams, from 9 Brown to Bridge
Winter, from 5 Brown to 101 Bridge
Winthrop, from 19 Broad to Mill Pond
Woodbury's court, from 15 Northey

WHARVES.

Almshouse, near the Almshouse on the Neck
Bancroft's, opens at 199 Derby
Bowker's, opens at 227 Derby
Brookhouse, opens 53 Derby
Brooks, opposite 109 Derby
Brown's, near North Bridge
Brown's, opens on Franklin
Buffum's, opens at 9 and 13 Front
Burley & Briggs', 18 to 36 Peabody
Carlton's, opens on Franklin

Central, opens at 117 Derby
Clark's, 169 Derby
Cushing's, 183 Derby
Derby, opposite Custom House, Derby st.
Dodge's, from 16 Lafayette
Faben's, opens 211 Derby
Farnham's, opens at 221 Derby
Felt's, near Orne's Point
Flint's, opens on Franklin
Frothingham's, opens at 25 Front
Hatch's, 113 Derby
Hunt's, opens at 53 Derby
Jewett's, opens at 205 Derby
Laboratory, opens on Franklin
Market, opens at 19 Front
Mill, opens at Mill street
Moore's, opens at 225 Derby
Naumkeag, opens on Peabody
North, near the North Bridge
Peabody's, 165 Derby, foot of Elm
Perkins, 153 Derby
Pierce's, opens at 171 Derby
Phillips, or India, opens 29 Derby
Putnam's, opens 157 Derby
Sanborn's, 115 Derby
Smith's, foot of Union
Smith's, n. Railway, South Salem
Tucker's, from 101 Derby
Union, foot of Union
Ward's, 121 Derby
Water's, opens on Franklin
Webb's, foot of Blaney
Whipple's, foot of Turner
West's, opens 15 Peabody
West's, opens at 215 Derby

HALLS, PUBLIC BUILDINGS, ETC.

Almshouse, on the Neck
Arrington building, Washington, near Depot
Asiatic building, 32 Washington
Athenæum, in Plummer Hall

Bowker building, 150 Essex
Browne's block, 222 to 226 Essex
City Fish Market, 21 Front
City Hall, 44 Washington
City Market, Derby square
City Mills, 35 to 43 Mill street
City Scales, Bridge, near St. Peter
City Watch House, 11 Front
Court Houses, Federal, corner Washington
Creamer's building, 243½ Essex
Custom House, 112 Derby
East India Marine Hall, 161 Essex
Essex Institute, in Plummer Hall
Frye's Mills, junction Goodhue and Beaver
Hamilton Hall, Cambridge, corner Chestnut
Hubon's block, 44 to 54 Washington
Lyceum Hall, 35 Church
Mechanic Hall, 285 Essex
Museum, 161 Essex
Phœnix building, Lafayette, corner Front
Phœnix Hall, in Phœnix building
Police Court, and station, 11 Front
Plummer Hall, 134 Essex
Post Office, 32 Washington
Town Hall, Derby square
Washington Hall, Hubon's Block
West's block, 188 Essex

BOUNDARIES OF WARDS.

WARD 1. That portion of the city south of Essex street, east of Washington street, excepting South Salem.

WARD 2. All north of Essex street, east of Washington street.

WARD 3. All west or south of Washington, and Essex, and eastern side of Turnpike.

WARD 4. Includes all north of Essex street, west of Washington (excepting North Salem), and all west of Turnpike.

WARD 5. All of South Salem.

WARD 6. All of North Salem.

GENERAL DIRECTORY.

ABBREVIATIONS. — St., for street; ct., court; ave., avenue; n., near; h., house; r., rear; opp., opposite; b., boards; c. and cor., corner; sq., square; (B.), Boston; Cal., California; U. S. A., United States Army; U. S. N., United States Navy. After the name of the street, the word street is omitted.

AARON JOHN, cabinetmaker, house 10 Broad
Aaron Samuel G. cooper, 36 Salem
Abbott Philip, painter, 9 Church, house 20 Williams
Abbott Abigail, widow, house rear 24 Hancock
Abbott Adolphus, baker, house 32 Essex   [Danvers
Abbott Alfred A. counsellor, 24 Washington, house at South
Abbott Annis, widow, house 6 Fowler
Abbott Benjamin, teamster, 30 Front, house 57 Bridge
Abbott Benjamin F. clerk, 40 Pleasant, boards 57 Bridge
Abbott Catharine, widow, house 61 Mason
Abbott Charles J. blacksmith, boards rear 24 Hancock
Abbott Eliza N. Miss, house 9 Becket
Abbott George, stonecutter, house 6 Gedney court
Abbott George B. master mariner, house 97 Bridge
Abbott George F. engineer, house 8 Prescott
Abbott Jacob A. milkman, boards 3 Lynn
Abbott John H. 12 Market square, house 40 Lafayette
Abbott Joseph C. clerk, 181 Essex, boards at South Danvers
Abbott Lydia Mrs. house 13 Winthrop
Abbott Mary Miss, house 35 Chestnut
Abbott Mary A. widow, house 97 Bridge
Abbott Moses C. carpenter, house 12 Conant
Abbott Nathaniel, trader, boards 55 Derby
Abbott Robert, teamster, house 3 Pond
Abbott Royal E. carder, boards 19 Turner
Abbott Royal H. laborer, house 19 Turner
Abbott Samuel D. painter, boards 20 Williams
Aborn J. Henry, carriage painter, house 1 Federal
Aborn Sarah S. widow, house 11 River
Adams Charles, tanner, house Adams, Mason Hill
Adams Charles H. house 7 at the F. R. Lead Mills
Adams Charles P. oil mill, boards 16 School
Adams George W. machinist (B.), house 17 Cambridge
Adams Henry, mariner, house 34 Endicott
Adams Henry J. teamster, Alms House, house 22 Derby

3

Adams (*Joseph*), Richardson (*C. M.*), & Co. (*H. E. Jocelyn*),
hardware, cutlery, and agricultural tools, 215 Essex, boards
Essex House
Adams Nahum, confectioner, house 24 Cedar
Adams Oliver, bill poster, house 33 Brown
Adams Peter F. carriagemaker, 23 Endicott, house 51 Summer
Adams Rebecca G. Mrs. house 16 School
Adams Sarah Miss, boards 29 Pleasant
Adams Thomas, house 16 Church
Adams William, house 11 May
Agge Jacob, blacksmith, 20 Peabody, house 96 Federal
Agge William, bookkeeper, First National Bank, b. 96 Federal
Agnes Thomas, laborer, house 11 Lynn
Ahern David, house at 6 F. R. Lead Mills
Ahern John, currier, boards rear 26 Beaver
Ahern Michael, laborer, house rear 26 Beaver
Ahern Thomas, watchman, house 14 Allen
Ahern William, track repairer, boards 14 Allen
Aiken William B. mariner, house Roslyn, near Lafayette
Alcott Richard, carpenter, house 24 Derby
Aldrich Moses, grocer, Harbor, c. Peabody, house 53 Harbor
Aldrich Moses H. clerk, house 50 Harbor
Allard Almon B. farmer, boards 3 Melcher court
Allard Thomas F. farmer, house 3 Melcher court
Allen Charles H. master mariner, house 24 Hardy
Allen Charles H. jr. captain, house 65 Lafayette
Allen David, cabinetmaker, house 8 Carlton
Allen Edward, merchant, house 19 Pickman
Allen Edward F. clerk, boards 19 Pickman
Allen Edward L. currier, house 5 Albion
Allen Elbridge B. baker, house 33 Barr
Allen Ephraim, measurer of leather, house 161 Federal
Allen Frank, dentist, at Habon block, bds. 38 Lafayette
Allen George H. merchant, 14 Asiatic building, h. 41 Endicott
Allen George W. currier, house 109 Boston
Allen Horatio D. boards 53 Charter
Allen Ira G. engineer, house 111 Boston
Allen Jacob H. carver, boards 10 Prince
Allen John F. grapery, Dean, house 31 Chestnut
Allen Joseph P. police, house 53 Charter
Allen Laura W. fancy goods, 368 Essex, house do.
Allen Manly, shoemaker, house 22 Derby
Allen Mary M. & Lydia A. house 13 Ash
Allen Michael, laborer, house 9 Tucker's wharf
Allen Nathaniel K. insurance agent, house 30 Lafayette
Allen Nathaniel M. watchmaker, 262 Essex, b. 24 St. Peter
Allen William A. baker, boards 10 Cedar
Allen William E. provisions, 50½ Derby, boards 103 Boston
Allen William E. Mrs. widow, house 34 Essex
Alley Alice Mrs. widow, house 27 Norman

Alley Benjamin M. billposter, house 25 High
Allie Abigail, nurse, house 22 Forrester
Almon Andrew B. counsellor (B.), house 79 Lafayette
Almy James F. & Co. (*S. E. Stacey, and W. K. Bigelow*),
   dry goods, 188 Essex, house 20 Harbor
Alton Currie S. widow, house 8 Ropes
Ames Edward B. painter, 3 Crombic, house 5 Cambridge
Ames George L. house 26 Pleasant, corner Pickman
Ames Mary, widow, house 32 St. Peter
Ames Mary L. Mrs. house 218 Essex
Ames Mary S. Mrs. house 26 Pleasant
Ames M. Eugene (India,) boards 218 Essex
Ames Peter, house 9 Curtis
Amidon Augustus R. tailor (125 Tremont, B.), house 6 ·Union
Amory Joanna Mrs. house 4 Pickman
Anderson Augustus M. butcher, house 3 Hardy
Anderson Edward, mariner, boards 9 Charter
Anderson George F. butcher, boards 57 Derby
Anderson Jacob, shipkeeper, house 57 Derby
Anderson James H. tailor, house 9 Charter
Anderson James H. jr. mariner, boards 9 Charter
Anderson John M. gluemaker, Salem turnpike, house do.
Anderson Mary C. house 306 Essex
Anderson Thomas B. mariner, boards 9 Charter
Anderson William, mariner, boards 9 Charter
Andrew Martha Mrs. house 15 Brown
Andrew Mary B. & Eunice W. Misses, house 16 Federal
Andrew Nathaniel Mrs. house 44 Pleasant
Andrews Caroline, boards 393 Essex
Andrews Daniel, house 24 Lynde
Andrews Dolly Ann W. house 24 Lynde
Andrews Eliza, house 24 Lynde
Andrews Esther H. Mrs. house 78 Mill
Andrews Gilman, blacksmith and carriage manufacturer and
   painter, 27 Beach, house 5 Oak
Andrews Gilman A. currier, 27 Beach, house 24 Mason
Andrews Hiram, patternmaker, and house joiner, h. 20 Salem
Andrews James H. Mrs. house 119 Lafayette
Andrews Jane, widow, house 77 Derby
Andrews John P. house 393 Essex
Andrews Joseph, currier, house 40 Phelps court
Andrews Mary, widow of Nehemiah, house 12 Mall
Andrews Mary Mrs. house 46 Federal
Andrews Mary Ann Mrs. house 12 Mall
Andrews Mary A. widow, house 21 High
Andrews Nehemiah W. clerk, 195 Essex, house 12 Mall
Andrews Samuel P. clerk, Police Court, Police Station, 11
   Front, house 8 Flint, near Warren
Anketele Edward, boarding house, 176 Derby
Annable Benj. R. millwright, house 144 Beaver

Annable Ephraim Mrs. house 73 North
Annable E. Augustus, clerk 222 Essex, boards 34 do.
Annable W. F. tinplate worker, boards 73 North
Anthony Harriet M. widow, house 41 North
Anthony Joseph H. boards 41 North (11th U. S. Regulars)
Appleton George B. watchmaker and jeweller, 187 Essex, h. 22
    Norman
Appleton George H. painter, boards 3 Woodbury's court
Appleton Nathaniel, shoemaker, boards 6 Woodbury's court
Appleton Nathaniel Mrs. house 14 Northey
Archer Augustus J. & Co., dry goods, 181 Essex, h. 134 Federal
Archer Elizabeth, widow, house 64 Mill
Archer Elizabeth Miss, house 12 Carlton
Archer Fidelia W. Mrs. house 6 Carpenter
Archer Henry Mrs. house 26 Williams
Archer John, house 6 Daniels
Archer Lydia, house 15 Federal
Archer Mary M. Mrs. house 40 Essex
Archer Rachel, house 15 Federal
Archer Rufus P. cooper, house 64 Mill
Archer Rufus P. jr. clerk, boards 64 Mill
Archer Samuel, machinist, house 67 Lafayette
Archer Samuel A. machinist, boards 67 Lafayette
Archer Sarah, house 45 St. Peter
Archer William Mrs. house 67 Lafayette
Archer William, auctioneer and commission merchant, 18 Wash.
    and 34 Front, house 67 Lafayette
Archer William H. mariner, house 10 Howard
Armstrong Eliza J. nurse, house 116 Derby
Armstrong George B. carriage smith, boards 16 Mechanic
Armstrong John Mrs. house 50 Charter
Armstrong Thomas, shoe manuf. 39 Federal, h. 16 Mechanic
Arnold Edward B. morocco manuf. house 87 Boston
Arnold Jabez R. overseer Naumkeag mill, house 25 Lafayette
Arnold James F. currier, house 163 Boston
Arnold James E. wheelwright, house 3 Palfrey court
Arnold Joseph E. morocco dresser, house 49 Warren
Arnold Mary E. nurse, house 38 Derby
Arnold Michael P. morocco dresser, house 8 Summit
Arnold Nicholas, laborer, house 426 Essex
Arnold Patrick, coachman, boards 176 Derby
Arnold Peter, grocer, 137 Derby, house do.
Arnold Thomas A. morocco dresser, house 9 May
Arnold William A., Naumkeag mill, boards 38 Harbor
Arnold William O. printer, 193 Essex, boards 38 Derby
Arrington Augusta, 1st asst. Brown school, boards 43 Lafayette
Arrington Benj. printer, 214 Essex, house 16 High
Arrington Benjamin R. house 56 Charter (U. S. A.)
Arrington George D. Mrs. house 17 Barr
Arrington George S. watchman, house 10 High

Arrington George S. jr. painter, 180 Bridge, boards 10 High
Arrington James, house 6 Andover
Arrington James jr. painter, house 8¼ Turner
Arrington John R. house 5 North court (U. S. N.)
Arrington Joseph Mrs. house 43 Lafayette
Arrington Samuel, boards 6 Andover
Arrington Walter R. painter, house 84 Summer
Arvedson George, clerk, 216 Essex, house 47 Federal
Arvedson Hannah Mrs. house 12 Broad   [Prescott
Arvedson William L. city liquor agent, 25 Washington, h. 12
Ashby Elias W. currier, 47 Boston, house 65 do.
Ashby John J. shoemaker, house 96 Essex
Ashby Josephus, carpenter, house Union place
Ashby Robert R. shoemaker, house 21¼ Salem
Ashby Sarah D. widow, house 206 Derby
Ashby Thomas, carpenter, house 1 Melcher's court
Ashby Thomas W. gardener, house 46 Broad
Ashton Francis M. currier, house 4 Walnut
Ashton Francis P. Mrs. house 5 Dearborn
Ashton William B. clothing, &c. 225 Essex, house 20 Central
Ashton William F. furnishing goods, 225 Essex, h. 17 Beckford
Atkins Hannah Mrs. house 43 Federal
Atkins John, house Walter
Atwell Hannah Miss, house 26 Turner
Atwill Isaac, at laboratory, house foot of Northey
Auld William, brakeman, E. R. R. boards 15 Crombie
Austerbery Ann, widow, house 7 Prince
Austerbery Thomas, heeler, boards 7 Prince
Atwood Edward S. Rev. house 31 Summer
Atwood Morrison, wheelwright, boards 112 Essex
Austin Eleazer, lumber, 16 Lafayette, house 58 do.
Austin Eugene F. joiner, house 19 Northey
Austin Everett E. clerk, 16 Lafayette, boards 58 do.
Austin Francis, tanner, house 41 Buffum
Austin George F. house 58 Lafayette (New Orleans)
Austin James L. tanner, house 49 Warren
Austin Josiah, watchmaker (B.), house 149 Federal
Austin Martha, widow, house rear 8 High
Austin Richard H. painter, 25 Front, house 4 N. Pine
Austin William, currier, rear May street ct. house 13 Boston
Austin William R. currier, boards 13 Boston
Averell Nathaniel P. Mrs. house 79 Boston
Averell Nathaniel S. currier, boards 79 Boston
Averill Benjamin, cooper, house 14 Mall
Averill Benjamin jr. distiller, house 4 Palfrey court
Averill Charles A. (Cox & A.), blacksmith, Bridge, cor. North,
    house 13 School
Averill Edward, engineer, house 68 Boston
Averill Eliza H. Mrs. house 317 Essex
Averill George H. provisions, 22 Central, house 317 Essex

Averill James W. painter, 18 Lafayette, house 11 Turner
Averill John J. sawyer, house 75 Mill
Averill Joseph J. painter, boards 12 Mall
Averill Moses A. watchman, house 2 Melcher court
Avery Mark B. farmer, house 140 Derby
Ayers Daniel, tanner, house 24 Beaver
Ayers James, miller, house 20 Porter
Ayers John, currier, house rear.Adams, Mason Hill
Aylward George G. engineer E. R. R. house 8 Botts court

BABBIDGE BENJAMIN, boatbuilder, house 106 Essex
Babbidge Benjamin A. Mrs. house 3 Federal
Babbidge Christopher, shipwright, house 21 Essex
Babbidge Elizabeth Mrs. house 3 Federal
Babbidge Eunice Mrs. house 12 Becket
Babbidge Francis Mrs. house 43 Broad
Babbidge William A. (*Thyng & Babbidge*), publishers Salem
    Witch, 182 Essex, house 3 Federal
Babcock Cecelia, hairwork, 188 Essex, house 59 Summer
Babcock (*Charles*) & Smith (*Robert*), hairdressers, 199 Essex,
    house 59 Summer
Babcock Charles F. blacksmith, boards 148 Federal
Babcock Elizabeth, widow, house 148 Federal
Babcock Joseph G. engineer, boards 148 Federal
Babcock Stanton, overseer Naumkeag Mills, house 23 Union
Badger B. Smith, watchman H. R. R. house 1 Allen
Baggs William, butcher, house Grafton near Hanson
Bailey Edwin, laborer, house 7 Park
Bailey George C. tanner, house 25 Beckford
Bailey George E. labbratory, house 32 Dearborn
Bailey Mary C. Mrs. house 31 Boston
Bailey Moses, house 30 Derby
Bailey M. Warren, baker's cart, house 30 Derby
Bailey R. T. Naumkeag Mills, boards Harbor
Bailey Warner, fancy painter, house 6 North court
Bailey William, laborer, house 152 Derby
Bain James, currier, house Grove near cemetery
Baker Abby A. teacher Brown School, boards 54 Mill
Baker Anna Mrs. house 12 Pickman   [Essex
Baker Ezra F. (*E. K. Noyes & Co.*), grocer, 6 Front, h. 280
Baker John, house 24 Lafayette (U. S. N.)
Baker Martha, widow, house 181 Bridge
Baker Mary Ann, widow, house 4 Barton   [Lafayette
Baker Mary A. at J. F. Almy & Co.'s, 188 Essex, boards 28
Baker Nellie F. cashier, 220 Essex, boards at South Danvers
Baker William H. painter, house 24 Liberty
Balch Benjamin Mrs. house Cherry, corner Cedar
Balch David M. chemist, boards Cedar, corner Cherry
Balch Edward F. ship broker (B.), b. Cherry, corner Cedar
Balch Harriet J. widow, house 89 Federal

Balcomb George W. carpenter, boards 21 Lafayette
Balcomb Henry W. carpenter, Phillips, n. Grove, h. 8 Phillips
Baldwin Ann Mrs. house 15 Pleasant
Baldwin Benjamin, carpenter, house 2 Beach
Baldwin Joseph, carpenter, house 64., North
Baldwin Mary Mrs. widow, house 24 Barr
Ball Mary Mrs. house 90 Federal
Ball William, flour, house 120 Derby
Ballard Barzillai, provisions 7¼ Winter, house 34 Pleasant
Ballard Francis A. shoemaker, house 7 Mall
Ballard Henry A. captain, house 96 Lafayette
Ballard James, house 96 Lafayette
Ballard James C. captain, house 7 Linden
Ballard Otis H. mariner, boards 3 Harbor   [Danvers
Bancroft Sydney C. counsellor, 27 Washington, house at South
Barker Benjamin, baker, house 7 Elm
Barker Charles F. clerk, 215 Essex, boards 4 Pearl
Barker George G. com. merchant (B.), boards 72 Lafayette
Barker Henry M. shipwright, house 17 Becket
Barker Jacob, carpenter, 39 North, house 34 Barr
Barker John, mariner, boards 129 Derby
Barker Joseph W. wheelwright, rear Essex House, h. 4 Pearl
Barker Ruth Mrs. house 12 Beckford
Barker Sarah D. & Hannah H. Misses, board 72 Lafayette
Barker Thomas H. clerk, 197 Essex, boards 17 Becket
Barker William G. oil (Penn.), house 72 Lafayette
Barlow John, house 11 Liberty
Barlow J. Henry, mariner, house 43 North
Barlow Lydia M. widow, house 43 North
Barnard Edwin M. carpenter, Naumkeag, house 56 Harbor
Barnard Mary J. widow, house 56 Derby
Barnard Samuel, farmer, boards 56 Derby
Barnard William H. mariner, boards 56 Derby
Barnes Alice A. Mrs. house 319 Essex
Barnes Joseph, shoemaker, rear 201 Essex, house 7 North ct.
Barnes Mary, widow, boards foot of Northey
Barnes Michael D. mariner, house 12 Becket   -
Barnes Nancy, nurse, boards 93 Bridge
Barnes Thomas H. teacher (S. B.), house 18 Church
Barnett Daniel, laborer, house 170 Derby
Barnett Michael, currier, house 16 Silver
Barnett Patrick, laborer, house 9 Herbert
Barney Leah, widow, house 10 English
Barney Mahala, widow, house 14 Cedar
Barney Samuel Mrs. house 9 English
Barney William, porter, boards 14 Cedar
Barney William jr. clerk 24 Front, boards 21 Cedar
Barr Eunice, house 21 Lynde
Barr Robert Mrs. house 36 Mason
Barr Robert Mrs. house 90 Essex

Barrenson Frank, baker, boards 15 Essex
Barrenson Jane Mrs. house 15 Essex
Barrett Mary, widow, house 9 Cherry
Barrett Matthew, laborer, house 14 Herbert
Barrett Patrick, laborer, house Tucker's wharf
Barrett Peter Mrs. house 174 Derby
Barrett William, laborer, house foot Ives
Barron Phœbe H. Mrs. nurse, house 45 Charter
Barry Edward, laborer, house 20 Charlton
Barry James, laborer, house 28 Peabody
Barry John, laborer, house 3 Ropes
Barry John, laborer, house rear 143 Boston
Barry Michael H. currier, house Adams, near Mason
Barstow Benjamin, counsellor, house 25 Chestnut
Barstow Josiah W. master mariner, house 24 Derby
Barstow Salome G. teacher, boards 19 Andrew
Bartlett Alexander, grocer, 82 Derby, house 4 Turner
Bartlett Dean R. shoemaker, house 74 Essex
Bartlett Fred. B. cigar manufacturer, house 4 Turner
Bartlett George W. clerk, 179 Essex, boards 24 Charter
Bartlett Gordon, merchant (B.), house 19 Broad
Bartlett Henry S. shoemaker, 5 North, house 24 Charter
Bartlett Moses, conductor, H. R. R. boards 14 Skerry
Bartlett M. W. Mrs. dressmaker, house 74 Essex
Bartlett William H. Mrs. house 3 Park
Bartlett William H. shoemaker, boards 24 Charter
Bartnet Michael, currier, house 7 Silver
Barton Gardner, apothecary, 124 Essex, house 88 Bridge
Barton John, mariner, boards 129 Derby
Barton William C. grocer, 8 Brown, house 2 Williams
Bassett Edward Mrs. house 27 Charter
Bassett John A. inventor, house Webb
Bassett John B. B. captain, house 8 Lemon
Bassett Robert C. Mrs. house 9 Mechanic
Batcheldor Anna, dry goods, 202 Essex, house 200 do.
Batchelder Augusta, widow, boards 24 St. Peter
Batchelder Barnard Mrs. house 6 Curtis
Batchelder Charles F. farmer, board 118 Lafayette
Batchelder Charles M. blacksmith, house 10 High
Batchelder David G. foreman, F. R. Lead Co. h. 3 Holly
Batchelder Elizabeth Mrs. house 55 Broad
Batchelder George E. clerk, house 147 Bridge
Batchelder George H. boards 14 Odell square
Batchelder George W. Mrs. boards 21 Williams
Batchelder Increase, laborer, house 7½ Prince
Batchelder John A. shoedealer, house 26 Lafayette
Batchelder John D. shoemaker, house 42 Broad
Batchelder John H. dentist, 20 Washington, house do.
Batchelder John H., Essex R. R. car shop, house 14 Odell sq.
Batchelder Joseph, wheelwright and carriagemaker, 35 North,
  house 17 Creek

Batchelder Nathan A. captain, house 4 Harbor street court
Batchelder Richard, blacksmith, house 71 Federal
Batchelder Samuel L. ticket master E. R. R. house 3 Cedar
Batchelder William Mrs. house 147 Bridge
Batchelder William L. steam gasfitter, house 47 Endicott
Bates Charles H. (B.), house Norman
Bates Elizabeth H. Mrs. house Norman
Bates Seth Mrs. widow, house 23 High
Bates Thomas, currier, house 19 Odell square
Bates William B. captain, house 76 Bridge
Bates William M. dentist, 46 Washington, house 38 Lafayette
Bathrick Josiah, laborer, house 23 High
Battis George J. cigarmaker, house 20 Mill
Battis (*James H.*) & Brown (*Willard H.*) tobacconists and cigar
    manufacturers, 30 Front, house 23 Liberty
Battis John, cooper, 147 Derby, house 24 Charter
Battis John H. clerk, 30 Front, boards 23 Liberty
Baxter Charles, laborer, house 127 Derby
Baxter John, teamster, house 10 Lagrange
Beadle Charles, mariner, boards 10 Hardy
Beadle Francis, mariner, boards 10 Hardy
Beadle John, boat builder, house 10 Hardy
Beadle John 3d, boards 10 Hardy (Denver, Colorado)
Beadle Josiah, shoemaker, house 17 Turner
Beadle William, mariner, boards 10 Hardy
Bean Michael, laborer, house 4 Perkins
Beane Arthur T. clerk, 173 Essex, boards 27 do.
Beane Samuel C. Rev. house 9 Williams
Beaseley Charles H. teamster, house 10 Congress
Beaver James, city watchman, house 20 Becket
Becker Peter, tailor, house 4 Turner
Becket Alfred H. cooper, boards 42 Derby
Becket (*Daniel C.*) & Fellows (*George*), boat builders and spar
    makers, Salem Marine Railway, house 42 Derby
Becket Daniel C. jr. gasfitter, house 24 Becket
Becket Jane H. Mrs. house 42 Derby
Becket Samuel Mrs. house 18 Carlton
Beckett Hannah Miss, house 21 Union
Beckford Asa N. provisions, 5 Boston, house 13 Fowler
Beckford Eben, watchman, house 15 Flint
Beckford Jefferson A. watchman, boards 2 Warren court
Beckford Josiah. grain and meal, 41 and 43 Mill and Grove,
    house 18 School
Beckford Penson, laborer, house 2 Warren court
Beckford Thomas F. Mrs. variety, Pleasant, cor. Bridge, h. do.
Beede Benjamin N. laborer, house 4 Downing
Beede Charles N. laborer, boards 4 Downing
Begg Sarah A. nurse, house 1 Hardy
Begg William H. teamster, house 8 Mechanic
Bell Charlotte, widow, house rear 8 Whittemore

5

Bell John H. carpenter, house 7 Lynn
Bell Mary, widow, house 7 Lynn
Bell William W. currier, boards 2 Jeffrey court
Bellew John B. engineer, house Aborn, near Boston
Bellow Catharine, widow, house 13 Congress
Bellow John, Naumkeag mill, boards 13 Congress
Bemis Nancy, widow, house 14 Daniels
Bennard Andrew A. cooper, house 7 Orange
Bennett Abraham, clothing, &c. 159 Essex, h. 12 St. Peter
Bennett George A. cooper, boards 168 Bridge
Bennett Geo. W. harness maker, 321 Essex, h. 168 Bridge
Bennett O. C. weaver, boards 38 Harbor
Bennett Patrick, laborer, house 18 Daniels
Benson Charles A. clerk, 18 and 20 Derby sq. h. 6 Creek
Benson Emery K. (B.), house 52 Forrester
Benson George W. (B.), house 52 Forrester
Benson Samuel Mrs. house 52 Forrester
Berg Nancy Mrs. nurse, house 163 Boston
Bermingham C. variety store, 30 Norman, house do.
Bermingham George, laborer, house 30 Norman
Berry Anna D. widow, house 8 Congress
Berry Betsey Mrs. house 5 High
Berry Charles F. clerk, 6 Front, boards 41 Essex
Berry Charles H. rigger, 20 Derby wharf, house 5 Northey
Berry Charles H. clerk, boards 2 Jeffrey court
Berry Charles H. building mover, house 6 Webb
Berry Ebenezer, master mariner, house 10 Allen
Berry Edwin, clerk, house 7 Dearborn
Berry George A. currier, house 12 Lafayette
Berry George E. captain, house 41 Essex
Berry George F. conductor H. R. R. house 17 Skerry
Berry Jacob, ass't keeper Salem Jail, house do.
Berry Nathaniel, house 1 Cambridge
Berry Oliver, shoemaker, house 13 Warren
Berry Silas P. shoemaker, house Summit
Berry William H. nurse, house 8 Cambridge
Bertram Henry, mariner, house 134 Derby
Bertram John, merchant, 22 Asiatic Building, h. 370 Essex
Bertram Joseph H. M. merchant, 22 Asiatic Building, house
    40 Chestnut
Beston James, shoemaker, house 44 Phelps court
Bethune Neal, currier, house 2 Mason court
Bettis John B. agent (C. A. Richards, B.), house 34 Turner .
Beyer Hannah, widow, house 146 Derby
Bickford John M. watchman, house 5 Phelps court
Bickford S. E. clerk, 42 North. house 113 do.   [23 Union
Bicknell Samuel F. (J. South & Co.), 33 Lafayette, house ·
Bigelow Edwin R. ass. U. S. assessor, boards 57 Washington
Bigelow Ira H. provisions, 12 and 13 Market House, house 27
    Summer   [57 Washington
Bigelow Walter K. (James F. Almy & Co.), 188 Essex, boards

Bird Benjamin M. painter. house 9 High
Bixby Henry M. clerk, 151 Essex, boards 11 Washington
Black Jessie, widow, house 210,Derby
Black (*Patrick W.*) & Co. dry goods, 149 Essex, house 1 Dodge
Blackburn James E. ship carpenter, house 20 Ward
Blake Augustus S. carpenter, 29 Liberty, house 14 Broad
Blake Darius G. house 1 at the F. R. Lead Mills
Blake George T. house 406 Essex (12 Cornhill, Boston)
Blake Hannah, widow, house Silver
Blake Jethro, house 5 at the F. R. Lead Mills
Blake Susan Mrs. widow, house 14 Broad
Blanchard Mehitable Miss, house 92 Federal
Blaney John, mariner, house 21 Becket
Blanigan Francis, Naumkeag mill, boards 59 Harbor
Blethen Andrew R. stonecutter, boards 25 Harbor
Blethen True G. stoneyard, 25 Peabody, boards 25 Harbor
Blinn George H. carpenter, 40 Bridge, house 86 do.
Blinn George H. jr. carpenter, boards 86 Bridge
Blinn John F. carpenter, house 152 North, near nursery
Bliss George H. shoemaker, house 51 Warren
Blunt Charles, cooper, boards 18 Salem
Blunt Thomas, laborer, house 18 Salem ·
Blunt Thomas jr. cooper, 20 Park
Bly Charity, widow, house rear 9 Aborn
Bly J. Franklin, insurance agent, 243½ Essex, house at Danvers
Bly Joseph P. morocco dresser, boards rear 9 Aborn
Boardman Benjamin S. currier, house 15 Mason
Boardman Francis, captain, boards 33 Summer
Boardman Francis G. shoemaker, boards 31 Williams
Boden Lucy A. dressmaker, house 100 Derby
Boden Sarah, widow, house 7 Dean
Boden Thomas C. morocco dresser, house 128 North
Bodwell George H. carpenter, house 47 Buffum
Bond Lewis, tanner, house 6 Boston
Boran Ann, widow, house 36 Ward
Bosson (*Abraham F.*) & Glover (*George D.*), boots and shoes,
    10 Lafayette, h. 3 Hancock
Bott James, tanner, rear 27 Boston, house 27 do.
Bott John C. house 95 Boston
Bott John C. currier, house 246½ Essex
Bott Thomas, boots and shoes, 46 Derby, house 11 Becket
Bott William, tanner, house Boston, above Federal
Bott William C. currier, rear 27 Boston, house 27 do.
Bousley Nathaniel C. artist, 208 Essex, house 4 Rust
Boutelle Augustus, leathercutter, house 4 Harrison avenue
Boutelle Luther, Rev. house 4 Harrison avenue
Bovey James, clerk, boards 38 Phelps' court
Bovey Thomas L. teamster, boards 142½ Essex
Bowditch Daniel C. shipwright, house 6 Hardy
Bowditch Elizabeth G. house 28 Turner

Bowditch Francis N. Mrs. boards 13 Walnut
Bowditch George jr. mason, house 9 Bentley
Bowditch Harriet, widow, house 8 Liberty
Bowditch Sarah S. widow, house 9 Bentley
Bowditch Thomas, mariner, boards 9 Bentley   [house 1 Rust
Bowditch William A. crockery and glass ware, 227 Essex,
Bowdoin David W. photographic artist, 175 Essex, h. 9 North
Bowdoin (*W. L.*) & Shepard (*Luther D.*), dentists, 208 Essex,
    house 57 Washington
Bowen Edward, currier, house 23 Fowler
Bowen Thomas, shoemaker, house Chestnut, cor. Cambridge
Bowen Thomas E. boards Chestnut, corner Cambridge
Bowker Brothers (*George & Charles*), flour, grain, and salt, 227
    and 229 Derby
Bowker Charles (*Bowker Brothers*), house 44 Essex
Bowker George (*Bowker Brothers*), house 9 Crombie
Bowland Hannah, teacher private school, 1 Walnut, house do.
Bowley Isaiah H. P. shoe heeler, house 16 High
Bowman James Mrs. house 15 High street court
Boyce Hugh, tanner, house 14 Margin
Boyce Hugh, hostler, house 325 Essex
Boyce James, tanner, house 14 Margin
Boyce Jonathan H. shoemaker, house 15 Warren
Boyd John, house 90 Essex
Boyer Charles, master mariner, house 4 Laboratory
Boyle Cornelius, laborer, house 36 Ward
Boyle James, sailor, house near foot of Congress
Brackett Thomas, teamster, house 1 Perkins
Bracey John B. morocco dresser, house 55½ Broad
Braden James, tanner & currier, 47 Boston, house 169 Federal
Bradley John Mrs. widow, house 39 Peabody
Brady James, shoemaker, house rear 35 Harbor
Brady John, laborer, house E. Gardner, cor. South Prospect
Brady John, house 12 Prince
Brady John, shoemaker. boards 433 Essex
Brady Mrs. widow, house 28 Ward
Brady Patrick, switchtender E. R. R. house 12 Prince
Brady Thomas, cooper, house 88 Derby
Bragg Hartson, laborer, boards 25 Cedar
Brainerd Sarah Mrs. house 3 Palfrey court
Branigan James, shoemaker, house 57 Charter
Bray Ann R. dry goods and piano fortes, 76 Federal, house do.
Bray Daniel Mrs. house Whittemore
Bray Daniel H. Mrs. house 10 Ash
Bray Guilford P. mariner, house 10 Becket
Bredeen Henry A. tobacconist, house 3 Park
Breed George J. music teacher, house 8 Mall
Breed Holton J. captain, house 8 Mall
Breed Hubbard, bookkeeper (B.), boards 57 Summer
Breed Rebecca Mrs. dressmaker, house 57 Summer

Breed Rebecca S. house 57 Summer
Breen John, currier, house 2 Warren court
Breen John jr. mason, boards 3 Lagrange
Brennan Bernard, tanner, house 12 Goodhue
Brennan George, currier, house rear 143 Boston
Brennan James, mason, house rear Adams, Mason Hill
Brennan Mary, widow, house Tucker's wharf
Brennan Richard, currier, house 121 Boston
Brennan Thomas, laborer, house 15 River
Brennan Thomas (*Madigan & Brennan*), curriers, Goodhue,
   house Summit, near Prospect
Brennan Walter, currier, house 83 Mason
Brick Margaret, widow, house 13 Becket
Brick Patrick, tanner, house Phillip, near Harrod
Brickley Honora, widow, house 88 Derby
Brickley Patrick, saloon, 96 Derby, house 88 do.
Bridges John B. carpenter, house 5 Warren
Bridges Samuel B. boards 5 Warren
Briggs Charles C. carpenter, house 11 Gardner court
Briggs Charles N. at laboratory, house 77 North
Briggs George W. Rev. house 9 Summer
Briggs Hepsibel Mrs. house 15 Washington
Briggs James B. Mrs. house 38 Forrester
Briggs James C. house 38 Forrester
Briggs John F. currier, house 22 Albion
Briggs Joseph B. boards 15½ River (4th Mass. Battery)
Briggs Lydia Mrs. house 15¼ River
Briggs Nelson T. Naumkeag mills, boards 9 Ward
Briggs Susan A. Mrs. house 24 Lafayette
Briggs William A. shoemaker, house 36 St. Peter
Bright Mary E. Mrs. house 12 Becket
Brimblecomb Philip H. mariner, house 166 Bridge
Brittney Jane, widow, house 7 Dean
Broadrick Bridget, widow, house 11 Tucker's wharf
Broadrick Dennis, currier, house Mason Hill
Broadrick Thomas, laborer, house rear Adams, Mason Hill
Brogan Patrick, laborer, house 2 Parker's court
Brookhouse Elizabeth T. Mrs. house 3 Lynn
Brookhouse Robert, merchant, 16 Asiatic building, h. 51 Wash.
Brookhouse Robert jr. (*Wm. Hunt & Co.*), merchant, 16 Asiatic
   building, and Phillips wharf, house 13 Lynde
Brooking Thomas, blacksmith, house 15 Creek
Brooks Alfred R. teamster, house 2 Bentley
Brooks Asa, clerk, Essex, corner Newbury, house 11 Andrew
Brooks Augustus T. flour, coal, &c. 117 Derby, h. 20 Federal
Brooks Caroline A. house 11 Washington
Brooks D. Brainerd & Brother (*L. B. Brooks*), books, station-
   ery, and music store, 201 Essex, h. 54 Lafayette
Brooks Charles W. currier, boards 11 Andrew
Brooks Elizabeth Miss, music teacher, house 8 Norman

Brooks George A. clerk, boards 20 Federal   [Andrew
Brooks George G. clerk at James F. Almy & Co.'s, b. rear 11
Brooks Henry M. clerk and treasurer Forest River Lead Co.
    243½ Essex, house 112 Lafayette
Brooks Horace A bookbinder, at 232 Essex, b. 11 Andrew
Brooks Isaac C. carpenter, house rear 11 Andrew
Brooks Jean M. widow, house 2 Walnut
Brooks John F. clerk (B.) house 15 Andrew
Brooks John F. (19 Doane, B.), house rear 26 Brown
Brooks John G. Mrs. house 11 Andrew
Brooks John H. clerk, 226 Essex, boards 11 Andrew
Brooks Joseph H. tanner, boards 9 Spring
Brooks Luke, com. merchant (77 Com'l. B.), house 7 Briggs
Brooks Luke jr. grocer, 178 Derby, house 18 Lynde
Brooks Lyman B. (D. B. Brooks & Bro.), house at Brookline
Brooks Nathaniel H. grocer, 178 Derby, h. 11 Washington
Brooks Susan E. widow, house 13 Andrew
Brooks Wm. A. apothecary, 33½ Lafayette, house 125 Essex
Brophy Michael, currier, house 85 Mason
Brophy Patrick, currier, house Odell square
Brown Albert W. currier, boards 8 Albion
Brown Alexander, laborer, house 10 Derby
Brown Ann, widow, house 12 Northey
Brown Augustus, clerk, 179 Essex, boards 34 St. Peter
Brown Benjamin, shoemaker, house 21 Cedar
Brown Benjamin, police, house 4 North court   [Derby
Brown Benjamin K. coffinmaker at H. G. Hubon's, boards 26
Brown (Calvin) & Son (F. C.), provisions, 22 Derby square,
    house 4 Endicott
Brown Catharine, widow, house rear 8 Essex
Brown Charles, ship carpenter, boards 5 Linden
Brown Charles A. (G. A. & C. A. Brown), carpenter, 158
    Derby, house rear 14 Webb
Brown Charles A. currier, house 20 Fowler
Brown Charles E. painter, 29 Liberty, house 13 Briggs
Brown Charles E. master mariner, boards 7 Becket
Brown Charles R. teacher, boards 13 Washington
Brown C. Warren, draftsman, boards 8 Northey
Brown Daniel, gatekeeper at almshouse, at the Neck
Brown Daniel, shoe heeling manuf. (Lynn), house 25 Winthrop
Brown Daniel jr. grocer, 16 Mill, house 8 do.
Brown Edward, captain, house 118 Bridge
Brown Edward F. clerk, house 22 Brown   [h. 31 Dearborn
Brown Edward F. (Sanborn & Brown), currier, rear 11 Mason,
Brown Elizabeth L. Miss, seamstress, house 26 Derby
Brown Ephraim, Register of Deeds, Court House, h. 11 Winter
Brown Ezra L. shoecutter, boards 20 Fowler
Brown Ezra W. boards 23 Briggs
Brown Frances S. Miss, tailoress, house 26 Derby
Brown Francis, house 5 Brown

Brown Frederick C. (*Calvin Brown & Son*), boards 4 Endicott
Brown George, house 49 St. Peter
Brown George jr. stairbuilder, 41 North, house 9 Northey
Brown Geo, A. & Charles A. carpenters, 158 Derby, house 59
    Bridge
Brown George B. clerk, house 9 Northey
Brown George F. & S. lumber, &c., 38 North, h. 31 Dearborn
Brown George H. provision, boards 13 Rust
Brown Hannah Mrs. house 11 Oliver
Brown Harry, boards 15 Salem
Brown Harvey Mrs. house 44 Forrester
Brown Henry, mason, house 7 Turner
Brown Henry jr. painter, house 12 Allen
Brown Henry 3d, house 4 Phelps court
Brown Henry A. bookkeeper (B.), house 1 Newbury
Brown Henry F. carpenter, house 22 Crombie   [Lafayette
Brown Jacob F. principal of Brown School, house Leach, near
Brown James, seaman, house 31 rear Derby   [Mall
Brown James M. carpenter, Bridge, opp. St. Peter, house 23
Brown James R. mason, boards 7 Turner
Brown John, laborer, house foot Lagrange
Brown John B. Mrs. house 8 Albion
Brown John D. cooper, house 11 Carlton
Brown John W. tanner, house 1 North Pine
Brown Jonathan, house 34 St. Peter
Brown Joseph A. driver bread cart, house 8 Mill
Brown Joshua, shipwright, E. Gardner, near 23 Daniels
Brown Judith Mrs. house 408 Essex
Brown Lawrence, refreshments, 6 Washington, house 42 Harbor
Brown Lucinda, widow, house 20 Andrew
Brown Martha A. house 44 Forrester
Brown Mary Mrs. widow, house 4 River
Brown Mary A. widow, house 5 Friend
Brown Nathan H. shoemaker, boards 1 Perkins
Brown Nathaniel, house 22 Brown
Brown Nathaniel jr, captain, house 52 Lafayette
Brown O. B. music teacher, Normal school, house at Malden
Brown Patrick, laborer, house Grove near Mason
Brown Paul, currier, house 25 Charter
Brown Phillip, tanner, house rear 8 Essex
Brown Robert, laborer, house 20 Odell square
Brown Robert L. painter, Washington, cor. Bridge, h. 45 Mill
Brown Samuel, tanner, house 40 Beaver
Brown Samuel (*G. F. & S. Brown*), house 11 Dearborn
Brown Sarah, widow, house 15 Salem
Brown Sarah Augusta, teacher, house 44 Forrester
Brown Theodore, carpenter, boards 9 Ward
Brown Thomas W. watchman, house 128 North
Brown Willard H. (*Battis & Brown*), cigar manuf., 30 Front,
    house 35 Charter

Brown William, ordnance sergeant at Ft. Pickering on the Neck
Brown William B. Mrs. house 86 Bridge
Brown William F. boards 20 Andrew
Brown William P. clothing, 198 Essex, boards 86 Bridge
Brown Winthrop, wool puller, house 13 Aborn
Browne Albert G. agent treasury dept. (Ga.), h. Broad, corner
    Summer
Browne Albert G.counsellor (10 State, B.), h. Broad, c. Summer
Browne Anna M. house 32 Andrew
Browne Benj. F. office 226 Essex, Browne's block, house 1
    Hamilton   [13 Pleasant
Browne J. Vincent, collector internal revenue, 175 Essex, house
Browning Clement A. boards 8 St. Peter
Browning George B. Mrs. house 8 St. Peter
Browning (*John P.*) & Long (*Isaac M.*), ladies' furnishing
    goods, 177 Essex, house 298½ Essex
Bruce Daniel Mrs. house 9 Linden
Bruce Francis, currier, house 51 Warren
Bruce George W. currier, 63 Boston, house 65 do.
Bruce Robert P. carpenter, house 1 Collins
Bruce Sarah Mrs. house 51 Warren
Bryant Hiram K. physician, house 8 carpenter
Bryant John, farmer, house Bryant near North   '
Bryant Lydia K. nurse, house 39 Summer
Bryant Phœbe, widow, house 47 Buffum
Bryant Timothy, house 31 Charter
Buckley Cornelius, laborer, house Irving
Buckley David, laborer, house 30 Peabody
Buckley James J. refreshments 3 Wash. house 18 Cambridge
Buckley John, currier, house Harrod near Phillips
Buckley Lawrence, laborer, house 13 Congress
Buckley Michael, laborer, house Irving
Buckley Michael J. clerk, boards 18 Cambridge
Buckley Patrick, laborer, house 60 Broad
Buckley Patrick, laborer, house foot Ropes
Buckley Patrick, laborer, house 18 Cambridge
Buckley William, laborer, house rear 16 Turner
Buckley William, laborer, house 12 Ward
Buckman Sarah Miss, house 25 Chestnut
Buffington James, master mariner, house 115 Boston
Buffum Caleb, supt. Naumkeag Cotton Co. house 14 Curtis
Buffum Caleb H. boards 16 Buffum (China)
Buffum Charles C. 9 Front, house 3 North court
Buffum Charles M. clerk, 206 Essex, boards 14 Curtis
Buffum Charles S. undertaker, 43 Washington, h. at S. Danvers
Buffum David, lumber and steam planing, 9 Front, house 59
    Lafayette
Buffum George W. shoe stiffenings, 14 Lafayette, b. 8 Munroe
Buffum Joshua jr. physician, house 8 Munroe
Buffum Sarah L. Mrs. house 1 Chestnut

Buffum Susan Mrs. house 11 Federal
Buffum William P. inspector, Custom House, house 25 Buffum
Buggy John, laborer, boards 129 Derby
Bullock Isaac, house 158 Boston
Bullock Martha, widow, house 158 Boston
Bullock Mary A. C. tailoress, house 21 Union
Bullock Samuel J. boards 4 Andover   [Derby
Bullock Sarah, Elizabeth, Hannah and Mary, Misses, house 73
Bunker Charles, expressman, 10 Wash. h. Everett, cor. Salem
Bunker Eli, expressman, 10 Washington, h. Everett, c. Salem
Bunker Lizzie A. music teacher, boards 5 Mason
Bunker Lyman W. currier, house 5 Mason
Burbank Charles W. driver, house 36 St. Peter
Burbank David H. cabinetmaker, boards 9 Higginson square
Burbank E. Augustus (*Eben G. & E. A. Burbank*), carriage
    painter, West pl. house 27 Buffum   [6 Buffum
Burbank Eben G. & E. A. carriage painters, West place, house
Burbank Elizabeth, widow, house 300 Essex
Burbank Eliza Mrs. house 1 Prospect
Burbank Nathan, boards 1 Prospect
Burbank Joseph L. painter, boards 44 Pleasant
Burbank William T. painter, house 8 Cambridge
Burbank ———, Naumkeag mill, boards 59 Harbor
Burbeck William H. merchant tailor, 249 Essex, h. 8 Barton sq.
Burchstead William H. hairdresser, 4 Central, h. at Beverly
Burchsted David W. shoemaker, boards 62 Buffum
Burchsted Job, shoemaker, house 62 Buffum
Burding Thomas, cooper, house 15 High street court
Burding William Mrs. house 122 Boston
Burditt James F. surgeon U. S. A. house 7 Cherry
Burgess James, fisherman, house 26 Turner
Burgess Joseph, Naumkeag mill, h. East Gardner, n. Harbor
Burgess Lucy, widow, house 17 Crombie
Burgess William H. machinist, house 8 Elm
Burke Michael, currier, house 411 Essex
Burke Patrick, currier, house 60 Broad
Burke William, at gas works, house 20 Walnut
Burke William jr. boards 20 Walnut (U. S. N.)
Burkinshaw Charles, horsenail maker, house foot E. Gardner
Burkinshaw George, horsenail maker, 51 Harbor, h. 2 Perkins
Burkinshaw Michael, horsenail maker, house foot E. Gardner
Burnham Charles F. mariner, house 18 Becket
Burnham Elizabeth G. Mrs. house 20 Northey
Burnham George H. shoemaker, house 20 Northey
Burnham John T. house 12 Williams
Burnham Joseph Mrs. house 30 Derby
Burnham Joseph P. Mrs. house 8 Margin
Burnham Lydia P. widow, boards 24 Brown
Burnham Morris, laborer, house 8 Pingree
Burnham Samuel N. shoemaker, house 1 English

6

Burns Caroline, widow, house 68 Essex
Burns Charles E. sailmaker, boards 2 Palfrey court
Burns Clifford C. teamster, 117 Derby, house 2 Palfrey court
Burns Cornelius, baker, house 36 Derby
Burns Edward H. currier, boards 2 English
Burns John, shoemaker, boards 13 Congress
Burns John H. cooper, boards 2 Palfrey court
Burns Marcella, widow, house 8 Lynn
Burns Margaret, widow, house 2 English
Burns Martha, widow, house 2 Tucker's wharf
Burns Mary, widow, house 9½ Prince
Burns Peter, cooper, boards 2 English
Burr Ephraim, Custom House, house 120 Derby
Burr S. Norwood, machinist, 142 Essex, boards 21 Lafayette
Burrill Bradford, Naumkeag mill, house 56 Harbor
Burrill Charles, boards 15 Winthrop
Burrill Francis A. shoemaker, house 12 Turner
Burrill Franklin, Naumkeag mill, boards 56 Harbor
Burrill Josiah S. clerk, 245 Essex, house 385 do.
Burrill Mary Mrs. nurse, house 15 Becket
Burt David W. teamster, house 44 Beaver
Burt Sarah H. teacher, house 44 Beaver
Burton Warren Rev. house 94 Federal
Bush Charles, currier, house 45 Endicott
Bush Sarah Mrs. house 45 Endicott
Bushby Mary, nurse, house 6 Whittemore
Buster Andrew, currier, house 2 Silver
Buster Andrew jr. currier, boards 2 Silver
Buster James, tanner, house 2 Silver
Buster William, shoemaker, house 29 Beaver   [h. 53 Broad
Buswell (Eben) & Morton (Henry), boots and shoes, 196 Essex,
Butler Benjamin F. currier, house 55 North
Butler (James S.), Davis (Daniel O.), & Merrill (J. H.), stone-
    cutters, 18 Lafayette, house 30 Winthrop
Butler John, mariner, house 24 Peabody
Butler John, laborer, house Grove near Mason
Butler John S. shoemaker, Boston, house 12 Carlton
Butler Pierce, currier, house 12 Goodhue
Butler Prentiss, boarding, house 59 Harbor
Butler Richard, currier, house Aborn near Boston
Butler Thomas, currier, house 23 Fowler
Butman Francis C. merchant (31 India st. B.), h. 18 Pleasant
Butman Luther C. shoemaker, house 7 Webb
Buttrick Franklin, building mover, house 16 Becket
Buttrick Samuel B. bookkeeper, house 54 Mill
Buxton Alonzo B. clerk, house 2 Downing
Buxton Charles H. currier, house Irving, near Grove
Buxton Edward, shoemaker, house 1 Aborn   [Hathorne
Buxton George H. wines, &c. 6 Derby square, house 18
Buxton George F. printer, house 1 Beach, corner Mason

Buxton John H. currier, house 1 Beach, corner Mason .
Buxton Joseph jr. tanner & currier, h. 1 Beach, cor. Mason
Buxton Joseph S. house 15 Friend
Buxton Mary C. widow, house 14 High
Byard Charles, cooper, boards 20 Oliver
Byrne Anna E. variety store, 77 Federal, house do.
Byrne Cornelius, baker, house 36 Derby
Byrne James Mrs. house 19 Daniels
Byrne Julia, dressmaker, house 36 Derby
Byrne Luke, currier, house 8 Vale

CABEEN JOHN, teamster, 198 Derby, house 18 Pickman
Cabeen William, weigher at W. P. Phillips, house 2 Milk
Cabot Joseph S. pres. Asiatic National Bank, house 29 Chestnut
Cahill Patrick, laborer, house Becket avenue
Cahill Thomas, tailor, 9 Herbert, house do.
Cahoon Lawrence, laborer, house 204 Derby
Cain Martha, widow, house foot Pingree
Cain William, laborer, house Felt, near Dearborn
Caldwell Elizabeth W. Mrs. house 23 Turner
Caldwell John Mrs. house rear 11 Andrew
Caldwell Patrick, shoemaker, boards 16 Congress
Caldwell Terrence, laborer, house 16 Congress
Calef John, grocer, 26 Washington, house 126 Federal
Call George A. printer, boards 14 Walnut
Call Mary A. Mrs. nurse, house 14 Walnut
Call Samuel L. mariner, house 2 Carlton
Call Samuel L. boards 14 Walnut
Call Thomas S. clerk, house 14 Walnut
Call William H. cooper, house 4 Woodbury court
Callahan Catharine, widow, house Congress, West side
Callahan Dennis, stone layer, house 24 High
Callahan John, tanner, house rear Adams
Callahan John, laborer, house 6 High street court
Callahan John, currier, house 24 High
Callahan John, tanner, house 85 Mason
Callahan John jr. boards rear Adams, Mason Hill
Callahan Patrick, currier, house Adams
Callahan Patrick, currier, house 15 River
Callahan Thomas, laborer, house 36 Ward
Callelly William, laborer, house rear 10 Congress
Callen Mary A. widow, house 20 Liberty
Caller James M. leather dealer, house 146 Boston
Calley Samuel, painter, 180 Bridge, house 11 Rust
Calnan Jeremiah, laborer, house 15 River
Campbell David, shoemaker, boards 5 Gardner court
Campbell Frances, widow, house Harbor, corner Congress
Campbell Francis, teamster, 14 Washington, house 89 North
Campbell James, teamster, 14 Washington
Campbell James, currier, boards 5 North Pine

Campbell Patrick, stonecutter, boards 55 Derby
Campbell Richard J. tanner, boards 30 Beaver ·
Campbell Robert, shoemaker, boards 5 Gardner court
Campion Edward, morocco dresser, house 10 Hanson
Canlan Thomas, mariner, house 26 .Congress
Canney Sylvester G. engineer, E. R. R. house 2 Cross
Cannon John, engineer, house 184 Federal
Cannon Susan Mrs. house 53 Warren
Canty John, laborer, house rear 34 Ward
Capela William, mariner, house 9 Pond
Capulla Joseph Mrs. house 13 Curtis
Caraway Catharine S. widow, variety store, 58 Derby
Carey George A. shoemaker, house 4 E. Webb
Carey Hugh, laborer, boards 14 High street court
Carey Mary, widow, house 85 Mason'
Carey Patrick, laborer, boards 14 High street court
Carey Robert H. house 16 St. Peter
Carey Sophia, widow, house 16 Sewall
Carey Timothy, currier, boards 85 Mason
Carey William, at laboratory, house 13 School
Carey William Mrs. widow, house 14 High street court
Carey William E. upholsterer, house 13 School   ·
Carlen Samuel F. shoemaker, boards 55 Mill
Carleton Edward F. tanner, 14 Franklin, house 15 Mason
Carleton Frazer, tanner, 14 Franklin, house 42 Federal
Carleton Henry W. tanner, 14 Franklin, house 14 Buffum
Carleton Mary I. teacher, boards 8 Leach
Carleton Michael Mrs. house 22 Lynde
Carleton William E. tanner, boards 15 Mason
Carlton Elizabeth, house 21 Union
Carlton John, variety store, 158 Essex, house 88 Federal
Carlton Jonathan F. carpenter, house 7 Friend
Carlton Lewis, machinist, Naumkeag mill, house 3 Park
Carlton Mary, private school, 8 Leach, house do
Carlton Oliver, teacher, house 28 St. Peter
Carney Catharine, widow, house 23 Fowler
Carney Joanna, widow, house 9 Beaver   ·
Carney John, shoemaker, boards 11 Flint
Carney Maurice, currier, house Varney, near Hanson
Carney Patrick, tanner, house 9 Beaver
Carney Richard, boards 9 Beaver
Carney Thomas, laborer, house 11 Flint
Carpenter Ann, widow, house 17 Dearborn
Carpenter Danford B. boards 17 Dearborn
Carpenter David P. clothing, &c., 211 Essex, h. 17 Dearborn
Carpenter Irving S. clerk, boards 17 Dearborn   ·
Carr Andrew, mariner, boards 44 Harbor
Carr Arthur, at jute factory, boards 3 English
Carr Dennis, Essex railroad, house 20 Northey
Carr Eliza, widow, house 44 Harbor

Carr John, gum copal worker, house 3 English
Carr Michael, machinist, house 11 Carlton
Carr Patrick, laborer, house 6 Pearl
Carr Peter, mariner, boards 44 Harbor
Carr Simon, gum copal worker, boards 3 English
Carr William H. engineer, boards 44 Harbor
Carroll Dennis, laborer, house 24 Peabody
Carroll Dennis, mariner, boards 19 Daniels
Carroll Ellen, widow, house 10 Congress
Carroll Hannah P. Miss, boards 183 Bridge
Carroll Joanna, house foot of Congress
Carroll John, peddler, house 19 Daniels
Carroll John, laborer, house 50 Derby
Carroll Margaret, widow, house 34 Derby
Carroll Michael, tanner, house 62 Mason
Carroll Michael, currier, house rear 24 Beaver
Carroll Peter, operative, house rear 19 Daniels
Carroll Thomas, mariner, boards 19 Daniels
Casey John, clerk, Derby, boards do.
Carson Matthew, laborer, house 8 Phelps court
Carter Eliza Mrs. house 5 Mall
Carter Henry W. shoemaker, house 14 Prescott
Carter James H. boards 5 Mall   [14 Hardy
Carter John A. (*Sumner & Carter*), teamster, 130 Derby, h.
Carter Simon, house 20 Daniels
Carter William, house 5 Mall
Cartwright Edmund G. W. house 14 Union
Carty James H. shoemaker, on Union bridge, house 8 Walnut
Carver Horatio B. master's mate, boards 2 Curtis
Casey James, laborer, house 6 Carlton
Casey Maximer, Naumkeag mill, boards 1 Pingree
Casey Michael, laborer, boards 31 Derby
Casey Michael T. laborer, house Odell square
Casey Thomas, laborer, house 31 Derby
Casey William, weaver, house foot East Gardner
Cashman Jeremiah Mrs. widow, house 28 Ward
Cass James, laborer, house rear 11 Whittemore
Cass John, peddler, house Phillips, near Grove
Cassell Charles C. stove polisher, house 27 Cedar
Cassell Edward P. waiter, house 6 Ropes
Cassell John, currier, house 44 Phelps court
Cassell John M. hairdresser, 9 Washington, house 22 Cedar
Cassidy Edward, shoe stiffenings (So. D.), boards 6 Aborn
Cassidy Hugh, laborer, house 4 Peabody
Cassidy James, laborer, house foot East Gardner
Cassidy Michael, shoe stiffenings (So. D.), house 6 Aborn
Cassidy Patrick, laborer, house 10 High street court
Cassion David, currier, boards 77 Mason
Cassion Edward, tanner, house 77 Mason
Cassion Robert, currier, house rear Adams, Mason Hill

Cassman Joanna, widow, house Ward, near Peabody
Castles John, currier, house 40 Phelps court
Caswell Edmund, wheelwright, house 29 Barr
Caswell George A. painter, boards 29 Barr
Caswell Joseph E. currier, boards 29 Barr
Cate Aaron J. steam planer, house 17 Crombie
Cate John H. laborer, boards 1 Allen
Cate Mary E. nurse, house 19 Warren
Cate Rachael C. widow, house 1 Allen
Cate Samuel A. currier, house 19 Warren
Cate Shadrach M. physician, 60 Washington, house 62 do.
Catin James, currier, house rear 141 Boston
Caulfield Anthony A. captain, house 18 Andrew
Caulfield James C. captain, house 90 Essex
Caulfield William Henry, captain, 18 Andrew
Cavanaugh Christopher, gardener, boards 24 Briggs
Cavin Patrick, laborer, house 12 Friend
Cawthorn William R. cooper, house 7 Woodbury court
Chadwick Ann & Catherine, house 396 Essex
Chadwick John, house 12 Summer
Chalk Henry T. shoemaker, 144 Essex, boards 4 Bridge
Chamberlain Benj. M. (*Smith & C.*), jeweller, 207 Essex, h.
    88 Summer
Chamberlain Charles P. house 22 Oliver
Chamberlain John, shoemaker, house 16 Lemon
Chamberlain Hazen, boards 52 Buffum
Chamberlain Henry P. clerk, boards 116 Federal
Chamberlain (*James*), Harris (*James*), & Co. (*John Chamber-
    lain*), grocers, 24 Front, cor. Derby sq. h. 16 Lynde
Chamberlain James A. clerk (B.), boards 16 Lynde
Chamberlain John (*Chamberlain, Harris & Co.*), h. 6 Liberty
Chamberlain Joseph W. apothecary, 1 Boston, b. 6 Liberty
Chamberlain Luther L. currier, house 86 Boston
Chamberlain Richard H. house 52 Buffum
Chamberlain Samuel, tailor, 282 Essex, house 116 Federal
Chambers George, laborer, house foot of Ropes
Chambers James, laborer, house 11 Warren
Chambers John, shoemaker, house 27 Ward
Chambers Thomas R. mariner, house 13 High street court
Chambers William, laborer, house rear 26 Peabody
Champon Charles Mrs. widow, house 3 Leach
Chandler Abby B. house 9 Margin
Chandler Ellen A. teacher, Normal School
Chandler Gardner L. house 8 Mount Vernon
Chandler George A. fireman, boards 9 Margin
Chandler (*James P.*) & Co. (*Irving Stone and James A. Saun-
    ders*), periodicals and newspapers, 4 Wash. h. 9 Mt. Vernon
Chandler John, grocer, 106 Federal, house 7 River
Chandler John, policeman, house 22 Mechanic
Chandler Joseph (11 Chatham, B.), house 5 River

Chandler Joseph D. confectioner, house 168 Bridge
Chandler Joseph D. Mrs. house 7 River
Chandler Joseph S. shoemaker, house 101 North
Chaney James, house 14 Liberty
Chaplin Orril R. patternmaker, house 54 Bridge
Chapman Francis N. (Boston), boards 38 Pleasant
Chapman George R. (B.), house 103 Federal
Chapman Henry A. clerk, 246 Essex, boards 3 Harrison av.
Chapman Isaac N. Mrs. house 38 Pleasant
Chapman (*John*) & Palfray (*Charles W.*), publishers "Salem
  Register," 193 Essex, house 103 Federal
Chapman John O. printer, 193 Essex, house 14 Lynde
Chapman Walter A. dentist, 208 Essex, house at Danvers Centre
Chapman William H. boots and shoes, 246 Essex, house 3 Har-
  rison avenue
Chapple John D. tobacconist, house 12 Lynn   [Essex
Chapple William F. assistant city marshal, 11 Front, h. 113
Charnce, Mary, widow, house 67 Mill
Chase Abigail, widow, house 23 Becket
Chase Charles H. junk, house Harrod, opp. Phillips
Chase Charles H. clerk, F. R. Lead Co. boards 69 Lafayette
Chase Charles P. boards 347 Essex (Co. B. 24th Reg't)
Chase Charles W. shoemaker, boards Harrod opp. Phillips
Chase Fidelia E. Mrs. house 109 Federal
Chase Francis A. hairdresser, Higginson sq. boards 8 Barton
Chase George C. agent Forest River Lead Company, 243½
  Essex, house 69 Lafayette
Chase George C. currier, house Prospect
Chase George E. shoemaker, boards Harrod opp. Phillips
Chase George H. house 83 Federal
Chase Hannah B. widow, house 6 Andrew
Chase Hannah G. Miss, house 11 Becket
Chase Henry A. clerk, boards 22 Federal
Chase Hiram, cooper, house 23 Becket
Chase Jacob C. tinsmith, boards 2 Osgood
Chase James, stonemason, house 8 Barton
Chase James C. carpenter, house 58 Harbor, cor. Perkins
Chase John R. boards 8 Barton
Chase Lyman H. clerk, house 33 Essex
Chase Maria Miss, house 21 Federal
Chase Mary Ann, house 2 Osgood
Chase Nathaniel S. overseer Naumkeag mill, house 58 Harbor
Chase Robert, supt. Salem Boot and Shoe Co. 42 Mill, house
  Roslyn near Lafayette
Chase Stephen A. house 138 Federal
Chase Ward, carpenter, boards Prospect near Summit
Chase William, hardware and carriages, 206 Essex, house 22
  Federal
Chase William W. upholsterer, house 19 Briggs
Cheever Abigail Mrs. house 113 Federal

Cheever Abigail F. widow, house 400 Essex
Cheever Edward C. clerk (B.), boards 8 Federal
Cheever George N. Mrs. house 20 Winter
Cheever Joseph Mrs. house 8 Federal
Cheever Joseph C. gasfitter, Federal, house 89½ North
Cheever Mary P. Mrs. nurse, house 25 North
Cheever Thomas H. Mrs. boards 11 Washington
Cheever, see Chever
Cheney Joseph H. cigar maker, house 20 Becket
Chesley Charles H. fireman, house 22 Forrester
Chesley Charles H. jr. boards 22 Forrester (24th Regt.)
Chesman Charles H. Mrs. house 33 Salem
Cheswell Samuel, cabinetmaker, house 26 Hardy
Chever George F. counsellor, 11 Hardy, house do.
Chever George N. Mrs. 20 Winter
Chever James W. Mrs. house 11 Hardy
Chever Mary Mrs. house 79 Bridge
Chew Annie J. Mrs. dressmaker, 150 Essex, house do.
Childs Charles N. mariner, house 64 Mill
Childs Warren F. shoemaker, house 29 Derby
Chipman Andrew A. tinsmith, boards 347 Essex
Chipman Andrew M. tinware, &c. 347 Essex, house do.
Chipman Anstiss, house 424 Essex
Chipman Hannah. widow, house 424 Essex
Chipman James G. house 7 Andrew
Chipman John M. Mrs. house 2½ Federal
Chipman William H. clerk, 190 Essex, boards 347 Essex
Chipman William T. P. heeler, boards 61 Derby
Chisholm Ann F. private school, house 7 Pond
Chisholm Joseph, line and twine factory, 68 Mill, h. 7 Pond
Chisholm Martha, teacher, boards 7 Pond
Chisholm William, currier, house 422 Essex
Choate David, physician, house 23 Norman
Choate Francis, boards 6 Lynde
Choate George, physician, house 257 Essex
Choate George F. Judge of Probate and Insolvency, Court
    House, house 2d in Roslyn
Church Jonathan B. shoemaker, house foot of Ropes
Church Lemuel, engineer, house 15 Salem
Church Mary, widow, house 36 Ward
Church P. E. Miss, teacher, Higginson school, house 31 Broad
Church Sally Mrs. house 8 Ropes
Church Samuel, blacksmith, house 4 Laboratory
Churchill Algernon H. Naumkeag mills, house 58 Harbor
Churchill George A. machinist, house 17 Saunders
Churchill William, mariner, house 2 Conant
Churchill William H. shoemaker, 58 Bridge, house 2 Conant
Clancey Mary, widow, house 174 Derby
Clapp Albert (L. & A. Clapp), house 6 Downing
Clapp Dexter Rev. house 11 Pleasant

Clapp Luther & A. sawing and turning, 5 Front, b. 30 Andrew
Clapp (*William A.*) & Wetherell (*Pliny*), bonnet bleachers,
   3 Sewall, house 250 Essex   [court
Clark Albion J. provisions, 48 Harbor, house 1 Harbor street
Clark Alvah, teamster, boards 2 Jeffrey court
Clark Andrew, laborer, house 13 Prince
Clark Betsey, widow, house 20 Mill
Clark Charles A. D. clerk, boards at Henry Clark's [22 Harbor
Clark Charles S. (*Wiggin & C.*) wood, &c. 29 Peabody, house
Clark Edward A. laborer, boards 206 Derby
Clark Elizabeth Mrs. nurse, house 5 Orange
Clark George C. carpenter, house 110 Bridge
Clark George W. clerk, boards 110 Bridge
Clark Henry, restaurant, house Putnam   [Danvers
Clark Henry C. fruits, &c. Essex, cor. Washington, house at S.
Clark Henry M. machinist, boards at Henry Clark's
Clark Hugh, currier, house 7 Hanson
Clark James, horseshoer, West place, house 75 North
Clark John, mariner, boards 3 Warren
Clark John Mrs. house 4 Chestnut
Clark John D. captain, house 24 Andrew
Clark John W. flour, 3 Phœnix Building, house 3 Harbor
Clark Joseph, shoemaker, house 202 Derby
Clark Joseph F. boards rear 76 Federal
Clark Mary, widow, house 35 Harbor
Clark Mary A. Miss, house 86 Mill
Clark Mary A. widow, house 7 Ropes
Clark Melissa Miss, clairvoyant physician, house 122 Bridge
Clark Patrick, coal, 169 Derby, house rear 76 Federal
Clark Roger, hostler, Essex House, house 13 Ash
Clark Samuel C. painter, 112 Essex, house 5 Winter
Clark Sarah F. variety store, 18 Mill, house 20 do.
Clark Susan Mrs. house 114 Federal
Clark Thomas, harnessmaker, house 13 River
Clark Thomas H. harnessmaker, boards 13 Lynn
Clark William B. mariner, boards 3 Harbor
Clarke N. A. insurance agent, house 14 Lynde
Cleaveland Ebenezer, blacksmith, E. R. R. house 16 Northey
Cleaves Joshua, merchant, boards at Essex House
Clement James W. peddler, house Lemon court
Cleveland Lucy H. Mrs. house 62 Lafayette
Cleveland William S treasurer, Salem Turnpike Co. 42 Washington, house 62 Lafayette
Clifford Dennis T. tailor, 3 West Block, house 57 Charter
Clifford Mary, house 32 Union
Cline Thomas, laborer, house 10 Lynn
Clough Benjamin P. mariner, house 11 Curtis [h. 9 Lagrange
Clough Daniel E. & F. S. tinsmiths, and stove dealers, 4 Front,
Clough Frank S. (*D. E. & F. S. Clough*), house 107 North
Clough Robert P. currier, house 16 Flint
7

Clough Thomas, mariner, house 13 Carlton
Clough William H. master mariner, house 11 Curtis
Cloutman Charles E. watchman, house 8 Congress
Cloutman George W. pilot, house 7 Margin
Cloutman Joseph, notary public, 150 Essex, house 10 Union
Cloutman Sally and Priscilla, tailoresses, house 21 Union
Cloutman Samuel, shoemaker, house 19 Northey
Cloutman Stephen, captain, house 71½ Bridge
Cloutman Thomas T. 212 Essex, house 7 Elm
Cloutman William R. boards 10 Union (China)
Clynes Frank H. billiard hall, 4 Derby square, b. 7 Lynn
Clynes John, clerk, 14½ Derby square, boards 10 Lynn
Clynes Michael, laborer, house 77 Mason
Coan Stephen M. mariner, house 1 Carlton
Coane Lawrence, porter, 166 Derby
Coburn Charles J. shoemaker, boards 59 Harbor
Coburn George E. laborer, house 142 Bridge
Cochran James, Naumkeag mill, house 2 Perkins
Cochran Mary, widow, house 101 Derby
Cochran Mary, widow, house 2½ Perkins
Cochran Thomas J. wines, &c. 14½ Derby square
Cochran William Mrs. wines, &c. 10 Derby square, house 16
    Buffum
Cody Ellen, house 407 Essex
Cody James, currier, house Varney, near Hansom
Coffee Martin, laborer, boards 2 Pingree   [house 61 Mill
Coffin Calvin, shipwright, S. Marine Railway, Gardner street,
Coffin Edward, mariner, boards 32 Derby
Coffin William, mariner, boards 61 Mill
Cogan John, painter, house 4 Pratt street court
Cogan Maurice, spinner, boards 38 Harbor
Cogswell Eliza G. teacher, boards 26 Federal
Cogswell Epes, carpenter, house 24 Derby
Cogswell Henry Mrs. house 26 Federal
Cogswell Robert Mrs. house 26 Federal
Cogswell William, counsellor, 214 Essex, boards 33 Summer
Cohane Michael, currier, house 30 Varney
Colbert John, laborer, house rear 41 Derby
Colbert John jr. laborer, boards rear 41 Derby
Colbert William, cabinetmaker, boards rear 41 Derby
Colby Charles, operator sew. machine, house 10 Becket
Colby Isaac N. tanner, house 171 Boston
Colby John W. Mrs. variety store, 46 Peabody, house do.
Colby William C. calker and graver, house 91 Federal
Colby William R. (Boston), boards 91 Federal
Colcord Joseph A. coachman, 212 Essex, house rear do.
Cole Caroline J. teacher, Normal school, boards 69 Mill
Cole Catharine Mrs. fur sewer, house 206 Derby
Cole George, coachman, house 10 Church
Cole John H. mariner, boards 3 March

Cole John W. Mrs. house 3 March
Cole Mary A. Mrs. nurse, boards 69 Mill
Cole Nicholas, fisherman, house 206 Derby
Cole Solomon D. shoemaker, house 12 Park
Cole Thomas Mrs. house 28 Chestnut
Collier Chas. D. printer, house rear 22 Lemon
Collier John Mrs. widow, house 16 Conant
Collier John F. baker, house 31 Hardy
Collier John H. inner soles, &c, 15 Lagrange, house 35 Buffum
Collier Lois Miss, house 7 North court
Collier Perry, upholsterer, 12 Sewall, boards 16 Conant
Colligan Patrick, tanner, house Mason Hill
Collins A. clerk, 80 Derby
Collins Charles, clerk, 44 Derby, house 31 Turner
Collins Charles H. fish, 80 Derby, house rear 18 Becket
Collins Daniel, laborer, house 2 Tucker's wharf
Collins Dennis Mrs. house 9 Tucker's wharf
Collins Edward Mrs. house 31 Turner
Collins Edward, clerk, 29 Peabody, house 22 Harbor
Collins Edward A. mariner, boards 14 English
Collins Ellen, widow, boards foot of Tucker's wharf
Collins George B. cooper, boards 14 English
Collins Hannah B. widow, house 14 English
Collins Henry, mariner, boards 146 Derby
Collins Honora, widow, house 171 Derby
Collins Jeremiah, laborer, boards East Webb
Collins Joanna, washerwoman, house Becket avenue
Collins John, real estate agent, house 16 Daniels
Collins John, shoemaker, house 22 Congress
Collins John, laborer, boards 98 Derby
Collins John, at gas house, boards 98 Derby
Collins John, laborer, house 90 Derby
Collins John L. H. cooper, boards 14 English
Collins John S. coachman, house 17½ Carlton
Collins Margaret, widow, house 26 Mill
Collins Mary, widow, house 23 Charter
Collins Thomas, laborer, house 35 Essex
Collins Thomas, laborer, boards 129 Derby
Collins Thomas, shoemaker, 85 Derby, house do.
Collins Thomas, moulder, boards 10 Prince
Collins Timothy, laborer, house East Webb
Colman Benjamin auct. and com. 7½ Washington, h. 3 Winter
Colman Benjamin F. clerk, boards 3 Winter
Colman Geo. B. hairdresser, house 12 Porter
Colman John, laborer, house 4 Elm
Colman Mary A. Miss, teacher, house 3 Winter
Colman Sarah, widow, house 12 Porter
Colwell Elizabeth, widow, house 23 Turner
Comer Charles, baker, boards 51 Derby
Comer Joseph D. mariner, boards 51 Derby

Comer Solomon H. mariner, boards 51 Derby
Comer Vincent, watchman, house 51 Derby
Comstock Caroline, widow, house rear 9 Lemon
Comstock John, machinist, house 89 Harbor
Comstock Sheridan, shoemaker, boards rear 9 Lemon
Conant Herbert T. mason, house 3 Mt. Vernon
Conant John, mason, house 5 Harbor
Condon Thomas, shoemaker, house near foot Congress
Cone George R. conductor, house 12 Buffum
Conhane John, tanner, house 2 May street court
Conlon John, gardener, house 24 Briggs
Connell Charles, mariner, house 32 Ward
Connell Cornelius, currier, house 34 Beaver
Connell Martin, harnessmaker, house 14 Williams
Connell Patrick, currier, house 46 Beaver
Connelly James, currier, house 75 Mason-
Connelly John, blacksmith, house 6 Ward
Connelly Patrick, shoemaker, house 9 Cross
Conner Charles T. janitor, house 4 Herbert
Conner James, mason, house 30 Albion
Conners Brian, laborer, house 10 Herbert
Conners Cornelius, currier, house rear 125 Boston
Conners Jeremiah, currier, house rear Adams, Mason Hill
Conners John, currier, house rear Adams, Mason Hill
Conners Michael, laborer, house Mason Hill
Conners William, currier, house 407 Essex
Connor Dennis, laborer, house rear Congress, east side
Connor William, currier, house 22 River
Connors John, shoemaker, house Congress, west side
Connors Mary, widow, house Becket avenue
Connors Michael, at gas house, boards 91 Derby
Connors Michael, hostler, house 4 Creek
Connors Owen, laborer, house 26 Peabody
Connors Timothy, tanner, house 24 Prospect
Conrad David, ladies' furnishing goods, 163 Essex, h. rear do.
Conrey James H. currier, foot of Buffum, house 98 North
Conroy James, laborer, house 6 Ropes
Conroy Patrick, clerk, 3 High, house 6 do.
Conroy Thomas, porter, 135 Derby, house 101 do.
Converse Augustus W. tinsmith, house 30 Beaver
Converse Elizabeth B. house 1 Rust
Converse Francis T. shoemaker, house 30 Beaver
Converse Frederick, fireman, E. R. R. house 8 Margin
Converse George A. fireman E. R. R. boards 118 Boston
Converse Lucinda, house 118 Boston
Converse Robert, shoemaker, house 118 Boston
Conway Anna Maria, teacher, boards 63 Broad
Conway Chaplin, captain, house 20 Beckford
Conway Charles, mariner, boards 7 Herbert
Conway Daniel, laborer, house 10 Congress

Conway Edward A. baker, house 7 Herbert
Conway Francis, currier, house 4 Mason
Conway Hugh, currier, house 3 Oak
Conway James H. carpenter, house 7 Beach
Conway John H. currier and tanner, r. 69 Mason; h. 8 Buffum
Cook Adelbert, clerk, boards 62 North
Cook Alonzo, mariner, house 23 Oliver
Cook Ariel, refreshments, E. R. R. depot, h. 62 North
Cook Benjamin C. boards 4 Buffum
Cook Caleb, student, boards 5 Hathorne
Cook George B. clerk, 106 Federal, boards 88 do.
Cook George T. fish dealer, 29 North, near the bridge, h. 37 do.
Cook Henry, cooper, house 7 Orange
Cook Humphrey, house Union place
Cook James Mrs. widow, house 10 Hathorne
Cook James P. merchant, boards 64 Bridge
Cook John Mrs. house 36 Pleasant
Cook Mary Mrs. nurse, house 23 Oliver
Cook Simon L. clerk, 211 Essex, house 44 Charter
Cook William Mrs. house 5 Hathorne   [Charter
Cook William Rev. author Eucleia and Neriah, house 44
Cook William S. boards 36 Pleasant
Coolidge James, house 24 Winter
Coombs Elizabeth Miss, dressmaker, boards 51 North
Coombs Frederick, harnessmaker, 81 North, house 61 do.
Coombs Lydia Mrs. house 51 North
Copeland George A. clerk, boards 16 Norman
Copeland Robert M. carpenter, 8 North, house 16 Norman
Corbett Mary, widow, boards 297 Essex
Corbett Mary, widow, house 16 Turner
Corcoran Patrick, laborer, house 23 Saunders
Corkery Jeremiah, laborer, house 38 Ward
Cornelius Alonzo E. clerk 3 West's block, boards 4 Cross
Cornelius Alonzo G. merchant tailor, 3 West's block, Essex,
    house 4 Cross
Cornell Charles, mariner, house 1 Turner
Corning Martha, widow, boards 161 Boston
Cornish John, horse-shoer, boards 8 Herbert
Corrigan James, currier, house 11 Oak
Corrigan John, laborer, house 13 Lynn
Cotter Edward, laborer, house 21 Becket
Cotter John, mariner, boards rear 87 Derby
Cotter James, switch tender, Essex R. R. house 27 Ward
Cotter James, hostler, Essex House, house 60 Bridge
Cotter Simon, hostler, house rear 89 Derby
Cotter Simon jr. mariner, house rear 89 Derby
Cottle Alfred Mrs. house 17 Webb
Cottle Edward, laborer, boards 17 Webb
Cottle Elizabeth, widow, house 24 Peabody
Cottle Erastus, fireman, boards 15 Crombie

Cottle Mary, widow, house 17 Webb
Cottle Samuel, cooper, boards 17 Webb
Cottle Wm. Henry, ship carpenter, house 17 Webb
Cottrell James, mariner, boards 25 Essex
Cottrell Judith Mrs. house 25 Essex
Cottrell William A. baker, house 25 Essex
Cottrell William A. baker, boards 416 Essex
Couch Daniel, carpenter, house 7 Whittemore
Coughlin Hannah, widow, house 8 Pratt
Coughlin Mary, widow, house Webb, corner East Webb
Coughlin Maurice, laborer, house foot Park
Coughlin Michael, tailor, house Webb, corner East Webb
Coughlin Patrick, laborer, house rear 168 Derby
Coughlin Patrick, laborer, house 23 Saunders
Coughlin Thomas H. boards Webb, cor. E. Webb (24th Regt.)
Coughlin Timothy, tailor, house Parker's court
Courtis Hannah Miss, house 19 North
Courtis Nancy Miss, house 117 Federal
Cousins Joseph H. clerk, 222 Essex, boards 8 English
Cousins Thomas, mariner, house 8 English
Cousins Thomas jr. clerk, 173 Essex, house 99 do.
Covell Thos. N. oysters, 1 Phœnix building, house 33 Charter
Coveney Eugene, shoemaker, boards 34 Beaver
Coveney Mary, widow, house 34 Beaver
Cowlan Patrick, currier, house 9 Hanson
Cowley John, laborer, house South Prospect, cor. Pingree
Cox Benjamin, physician, house 132 Essex
Cox Eliza and Mary Ann, house 21 Norman
Cox Benjamin Mrs. widow, house 21 Norman
Cox Edward S. accountant, house 21 Norman
Cox Francis, treas, O. P. Co. (160 State, B.), h. 1 Chestnut
Cox (*Francis R.*) & Averill (*Charles A.*) blacksmiths, Bridge,
   corner North, house 105 North
Cox Mary G. Mrs. house 16 High
Cox Olivia, widow, house 11 Osgood
Coyle Rachel Miss, house 7 Prince
Crafts George, junk, 43 Derby, boards 4 St. Peter court
Craig Catharine Mrs. house 38 Essex
Craig Samuel, house 210 Derby
Crandell Charles A. Mrs. house 17½ Carlton
Crandell John, sailmaker, house 12 Becket
Crane Cornelius, Naumkeag mill, house 30 Congress
Crane Fanny, widow, house 19 Boston
Crane Mary E. milliner, 168 Essex, house at So. Danvers
Craney John, mechanic, house Varney
Cread James, tailor, house High
Creamer Benjamin Mrs. house 361 Essex
Creamer Frederick M. house 9 Newbury
Creamer George, house 126 Essex
Creamer Hannah Mrs. house 12 Walnut

Creamer Jeremiah, laborer, house Congress, near Harbor
Creamer Lawrence H. laborer, boards 1 Turner
Creamer Matthew, laborer, house 1 Turner
Creamer Matthew, laborer, boards Congress, near Harbor
Crean Jeremiah, tanner, house 23 Beaver
Crean Timothy, currier, house 27 Prospect
Credon John, laborer, house 42 Ward
Credon Mary, widow, house rear Adams, Mason Hill
Creed James, tailor, house 7 High
Creesy Charles, sup't Harmony Grove, house 8 Grove
Cresoe Henry, laborer, house 6 Prince
Cresoe Michael, ropemaker, house 17 Pond
Cressey J. Jewett, clerk, 173 Essex, boards 15 Briggs
Cressey Lyman M. (B.), boards 24½ Brown
Cressey William B. (B.), house 24½ Brown
Cressy John W. carpenter, house 75 Mason
Cressy Mehitable Miss, Home for Aged Females
Crierie Archelaus, house 11 Norman (Cal.)
Crocker Josiah, house 18 Mall
Crocker Josiah M. currier, boards 18 Mall
Crocker William, provisions, 9 Newbury, house 10 Williams
Cronan Daniel, currier, house 136 Boston
Cronan Edward, Naumkeag mill, house 5 Perkins
Cronan Hannah, widow, house 411 Essex
Cronan Jeremiah, mariner, house 58 St. Peter
Cronan John, mariner, boards foot Pingree
Cronan John, tanner, house rear Adams, Mason Hill
Cronan Michael, currier, house 136 Boston
Cronan Michael, laborer, house 82 Union
Cronan Michael, grocer, 2 and 3 Norman, house 5 May
Cronan Patrick, laborer, house Becket avenue
Crone Charles, mariner, house 22 Daniels
Crooks Paul, shoemaker, house 118 Boston
Crosby Alpheus (B.), house 109 Federal
Crosby George W. produce dealer, house 18 Sewall
Crosby Mary Ann, widow, house foot Perkins
Crosby Sarah, nurse, house 50 Mill
Cross Ann C. widow, house 19 Williams
Cross Anna C. bookkeeper, 243 Essex, boards 19 Williams
Cross Chas. B. shoemaker, Frye Mills Crossing, house 24 Vale
Cross George, tanner, boards 24 Vale
Cross George W. Mrs. house 1 Turner
Cross Hannah and Lucy, house 9 Liberty
Cross Henry J. City Treasurer, City Hall, h. Liberty Hill road
Cross Joseph S. clothing, 219 Essex, house 8 Union
Cross Joshua H. house 50 Lafayette
Cross Mary A. teacher, Pickering School, house 13 Liberty
Cross Parker, farmer, house Liberty Hill road
Cross Sarah E. teacher, boards 45 Endicott
Cross William Mrs. house 13 Liberty

Cross William T. clerk, 215 Essex, boards 19 Williams
Crowdis George R. currier, house Grove corner Phillips
Crowell Loranus Rev. house 2 Harbor street court
Crowley Ellen, widow, house 7 Ropes
Crowley John, tanner, house 27 Beaver
Crowley John J. laborer, house 4 High street court
Crowley John H. laborer, house 7 Ropes
Crowley Joseph O. currier, house Mason Hill   '
Crowley Patrick, tailor, house 383 Essex
Crowley Timothy, laborer, house 2 Friend
Cuff John, currier, house 38 Phelps court
Cullen James, laborer, house 136 North
Cullen James, laborer, house Tucker's wharf
Cullen John, shoemaker, house 132 North
Culliton John, tanner and currier, r. 91 Mason, h. 145 Federal
Cumings Susan S. Mrs. nurse and watcher, house 13 Ward
Cummings Edward, sailmaker, boards 13 Ward
Cumming Helen, widow, house 27 Charter
Cummins John, currier, house Mason, corner Friend
Cummisky Mary, widow, house 21 Ward
Cunning George, engineer, house Grove, near Mason
Cunningham Dorothy, widow, house rear 19 Daniels
Cunningham Eliza, house 46 Phelps court
Cunningham Francis M. mariner, boards 93 Derby
Cunningham Henry, morocco dresser, boards 93 Boston
Cunningham James, blacksmith, house 47 Harbor
Cunningham John, harnessmaker, 17 Daniels, house 93 Derby
Cunningham John, mariner, boards 93 Derby
Cunningham Lawrence (*Martin & C.*), boots and shoes, 145
    Essex, boards 8 Ward
Cunningham Margaret, widow, house 136 Boston
Cunningham Mary, widow, boards 177 North
Cunningham Mary, widow, house 46 Phelps court
Cunningham Matthew, currier boards 93 Derby
Cunningham Nicholas, shoemaker, boards 10 Prince
Cunningham William H. mariner, boards 93 Derby
Curran Catharine, widow, house 32 Union
Curran Hannah Mrs. house 22 Dearborn
Curran Stephen, chemist, house 22 Dearborn
Currier Daniel, laborer, house 39 Essex
Currier George H. dentist, 22 Washington, house at Hamilton
Currier George L. confectioner, 170 Essex, boards 39 do.
Currier (*Seth S.*) & Millett (*B. R.*), furniture, 259 and 261
    Essex, house 118 Federal
Currin Francis, tanner, house 32 Phelps court
Currin John A. mason, house 4 St. Peter court
Curtin John, upholsterer, house 17 Mason
Curtin Patrick, currier, house 9 Silver
Curtis Austin, currier, boards 40 St. Peter
Curtis Emanuel, trader, house 49 Broad

Curtis Lydia Mrs. house 40 St. Peter
Curtis Stephen W. shoemaker, house 28 Derby.
Curtis, see Courtis
Curwen George R. clerk Register of Deeds, house 21 Lynde
Curwen Henry, clerk, Asiatic Nat. Bank, boards 333 Essex
Curwen Jas. B. merchant, 22 Asiatic building, h. 331 Essex
Curwen Samuel R. captain, house 333 Essex
Cushing Maria, teacher, house 183 Bridge
Cushing Nancy P. Mrs. house 183 Bridge
Cushman Charles S. foreman at H. G. Hubons, h. 1 Jeffrey ct.
Cushman Silas S. machinist, house 164 Federal
Cusick Patrick, shoe stiffenings, rear 55 Warren, h. 55 do.
Cutler Nathan P. pocketbookmaker, boards 130 Boston
Cutler William, pocketbookmanufac., 138 Boston, h. 105 do.
Cutts Benj. blacksmith, 8 Sewall, house 30 Beckford
Cutts Love P. music teacher, house 30 Beckford

DABNEY MARGARET P. Miss, boards 20 Beckford
Dadd Patrick, laborer, house 30 Peabody
Dady William, currier, house 9 Beaver
Dagnan James, laborer, house Lynch, cor. Perkins
Dagnan Rose, widow, boards Lynch, corner Perkins
Dailey Robert, city express, 5 Arrington building, h. 8 Porter
Daily William, laborer, house Thorndike
Dakin Rachel Mrs. house 77 Summer
Daland Charles, mariner, house 109 Essex
Daland Joanna Miss, carpetmaker, 12 Beckford, h. 14 do.
Daland Mary, tailoress, house 14 Beckford
Daley Catharine, widow, house 2 Perkins
Daley Daniel, watchman 212 Essex, house 11 Gedney court
Daley James P. Peabody's mill, house 4 Bartlett
Daley Jeremiah, laborer, house 18 Charter
Daley Jeremiah, laborer, house 23 Congress
Daley John, baker, house 9 Ropes
Daley Margaret, widow, house 160 Bridge
Daley Michael, baker, house 2 Pratt
Daley Patrick, currier, house 23 Congress
Daley Timothy, currier, house Adams
Dalrymple George W. machinist, boards 6 Herbert
Dalrymple James, asst. city marshal, police station, h. 6 Herbert
Dalrymple John J. boards 6 Herbert (Oregon)
Dalrymple John J. jr. house 19 Daniels (Cal.)
Dalrymple Margaret Miss, house 10 Essex
Dalrymple Simon O. weigher & gauger, Custom House, house
    99 Essex
Dalrymple Simon O. boards 6 Herbert (China)
Dalrymple William H. attorney (Lynn), boards 6 Herbert
Dalton Caroline P. teacher, boards 56 Forrester
Dalton Charles H. cutter, house rear 18 Beckford
Dalton David, currier, house 36 Mill

Dalton Edward, currier, house 4 Creek
Dalton Edward A. calker, house 127 Essex
Dalton Edward E. tailor (B.), house 88 North
Dalton Eleazer M. clerk 212 Essex, house 58 Forrester
Dalton James, laborer, boards 36 Mill
Dalton John C. coaches, house 7 Everett
Dalton Joseph A. currier, 61 Mason, house 75 Boston
Dalton J. Frank, clerk Custom House, boards 75 Boston
Dalton Lucy F. widow, house 163 Boston
Dalton Patrick, bootmaker, 19 Ward, house 17 Salem
Dalton Patrick, shoemaker, house 17 Salem
Dalton Samuel, leather dealer (B.), boards 115 Boston
Dalton Sarah N. Mrs. nurse, house 127 Essex
Dalton Sepherino M.'currier, house 2 Beaver
Dalton William T. currier, house 19 Creek
Daly William J. Rev. house 152 Federal
Damon Samuel H. second hand clothing, 5 Liberty, boards 26
     Essex
Dane Joseph F. shoes and leather (69 Pearl, B.), house Essex,
     cor. Summer
Danforth Edward F. provisions, 33 Endicott, h. Osborne Hill
Danforth Joseph A. carpenter, house 43 Forrester
Danforth Samuel G. carpenter, 31 Endicott, house 13 Winthrop
Danhey Lawrence, confectioner, boards Essex
Daniels Alonzo L. shoemaker, boards 125 Lafayette
Daniels Charles H. clerk, 70 Federal, house 3 Dean
Daniels Edward A. house 125 Lafayette
Daniels George P. & William K. dry goods, 190 Essex, h. 112
     Federal
Daniels John, shoemaker, house 125 Lafayette
Daniels John B. house 126 Lafayette (48 Regt. M. V.)
Daniels Stephen, provisions, 70 Federal, house 68 do.
Daniels Warren, shoemaker, house 128 Lafayette
Daniels William, shoemaker, house 64 Broad
Daniels William F. hairdresser, 22 Washington, bds. 64 Broad
Daniels William K. (Geo. P. & W. K. Daniels), 190 Essex,
     boards 26 Washington, So. Danvers
Darcy John, shoemaker, Aborn near Boston, house do.
Darling Charles L. shoecutter, boards 14 Odell sq.
Davenport David, currier, house 20 Vale
Davenport Jonathan K. brakeman, boards 17 Harbor
Davenport J. Kingsbury, provisions, 46 Pleasant, h. 6 Cross
Davenport Mary, widow, house 59 Mill
Davenport Wesley C. teamster, boards 59 Mill
Davidson Henry, tanner, house 57½ Broad
Davidson Henry jr. tanner, boards 57½ Broad ·
Davidson John, tanner, house 75 Mason
Davidson Moses coach painter, house 20 Albion
Davidson Theodore, machinist, boards 20 Albion
Davidson Thomas F. h. 20 Albion

Davis Alice N. Mrs. house 27 Forrester
Davis Benjamin T. Mrs. house 15 Mall
Davis Charles H. painter and glazier, 85 North, house Walter
  cor. Dodge
Davies Charles W. boards 12 Upham
Davis Christopher C., E. R. R. house 60 North
Davis Daniel C. (*Butler, Davis, & Merrill*), house at Chelsea
Davis Daniel M. carpenter, house 12 Upham
Davis Daniel W. shoemaker, boards 64 North
Davis Dudley B. captain, house 15 Osgood
Davis George H. clerk, boards 108 North
Davis George L. shoemaker, boards 12 Upham
Davis H. teacher, High school, boards 33 Summer
Davis Hannah T. fancy goods, dressmaking, 155 Essex, h. do.
Davis Horatio G. hackman, Essex House
Davis Jacob P. express, 8 Washington, house 396 Essex
Davis James B. clerk, 237 Essex, boards 16 Williams
Davis James P. carpenter, house 110 Essex
Davis John Mrs. house 16 Williams
Davis John, fisherman, boards 15 Osgood
Davis John, boards 16 Williams
Davis John H. junk, house 20 Pickman
Davis Jonathan, mason, house 6 Dearborn
Davis Joseph W. Mrs. house 12 Upham
Davis J. P. Mrs. milliner, 110 Essex, house do.
Davis Mary Mrs. house 21 Buffum
Davis Mary C. widow, house 4 Palfrey court
Davis Mary E. teacher, house 7 Buffum
Davis Nancy P. widow, house 8 Hardy
Davis Nathaniel R. fisherman, house 1 Warner
Davis Paine M. shoemaker, house 64 North
Davis Richard, merchant, house 19 Hardy
Davis Sarah P. house Dean
Davis Stephen L., E. R. R. car shop, house 149 Bridge
Davis Stephen W. clerk, 12 Washington, house 7 Margin
Davis Sylvester P. engineer, house 108 North
Davis Warren P. currier, house 70 Boston
Dawes Mary, widow, house 58 Federal
Dawson George, shipkeeper, house 22 Carlton
Day Albert, carpenter, 16 Lafayette, house 3 Mount Vernon
Day Amos P. (*Goldthwait & D.*), 221 Derby, h. 35 Lafayette
Day Aziel, currier, house 9 Albion
Day Benjamin Mrs. house 18 Walnut
Day Catharine, widow, house 18 Charter
Day Elizabeth B. Miss, dressmaker, house 18 Walnut
Day James, farmer, house Mason Hill
Day John, captain, house 15 North
Day Mary, widow, house 18 Charter
Day Mary, widow, house 24 Beaver
Day Samuel, house 57 Washington

Day Thomas Mrs. house Grove, near School
Dayton Isaac, harnessmaker, house 108 Boston
Dean George Mrs. house 45 Broad
Dean James, laborer, house foot of Northey
Dean Sarah B. widow, house 120 Bridge
Dearborn Charles A. clerk (B.), house 12 Nursery
Dearborn Henry C. Mrs. house 4 May
Dearborn John R. laborer, house 7 Nursery
Dease Lawrence, tailor, 21 Central, house 76 Federal
Debaker Victor F. captain, house 36 Essex
Deboe James, currier, house 29 Boston
Decker Jefford M. house 11 Margin
Decker Robert M. carver, house 10 Winthrop
Decker Samuel E. clerk, boards 11 Margin
De Costa Emanuel, bowling saloon, 6 Washington, b. 6 Norman
Deffel Joseph, mariner, house 51 Derby
De Forrest Daniel, wood sawyer, house 9 Tucker's wharf
Defreace Jacob H. hairdresser, house 12 Cedar
De Gersdorff B. physician, 255 Essex, house do.
Deland Eliza and Helen Misses, house 109 Essex
Deland Mary Miss, house 155 Bridge
Deland Samuel D. shoemaker, house 155 Bridge
Deland Susan Miss, house 2 Church
Delaney Thomas, currier, house 9 Hanson
Delaney Thomas, currier, house 36 Phelps' court
Delong James, Naumkeag mill, boards 59 Harbor
Delong James W. machinist, house 14 Park
Delury David Mrs. widow, house 4 High
Delvecho Petro, currier, house 8 Phillips
Dempsey Catherine, widow, house 7 Hanson
Dempsey James, boards 7 Hanson
Dempsey Patrick, currier, house rear Hanson
Dempsey William, express, house 82 Mill
Dennehey Michael, shoemaker, house rear 7 Charter
Dennen Joseph, farmer, house Tremont, n. S. Danvers line
Dennett Ruth, widow, house 28 Harbor
Dennis Benjamin S. clerk, 16 Market House, house 7 Curtis
Dennis Devereux, carpenter, r. 17 Lafayette, h. 15 Dearborn
Dennis George F. conductor H. R. R. boards 7 Curtis
Dennis William D. architect, 243½ Essex, boards 15 Dearborn
Denny Timothy Mrs. widow, house 16 Congress
Denton Charles A. carpenter, boards 59 Harbor
Derby Abigail Mrs. house 4 Blaney
Derby Caroline R. Miss, house 122 Lafayette
Derby Charles, house 30 Williams
Derby Charles, watchmaker, 287 Essex, house 47 St. Peter
Derby Charles jr. (Sandwich Islands), house 4 Blaney
Derby Elizabeth D. Mrs. house 79 Lafayette
Derby Henry, house 59 Federal
Derby H. Matilda Miss, house 122 Lafayette

Derby John H. insurance agent, 214 Essex, house 59 Federal
Derby Marianne B. Miss, house 122 Lafayette
Derby Mary, artist, house 4 Blaney
Derby Perley, dentist, 208 Essex, house 15 Northey
Derby Putnam T. boards 6 Andrews
Derby Susan A. Mrs. house 118 Federal
Derby William H. clerk, boards 59 Federal
Desmond Daniel, boards 170 Derby (U. S. N.)
Desmond Jeremiah, mariner, boards 174 Derby
Desmond John, shoemaker, house 170 Derby
Devereux Charles U. boards 19 School
Devereux Elizabeth I. Miss, house 8 Pleasant
Devereux George H. counsellor, house 19 School
Devereux Henry, house North Salem
Devereux Humphrey, merchant, boards 33 Summer
Devereux John F. counsellor, boards 19 School
Devereux Walter F. student, boards 19 School
Devine Henry P. clerk, 14½ Front, house 29 Cedar
Devine James, Naumkeag mill, house 49 Harbor
Devine John, laborer, house 9 Tucker's wharf
Devine John, laborer, boards 49 Harbor
Devine Michael, clerk, boards 49 Harbor
Devine William Henry, wines, &c., house 29 Cedar
Devlin Jones Mrs. house 11 Park
Devlin Mark H. clock repairer, house 47 Harbor
Dewing Dolly, dressmaker, house 16 Central
Dewing Joseph Mrs. house 28 Beckford
Dewing Josiah, captain, house 93 Federal
Dexter Benjamin W. Mrs. house 8 Church
Dickerson George, stoveworker, 29 Front, h. r. 8 Whittemore
Dickerson Ovid, laborer, house rear 8 Whittemore
Dickson Thomas Mrs. house 2 Mason
Dickson Walter S. shoeheeler, boards 2 Mason
Dike John, merchant, house 52 Federal
Dimond Abigail Mrs. house 2 Botts court
Dimond Abigail, dressmaker, house 2 Botts court
Ditmore Sarah, widow, house 12 Oliver
Dix Asa C. dry goods, 245 Essex, house 78 Summer
Dix Charles E. mariner, boards 55 Derby
Dix Edward D. Mrs. house 83 Summer
Dix Eliza A. widow, nurse, house 55 Derby
Dix George A. currier, house 424 Essex
Dix Thomas M. supt. Mechanics' Hall, house 86 Summer
Dix Thomas M. jr. clerk, 178 Derby, boards 86 Summer
Dixon Henry, tailor, 3 West block, house rear 9 Charter
Dlury Daniel, laborer, house 7 Ward
Dockham Eliza, house 397 Essex
Dockham Elizabeth, nurse, house 12 Essex
Dockham Mary Ann, dressmaker, house 397 Essex
Dockham Mary E. teacher, boards 397 Essex

Dockham William S. teamster, house 11 Congress
Dodd John, hostler, 212 Essex, house 12 Ash
Dodd Patrick, laborer, house rear 18 Lafayette
Dodd Patrick, laborer, house 36 Peabody
Dodd Thomas, switchman, E. R. R. house 31 Mill
Dodge Allen W. county treasurer, Court-house, h. at Hamilton
Dodge Charles H. mariner, house 9 Federal
Dodge Charles H. boards 9 Federal
Dodge Charles H. mariner, house 5 Orange
Dodge Charles T. supt. Alms-house
Dodge Charles W. tinsmith, 29 Front, boards 5 Lemon
Dodge Clara Miss, house 375 Essex
Dodge David Mrs. house 5 Orange
Dodge Eben, house 4 Federal court
Dodge Edwin H. bookkeeper at C. A. Ropes's, boards 3 Brown
Dodge Ellen M. teacher Normal school, house 5 Lemon
Dodge Emma Miss, tailoress, boards 5 Hardy
Dodge George, house 3 Brown
Dodge George A. currier, house 93 Bridge
Dodge George A. house 2 Conant
Dodge Isaac B. shoemaker, house 113 Boston
Dodge Jacob L. wood and coal, 17 Lafayette, house 18 do.
Dodge James A. clerk war dept. house 4 Federal court
Dodge John N. carpenter, house 24 Derby
Dodge John P. Mrs. house 12 Church
Dodge John W. carriage maker, 29 & 31 Liberty, h. 26 do.
Dodge Joseph S. tanner, house 6 Silver
Dodge Josiah, carpenter, house 8 Conant
Dodge Josiah S. painter, house 8 Conant
Dodge Judson F. machinist, boards 38 Harbor
Dodge Leverett, painter, house 76 Mill
Dodge Lucy, widow, house 18 Lafayette
Dodge Mary Mrs. at Home for Aged Females
Dodge Mary Ann Mrs. seamstress, house 9 Federal
Dodge Richard F. captain, house 8 Saunders
Dodge Temple Mrs. seamstress, house 91 North
Dodge Thomas F. carpenter, house 55 Federal
Dodge Thomas S. coachman, 9 Hamilton, house 9 Bott's court
Dodge Thomas W. carpenter, house 55 Federal
Dodge Wm. baggage master, E. R. R. house 7 Federal
Dodge William M. shoemaker, 3 Lemon, house 5 do.
Doggett William, laborer, house 2 Pratt street court
Doherty Charles, house 24 Ward
Doherty Charles Mrs. house 24 Ward
Doherty George, laborer, house 24 Northey
Doherty John, laborer, house 24 Northey
Doherty Lawrence, laborer, house 21 Ward
Doherty Patrick, laborer, house 22 Daniels
Doherty William, laborer, house 34 Derby
Dolan Catharine, widow, house Pratt

Dolan Edward, laborer, house rear Adams
Dolan Morris Mrs. house 30 North
Dolan Patrick, currier, house 6 High street court
Dolan Patrick, currier, house 9 Beach
Dolan Patrick, currier, house Pratt
Dolan William, gardener, house 89 North
Dole Lydia A. Mrs. house 4 Andover
Dolliver John, shoemaker, house 14 Norman
Domican Ellen, widow, boards 30 Williams
Domican George, upholsterer, house 30 Williams
Dominick Michael Mrs. house 24 Essex
Donaghan John, laborer, house foot Pingree
Donahoe John, laborer, house 31 Derby
Donahoe Michael, teamster, D. H. Jewett's, house 36 Mill
Donahoe William Mrs. house 26 Union
Donahue Patrick, machinist, boards 176 Derby
Donahue Patrick, laborer, boards 26 Union
Donahue William, laborer, house 21 Ward   [Bridge
Donaldson Alex. pump and block maker, 141 Derby, house 99
Donaldson James, currier, house 19 Mason   [Bridge
Donaldson John, pump and block maker, 141 Derby, house 99
Donlian Malachi, currier, house 3 Silver
Donovan Catharine, widow, house rear 19 Daniels
Donovan Catherine, widow, house 40 Peabody
Donovan Dennis, laborer, house 29 Prospect
Donovan Ellen, widow, house 28 Carlton
Donovan Jeremiah, wheelwright, house 64 Mason
Donovan John, laborer, house 144 Derby
Donovan John, currier, house rear 133 Boston
Donovan John, laborer, house rear 19 Daniels
Donovan John, machinist, boards 23 Charter
Donovan Michael, currier, house 16 Avon
Donovan Michael, shoemaker, rear 168 Derby, h. 23 Charter
Donovan Michael, laborer, boards 23 Charter
Donovan Patrick, laborer, house 5 Ward
Doody John, currier, house 12 Friend
Doreum Melvin E. baggage, E. R. R. boards 6 Cross
Doren Catharine, widow, boards Varney near Putnam
Doret Stephen, mariner, house 29 Turner
Dorman Joseph, boarding, house 24 St. Peter
Dorsey Alice, widow, house 20 Carlton
Dorsey Michael, currier, house 42 Beaver
Dorsey ———, mariner, house 11 Albion
Doucet Joseph, foreman, house 3 Lynn road
Douglass Albert C. clerk (B.), boards 11 North
Douglass Albert L. mariner, boards 48 Derby
Douglass George W. mariner, house 27 Carlton
Douglass Joseph P. laborer, boards 48 Derby
Douglass William, laborer, house 48 Derby
Douglass William Mrs. boards 16 Sewall

Dow George W. laborer, house rear 24 Hancock
Dow Zilpha M. Mrs. house 10 Whittemore
Dowbridge Andrew, lobsters, house 9 Gardner court
Dowbridge Andrew jr. fish, 21 Front, house 33 Pleasant
Dowbridge Henry F. mason, house 11 Gardner court
Dowdell Elizabeth, widow, house 44 Union
Downey Nancy, widow, house foot Pingree
Downie E. A. Mrs. milliner and fancy goods, 264 Essex, h. do.
Downs Joshua D. painter, boards 25 Essex   [11 Washington
Downs S. M. teacher of singing and pianoforte, 175 Essex, b.
Downs Nathaniel, carpenter, house Cabot, cor. Hancock
Downs William, tin peddler, house 4 Union place
Downing Catharine, widow, house 22 Williams
Downing Charles M. cook, house 68 North
Downing Henry W. currier, house 14 Salem
Downing John H. (*Thos. W. Downing & Co.*), house 20 Brown
Downing John P. clerk (U. S. Asst. Treas. Office, B.), boards
   14 Salem
Downing John W. Mrs. house 14 Salem
Downing Thos. W. & Co. (*J. H. Downing*), dry goods and car-
   petings, 179 Essex, house 20 Brown
Dowst David, baker, house 23 North
Dowst David B. teamster, Charter, c. Central, h. Dodge's ct.
Dowst Jesse, teamster, boards 21 Lafayette
Dowst Joseph A. lastmaker (Lynn), house 10 Upham
Dowst Justin M. expressman, 10 Washington, b. 21 Lafayette
Dowst Richard, expressman, house 2 Vale
Dowst Richard jr. carpenter, house 8 Nursery
Doyle Edward, laborer, house 38 Ward
Doyle John, laborer, house 99 Derby
Doyle John, currier, house 27 Albion
Doyle Thomas, lumber, 157 Derby, house 33 Summer
Draper Arnold Mrs. millinery, 260 Essex, house do.   [Union
Dresser Augustus, jewelry and fancy goods, 152 Essex, h. 31
Drew Harrison, shoecutter, house 18 River
Drew James, laborer, boards 16 Ward
Drew Mary A. Mrs. house 16 High
Drew ———, shoemaker, house 18 River
Drinan John, charcoal, house Irving
Drinkwater James, laborer, house rear Congress, east side
Driscoll Cornelius, hatter, 128 Derby, house do.
Driscoll Cornelius, hostler, boards 5 Buffum
Driscoll Daniel, at fish market, boards 92 Derby
Driscoll Daniel, laborer, house 5 Ward
Driscoll Joanna, widow, house 92 Derby
Driscoll John, house rear 7 English
Driscoll Margaret, widow, house 10 Herbert
Driscoll Mary, widow, house Nichols, cor. Varney
Driscoll Patrick, laborer, house 98 Derby
Driscoll Patrick, laborer, house 95 Derby

Driscoll Thomas, laborer, house Tucker's wharf
Driscoll Timothy, at machine shop, boards 92 Derby
Driver George, foreman, 16 Washington, h. Cedar, cor. Cherry
Driver Samuel, 34½ Front, boards 24 St. Peter
Driver Stephen, shoe manufacturer, 16 Washington and 34½
  Front, house Beaver Brook, North Danvers
Driver Stephen P. (39 Pearl street, B.), house 10 Barton sq.
Drown William P. blacksmith, boards 1 Blaney
Drumey Jeremiah, laborer, boards Prospect, near Summit
Ducey John, currier, house 11 Beaver   [Danvers
Dudley Albion M. (A. S. Dudley & Co.), 224 Essex, boards at
Dudley A. S. & Co. (Thomas Walwork and Albion M. Dudley),
  dentists, 224 Essex, house at Danvers
Dudley Susan J. milliner, 224 Essex, boards 29 Brown
Duffie John, tanner, house 11 Beaver
Duffy Peter, laborer, boards 47 Harbor
Dufries Henry, Naumkeag mill, boards 70 Harbor
Dufries William, Naumkeag mill, boards 70 Harbor
Dugan Bernard, currier, house 14 Oak
Dugan Dennis, laborer, house 30 Ward
Dugan James, currier, rear 95 Mason, house 101 Mason
Dugan John, Naumkeag mill, house foot Pingree
Dugan Timothy, laborer, house rear 1 Pingree
Dugan William, laborer, house 6 Allen
Dummer John S. fish dealer, 21 Front, b. Farmers' Exchange
Dunbar Henry, carpenter, house 21 Creek
Duncklee Elizabeth, house 121 North
Dunham Charles, cigar maker, boards 55 Derby
Dunham Margaret, nurse, boards 1 Perkins
Dunn Margaret A. teacher, house 19 Becket
Dunn Mary, widow, house 50 Broad
Dunnihy Lawrence, servant, boards 36 Ward
Dunnihy Mary, widow, house 36 Ward
Dunzack Daniel N. painter, house 7 Winter
Dunzack Sarah Mrs. house 54 Endicott
Duperre Julius, currier, house rear Adams, Mason Hill
Durgin John, peddler, house Tucker's wharf
Durgin Mary T. widow, house 56 Charter
Durgin Thomas, mariner, boards Tucker's wharf
Durgin William P. calker, house 17 Lynde
Dutra Francis, shipkeeper, house 8 Pearl
Dutra Theodore, shoemaker, boards 8 Pearl
Duvall Mitchell Mrs. house 84 Derby
Dwinell David L. M. painter, 37 North, house 70 North
Dwyer Edward, bootmaker, house 8 Peabody
Dwyer John, merchant (27 Union whf. B.), house 336 Essex
Dwyer John F. Mrs. house 364 Essex
Dyer Charles E. baggage master E. R. R. boards 6 Cross

9

EAGAN JAMES, gardener, house 4 High
Eagan James B. wines, &c. 10 Derby square, house 16 Buffum
Eagan Patrick D. currier, house Mason Hill
Eagan Richard, currier, house rear Adams, Mason Hill
Eagan William H. grocer, house 12 Pingree
Engleston John H. captain, house 10 Salem
Earle Alice C. house 136 Federal
Earl Charles H. carpenter, house 3 Harbor street court
Earl John, currier, house rear Hanson
Easson William Henry, carpenter, house 8 Beach
Eastman Nancy T. widow, house 71 Federal
Eaton Charles F. merchant (Boston), house 22 Beckford
Eaton Horace D. carpenter, boards 29 Brown
Eaton John D. (*J. W. Eaton & Co.*), house 38 Buffum
Eaton Joseph W. & Co. (*J. D. Eaton*), stoves and tinware, 34
    North, boards 16 Upham
Eaton Martin V. B. peddler, house 44 Buffum
Eaton Nathaniel J. baker, 29 Brown, house do.
Eaton William B. artist, 188 Essex, house 9 Skerry
Eddy Jessie B. cotton mill, house 32 Mill
Edgerly Charles E. currier, boards 4 North court
Edgerly Peter Mrs. Home for Aged Females
Edgerley Samuel, captain, house 2 North court
Edgerly S. Augustus, carpenter, house 11 Prescott
Edwards Abraham jr. Naumkeag mill, house 12 Barton
Edwards Anastasia, widow, house rear 9 Rust
Edwards Benjamin (Boston), house 1 Harrison avenue
Edwards Charles W. house 5 Woodbury court
Edwards Jesse B. building mover, house 21 Andrew
Edwards John B. clerk, 18 Washington, house 2 Franklin
Edwards John B. shoemaker, 16 English, house do.
Edwards John S. carpenter, 8 North, house 49 Summer
Edwards Joseph, boards 43 Charter
Edwards Martha P. Mrs. house 4 Curtis
Edwards Mary Mrs. house 1 Daniels
Edwards Richard L. house 43 Charter (Co. H. 24 Regt.)
Edwards William, painter, house 80 Mill
Edwards William P. mariner, boards 4 Curtis
Egan Martin, currier and tanner, foot Buffum, h. 43 North
Egan William, hostler, 212 Essex, house 15 Ash
Eiffe John, currier, house 15 Flint
Elliot Andrew, mason, house 7 Gedney court
Ellis John, sheriff's keeper, house rear 220 Essex
Ellis Linda M. Mrs. house rear 9 Aborn
Ellsworth William E. shoemaker, house rear Bridge, n. Osgood
Elsworth Caroline, widow, house 13 Rust
Elwell Caroline, widow, house 167 Bridge
Elwell Charles B. carpenter, 88 Peabody, house 58 Mill
Elwell Charles H. mariner, boards 58 Mill
Emerson Brown Rev. D. D. house 377 Essex

Emerson Daniel P. provisions, 17 & 18 Market house, house at
   South Reading
Emerson Elizabeth Mrs. house 23 Albion
Emerson George B. bookkeeper (Boston), house 377 Essex
Emerson George E. engineer, E. R. R. house 4 Downing
Emerson Gilbert B. baggagemaster E. R. R. h. 7 Bott's court
Emerson Hiram G. tanner, house 23 Albion
Emerson Huldah & Olive Mrs. Home for Aged Females
Emerson John P. shoemaker, house Shillaber
Emerson Nathan, grocer, 134 Boston, house do.
Emerson Pamelia Mrs. house 3 Fowler
Emerson Putnam, 17 City Market, boards Essex House
Emerton Hannah M. Mrs. house 1 Elm
Emerton James, apothecary, 119 Essex, house 1 Elm
Emerton James H. clerk, 119 Essex, boards 1 Elm
Emery Cyrus K. mariner, boards 18 March   [131 Federal
Emery Samuel, nautical instrument maker, 162 Derby, house
Emilio Louis, clerk, boards 76 Essex
Emilio Manuel, teacher of music, 7 Central, house 76 Essex
Emmerton Charles S. boards 13 Summer
Emmerton Daniel S., house 13 Summer
Emmerton Ephraim, merchant, house 13 Summer
Emmerton Ephraim A. (Boston), house 175 Federal
Emmerton George R. merchant (33 India, B.), h. 7 Summer
Emmerton James A. house 13 Summer
Emmerton William, house 114 Essex
Emmerton (*Wm. H.*) & Foster (*J. C.*) architects and engineers,
   26 Asiatic building, house 10 Andrew
Endicott Aaron Mrs. house 90 Bridge
Endicott Charles Mrs. boards 76 Essex
Endicott Nathan Mrs. house 22 Chestnut   [h. 365 do.
Endicott William C. (*Perry & Endicott*), counsellors, 182 Essex,
Endicott William P. house 359 Essex
English Philip Mrs. house 11 Northey
English William G. curled hair, rear 40 Bridge, house 79 do.
Entwistle Thomas, shoemaker, house foot East Gardner
Erickson Christopher Mrs. house rear 11 Andrew
Estes Charles A. printer, 193 Essex, boards 8 Howard
Estes George H. express, 14 Wash. b. Barr, beyond School
Estes George W. house 8 Howard
Estes Geo. W. jr. fruit and oysters, 3 Newbury, h. 8 Howard
Estes John F. boards 20 Conant
Estes J. Frank, clerk, 181 Essex, house 47 St. Peter
Estes Joshua P. ketchup maker, house 20 Conant
Estes Nathaniel K. shoemaker, house Barr, beyond School
Estes William P. R. boards 20 Conant
Esty Jeremiah A. restorator, 17 Derby sq. h. at Middleton
Esty Warren A. 17 Derby square, house at Middleton
Eustis Abigail, widow, house 11 Norman
Eustis Betsey, house 154 Boston

Eustis Nancy, teacher, house 154 Boston
Evans Alvan A. & Sons (*Alvan A. and John W.*), curriers,
   rear 9 Mason, h. 11 Mason   [house 11 Mason
Evans Alvan A. (*A. A. Evans & Sons*), currier, rear 9 Mason,
Evans Andrew, teamster, house 16 Carlton
Evans Eliza A. nurse, house 25 Salem
Evans George E. mariner, boards 19 Daniels
Evans James G. teamster, house 1 English
Evans John A. laborer, house 9 Tucker's wharf
Evans John H. peddler, boards 54 Buffum
Evans John W. (*A. A. Evans & Sons*), currier, boards 11 Mason
Evans Lucy, widow, house 19 Daniels
Evans William A. cigarmaker, boards 1 Park
Evans William H. mariner, house 19 Daniels
Evans Winslow, mariner, boards 32 Derby
Ewings Sarah, widow, house 12 Daniels

FABENS BENJ. merchant, 211 Derby, house 87 Lafayette
Fabens Benj. F. merchant, house 73 Lafayette
Fabens Benj. H. messenger, Naumkeag Bank, b. 81 Lafayette
Fabens B. Louis (Eliot Nat. Bank, B.), house 87 Lafayette
Fabens Charles E. clerk, boards 81 Lafayette
Fabens Charles H. merchant, 211 Derby, house 81 Lafayette
Fabens Elias W. Mrs. house 16 Williams
Fabens George, currier, boards 18 Vale
Fabens George O. boards 10 Hathorne
Fabens John, house 61 Broad
Fabens John W. shoemaker, house 18 Vale
Fabens Mary T. Mrs. house 33 Summer
Fabens Sarah Mrs. house 6 Norman
Fagan Matthew, laborer, house rear 10 Congress
Fairbanks Joseph, sashmaker, house 4 Pearl
Fairfield Elizabeth Mrs. boards 3 Federal
Fairfield Hester Mrs. house Hanson, near Boston
Fairfield James, master mariner, house 7 Carlton
Fairfield James jr. carpenter, head Derby wharf, h. 3 Becket
Fairfield Margaret Mrs. house 67 Essex
Fairfield Samuel G. house 4 Becket'   [Boston, h. 20 do.
Fairfield (*Samuel W.*) & Getchell (*Charles E.*), machinists, 41
Fall William A. machinist, house 1 Peabody
Fallon Anthony, tanner, house Grove, above Mason
Fallon James, shoemaker, house 18 Northey
Fallon James, laborer, house Grove, above Mason
Fallon Malachi, currier, house rear 170 Federal
Fallon Thomas, currier, house 14 Flint
Fanning James, currier, rear 46 Boston, house 10 Hanson
Fanning James, carpenter, house Maple
Fanning Samuel, currier, house 32 Phelps court
Farless James A. clerk (B.), house 120 Derby
Farless Thomas Mrs. house 120 Derby

Farley Charles M. cooper, house 21 Harbor
Farley Henry, cooper, 10 Hancock, house 7 Lagrange
Farley James, cooper, boards 130 Lafayette
Farley Joseph L. cooper, house 5 Everett
Farmer Charles P. mariner, house 9 English
Farmer George S. Mrs. house rear 59 North
Farmer James D. shoemaker, house 1 Downing
Farmer (*Joseph*) & Harris (*Walter S.*), masons, 72 Washington, house 47 North
Farmer Joseph P. mason, house 66 North
Farmer Mary H. tailoress, house 9 English
Farmer Moses G. telegraphic engineer, house 403 Essex
Farnham Jonathan M. house 8 Lynde
Farnham Wm. H. P. clerk, 179 Essex, boards Essex House
Farnsworth Elizabeth, widow, house 9 Cedar
Farnsworth Joseph A. clerk, house 9 Cedar
Farnham Charles, carpenter, 10 Prince
Farnum George W. A. currier, house Grove, rear Cemetery
Farnum Henry A. carpenter, house 21 School
Farnum Joseph Mrs. house 143 Federal
Farnum Joseph, dentist, 22 Washington, house 143 Federal
Farnum Nathan, house 13 Winthrop
Farrant Mary Mrs. boards 114 Essex
Farrell Ellen, widow, house 22 Congress
Farrell Hugh, house 8 Vale
Farrell John, shoemaker, house Congress
Farrell John, tailor, 7 Derby sq. house 176 Derby
Farrell Sylvester, laborer, house 5 Perkins
Farrell William, boards 176 Derby
Farrell William H. clerk, 2 Washington
Farrington Charles W. captain, house 346 Essex
Farrington George P. druggist, 310 Essex, corner North, house 114 Federal
Farrington George P. jr. 310 Essex, house 114 Federal
Farrington Leonard Mrs. house 28 Chestnut
Farrington Mary Mrs. house 16 Hathorne
Farrington Timothy, farmer, rear 9 Aborn
Farrington William H. harnessmaker, boards 12½ Hathorne
Faunce Moses D. house 10 Ash   [h. 3 Cambridge
Faxon (*Elisha J.*) & Locke (*Milton P.*), stairbuilders, 72 Wash.
Faxon James, shoemaker, house 70 Summer
Fay Ann, widow, house 10 Derby
Fay Frank M. (15 Central, B.), boards 14 Elm
Fell Thomas, cooper, house 9 Hardy
Feely James Mrs. house 16 Elm   •
Fellows George (*Becket & F.*), boatbuilder, Salem Marine Railway, house 17 Lynde
Fellows Israel, furniture warehouse, 205 Essex, house 10 Mall
Fellows Jeremiah B. laborer, house Harbor, near Peabody
Fellows Oliver Mrs. house 16 Crombie

Fellows Thomas B. boards 10 Mall
Felt Augusta and Caroline, house 13 Norman
Felt Benjamin, house 8 Curtis
Felt Benjamin W. cigar maker, boards 16 Curtis
Felt Betsey Miss, house 1 Cambridge
Felt Betsey Mrs. house 6 Lynde
Felt Catharine Miss, house 113 Federal
Felt Charles H. clerk, 181 Essex, boards 10 Hardy
Felt Charles W. inventor, house 30 Bridge
Felt Edward A. mariner, boards 16 Curtis
Felt Eliza Miss, tailoress, house 32 Charter
Felt Ephraim, inspector Custom House, house 8 Norman
Felt George R. bookkeeper, Naumkeag National Bank, house
     9 Norman
Felt George W. cooper, house 10 Hardy
Felt John, asst. supt. 188 Essex, house 6 Federal court
Felt John G. painter, 27 Front, house 2 Church
Felt John H. clerk, boards 2 Church
Felt John P. clerk Gas Co. boards 6 Federal court
Felt John V. clerk at Gayle & Co.'s, house 1 Hardy
Felt Joseph B. Rev. house 17 Norman
Felt Lucy B. widow, house 10 Hardy
Felt Martha D. Miss, milliner, house 32 Charter
Felt Samuel Q. house 2 Church
Felt Sarah and Nancy S. house 118 Derby
Felt Susan Miss, house 1 Cambridge
Felton Francis A. sailmaker, house 13 Allen
Felton Harriet S. teacher, boards 20 Winthrop
Felton John S. house 104 Federal
Felton Mary J. dressmaker, boards 20 Howard
Felton Nancy Mrs. house 20 Howard
Felton William S. clerk 42 Washington, boards 20 Winthrop
Fennell Mary, widow, boards 3 Tucker's wharf
Fenollosa Manuel, music teacher, and pianos and cabinet organs,
     286 Essex, house 5 Chestnut
Ferguson Edward A. machinist (B.), boards 10 Carpenter
Ferguson George B. gasfitter, 41 Boston, house 3 Fowler
Ferguson George P. confectioner, boards 164 Boston [Monroe
Ferguson James B. painter, Essex, corner Beckford, house 6
Ferguson John F. painter, Essex, cor. Beckford, house 10 Car-
     penter
Ferguson Michael, shoemaker, house rear 168 Derby
Ferguson Samuel, soap manufacturer, house 164 Boston
Ferguson Samuel A. painter, boards 164 Boston
Ferguson Thomas B. rubber mittens and leather, 5 Washington,
     house 4 Bott's court
Ferguson Wesley B. tanner, house 11 Boston
Fernald Giles C. currier, house 12 Beaver
Fernandez William D. cabinetmaker, house 4 Bridge
Fettyplace Misses, house 16 Winter

Field Louisa, nurse, boards 14 Salem
Field Lucinda B. house 17 Upham
Field Sally Mrs. house 17 Upham
Field Sarah E. saleswoman, 186 Essex, boards 8 Carpenter
Fields Robert M. shoemaker, house Grove near Mason
Fifield Charles H. (*Thos. H. Frothingham & Co.*), stoves, &c.,
    29 and 31 Front, house 51 St. Peter
Fifield David P. clerk, boards 5 Salem
Fifield Perkins, laborer, house 5 Salem
Fifield Richard, farmer, house 18 March
Fielden Thomas, machinist, house 18 Howard
Fillebrown Charles F. varnisher, house 10 Becket
Fillie Patrick, Naumkeag mill, boards 70 Harbor
Findley John Mrs. house 142 Bridge
Finn Patrick, laborer, house 172 Derby
Finegan John, laborer, house rear 7 Charter
Finnegan Mary, widow, house 12 Ash
Finnegan Michael, moulder, boards 95 Derby
Fish George S. mason, boards 3 Pleasant
Fish Rachel P. nurse, house 23 Pleasant
Fisher Charles, house 108 Bridge
Fisher George A. boards 24 St Peter
Fisher J. Augusta Miss, teacher, Fowler street school, boards
    Norman, cor. Summer
Fisher Thorpe, house 115 Federal
Fisk Augustus, mariner, house 16 Mason
Fisk Elsy, house 10 Church
Fisk John B. captain, house 16 Mason
Fisk Joseph E. dentist, 11 Washington, house do.
Fitz Daniel P. clerk, Overseers Poor, house 13 Harbor
Fitz Joseph L. shipjoiner, house 10 Curtis
Fitz Josiah, house 21 Forrester
Fitz Mary Jane, principal Bentley school, house 21 Forrester
Fitzgerald John, currier, house 433 Essex
Fitzgerald Michael, shoemaker, house 22 Congress
Fitzgerald Michael, laborer, house 15 Turner
Fitzgerald Morris, laborer, house 24 Herbert
Fitzgerald Morris, laborer, boards 15 Turner
Fitzgerald Patrick, laborer, house 23 Congress
Fitzgerald Patrick, laborer, boards 15 Turner
Fitzgerald William, laborer, house rear 142 Bridge
Fitzgerald William, umbrellas, &c. 244 Essex, house 12 Prince
Fitzpatrick Cornelius, laborer, house rear 170 Derby
Fitzpatrick Edward, currier, house 95 Mason
Fitzpatrick James, currier, house Varney, near Hanson
Fitzpatrick Patrick, currier, house rear 141 Boston
Fitzpatrick Timothy, shoemaker, house Prospect, near Aborn
Flaherty Hugh, laborer, house 4½ Turner
Flaherty Mary, milliner, 291 Essex, house do.
Flakefield John, sailmaker, house 11 Cross

Flakefield John jr. ropemaker, boards 11 Cross
Flanders Hezekiah B. peddler, house 113 North
Flannigan Edward, mariner, house 40 Union
Flannigan James, currier, house Varney, near Hanson
Flannigan John, currier, house 8 Lynn
Flannigan Maria, dressmaker, house 40 Union
Flannigan Mary, widow, house 24 Herbert
Flannigan Nicholas, currier, house 24 Herbert
Flannigan Thomas, currier, house 24 Herbert
Fleet George E. Mrs. house 310 Essex
Fletcher Francis H. 150 Essex, boards 2 Pratt
Fletcher M. M. Mrs. house 2 Margin
Fling John, laborer, house rear 7 Charter
Flinn James Mrs. widow, house Congress, west side
Flinn Jeremiah, laborer, house 8 Pratt
Flinn Patrick, currier, boards Congress, west side
Flinn Thomas, laborer, house Mason Hill
Flinn William, laborer, house 24 Ward
Flint Charles F. farmer. house 12 Laboratory
Flint Elizabeth, widow, boards 16 Pickman
Flint George, farmer, house 12 Laboratory
Flint George F. counsellor, 194 Essex, boards 23 Summer
Flint Harrison O. boots, shoes, &c. 210 Essex, house 2 Ash
Flint (H. O.) & Goldthwait (E. A.), patent medicines, 4 Cam-
    bridge
Flint James Mrs. house 76 Bridge
Flint John F. farmer, house 12 Laboratory
Flint Samuel P. house 12 Laboratory
Flint Simeon, mason, 221 Derby, house 53 Lafayette
Flockhart John, in oil mill, house 22 Pingree
Florance Elizabeth, widow, house 5 Everett
Florance Henry, cooper, boards 5 Everett
Florance Thomas T. cooper, 22 Cedar. house 5 Everett
Florentine Nicholas, carpenter, house 11½ English
Flowers Matilda, widow, boards 77 Mill
Flowers William H. cabinetmaker, 205 Essex, house 327 do.
Flowers William H. jr. clerk, P. O. house 24 St. Peter
Floyd Abigail and Hannah, house 18 Crombie
Floyd Reuben H. flagman E. R. R. house 20 Vale
Floyd Samuel P. fish, 56 Bridge, house do.
Flynn P. Edward, hostler, house 53 Warren
Flynn James, laborer, house 105 Derby
Flynn John, morocco dresser, boards 15 Turner
Flynn Mary, widow, house 15 Turner
Flynn Michael, laborer, house 105 Derby
Flynn Patrick, currier, house Watson, cor. Beaver
Flynn Thomas, hostler, Essex House, house 13 Ash
Fogg Frederic (Julian A. Fogg & Co.), house 24 Harbor
Fogg Frederick L. P. com. merchant, house Harbor, cor. Salem
Fogg Frederick O. engraver, boards 26 Harbor

Fogg James, boards 83 Derby (U. S. N.)
Fogg John M. Mrs. house 83 Derby
Fogg Julian A. & Co. (*Frederick Fogg*), watches and jewelry
    and engravers, 237 Essex, house 24 Harbor
Fogg Stephen Mrs. house 4 Flint
Fogherty Joanna, widow, house 21 Ward
Fogherty John, machinist, house rear 34 Ward
Foley Cornelius, laborer, house 383 Essex
Foley Daniel, laborer, house 11 Lynn
Foley Edward, painter, 32 Endicott, house 20 Charter
Foley John, machinist, boards 10 Ward
Foley Mark, laborer, house 11 Lynn
Foley Michael, house 10 Ward
Foley Patrick, currier, house Phillip, near Harrod
Follette Lewis B. wholesale dealer in hoop skirts, 186 Essex,
    boards Essex House
Foote (*Caleb*) & Horton (*N. A.*), publishers of " Salem Gazette
    and Essex County Mercury," 199 Essex, h. 44 Warren
Foote George F. tanner, boards Putnam, cor. Hanson
Foote Frazier C. teamster, house Putnam, cor. Hanson
Foote John C. currier, boards Putnam, cor. Hanson
Forbush Jonathan C. Mrs. house 67 Bridge,
Ford Daniel, blacksmith, house 4 High street court
Ford Jeremiah L. currier, house 19 Warren
Ford S. Augustus, morocco dresser, house 2 North Pine
Ford John F. morocco dresser, boards 18 Fowler
Ford Martin, tanner, house 21 Fowler
Ford Mary L. dressmaker, house 18 Fowler
Ford Thomas Mrs. house Varney, near Hanson
Forness Augustus W. morocco dresser, house 8 Daniel
Forness Charles, mariner, house 5 Gardner court
Forrester Charlotte S. Mrs. house 9 Oliver
Forsyth Nelson S. peddler, house 19 Turner
Forsyth William Mrs. house 166 Federal
Foss John G. farmer, house 23 North
Foss Jonathan T. teamster, house 60 Mason
Foss Nathaniel M. express, 14 Washington, house 60 Mason
Foster Adaline Miss, house 23 Summer
Foster Charles H. boards 20 Hardy
Foster Isaac P. grocer, 109 Derby, house 12 Charter
Foster Isaac P. jr. 109 Derby, house 13 Walnut   [357 Essex
Foster Joseph C. (*Emmerton & Foster*), 26 Asiatic building, b.
Foster Joshua L. cigar maker, house 20 Hardy
Foster Josiah, cooper, house 10 Mechanic
Foster Mary Mrs. house 7 Buffum
Foster Matilda L. milliner, 174 Essex, house 14 Walnut
Foster William H. cashier, Asiatic Bank, 32 Washington, house
    357 Essex
Foster William J. bookkeeper, Asiatic Bank, house 357 Essex
Fountain James W. hairdresser, 9 Washington, h. 14 Porter

Fowler Charles B. clerk, 27 Washington, house 13 Barr
Fowler Edward E. boards 31 North
Fowler Elizabeth B. house 16 Boston
Fowler George & Co. (*Geo. P. Fowler*), slaters, house 2 St.
    Peter's court
Fowler George P. (*George Fowler & Co.*), h. 2 St. Peter's ct.
Fowler Hannah B. Mrs. house 31 North
Fowler Henry P. Naumkeag mill, house 38 Harbor
Fowler Joseph, baker, house 18 Endicott
Fowler Joseph, cooper, boards 55 Derby
Fowler Joseph H. cigar maker, house 16 Norman
Fowler Phœbe A. boarding house, house 38 Harbor
Fowler William T. Mrs. house 11 Creek
Fox Ebenezer Mrs. house 11 Creek
Fox Joanna, widow, house rear 22 Charter
Fox Margaret, widow, house 22 Congress
Foye Deborah, teacher, private school, house rear 28 Church
Foye Edward, laborer, house 16 Salem
Foye Geo. H., Naumkeag mill, h. East Gardner, near Harbor
Foye James F. treasurer Salem & So. Danvers H. R. R. 243½
    Essex, house 75 Derby
Foye Samuel, house 75 Derby
Foye Samuel A. currier, house 7 Hardy
Foye William P. carpenter, boards 75 Derby
Francis Anthony, mariner, house 3 Turner
Francis Augustus B. teacher of French, house 10 Pearl
Francis Ephraim F. Mrs. house 3 Barton
Francis George H. shoemaker, boards 10 Pearl
Francis Henry H. farmer, boards 97 Bridge
Francis John Mrs. house 29 St. Peter
Francis John E. mariner, house 29 St. Peter
Francis Lucy, widow, house 97 Bridge
Francis Maria Miss, nurse, house 20 Pickman
Francis Mary Mrs. nurse, house 19 Becket
Francis Margaret C. clerk, 170 Essex, boards 97 Bridge
Francks Rachel Mrs. house 16 Becket
Francois Dorlice J. expressman, house 8 Pond
Frazier John Mrs. house 21 Northey
Freeman Ezra, tinsmith, house 16 Upham
Freeman Thomas C. clerk, boards 33 Charter
Freeman Truman, machinist, house 11 Oliver
Freeman Sylvester, flagman E. R. R. house 158 Bridge
Freeman V. O. weaver, boards 38 Harbor
Freening Aurora S. B. Mrs. house 18 Sewall
Freese Annie Mrs. house 16 Curtis
French Charles, baker, boards 416 Essex
Friend Franklin, grocer, 33 Bridge, house do.
Friend Joel, shoemanuf. Aborn, near Boston, house 152 Boston
Friend Joel M. clerk, boards 152 Boston
Friend Luke E. cook, house Ord

Friend Sarah A. widow, house 152 Boston
Frost John, merchant, house 73 Lafayette
Frost John, tanner and currier, So. Danvers, house 140 Boston
Frothingham Joseph, boards 23 Church
Frothingham Gustavus Mrs. boards 19 Oliver
Frothingham Lydia Miss, house 23 Church
Frothingham Nathaniel, house 12 Federal
Frothingham Thomas H. & Co. (*Charles H. Fifield*), stoves,
    tin ware, &c., 29 & 31 Front, house 43 Federal
Frye Benjamin, house 30 Beckford
Frye Daniel, currier, Grove near Goodhue, house 2 Beaver
Frye Daniel M. cooper, boards 11 Daniels
Frye Elizabeth and Marion, Misses, house 10 Daniels
Frye Frederick A. tanner, foot of Dean, house 6 Oak
Frye George H. baker, house 11 Prince
Frye Henry L. engineer, house 8 Beckford
Frye James, tanner, Grove near Goodhue, house 8 Silver
Frye John N. house 11 Daniels   [Boston
Frye Joseph S. bark grinding mill, Grove foot Mason, house 90
Frye Nathan, captain, house 354 Essex
Frye Nathan A. (*William Hunt & Co.*), merchants, 16 Asiatic
    building, and Phillip's wharf, house 356 Essex
Frye Nathan A. jr. boards 356 Essex
Frye Phillip, boards 2 Beaver
Frye Sally, house 139 Federal
Frye William, currier, house 8 Aborn
Frye William Mrs. house 2 Beaver
Full Joseph F. hairdresser, 22 Washington, house 53 Endicott
Full William L. teamster, house 13 Curtis
Fullam Thomas, mariner, house 148 Derby
Fuller Christopher G. house 11 Ash
Fuller David, porter, house 9 High street court
Fuller Enoch P. carpenter, 11 Beckford, house 7 South Pine
Fuller George A. (*Lord & Fuller*), architects, 243½ Essex, h.
    7 South Pine
Fuller George H. at car shop, house 15 Hardy
Fuller Joseph Mrs. house 2 May street court
Fuller Joseph T. currier, house 9 Dean
Fuller Henry O. clerk Merchants' National Bank, bds. 11 Ash
Fuller Mary A., Henrietta and Lucy Misses, h. 22 Andrew
Fuller Nancy, widow, house 23 High
Fuller Sylvester B. shoe dealer, house 7 Lagrange
Fuller Thomas, captain, house 13 Mount Vernon   [ard
Fuller Wm. P. stoves and tinware, 17 St. Peter's, h. 12 How-
Fuller William P. jr. mariner, boards 12 Howard
Fullum William, laborer, house 97 Derby

GADBYS THEOPHILUS, boarding house, 1 Pingree
Gaffney Ellen, widow, house 21 Ward
Gage Andrew jr. clerk, Hubon's block, house 18 Hardy

Gahagan John, tanner, house 29 Boston
Gahagan Patrick, tanner, house Pope's court
Galaher Patrick, laborer, house 156 Bridge
Gale Levi B. Mrs. house 49 Derby
Gallagher John, house 4 Elm
Gallagher Thomas A. Mrs. house 7 Church
Gallagher William, bootmaker, house 24 Ward
Gallen Thomas, shoemaker, house 141 Boston
Gallivan Dennis, currier, house 16 Vale
Gallivan Edward J. currier, boards 5 Beach
Gallison Joseph E. shoemaker, rear 39 Essex, house 9 Hardy
Gallivan John, currier, house 5 Beach
Gallivan John, laborer, house 11 Tucker s wharf
Gallivan Michael, tanner, house 9 Beaver
Galloway John H. shoemaker, 60 Derby, boards 56 do.
Gallup George M. foreman oil works, house 13 Briggs
Galvan John, tanner, house 7 High street court
Galway Thomas, laborer, house Putnam
Gangner Joseph, Naumkeag mill, boards 1 Pingree
Ganey Catharine, house 3 Ropes
Ganey Michael, tinsmith, 29 Front, house 3 Ropes
Ganley Patrick, currier, house rear 56 Broad
Gannan James, gardener, house 18 River
Gannon Alexander, currier, boards 6 May
Gannon Thomas, currier, house 6 May
Gardner Abel, currier, boards 99 Federal
Gardner Benjamin, house 99 Federal
Gardner Benjamin S. shoemaker, boards 6 North court
Gardner Charles W. currier, house 31 Turner
Gardner Charles W. clerk, boards 59 Mill
Gardner Daniel B. merchant, 14 Front, house 21 Washington
Gardner Daniel B. jr. (*M. C. Reynolds & Co.*), grocer, 20 Front,
    boards Essex House   [court
Gardner Edward E. bath house, 148 Bridge, boards 6 North
Gardner George H. photographer, 241 Essex, house 168 Bridge
Gardner George W. Mrs. house 86 Summer
Gardner Henry, captain, house 16 Crombie
Gardner Henry, house 24 Chestnut
Gardner Henry R. clerk (Boston), boards 33 Summer
Gardner Horace B. currier, boards 24 Turner
Gardner Howell P. baker, boards 24 Turner
Gardner James W. carpenter, boards 99 Federal
Gardner John, shoe stiffenings, 137 Boston, house 22 Prospect
Gardner John, laborer, boards Prospect, near Summit
Gardner John, tailor, house 28 Winthrop
Gardner Jonathan, cooper, house 66 North
Gardner Joseph 1st, house 19 Crombie
Gardner Joseph 2d, house 13 Margin
Gardner Joseph D. tanner, house 67 North
Gardner Martha, cloak and dress maker, house 59 Mill

Gardner Nathaniel, at oil factory, house 49 Buffum
Gardner Richard, clerk Gas Co. 188 Essex, house 33 Summer
Gardner Sarah Mrs. house 6 North court
Gardner Simon, baker, 24 Turner, house do.
Gardner Stephen W. currier, house 67 North
Gardner Thomas N. liquors, 14½ Front, house 49 Lafayette
Gardner William D. carpenter, house 55 Endicott
Gardner William F. Mrs. house 72 Lafayette
Gardner William F. carpenter, 32 Norman, house 55 Endicott
Gardner William H. florist, boards 6 North court
Gardner William H. gilder, boards 59 Mill
Garland Mary Ann Miss, boards 12 Pickman
Garrity John, laborer, house 152 Derby
Garrity Patrick, laborer, house Mason Hill
Gass James, stonecutter, house 317 Essex
Gately John, tanner, house 21 Ward
Gass Philemon, baggage master E. R. R. (Lynn), b. 317 Essex
Gauss Ruth B. widow, house 36 Derby
Gauss Stephen, cooper, house rear 36 Derby
Gavett Charles (10 Summer, B.), house 21 Turner
Gavett Clara, and Mary Augusta Misses, house 19 North
Gavett Henry, currier, house 62 Mason
Gavett Jonathan, house 19 North
Gavett Mary A. saleswoman, 192 Essex, house 19 North
Gavett William F. (27 Federal, B.), house 85 Lafayette
Gavett Wm. R. dry goods, 192 Essex, h. 20 Turner, c. Derby
Gayle Edward Mrs. house 12 Brown [wharf, house 12 Brown
Gayle (*Edward F. W.*) & Co. flour grain, and produce, Phillips
Gearing James B. currier, house rear 93 Boston
Geary Joanna, widow, house 18 High
Geary John, laborer, house 18 High
Geary Maurice, laborer, house 21 High
Geary Owen, harnessmaker, house 18 High
Gebow James, building mover, boards 83 Derby
Gebow John, laborer, house 83 Derby
Gebow Richard, shoemaker, house 5 E. Webb
Gebow William H. waiter, boards 83 Derby
Gendrot Peter, carver, house 11 Pearl
Gerald Jeanette, teacher, boards 29 Brown
Gerghan William, currier, house 405 Essex
Getchell Benjamin W. cooper, head Phillips wharf, h. 9 Carlton
Getchell Charles E. (*Fairfield & Getchell*), carpenter, 14 Boston,
   boards 19 Boston
Getchell Edward E. painter, 18 Lafayette, house 7 Prince
Getchell George F. cooper, house 72 Essex
Getchell George H. clerk, boards 17 English
Getchell Josiah B. laborer, boards 17 English
Getchell Josiah W. sup. Marine Railway, house 17 English
Getchell Stephen O. carpenter, house 46 Beaver
Getchell William Mrs. house 17 English

Getchell William Henry, musician, house 2 Becket
Gibbon James, house 16 Turner (Cal.)
Gibbons Michael, laborer, house 97 Derby
Gibney Charles T. currier, house 14 Beach
Gibney James B. tanner and currier, house 3 Beach
Gibney John, tanner and currier, Beach, house 14 do.
Gibney John A. tanner, house 9 Friend
Gibson John F. house 26 Endicott
Giddings Aaron Mrs. house 24 Dearborn
Giffin Bridget, widow, house 14 Pingree
Gifford James B. (*T. J. Gifford & Co.*), house 18 Mason
Gifford Rufus B. (*T. J. Gifford & Co.*), house 149 Federal, cor.
    Dean
Gifford Thomas J. & Co. (*J. B. & R. B. Gifford*), carpenters,
    rear 12 Carpenter, house 20 Mason
Gifford Thomas S. Mrs. house 59 North
Gilbert James, captain, house 3 Spring
Gilbert James, teamster, house 177 Boston
Giles Lydia G. Mrs. house 28 Lynde
Giles William, Naumkeag mill, boards foot E. Gardner
Gill Catharine, widow, house foot Congress, west side
Gill Harriet P. private school, Holly street, b. 4 Harbor st. ct
Gillan John, captain, house 4 Prescott
Gillespie John W. hairdresser, Higginson sq. house 49 Mill
Gillespie Joseph A. hairdresser, Higginson sq. house 49 Mill
Gillespie Louisa, widow, house 18 Central
Gilligan Daniel, mariner, boards 10 Pingree
Gilligan Matthew, machinist, boards Lynch, corner Perkins
Gilligan John, laborer, house 10 Pingree
Gilligan Michael, boards 10 Pingree   [32 Forrester
Gillis James A. (*Phillips & G.*), counsellor, 243½ Essex, house
Gillis Lydia D. Mrs. house 32 Forrester   [Carpenter
Gillpatrick Azuba Mrs. matron Seaman's Orphan Society, 7
Gilman Alfred J. wool puller, boards 3 Ord
Gilman Daniel M. ropemaker, house 5 English
Gilman John H. mariner, house 28 Essex
Gilman Joseph, laborer, house 5 English
Gilman Joseph jr. ropemaker, boards 5 English
Glazier Charles H. (*E. Glazier & Son*), house 11 Lagrange
Glazier Ezra & Son (*C. H. Glazier*), furniture, crockery, &c.
    Central, cor. Charter, house 11 Lagrange
Glazier George W. machinist, house 31 Harbor
Gleeson John, currier, house 7 Hanson
Glidden Bethuel, trader, house 144 North
Glidden Israel, shoecutter, house 15 Lemon
Glidden Joseph H. grocer, 18 Boston, house 12 Albion
Glidden Joseph P. Mrs. house 99 Federal
Glover Deborah M. Mrs. house 14 Salem   [cock
Glover Geo. D. (*Bosson & G.*), shoes, 10 Lafayette, h. 1 Han-
Glover Geo. H. currier, boards 86 North

Glover Joseph E. station agent, E. R. R. house 46 Endicott
Glover Joseph N. painter, house 15 Hathorne
Glover Nancy, widow, house 15 Hathorne
Glover Rebecca Mrs. house 140 Federal
Glover Susan S. Mrs. house 86 North
Glover William H. conductor, H. R. R. boards 15 Hathorne
Glover William H. painter, house 86 North
Godden Mary E. teacher, b. Everett, cor. Lafayette
Goff Walter, shoemaker, house 18 Park
Gogin Ellen, widow, house foot Park
Gogin Thomas, laborer, boards foot Park
Goldsmith Albert, carder, house 15 Oliver
Goldsmith Charles B. cabinetmaker, boards 7 Mall
Goldsmith Cordelia Miss, boards 22 Lynde
Goldsmith Edwin C. cabinetmaker, boards 15 Oliver
Goldsmith George W. polisher, house 39 Buffum
Goldsmith James T. carpenter, house 17 Hardy
Goldsmith John, captain, house 1 Arabella
Goldsmith John H. captain, house 1 Arabella
Goldthwait (*Aaron and Aaron jr.*) & Day (*Amos P.*), carpen-
 ters, 221 Derby, house 43 Broad
Goldthwait Aaron jr. (*Goldthwait & Day*), house 7 Cedar
Goldthwait Charles M. butcher, house 1 High
Goldthwait Edward A. (*Flint & Goldthwait*) patent medicines,
 4 Cambridge, house 3 Phelps court
Goldthwait Edward A. (S. Danvers), boards 7 Cedar
Goldthwait George C. painter, house 3 Woodbury's court
Goldthwait George E. house 75 Summer
Goldthwait James G. carpenter, E. R. R. house 17 Conant
Goldthwait Joseph A. house 23 Federal
Goldthwait Joseph W. shoemaker, house 3 Woodbury's court
Goldthwait Luther M. lather, boards 17 March
Goldthwait Samuel F. Mrs. house 3 Woodbury's court
Goldthwait Willard, carpets, upholstery goods, 151 Essex, house
 64 Summer
Goldthwait William J. tinsmith, house 27 Andrew
Goldthwait William W. clerk, 9 Newbury, house 30 Turner
Gomes Anna, private school, 8 Cherry
Gomes Charles H. agent, boards 8 Cherry
Gomes Joseph, house 8 Cherry
Goodacre Jemima, widow, house 130 North
Goodell Abner C. machinist, house 4 Federal
Goodell A. C. jr. Register of Court of Probate and Insolvency,
 Court House, boards 4 Federal
Goodell Elizabeth C. Mrs. boards 12 Pickman
Goodell Zina, machinist, 16 Lafayette, house 13 Federal
Goodhue Abner Mrs. house 2 Liberty
Goodhue Albert P. clerk, boards 51 Essex
Goodhue George C. clerk (8 Comm'l whf., B.), h. 2 Liberty
Goodhue James B. blacksmith, 3 Camb. house 6 Hathorne

Goodhue John E. shoemaker, boards 14 Creek
Goodhue Joseph, feather-bed renovator, rear 274 Essex, house
   19 Lemon
Goodhue Mary T. house 99 Bridge
Goodhue Priscilla, house 99 Bridge
Goodhue Robert W. shoemaker, house 8 Hathorne
Goodhue Samuel V. clerk (82 Milk, B.), house 106 Lafayette
Goodhue Sarah Mrs. house 14 Creek
Goodhue William P. ship chandler and grocer, 44 Derby, house
   51 Essex
Goodhue William W. (Zanzibar), boards 51 Essex
Goodridge George A. periodicals and papers, 4 Washington,
   boards 4 Peabody
Goodridge John W. master mariner, house 8 Becket
Goodridge Joshua Mrs. house 5 Gerrish place
Goodridge Mary L. Mrs. house 8 Becket
Goodwin Elizabeth D. Mrs. house 81 Derby
Goodwin Isaac, cooper, house 17 Becket
Goodwin Isaac B. mariner, boards 81 Derby
Goodwin James B. house Lafayette, near F. R. Lead Mills
Goodwin Paul, cooper, house 5 Carlton
Gordon Caroline A. dressmaker, boards 23 Daniels
Gordon George E. seaman, boards 23 Daniels
Gordon Hiram E. dyer, house near foot Laboratory   [Daniels
Gordon Rufus L. wood and bark measurer, 11 Front, house 23
Gorman Joanna, widow, house 30 Union
Gorman John, laborer, house 8 Herbert
Gorman John, mariner, boards 30 Union
Gorman Michael, mariner, boards 30 Union
Gorman Patrick Mrs. house 50 Derby
Gorman Thomas, carpenter, boards 30 Union
Gorman Thomas, helper, boards 8 Herbert
Gormley Michael, shoemaker, 16 Peabody
Goss Charles Henry, clerk, 16 Asiatic building, bds. 2 Brown
Goss (*Charles H.*), Frye (*George H.*) & Co. (*George L. Goss*),
   bakers, 87 North, house 15 Dearborn
Goss (*Ezra L.*) & Pepper (*Charles H.*), photographers, 46
   Washington, boards 87 North
Goss Francis, house 9 Rust
Goss Francis jr. plumber, 7 St. Peter, house 77 Bridge
Goss Francis P. plumber, 7 St. Peter, house 2 Brown
Goss George L. (*Goss, Frye, & Co.*), boards 87 North
Goss Richard G. house 87 North
Goss Samuel T. carpenter, house 8 Dearborn
Gould George Mrs. house rear 18 Charter
Gould Irene C. widow, house 4 Laboratory
Gould Robert W. house 10 Monroe
Gove Hiram, physician, boards 13 Washington
Gove Lydia B. Mrs. house 13 Margin
Govea Augustus E. B. clerk, house 30 Pleasant

Gower George, ropemaker, house 62 Mill
Grace Mary, widow, house 172 Derby
Gracie Henry A. mariner, house Barr, near Mason
Grady Henry, laborer, house rear Adams, Mason Hill
Grady James, laborer, house rear Adams, Mason Hill
Grady Jeremiah, laborer, house 7 Creek
Grady Julia, widow, house 7 Creek
Grafton William B. insurance agent, boards 12 Pickman
Graham John, laborer, house 24 River
Graham Mary, widow, house 11 Bentley
Graham Thomas, mariner, boards 11 Bentley
Grant Abigail H. widow, house 6 Andrew
Grant Benj. H. painter, house 6 Andrew
Grant Franklin, paper boxes (B.), boards 26 Williams
Grant Frederick, bookkeeper, house 6 Andrew
Grant Henry, house 9 Boston
Grant Henry Mrs. widow, house 9 Boston
Grant John C. pattern and model maker, 15½ Lafayette, boards
     98 Federal
Grant John W. house 1 Fowler   [at Ipswich
Grant Joshua B. curriers' tools manufacturer, 51 Boston, house
Grant Samuel Mrs. house 6 Andrew
Grant Samuel jr. machinist, 17 St. Peter, house 6 Andrew
Graves William B. captain, house 5 Everett
Gray Benjamin Mrs. house 72 Derby   [Mall
Gray Benjamin A. constable and janitor, Court-house, house 13
Gray Charles, boards 16 Allen
Gray Daniel C. mariner, boards 16 Allen
Gray Elizabeth Miss, millinery, 295 Essex, boards 57 Federal
Gray Elizabeth Mrs. house 25 Williams
Gray Everard W. cooper, house 12 English
Gray George A. mariner, house 5 Gedney court
Gray George C. sash and blinds, boards 13 Mall   [Federal
Gray Harriet C. teacher, Browne grammar school, boards 57
Gray John, boards 13 Mall
Gray John, cooper, boards 16 Allen
Gray Joseph, currier, house 41 Beaver
Gray Melinda R. widow, boards 8½ Turner
Gray Nathaniel A. grocer, 15 English, boards 16 Allen
Gray Robert, laborer, house 68 Mason
Gray Susan P. Mrs. house 57 Federal
Gray William, clerk, 44 Derby, boards 16 Allen
Gray William B. house 16 Allen
Greamer Michael, shipkeeper, house 7 Allen
Greeley Erastus P. shoemaker, boards 4 Becket
Greeley Mariam Mrs. house 4 Becket
Greeley Thomas J. boards 4 Becket (24th Regt.)
Gregg Catharine, widow, house 38 Essex
Green Alexander, captain, house 7 Everett
Green Eliza, widow, boards 7½ Turner

11

Green G. Patrick, house opposite 165 Derby
Green James Mrs. widow, house rear foot Congress
Green (*James W.*) & McCarty (*Patrick J.*), shoe findings, 123 Boston, house 126 do.
Green John, laborer, house 2 English
Green John, mariner, house near foot E. Gardner
Green Joseph H. Mrs. house 32 Essex
Green Margaret, widow, house 101 Derby
Green Patrick, laborer, house 170 Derby
Green Rebecca, widow, house 38 Phelps court
Green Rufus, carpenter, boards 59 Harbor
Green Thomas Mrs. house 99 Derby
Green Thomas, shoemaker, house 28 Congress
Greenleaf Mary V. Mrs. nurse, house 23 Becket
Greenough John W. carpenter, house 4 Everett
Grey William S. clerk, 173 Essex, boards 27 do.
Griffen John S. 2d, clerk, house 26 Charter
Griffen Thomas J. (B.), house 7 Pratt
Griffin Benjamin, laborer, house rear 142 Bridge
Griffin Daniel, laborer, house foot Park
Griffin Eben, repairer, house 3 Webb   [Lynde
Griffin Hosea B. (*Reeves & G.*), fish oils, 13 Front, house 19
Griffin James, plastering hair manufacturer, rear 20 Beaver, house 20 do.
Griffin John, tanner, house 47 Beaver
Griffin John Mrs. house 101 North
Griffin Maurice, mariner, boards 3 Tucker's wharf
Griffin Nathaniel, house 1 Winter
Griffin Patrick, shoemaker, boards 47 Harbor
Griffin Timothy J. currier, house 11 Beaver
Griffin William, laborer, house 3 Tucker's wharf
Grimes Charles, currier, house 4 Thorndike
Grimes Israel, currier, house 2 Thorndike
Grimes Oliver, laborer, house 4 Thorndike
Grimes Robert, baker, house 13 Prince
Grindal Stover, paper bags, house 149 Bridge
Griswold Benoni L. sewing machines, 142 Essex, h. 142½ do.
Griswold John A. machinist, 142 Essex, house 97 do.
Griswold Rhoda L. widow, boards 97 Essex
Grogan James, Naumkeag mill, house 4 Elm
Grogan Nicholas, laborer, house 1 Thorndike
Grover Albert, teamster, boards 18 Becket
Grover Benjamin, house 8 North court
Grover James, currier, house 11 Phelps court
Grover Jane, widow, house rear 18 Becket
Grover John, wood and coal, Hunt's wharf, house 18 Becket
Grover John jr. bookkeeper, house 57 Derby
Grover John C. mariner, house 16 Carlton
Grover Lucy Miss, boards 22 Williams
Groves Henry B. (65 State, Boston), house 21 Winter

Grush Benjamin S. mason, house foot of Lemon
Grush Michael, mason, house 14 Howard
Guilford Elbridge G. shoemaker, house rear 264 Essex
Guilford Elbridge W. shoemaker, house 134 North
Guilford Levi S. mariner, house 3 E. Webb
Guilford Samuel W. Mrs. boards 2 Jeffrey court
Guilford William H. H. shoemaker, house 134 North
Gunn Bridget, widow, house Pingree, corner S. Prospect
Gurney George, laborer, boards 1 Perkins
Guinn Nicholas, farmer, boards 10 March
Gwinn James F. twine factory, 38 Bridge, house 51 do.
Gwinn James S. grocer, house 57 Warren
Gwinn Mary A. millinery, 294 Essex, house 171 Federal
Gwinn Thomas W. grocer, 410 Essex, house 408 do.
Gynan John A. shoemaker, Ward, boards 2 Jeffrey court

HACKETT WILLIAM, currier, house Aborn, near Boston
Haddock James M. master mariner, house 29 Union
Hadley George S. tanner, rear 2 Goodhue, house Beaver,
    opposite Silver
Hadley Willis, currier, house 5 Albion
Hafey James, laborer, house rear 10 Herbert
Hagar Daniel B. prin. Normal School, house 26 Lynde
Hagar John M. (Boston), boards 26 Lynde
Hagan John W. mariner, house 16 Derby
Hagan Martha, widow, house 49 Derby
Hagerty Bartholomew, laborer, house 11 Hanson
Hagerty Cornelius, tanner, house 11 Hanson
Hagerty Daniel, harness maker, house 127 Boston
Hagerty Dennis, laborer, house foot of Tucker's wharf
Hagerty Michael, clerk, boards foot of Tucker's wharf
Hagerty Patrick, porter, Essex House, boards do.
Hale Francis H. baker, boards 26 Essex
Hale Henry, hardware, cutlery, and agricultural tools, 223 Es-
    sex, house 12 Northey
Hale Henry A. boards 12 Northey (Maj. U. S. A.)
Hale James F. grocer, 27 Summer, house 8 Winthrop
Hale Moses H. super. H. R. R. office Webb, corner Webster,
    house 3 Webster
Hale Pemberton, grocer, 27 Summer, house 11 Cambridge
Hale William H. baker, house 26 Essex
Haley Bridget, widow, house 26 Beaver
Haley Dennis, laborer, house 64 Mason
Haley James, mariner, boards 23½ Harbor
Haley Owen, shoemaker, house 24 Peabody
Haley Shillaber, house 23½ Harbor
Hall Alvan, tea, coffee & sugar, 195 Essex, house 11 Central
Hall Arthur C. watchmaker, 237 Essex, house 26 Harbor
Hall Arthur C. jeweller, house 26 Harbor
Hall David, blacksmith, house 90 Federal

Hall Edward, teamster, boards rear 26 Harbor
Hall Edwin A. shoecutter, house 8 Hathorne
Hall Eliphalet, carpenter, house 97 Boston
Hall Gilman B. currier, boards 97 Boston
Hall John, teamster, house 2 Downing
Hall Margaret, widow, house rear 26 Harbor
Hall Thomas H. shoemaker, house 170 Bridge
Hall William H. master mariner, house 25 Essex
Hall William H. clerk, boards 97 Boston
Hallahan John, laborer, house 25 Ward
Halliscy John, gardener, house 8 Perkins
Halliscy Thomas, marble worker, house 4 High street court
Ham Albert, shoemaker, house 8 English
Ham Henry E. milkman, boards H. C. Ware, Salem turnpike
Ham Joseph, mason, boards 21 Lafayette
Hamblett Malvina L. widow, house 34 Charter
Hamblett Philip A. currier, house 34 Charter
Hamblett Samuel H. (N. C.), boards 34 Charter
Hamilton Alexander, laborer, house 34 Mill
Hamilton John C. at laboratory, house foot of Ives
Hamilton Joseph R. laborer, house rear 34 Mill
Hamilton Mary Mrs. house 34 Mill
Hamlen John P. tanner, house 14 Goodhue
Hammar Martin, hostler, Essex House, boards do.
Hammond Hannah Mrs. house 12 Winthrop
Hammond John D. clerk 179 Essex, house 8 Broad
Hammond Joseph, captain, house 17 Washington
Hammond Joseph L. (China), boards 17 Washington
Hammond Mary Mrs. Home for Aged Females
Hamond William C. carpenter, 113 Derby, house 7 Carlton
Hamond William G. carpenter, house 7 Lemon
Hancock John, mariner, house 33 Derby
Hancock (*John E.*) & Morse (*George F.*), provisions, 39 Derby,
    boards 33 do.
Hand Julia, widow, house 10 Herbert
Handy Frank D. clerk 151 Essex, boards 6 Norman
Hannabell Thomas W. shoemaker, house 43 Bridge
Hannah Robert, laborer, house 3 Ward
Hannam Thomas, tailor, 64 Boston, house Hanson, cor. Varney
Hannan Dennis B. surgeon, house 15 Winthrop
Hannan George G. clerk, boards 15 Winthrop
Hannan John, gardener, house 39 Dearborn
Hannan Patrick, mariner, house 34 Beaver
Hanscom James Mrs. boards 3 Melcher court
Hanson Albert H. clerk (B.), boards 355 Essex
Hanson Charles J. clerk, 6 Front, house 31 Harbor
Hanson Elijah A. tanner, house 96 Boston
Hanson George H. A. lamplighter, house 15 Friend   [Buffum
Hanson Job V. & John, grain and meal, 1 & 3 Front, house 28
Hanson John (*J. V. & J. Hanson*), 1 Front, house 38 Buffum

Hanson John B. captain, house 7 Salem
Hanson Joseph H. (*Wm. Hunt & Co.*), merchant, 16 Asiatic
    building, house 355 Essex
Hanson Lizzie, music teacher, house 20 Union
Hanson Lydia Mrs. house 7 Phelps court
Hanson Sarah, widow, house 33 Harbor
Hanson Tobias, butcher, house 32 Beaver
Hanson William, boards 20 Union (ensign U. S. A.)
Haraden Andrew, Boston Express, basement Asiatic building,
    house 6 Barton square
Haraden Jonathan, house 19 Washington
Haraden Stephen, captain, house 3 Ash
Hardin William, laborer, house 14 Turner
Harding David, horse shoer, rear 25 Front, house 20 Charter
Harding James Mrs. house 14 Williams
Harding John B. horse shoer, boards 20 Charter
Hardy Abner H. painter, house 121 North
Hardy Harrison, shoemaker, house rear 161 Boston
Hardy Temple, house 74 Federal   [Federal
Hardy Temple jr. doors, sashes and blinds, 26 Front, house 74
Hardy T. Alvah, clerk, 173 Essex, house 20 Lynde
Hardy Warren B. shoemaker, boards rear 161 Boston
Hardy William W. (Boston), boards 74 Federal
Harraden Samuel L. boarding, house 66 Harbor
Harrigan John, laborer, house 16 Derby
Harrigan Michael, laborer, house 23 Carlton
Harrigan Patrick, laborer, boards 107 Derby
Harrington Charles, currier, Boston st., house 179 Federal
Harrington Francis, teller (Eliot Bank, B.) boards 16 Beaver
Harrington George, master mariner, house 7 Liberty
Harrington Henry, clerk, 428 Essex, house 153 Federal
Harrington Jonas B. gardener, house 16 Beaver
Harrington Leonard, clerk (B.), boards 153 Federal
Harrington Leonard B. currier, 428 Essex, house 153 Federal
Harrington Patrick, house 28 Congress
Harrington Richard, tanner, 11 Franklin, house 13 Mason
Harrington Samuel B. Mrs. house Salem Turnpike
Harrington William H. tanner (North Becket,) h. 116 Boston
Harrington William H. jr. currier, boards 116 Boston
Harris Andrew J. machinist, boards 13 River
Harris Alphonso S. clerk (B.), house 84 North
Harris Clayton, clerk, 137 Essex, boards 14 Sewall
Harris Daniel Mrs. boards 23 Brown
Harris Daniel M. carpenter, 41 North, house 12 Upham
Harris Franklin D. carpenter, boards 84 North
Harris George M. clerk, 245 Essex, boards 84 North
Harris George R. bookkeeper, 170 Essex, house 105 Bridge
Harris Israel P. grocer, 6 St. Peter, house 28 Brown
Harris James (*Chamberlain, Harris & Co.*), grocer, 24 Front,
    house 3 Linden, near Holly •

Harris John jr. harnessmaker, 11 Church, b. Washington
Harris Nathaniel, clerk, boards 200 Essex
Harris R. Anna, teacher, house 15 Federal
Harris Thomas H. shoe manuf. (Lynn), h. 77 Summer
Harris Simon A. shoemaker, house 14 Sewall   [North
Harris Walter S. (*Farmer & Harris*), mason, 72 Wash. h. 84
Harris William B. house Walter, near Orne
Harris William S. carpenter, boards Walter, near Orne
Harrison Eunice Mrs. house 19 Federal
Hart Daniel, laborer, house 10 Webb
Hart David jr. ship carpenter, house 16 Conant
Hart George A. tailor, boards 2 Becket
Hart John, morocco dresser, house 435 Essex
Hart John W. currier, house 21 Turner
Hart Hannah W. Mrs. nurse, house 48 Derby
Hart Sarah Mrs. house 36 Pleasant
Hart Susan E. widow, house 2 Harrison avenue
Hart William H. plumber, 13 Central, boards 2 Becket
Hartigan Patrick, horse shoer, Jeffrey court, h. 8 Herbert
Hartnet Michael, currier, house 51 Broad
Hartney Michael Rev. house 22 Union
Hartwell Lydia B. widow, house 7 Park
Harvey Eleanor C. at 306 Essex
Harvey Isaac, whitewasher, house 32 St. Peter
Haskell Augustus M. Rev. house 5 Carpenter
Haskell Daniel C. currier, 73 Mason, house 174 Federal
Haskell Edward B. currier, boards 100 Derby
Haskell Elijah (gunner, U. S. N.), house 17 North
Haskell George, ice, boards 22 Ward
Haskell Hannah B. widow, house 100 Derby
Haskell Jacob, ice, 2 Lafayette, house 22 Ward   [325 do.
Haskell (*Jacob S.*) & Lougee (*J. L.*), furniture 279 Essex, h.
Haskell Mark, clerk, 172 Essex, house 9 Ash
Haskell William H. shoemaker, house 163 Federal
Haskell William R. clerk, house 9 Ash
Haskins Jason A. hairdresser, Higginson sq. b. 14 Prescott
Haskins Susan L. Mrs. machine stitching, 72 Mill, house do.
Haslan Joseph, boilermaker, house 19 Harbor
Hatch Charles F. mariner, boards 3 Phelps court
Hatch Henry J. machinist, house rear 23 Cedar
Hatch Lemuel B. wood & coal, and wharfinger, 113 Derby,
          house 2 Arabella
Hatch William P., Naumkeag mill, boards 59 Harbor
Hathaway Eleazer, baker, 72 Washington, house do.
Hathaway James, currier, house 7 Albion
Hathaway James E. baker, boards 72 Washington
Hathaway John, baker, 416 Essex, house do.
Hathaway Samuel R. inspector Custom House, h. 41 Essex
Havey William, laborer, house foot Congress, west side
Hawes John Q. carpenter, house Prospect, near Summit

Hawes William, carpenter, Prospect, house 4 Beaver
Hawkes Louisa M. teacher, private school, house 28 Broad
Hay John, laborer, house Thorndike
Hay John A. shoemaker, 81 Bridge, house 12 Pearl
Hayes Bartholomew, laborer, house 27 Carlton
Hayes Catharine, widow, house 2 Tucker's wharf
Hayes Ellen, widow, house 6 Tucker's wharf
Hayes Hannah, widow, house 14 Turner
Hayes Honora, widow, boards 28 Peabody
Hayes Jeremiah, laborer, house 28 Peabody
Hayes James, laborer, boards 129 Derby
Hayes John, laborer, house 28 Ward
Hayes John, servant, 14 Chestnut, house 64 Mason
Hayes John, laborer, house 23 Carlton
Hayes John jr. laborer, house 2 Tucker's wharf
Hayes John jr. plumber, boards 23 Carlton
Hayes Margaret, widow, house Tucker's wharf
Hayes Matthew, laborer, boards 3 Tucker's wharf
Hayes Maurice, laborer, house 22 Becket
Hayes Michael, laborer, boards 23 Carlton
Hayes Michael, laborer, house rear 39 Derby
Hayes Michael, laborer, house 16 Turner
Hayes Patrick, laborer, house 9 Tucker's wharf
Hayes Patrick, laborer, house 23 Carlton
Hayes Thomas, morocco dresser, house 26 Peabody
Hayes Thomas, laborer, boards 16 Turner
Hayford Asa, house rear 18 Beckford
Hayford William B. carpenter, house foot Leach
Hayman John, captain, house 42 Essex
Haynes Robert Z. carpenter, house 14 Becket
Hayward Aaron, mason, house 82 Summer
Hayward Charles E. moulder (B.), boards 10 Prince
Hayward Charles H. bookkeeper (B.), house 20 Winthrop
Hayward Cyrus Mrs. house 13 River
Hayward Cyrus L. clerk, boards 13 River
Hayward James, laborer, boards 5 Buffum
Hayward Josiah, mason, house 120 Federal ⁣ [Bridge
Hayward William P. principal Pickering School, house 138
Haywood George, teamster, house foot East Gardner
Hazelton Andrew, tanner, house Putnam, near Hanson
Hazelton Augustus, tanner, house 15 May
Hazelton John, tanner, May, house 12 do.
Hazelton Joseph, currier, house 15 May
Heard, see Hurd
Heath Sarah A. widow, house 402 Essex
Hebard William H. blacksmith, house 8 Cross
Heborn James, machinist, boards 2 Pingree
Heborn Mary, widow, house 2 Pingree
Heaney Michael, currier, boards 89 Mason
Heeney Bridget, widow, house 61 Essex

Heeney Mary E. teacher, boards 61 Essex
Heeney Thomas, shoemaker, house 99 Derby
Heferan Patrick, Naumkeag mill, house rear foot Pingree
Heferan William, currier, boards 53 St. Peter
Heferen John, shoemaker, 51½ St. Peter, house do.
Heferen Michael, laborer, house 53 St. Peter
Helt Benjamin G. cigar maker, house 14 Daniels
Henderson Benjamin I. painter, boards 56 Forrester
Henderson Charles A. clerk, 6 St. Peter, boards 14 do.
Henderson Charles H. clerk, Internal Revenue Office, boards
    11 Mount Vernon
Henderson Daniel, painter, 3 Walnut
Henderson & Co. (*J. H. Richards*), inner soles, heels and stiff-
    ening, 150 Essex
Henderson John S. carpenter, house 4 Dow
Henderson Margaret Miss, house 27 Liberty   [Peter
Henderson Samuel, boots and shoes, 37 Brown, house 14 St.
Henderson (*Thomas*) & Thurston (*H. W.*), furniture dealers,
    38 & 40 Washington, house 11 Mount Vernon
Henderson William, clerk, house 2 Rust
Henderson William C. paper box manufacturer, 150 Essex,
    house 18 Winter
Hendley John, pocketbook maker, house 136 Boston
Henfield Amos, wheelwright, house 26 Endicott
Henfield James H. wheelwright, 18 Central
Henfield John, house 32 Lafayette
Henfield John jr. letter carrier, house 6 Prescott
Henfield Joseph H. house 32 Lafayette
Hennessey Catharine, widow, house 172 Derby
Hennessey David, currier, house 62 Mason Hill
Hennessey John, tanner, house 95 Mason
Hennessey Julia, cook, boards 80 Mason
Hennessey Margaret, widow, house 4 Beach
Hennessey Mary, widow, boards Grafton, near Hanson
Hennessey Patrick, laborer, house 151 Bridge
Hennessey Patrick, laborer, house 3 North Pine
Hennessey William, currier, house 4 Beach
Hennessey William, laborer, house Grafton, near Hanson
Henry Elizabeth Mrs. house 27 Essex
Henry John, currier, house rear Adams, Mason Hill
Henry William, currier, house rear Adams, Mason Hill
Henshion Mary, widow, house 57 Mill
Hensman George, shoemaker, house 24 Cedar
Hensman John C. lobsters and fish, house 56 Charter
Herlihey Patrick, currier, house 3 Warren court
Herman Martha Mrs. house 7 Hardy
Herrick Mary, widow, house 7 Dean
Hersey Benjamin, fisherman, house 7 Webb
Hersey Nancy L. widow, boards 11 Beaver
Hewes Orrin, shoecutter, house Cabot, corner Hancock

Hewett Delight R. Mrs. dressmaker, 183 Essex, house 36 St. Peter
Hewett Edward W. boards 36 St. Peter
Hewitt Henry C. clerk, 228 Essex, boards 36 St. Peter
Hickey Patrick, coachman, house 20 Liberty
Hifield John, laborer, house 8 English
Hifield Thomas, boards 8 English (U. S. N.)
Higbee Betsey Mrs. house 64 Broad
Higbee Charles, leather (94 Pearl, Boston), house 155 Federal
Higbee Lemuel, leather (30½ Pearl, B.), house 387 Essex
Higgins Barnard, rag gatherer, house 67 Mill
Hildreth Elbridge H. driver, house 97 Bridge
Hill Abner E. house 30 Derby
Hill Anstiss P. widow, house 28 Turner
Hill Bradley, peddler, boards 10 Prince
Hill Edwin R. Mrs. house 97 Bridge
Hill Elizabeth H. widow, house 65 Essex
Hill Elizabeth Mrs. house 4 Palfrey court
Hill George H. clerk, 54 Essex, boards 1 Fowler
Hill George W. clerk, boards 4 Winthrop·
Hill Ira, carpenter, house 4 Winthrop
Hill J. Archer, currier, house 1 Fowler
Hill Joseph T. mariner, boards 11 Salem
Hill Oliver A. shoemaker, boards 65 Essex
Hill Robert (W. & R. Hill), house 8 Bentley
Hill Samuel, captain, house 41 Lafayette
Hill Sarah E. widow, house 11 Salem
Hill Thomas, gasfitter, house rear 25 Salem
Hill Thomas, painter, house foot Pingree
Hill William Mrs. house 20 Beckford
Hill William & R. dry goods, 277 Essex, house 10 Walter
Hill William M. currier, house 15 Buffum
Hinckley George O. Mrs. house 22 Forrester
Hinkley Ezekiel F. junk, 170 Bridge, house do.
Hinds Edward, laborer, house 5 Pratt street court
Hinds Justin, supt. Salem Type Machine Co. house 85 Essex
Hines Edward, fireman, E. R. R. house 105 North
Hines Richard, laborer, house 6 High street court
Hinman Hannah K. widow, house 13 Curtis
Hitchens Richard, laborer, house 8½ English
Hitchings Abijah, carpenter, house 12 Allen
Hitchings Abijah jr. Mrs. nurse, house rear 22 Hardy
Hitchings Abijah F. sailmaker, house 18 Hardy
Hitchings Mary Mrs. house 7 Becket
Hoar Eugene, foundryman, boards 6 Tucker's wharf
Hoar John, laborer, house 13 Becket
Hobart Sarah Miss, house 8 Allen
Hobart Sarah, widow, house 8 Allen
Hobbs Edward, clerk, 223 Essex, boards Essex House
Hobbs George, house 21 Mall

Hobbs James S. Mrs. house 9 Rust
Hobbs William H. expressman, house 30 Mill
Hodgdon David, captain, boards 199 Bridge
Hodgdon George C. clerk (B.), house 65 Mill
Hodgdon (*Robert H.*) & Stedman (*S. L.*), tailors, 39 Washington,
    boards 1 North Pine
Hodges Edward, inspector, Custom House, house 845 Essex
Hodges Gamaliel, machinist, house 7 Barton
Hodges John, merchant, house 266 Essex
Hodges John, moulder, boards 10 Prince
Hodges Joseph Mrs. house 95 Essex
Hodges Samuel R. distiller, house 4 Chestnut
Hodges Sarah E. boards 102 Bridge   [Vols.
Hodges Thorndike D. house 266 Essex (Capt. Co. C. 1st N. C.
Hodgkins George L. grocer, 40 Pleasant, house 91 Bridge
Hodgkins Sarah, tailoress, house 71 Federal
Hodskinson Jabez, machinist, house 20 School
Hoffman Charles, merchant, 12 Derby wharf, h. 26 Chestnut
Hogan James Mrs. widow, house Grove, near Cemetery
Hogan James H. Mrs. house 51 Mill
Hogan Michael, farmer, house 3 Lynn road
Holbrook Joseph, oysters, &c. 5 Derby square, house 7 Oliver
Holbrook J. M. milliner, 238 Essex, boards 7 Oliver
Holbrook Solomon H. physician, house 122 Bridge
Holden Charles, shoemaker, house 15 Carlton
Holden Charles J. boards 17 Briggs
Holden Joshua F. shoemaker, boards 15 Carlton
Holden Nathaniel J. counsellor, 218 Essex, h. 17 Briggs
Holden Nathaniel Mrs. house 17 Briggs
Holland John, laborer, house 20 Carlton
Holland William W. clairvoyant physician, house 86 Mill
Hollin David, carpenter, house 12 Aborn
Holman Lydia Mrs. house 93 Lafayette
Holman Lyman, building mover, house 175 Boston
Holmes Frances, widow, house 8 High
Holmes George H. carpenter, house 46 Charter
Holmes Mary M. Mrs. boys' clothing, house 46 Charter
Holmes William F. currier, house 16 High
Holt Lucy W. Mrs. house 80 Mill
Holt Sophia Miss, house 20 North
Homan Abigail, house 368 Essex
Honeycomb Samuel R. carpenter, 21 Margin, house 2 Collins
Honeycomb Sarah E. teacher, house 7 Lemon
Honeycomb Thomas P. carpenter, 27 North, house 100 do.
Honeycomb William H. carpenter, 14 Cross, house 7 Lemon
Hood Abraham, gardener, house 9 Webb
Hood Asa, hats, caps, and furs, 178 Essex, house 102 Federal
Hood David B. carpenter, foot of Turner, house 9 Webb
Hood Henry P. dentist, boards 9 Webb
Hood Nathaniel S. cooper, house 12 Daniels

Hooper Hannah, house 12 Beckford
Hooper John, laborer, house 7 High
Hooper Nathaniel, shoemaker, house 96 Essex
Hooper Nathaniel M. inspector, Custom House, h. 19 Pickman
Hooper Stephen G. shoemaker, house 70 North
Hopkins John, currier, house 81 Boston
Horden Michael, stonecutter, boards 55 Derby
Horne Betsey, widow, house 218 Essex
Horrigan Jeremiah, house Watson, near Beaver
Horton George, currier, house 44 Boston
Horton (*Nathaniel*) & Crocker (*Josiah M.*), curriers, foot Buffum, h. 22 do.
Horton Nathaniel A. (*Foote & Horton*), publisher "Salem Gazette," 199 Essex, house 22 Buffum
Horton William C. accountant, h. Leach, n. Lafayette
Howard David A. shoemaker, boards 206 Derby
Howard David R. shoemaker, house 206 Derby
Howard Dorcas, widow, house foot Pingree
Howard Eben M. clerk, Essex, cor. Newbury, b. 7 Northey
Howard Frederick P. (*South & H.*), boot and shoe manuf. 19 Lafayette, house 1 Salem
Howard John D. clerk, house 38 Beaver
Howard John Mrs. house 2 Winter
Howarth Austin S. student, boards 23 Briggs
Howarth John, house 23 Briggs
Howe Edward, laborer, boards 42 Harbor
Howe William T. boards 355 Essex
Howes William jr. mariner, boards 6 Whittemore
Howley John, house 3 Tucker's wharf (U. S. N.)
Hoyt Charles C. 24 Front, house 13 Cambridge
Hoyt Erastus, teamster, Central, corner Front, house 34 Essex
Hoyt Esther & Sally Misses, house 28 Harbor
Hoyt George R. carpenter, house 28 Harbor
Hoyt Ichabod R. ship carpenter, house 28 Harbor
Hubbard Mary, house 369 Essex
Hubon Frederick, carpenter, house 6 Everett
Hubon Henry Mrs. house 9 Dearborn
Hubon Henry G. coffin warehouse, 56 Washington, house 52 do.
Huddell William, laborer, house foot of Ives
Hughes James, shoemaker, house 32 Phelps' court
Hughes James, laborer, house East Webb
Hughes James H. laborer, boards East Webb
Hughes John H. fireman, house 22 Becket
Hultman Samuel Mrs. house 48 Lafayette
Humphrey Simon P. moulder, house 10 Becket
Hunt Frederick H. police, house 23 Hardy
Hunt Joseph Mrs. house 19 Church
Hunt Lewis, clerk, boards 1 Brown
Hunt Thomas, merchant, house 64 Bridge, corner Pearl
Hunt Thomas F. 243½ Essex, boards 64 Bridge

Hunt William & Co. (*Joseph H. Hanson, N. A. Frye, and R. Brookhouse jr.*), merchants, 16 Asiatic building, house 1 Brown
Hunt William D. (Boston), house 10½ Lynde
Hunter William, Naumkeag mill, boards 59 Harbor
Huntington Asahel, clerk of the courts, Court House, and president, Naumkeag mills, house 35 Chestnut
Huntoon F. W. L. dry goods, 222 Essex, h. at Marblehead
Huntress Charles W. printer, 199 Essex, boards 100 Derby
Huntress Darling, teamster, house 100 Derby
Huntress John E. shoemaker, boards 100 Derby
Hurd Thomas, stone mason, house 24 Hathorne
Hurd William H. mason, boards 17 Harbor
Hurd, see Heard
Hurlburt Oscar B. machinist, boards 5 Mall
Hurley Cornelius, blacksmith, house 41 Union
Hurley Elizabeth, widow, house Congress, West side
Hurley James, laborer, house 4 Elm
Hurley John, ales, liquors, &c. 3 High, house 6 do.
Hurley John, blacksmith, house 41 Union
Hurley John, clerk, 6 Derby square, boards 3 Bridge
Hurley John, currier, house 26 Beaver
Hurley John, laborer, house 1 Thorndike
Hurley Margaret, widow, house 36 Ward
Hurley Thomas, laborer, house 3 Bridge
Hurley William Mrs. house 1 Thorndike
Hurnan Kate, widow, house 21 Ward
Huse John, currier, 59 Boston, house 171 Federal
Hussey George B. carpenter, house 3 Cedar street court
Hussey Robert, captain, house 7 Orange   [89½ do.
Hutchings Augustus (*Harris & H.*), carpenter, 33 North, house
Hutchings Charles W. captain, house 3 Mechanic
Hutchinson Benjamin, mariner, boards 35 Lafayette
Hutchinson Charles E. stove worker, 29 Front, h. 83 Summer
Hutchinson Daniel H. captain, house 45 Endicott
Hutchinson George C. carpenter, house 30 Turner
Hutchinson Hannah, widow, house 208 Derby
Hutchinson Horace, peddler, house 208 Derby
Hutchinson John I. (Boston), house 94 Bridge
Hutchinson John L. shoemaker, house 4 Dow
Hutchinson Samuel, captain, house 96 Bridge
Hutchinson Samuel jr. captain, house 52 Bridge
Hutchinson Sarah, widow, house 30 Turner
Hutchinson Thomas, cabinetmaker, 205 Essex, h. 18 Walnut
Hutchinson Thomas J. job printer, 183 Essex, h. 60 Federal
Hyde Daniel, laborer, boards 156 Derby
Hyde Thomas, laborer, house 156 Derby
Hyland Edward, tanner, Grafton, near Hanson
Hynes Patrick J. furniture, 10 Front, house 6 High street court

IDE EDWIN R. carpetings and dry goods, 229 Essex, house
   10 Mason   [Derby, corner Orange
Imperial Harriet Mrs. matron Home of Aged Females, 114
Imperial S. Francis, machinist, house 2 Prince
Ingalls C. H. (ink manufacturer, B.), house 11 Prescott
Ingalls Elizabeth, widow, house 68 Essex
Ingalls Ira Mrs. house 33 Buffum
Ingalls Ira F. house Tremont, near S. Danvers line
Ingalls Mary Mrs. house 7 Pratt
Ingalls Mary Mrs. house 66 Mill
Ingalls Nathaniel, moulder, boards foot East Gardner
Ingalls Wilson H. cooper, house 4 Cabot
Ingersoll Nathaniel, captain, house 77½ Bridge
Ingersoll Nathaniel Mrs. house 77½ Bridge
Innis John A. newspaper and book agent, house 18 Beckford
Innis John, city watch, house 72 Essex
Ireland Eliza S. Mrs. house 90 Mill
Ireland Mary Mrs. house 6 River
Ireland William A. clerk, 214 Essex, house 188 Federal
Isaackson Sarah A. Mrs. nurse, house 29 Norman [19 Winter
Ives Benjamin H. dep. col. internal revenue, 175 Essex, house
Ives D. Perkins, fancy goods (47 Milk, B.), house 85 Federal
Ives Henry P. bookstore and bindery, 232 Essex, house 301 do.
Ives John M. house 17 Pickman [Essex, house 123 Lafayette
Ives John S. books, stationery, fancy goods, and seeds, 281
Ives Lydia A. Mrs. house 19 Washington
Ives Mary M. Miss, house 368 Essex
Ives Stephen B. bookbinder, house 26 Brown
Ives (*Stephen B. jr.*) & Lincoln (*Solmon jr.*), counsellors, 27
    Washington, house 24 Brown
Ives William, 226½ Essex, house 390 do.

JACKMAN NATHANIEL M. printer, house 18 Church
Jackson Andrew, mariner, house 47 Federal
Jackson Eben, salesman, house 1 Harbor street court
Jackson James, laborer, boards foot Perkins
Jackson John, lastmaker (Lynn), house 2 Mount Vernon
Jackson Nancy, house 20 Oliver
Jackson Wm. H. merchant (160 State, B.), h. 93 Lafayette
James Abraham, tanner, house 4 Pratt street court
James Daniel, pattern maker, Naumkeag mill, b. 59 Harbor
Jameson Mary Mrs. house 55 North
Janes Edwin, painter, boards 59 Winthrop
Janes John, printer, 241 Essex, house Salem Turnpike
Janes John, carpenter, house 59 Winthrop
Janes Joshua D. carpenter, house 19 Winthrop
Janes Sarah Mrs. house 59 Winthrop
Jaques Bridget, widow, house rear 34 Ward
Jaques John, laborer, boards rear 34 Ward
Jaques Joseph, laborer, boards rear 34 Ward

Jarvis William, house 4 Woodbury court
Jay Martin, laborer, house Mason Hill
Jeffers George, laborer, house 182 Federal
Jeffrey John jr. teamster, house 22 Vale
Jeffrey John B. teamster, house 22 Vale
Jeffs A. Perry, shoemaker, house 11 Aborn
Jelly Charles, coachman, house 12 Winthrop
Jelly Charles H. baker, 10 Cedar, house do.
Jelly Caroline, cashier, 190 Essex, boards 10 Beckford
Jelly George F. student, boards 10 Beckford
Jelly George G. gasfitter, 147 Essex, house 65 Mill
Jelly John A. captain, house 20 Endicott
Jelly Mary H. Mrs. dressmaker, house 12 Winthrop
Jelly Samuel S. cabman, house 3 Winter   [Beckford.
Jelly William, collector, Aqueduct Co. 280½ Essex, house 10
Jelly William F. mariner, house 58 Endicott
Jelly William H. house 73 Essex
Jenkins Michael, laborer, house 15 Turner
Jenks Lydia Mrs. house 30 Harbor
Jennis J. C. overseer, Naumkeag mill, boards 38 Harbor
Jerome N. H. Mrs. house 81 Lafayette
Jewell Benjamin, laborer, house 13 Skerry
Jewell Charles, currier, boards 2 Jeffrey court
Jewett Daniel H. wood, lumber, &c. 205 Derby, h. 61 Charter
Jewett George B. Rev. house 50 Federal
Jewett John, house 24 Winter
Jewett Lewis T. boards 8 Margin
Jewett Thomas S. assessor, city hall, house 45 St. Peter
Jillson Abel S. shoemaker, house 7 Salem
Jocelyn Henry E. (*Adams, Richardson, & Co.*), hardware, 215
      Essex, boards Essex House
Jocelyn Mary E. W. Miss, boards 11 Washington
Johnson Daniel H. shipbroker, house 10 North
Johnson Daniel H. jr. provost marshal, 5th District, 46 Wash-
      ington, house 12 North
Johnson Emery Mrs. house 362 Essex
Johnson Emery S. house 360 Essex
Johnson Flemming T. porter, house 12 Cedar
Johnson Francis D. clerk (B.), boards 2 Chestnut
Johnson Franklin, mariner, house 38 Essex
Johnson Frederick, master mariner, house 6 Winthrop
Johnson Frederick A. shoemaker, house foot of Northey
Johnson Hannah, Miss, house 406 Essex
Johnson Helen M. Mrs. house 84 Bridge
Johnson Henry D. (Boston), house 10 North
Johnson Henry L. captain, house 3 Spring
Johnson Job, Naumkeag mill, house 22 Ward
Johnson Peter, laborer, house 17 Pond
Johnson Samuel, physician, house 2 Chestnut
Johnson Samuel jr. Rev. house 2 Chestnut

Johnson Thos. H. sec'y Holyoke Ins. Co. 27 Wash. h. 94 Essex
Johnson William H. clothes cleanser and repairer, 9½ Central, house 15 Cambridge
Johnson William Henry, bookkeeper (B.), house 24 Pleasant
Johnson ——, solemaker, house 6 Woodbury's court
Jones George W. surveyor, house 16 Park
Jones Hugh, rigger, house 8 Pingree
Jones John S. & Co. commission merchants, head of Pierce's wharf, house 29 Broad
Jones Lewis, mariner, house 7 Park
Jones Reuben, engineer, E. R. R. house 9 Margin
Jones Samuel G. merchant tailor, 185 Essex, h. 16 Howard
Jones Sophronia, saleswoman, 184 Essex, house So. Danvers
Jones Sarah V. house 3 Salem
Jones William F. cabinetmaker, house 49 Endicott
Joplin William Mrs. house 61 Summer
Jordan Betsey Mrs. house 6 Norman
Jordan James, shoemaker, house Mason Hill
Jordan Michael, shoemaker, 34 Union, house 32 do.
Jordan William, shoemaker, boards 32 Union
Josephs Nancy, widow, house 30 Essex
Jowders Alexander, shoe manuf. house 6 Beach
Jowders E. Austin, shoemaker, house 51 Broad
Jowders James B. shoecutter, house 23 Flint
Joye Joseph, shoemaker, house 129 North
Joye Robert H. painter, boards 129 North
Julyn Charles R. ice, house 10 March

KALER MICHAEL, currier, house 27 Prospect
Kane John, laborer, house Phillips, near Grove
Kane Michael, laborer, house foot Perkins
Kaneley Patrick, cane-chairseater, house 12 Ward
Kaula John A. teacher of music, house 36 Charter
Keating Edward, tanner, house 7 Grove
Keating Thomas, laborer, house 407 Essex
Keating William, currier, house 106 Boston
Keefe John, currier, house 94 Mason
Keefe John, laborer, house 30 Peabody
Keefe Patrick, laborer, house rear 10 Herbert
Keegan Michael, shoemaker, house Boston
Kehew Aaron jr. Mrs. house 114 Bridge
Kehew Charles, laborer, house rear 34 Endicott
Kehew Ella F. teacher, Broad street primary, b. 19 Becket
Kehew Francis A. cooper, house 48 Hardy
Kehew Joseph C. carpenter, house 114 Bridge
Kehew Mary A. widow, house 19 Becket
Kehew Samuel B. cooper, house 12 Albion
Kehew Samuel Mrs. house 11 Herbert
Kehew William B. mason, house 24 North
Kehew William H. watchmaker, 230 Essex, h. 177 Federal

Kehoe James, laborer, house 21 Saunders
Keiran Owen, laborer, house 172 Derby
Kell William, shoecutter, boards 20 Fowler
Kellaher Hannah, widow, house 13 Becket
Kellaher Jeremiah, mariner, house 13 Becket
Kellaher John, laborer, house 8 Friend
Kellaher Mary, widow, house 21 High
Kellaher William, currier, house May street
Kelley Andrew, currier, house 2 Adams, Mason Hill
Kelley Andrew, currier, house Mason Hill
Kelley Betsey, widow, house rear 36 Charter
Kelley Catharine, widow, house 172 Derby
Kelley Daniel, stoveworker, 29 Front, house Jeffrey court
Kelley David H. stoveworker, house 3 Jeffrey court
Kelley David, currier, boards 86 Mill
Kelley Edmund, currier, house 34 Beaver
Kelley James, laborer, boards rear 36 Charter
Kelley James (*Quinn & K.*), tailor, 203 Essex, house 9 Barr
Kelley James, currier, house Prospect, near Ord
Kelley James H. mariner, house 15 Brown
Kelley John, butcher, house 27 Albion
Kelley John Mrs. house 160 Bridge
Kelley John, laborer, house rear 21 Becket
Kelley John, laborer, house 36 Mill
Kelley John, plumber, 7 St. Peter, boards 176 Derby
Kelley John (Cal.), house 172 Derby
Kelley John, laborer, house 26 Peabody
Kelley Jonathan D. farmer, h. 2 Lynn road, near Lafayette
Kelley Mary, widow, house 30 North
Kelley Mary, widow, house 34 Beaver
Kelley Mary, widow, house 86 Mill
Kelley Michael, currier, boards 13 River
Kelley Michael, laborer, house 96 Derby
Kelley Nathaniel, farmer, house Lynn road, near Lafayette
Kelley Nathaniel jr. carder, house 6 Cabot
Kelley Patrick, laborer, house rear 21 Becket
Kelley Simon P. morocco dresser, boards 86 Mill
Kelley Timothy, laborer, boards rear 36 Charter
Kelley Thomas, currier, house Prospect, near Ord
Kelley Thomas, house 156 Bridge (U. S. A.)
Kelman John, mariner, house 28 Essex
Kelman John Mrs. house 28 Essex
Kelman William W. broker (B.), house 181 Bridge
Kelsey Isaac, house 2 Pratt (Cal.)
Kemble Arthur, physician, over 174 Essex, b. Essex House
Kemp Frank B. clerk, boards 102 Bridge
Kemp Samuel, sailmaker (B.), house 102 Bridge
Kemp Samuel jr. currier, boards 102 Bridge
Kendall Alvah, stairbuilder, house 11 Hathorne
Kendall William H. clerk, boards 11 Hathorne

Kennedy Cornelius, laborer, house 4 Gerrish place
Kennedy John, laborer, house 23 Carlton
Kennedy Mary J. Miss, house 18 Norman
Kennedy Patrick, stonecutter, boards 55 Derby
Kennedy ————, mason, boards 9 Higginson square
Kenneilly David, saloon, house 43 Union
Kenney Alanson, supt. street lamps, house 12 Harbor
Kenney Benjamin M. machinist, 142 Essex, house 16 Salem
Kenney Bridget, widow, house 17 River
Kenney Edward W. machinist, boards 21 Lafayette
Kenney Emily Mrs. house 6 River
Kenney Francis, 5 Derby square, house 14 Howard
Kenney George, tanner, house 55 Warren
Kenney Heman A. shipcarpenter, house 8 Ropes
Kenney James, 5 Derby square, house 19 Oliver
Kenney John, laborer, house 11 Tucker's wharf
Kenney John, laborer, house 24 Ward
Kenney John J. waiter, at Essex House, house 6 Ward
Kenney Jonathan A. treas. Salem boot and shoe Co. 42 Mill, house 8 Pond
Kenney Michael, harnessmaker, boards 17 River
Kenney Michael, mariner, house 35 Harbor
Kenney Patrick, currier, house 93 Mason
Kenney Patrick, operative, house 11 Tucker's wharf
Kenney Thomas, carpenter, house 20 Union
Kenney William, tanner, rear turnpike, house 421 Essex
Kenney William, Naumkeag mill, boards 59 Harbor
Kenny Michael, harness maker, boards 17 River
Kent Otis L. clerk, 225 Essex, boards 20 Central
Kettlewell Peter, farmer, house 19 Salem
Keyes Michael, currier, house Silver
Kezar Albert A. currier, boards 17 Warren
Kezar Alonzo C. clerk, boards 38 St. Peter
Kezar Charles H. clerk, Higginson square, h. 1 Mason court
Kezar George L. baker, house 61 Derby
Kezar Sarah B. widow, house 38 St. Peter
Kezar Walter A. clerk, Adj. Gen'l. Office, house 17 Warren
Kiely David, laborer, house 44 Phelps' court
Kiely Ellen, widow, boards 50 Derby
Kiely Michael, carpenter, house 50 Derby
Kiely Peter, scissors grinder, house 9 Turner
Kiely Robert, clerk, boards 9 Turner
Kiely Richard, clerk, 4 Washington, boards 44 Phelps' court
Kiernan Patrick, teacher, house 8 North Pine
Kiernans John, currier, house 8 Vale
Kilbride Daniel, peddler, house rear 19 Daniels
Kilburn John, agent, Naumkeag mills, house 107 Lafayette
Kilby Christopher Mrs. house 18 Lynde
Kilham Alexander S. boards 10 Ash
Kilham William G. currier, house 1 Phelps' court
13

Killam Sylvester, carpenter, house 10 Ash
Kilroy John, Naumkeag mill, house 16 Congress
Kimball Adam W. clerk, 217 Essex, boards at Beverly
Kimball Alfred M. shoemaker, 23 North, boards do.
Kimball Augustus H. carpenter, house 80 Mill
Kimball Charles, counsellor, 226½ Essex, house at Ipswich
Kimball Charles A. counsellor, 226½ Essex, house at Ipswich
Kimball Charles A. (Boston), boards 36 Pleasant
Kimball Charles E. carpenter, house 18 Webb
Kimball David B. counsellor, 24 Washington, h. at Manchester
Kimball Dorcas Mrs. boarding, house 23 North
Kimball Edward D. house 16 Pleasant
Kimball Elizabeth H. house 55 Washington
Kimball George, printer and publisher, Essex Statesman, 224
    Essex, house 30 Pleasant
Kimball George, brakeman, E. R. R. boards 17 Crombie
Kimball George, clerk, boards 145 Boston
Kimball George S. painter, house 16 Harbor
Kimball Hannah W. Mrs. house Congress, near Harbor
Kimball Hiram, stonecutter, boards 30 Winthrop
Kimball Jacob, captain, house 9 Salem
Kimball James, county commissioner, house 123 Essex
Kimball James Mrs. house 8 Turner
Kimball James S. captain, house 14 Pickman
Kimball John, sailmaker, house 9 Rust
Kimball John S. house 17 Pleasant
Kimball Jonathan C. Mrs. house 29 Pleasant
Kimball Joseph Mrs. house 26 Charter
Kimball Joseph Mrs. house 4 School
Kimball Margaret Mrs. house 82 Essex
Kimball Margaret Mrs. house 59 North
Kimball Mark, house 1 Harbor
Kimball Mary, widow, house 15 Whittemore
Kimball Nathaniel, boards 6 Herbert
Kimball Nathaniel A. estate of, house 19 Pleasant
Kimball Philip H. clerk, 230 Essex, boards at South Danvers
Kimball Samuel T. house 16 Pickman
Kimball Thomas, captain, house 14 Pickman
Kimball Warren, house 91 Bridge
Kimball William, hats, caps, &c. 217 Essex, house 10 Charter
Kimball William jr. 217 Essex, house 26 Hardy
King Caroline and Susan, house 258 Essex
King Elizabeth Mrs. house 85 Essex·
King Esther L. widow, boards 15 Allen
King Hannah H. house 85 Essex
King Henry F. captain, house 389 Essex
King Henry Mrs. house 389 Essex
King James, house 34 Harbor
King James Mrs. house 15 Allen
King James B. Mrs. house 38 Chestnut

King John, currier, house rear Adams, Mason Hill
King John, shoemaker, 60 Derby, house 13 Allen . .
King John Gallison, counsellor (Boston), house 258 Essex
Kingman Christopher D. junk, house 132 North
Kingsley David P. clerk, 206 Essex, boards 1 Summer
Kingsley George W. baker, house 53 Summer
Kingsley Thomas P. house 21 Beckford
Kingsley Thomas S. mariner, boards 21 Beckford
Kinsley George W. currier, boards 12 Turner
Kinsley James, laborer, house 6 Park
Kinsley John, mariner, house 12 Turner
Kinsley William P. sashmaker, house 7 Beach   [h. 78 Bridge
Kinsman John, agent Salem and South Danvers Aqueduct Co.
Kinsman John, 251 Essex, house Bridge
Kinsman John C. house 7 Spring
Kinsman Joseph, shoemaker, house 31 Williams
Kinsman Joshua Mrs. house 22 Brown
Kinsman Nathaniel (38 India wharf, B.), house 24 Church
Kinsman Nathaniel J. captain, house 22 Brown
Kinsman Samuel, qurrier, house 59 North
Kinsman Samuel A. carpenter, house 74 Federal
Kinsman William L. (55 Comm'l wharf, B.), house 24 Church
Kirby Mary, widow, house 13 Ash
Kirby Mary Mrs. house 4 Ward
Kirwin John, currier, house 13 Rust
Kisskalt Maurice, confectioner, boards 269 Essex
Kittlewell Peter, house 19 Salem
Kittredge Gilbert H. clerk, boards 27 Essex
Kittredge Henry A. Mrs. house 27 Essex
Kittredge Jonathan, laborer, house rear 7 English
Knapp Joseph J. Mrs. house 85 Essex   .
Knapp William H. shoecutter, boarding house 1 Sewall
Knight Albert, baggage master, E. R. R. depot, h. 13 Salem
Knight Ann Mrs. house 168 Bridge
Knight Anna Mrs. tailoress, house 7 Cross
Knight Anthony laborer, house foot Pingree
Knight Charles, Mrs. house 60 North
Knight David A. painter, boards 168 Bridge
Knight Edward A. pressman, boards 168 Bridge
Knight Edward H. wharfinger and freight agent, Phillips
    wharf, house 10 St. Peter
Knight Jeremiah, shoemaker, house 4 Nursery
Knight Joseph F. currier, house 60 North
Knight Mary Ellen, boards 34 broad
Knight M. B. & M. Misses, fancy goods, 5 Pleasant, house do
Knight Nathaniel, laborer, house 13 Wittemore
Knight Nathaniel jr. laborer, boards 13 Whittemore .
Knight Richard N. clerk, 10 Washington, house 4 Cabot
Knight R. Foster, provisions, 48 North, house do.
Knight Sally, widow, house 60 North

Knight William Mrs. house 6 River
Knowlton George, blacksmith, house 53 Charter
Knowlton George W. stonecutter, boards 25 Harbor
Knowlton Marcus A. cabinetmaker, boards 10 Barton
Knowlton William A. boards 65 Lafayette
Knowlton William Mrs. boards 65 Lafayette
Knowlton W. Sargent, cabinetmaker, boards 10 Barton
Kyle Rachel Miss, house 7 Prince

LABREE EUNICE, widow, house Water, near Mechanic
Ladd Daniel W. messenger, State House (B.), h. 6 Gedney ct.
Ladd Mary Mrs. house 7 Gedney court
Lahan John, laborer, house 16 Turner
Lahan Patrick, laborer, house 34 Derby
Lahey Bartholomew, operative, house foot of Tucker's wharf
Lahey Catharine, widow, house 3 Tucker's wharf
Lahey Daniel, laborer, house foot of Tucker's wharf
Lahey Dennis, laborer, house 28 Peabody
Lahey James, laborer, house 3 Tucker's wharf
Lahey James, mariner, house 22 Pingree
Lahey Jeremiah, laborer, house 26 Peabody
Lahey Joanna, widow, house foot of Tucker's wharf
Lahey Mary, widow, house 3 Tucker's wharf
Lahey Patrick, laborer, house rear Leach, near Lafayette
Lake A. F. milliner, 256 Essex
Lake Calvin H. shoe manuf. (Lynn), house 17 Pickman
Lake George C. shoe manuf. 150 Essex, boards 17 Pickman
Lake Harrison H. shoe heeler, 150 Essex, house 19 Andrew
Lake Herman, boards 110 Essex
Lakeman Asa, teamster, boards 32 Derby
Lakeman Eben K. Mrs. house 12 Elm
Lakeman John R. clerk, 181 Essex, boards 28½ Harbor
Lakeman Nathan, currier, house 154 Boston
Lamb Hiram O. clerk, 232 Essex, house 31 Norman
Lambert Horace P. (B.), boards 4 Howard
Lambert John Mrs. house 22 Hathorne
Lambert Laura L. Mrs. house 98 Essex
Lambert Porter, leather dealer, house 4 Howard
LaMont Daniel G. physician, 243½ Essex, house at 41 Malden
    street, Boston
Lamprey John M. junk, boards 166 Bridge
Lamson Asa, house 4 Northey
Lamson Charles, watchmaker, 234 Essex, house 5 Northey
Lamson Frederick, florist and seedsman, 4 Northey, house do.
Lamson George A. 234 Essex, boards 5 Northey
Lander Benjamin W. printer, house 51 Summer
Lander Misses, house 5 Summer
Lander Henry R. clerk, 190 Essex, boards 51 Summer
Lander William T. clerk, boards 51 Summer
Lander William W. boards 106 Essex (Alexandria)

Landergan Edward, currier, house Grove, near Mason
Landergan James, laborer, house 53 St. Peter
Landergan John, currier, house Grove, above Mason
Landergan Patrick, hostler, house 7 Ward
Landergan William Mrs. 151 Bridge
Lane Caroline M. and Harriet P. Misses, house 21 Turner
Lane Charles H. boards 27 Charter
Lane Edward, clerk (B.), boards 12 Union
Lane Edward B. sailmaker, 57 Union, house 12 do.
Lane George N. clerk, boards 27 Charter
Lane Henry J. shoemaker, house 58 Endicott
Lane Mary, tailoress, house 27 Charter
Lane Mehitable Mrs. house 27 Charter
Lane Patrick, Naumkeag mill, house foot Pingree
Lang Elizabeth Miss, house 156 Federal
Lang Joseph, mariner, boards 15 Essex
Langdell Charles, clerk (B.), boards 5 Rust
Langdell George W. painter, 180 Bridge, boards 5 Rust
Langdell Mary, widow, house 5 Rust
Langmaid John P. lumber, 16 Lafayette, house 42 Charter
Langmaid J. Henry (Mt. Vernon Nat. Bank, B.), b. 42 Charter
Lannon Thomas, currier, house Peabody, near Ward
Larkin Matthew, currier, boards 63 Broad
Larrabee Charles W. shoemaker, house 5 Friend
Larrabee Edward W. expressman, boards 10 Oak
Larrabee George B. shoemaker, house 112 Bridge
Larrabee Henry A. shoemaker, boards 12 Lynn
Larrabee Joseph N. shoemaker, 37 North, house do.
Larrabee Samuel F. clerk, 42 Washington, boards 11 North
Larrabee Samuel H. house 11 North
Larrabee Samuel W. shoemaker, boards 77 North
Larrabee Sarah Miss, Home for Aged Females
Larrabee Somers N. shoe heeler, 37 North, house rear 70 do.
Larrabee Warren, house 5 Gardner court
Larrabee William H. shoemaker, boards 112 Bridge
Lasanby Maria, house 35 Essex
Laskey Esther Mrs. tailoress, house 18 Walnut
Laskey John, tobacconist, house 45 Mill
Laskey Mary E. dressmaker, 182 Essex, house 45 Mill
Lassan Peter, master mariner, house 7 Becket
Last John, mariner, house 14 Becket
Lations Jonathan P. wheelwright, Jeffrey court, h. 38 St. Peter
Lavers Richard, clerk, boards 2 Jeffrey court
Law George D. shoemaker, 12 Norman, house do.
Lawless Timothy, shoemaker, house 4 Barton
Lawrence Eliza A. Mrs. house 12 Essex
Lawrence George, mason, house 42 Endicott
Lawrence James, currier, house 22 River
Lawrence John, shoemaker, house 153 Bridge
Lawrence Joseph, clerk, 44 Derby, house 19 Carlton

Lawrence Joseph L. laborer, boards 19 Carlton
Lawrence Lewis, watchman, Phillips' wharf, house 35 Derby
Lawrence Lewis jr. cooper, house 20 Derby
Lawrence Michael, currier, house 20 River
Lawrence Patrick, restaurant, 4 Washington, boards 20 River
Leach Sarah H. Mrs. house 78 Federal
Learock John M. shoemaker, house 22 Derby
Leary Bartholomew, laborer, house 26 Union
Leary Daniel, coachman, house 16 Vale
Leary Jeremiah, mason, house 21 High
Leary Timothy, currier, house 1 Friend
Leavers Richard, grocer, boards 2 Jeffrey court
Leavitt Eunice Mrs. house 6 Walnut
Leavitt Henry J. express, boards 15 Crombie
Leavitt Israel P. shoemaker, house 107 Boston
Leavitt Joseph H. clerk, Essex House, 176 Essex
Leavitt Joseph S. proprietor Essex house, 176 Essex
Leavitt Walter, carpenter (B.), house 79 North
Leavitt William, teacher of navigation, 153 Essex, house 26
    Church
Lecraw Mary Mrs. house 9 Dean
Lee Elizabeth E. Miss, boards 12 Barton
Lee Francis H. house 14 Chestnut
Lee George Mrs. house 14 Curtis
Lee George W. Mrs. house 7 Elm
Lee Israel S. clerk, 58 Washington, house 10 Saunders
Lee John C. (40 State, B.), house 14 Chestnut
Lee John W. house 8 Phillips (Port Royal)
Lee Joseph laborer, house 16 Williams
Lee Joseph jr. house 11 Pearl
Lee Joseph L. machinist, house 90 Mill
Lee Lois D. Mrs. house 18 Saunders
Lee Mary D. Miss, house 90 Mill
Lee Robert G. boards 16 Williams
Lee Thomas, laborer, house 8 Phillips
Lee William J. hairdresser, house 10 Saunders
Lee William S. currier, boards 16 Williams
Leech William, boats, house 25 Turner
Lefavor B. Frank, house 23 Pleasant
Lefavor Samuel H. captain, house 58 Charter
Lefavour George B. mariner, boards 12 Winter
Lefavour John S. musician, house 15 Essex
Lefavour John W. Mrs. widow, house 9 Barton square
Lefavour Joseph Mrs. house 28 Pleasant
Lefavour Joseph A. clerk, 117 Essex, boards 17 Andrew
Lefavour Mary, house 18 Williams
Lefavour Richard M. mariner, boards 12 Winter
Lefavour Thomas H. clothing 197 Essex, house 12 Winter
Lefavour William, captain, house 17 Andrew
Legrand Matilda C. widow, house 12 Daniels

Lemasney John, laborer, house 7 Charter
Lemasney Thomas, laborer, house 42 Ward
Lemon Helen W. variety store, 2 Walnut, house do.
Lemon James B. tanner, boards 6 Beaver
Lendall Eliza, widow, house 28 May
Lendall George A. engineer, house 28 May
Lendall Jacob H. tanner, house 5 May
Lendall John G. tanner, house 28 May
Lendholm Charles F. mariner, boards 57 Lafayette
Lendholm Frederick Mrs. widow, house 57 Lafayette
Lennox Patrick, currier, house grove near Mason
Leonard James, shoemaker, house 14 Central
Leonard Lucius H. junk dealer, house 154 Federal
Leonard William, shoemaker, 196 Essex, house 25 Harbor
Levy Ole, mariner, house 42 Union
Lewellyn James, currier, house Salem Turnpike
Lewellyn Patrick, morocco dresser, boards Salem Turnpike
Lewellen Thomas J. currier, boards Salem Turnpike
Lewis Dana Mrs. house 20 Winter
Lewis Eliza A. widow, house 14 Allen
Lewis George A. Mrs. boards 3 March
Lewis George B. at Lynn depot, house 9 Hardy
Lewis Harriet E. teacher, Brown school, boards 18 Ward
Lewis Henry, house 16 Turner (U. S. N.)
Lewis Jesse W. oyster saloon, 7 Franklin building, h. 18 Howard
Lewis Louisa Miss, boards 80 Bridge
Lewis Lydia C. widow, house 170 Bridge
Lewis Martha Ann W. widow, house 319 Essex
Lewis Peter, mariner, house 28 High
Lewis Roland F. jig sawyer, boards 5 Hardy
Lewis Samuel, shipwright, house 18 Ward
Lewis Samuel A. clerk, house 5 Hardy
Lewis Samuel A. shipwright, boards 18 Ward
Lewis Samuel A. jr. clerk, 5 Derby square, house 5 Hardy
Lewis Thomas R. artist, boards 5 Hardy
Lewis William, Custom House, house 5 Hardy
Libbey John W. police, house 4 Herbert
Libby Frederick M. clerk, Naumkeag mill, boards rear 86 Mill
Libby Henry, morocco dresser, house 93 Boston
Libby John F. clerk, house 185 Federal
Lillis Owen, laborer, house 12 Ward
Lillis James, bootmaker, boards 12 Ward   [house 3 Gardner
Lincoln Solomon jr. (*Ives & L.*), counsellors, 27 Washington,
Lindegard Mary P. widow, house 8½ Carpenter
Lindsay Robert M. cutter, 282 Essex, house 12 Conant
Lindsey (*Richard*) & Durgin (*Horace W.*), grocers, 25 Lafayette,
        house 4 Broad   [4 Broad
Lindsey Richard F. bookkeeper, at John S. Jones & Co. boards
Liebsch Anton M. sailmaker, house 18 Carlton
Linehan Hannah, widow, house 36 Ward

Linehan Jeremiah Mrs. house 13 Park
Linehan John, laborer, house foot Pingree
Linehan John, boards 14 Park
Linehan Thomas, shoemaker, house 14 Park
Linehan William Mrs. house 7 Ward
Liner Margaret, widow, house 16 Ward
Lines John, laborer, house 3 Park
Linskey Patrick, currier, house 28 Ward
Little John, currier, house 13 River
Little Joshua B. Mrs. house 344 Essex
Little Michael, laborer, house 15 River
Littlefield Daniel, fish, house 19 Daniels   [Essex, h. 14 Curtis
Littlefield Edson L. riding school, and gymnasium, rear 161
Littlefield Edson L. jr. clerk, 14 Front, boards 14 Curtis
Littlefield Elmer, liquor (Boston), boards 14 Curtis
Littlefield Emeline M. teacher, boards 96 North
Littlefield Eri, Salem and South Danvers express, office 15
    Central, and 5 Washington
Littlefield Hannah Mrs. nurse, house 6 River
Littlefield Joseph, mariner, boards 19 Daniels
Littlefield Thomas A. house 16 Cambridge
Lloyd William H. mariner, house 2 Bentley   [4 Rust
Locke Milton P. (*Faxon & Locke*), stair builder, 72 Wash. h.
Locke Nathaniel B. carpenter, house 13 Saunders
Locke William, shoemaker, boards 6 Norman
Lockwood Elizabeth L. Mrs. widow, house 6 Becket
Loesch Gervas, ordnance sergt. of Fort Lee, at the Neck
Loflin Lydia A. widow, nurse, house 91 Essex
Logan Jeremiah, currier, house rear Adams, Mason Hill
Logan Thomas, laborer, house 23 Carlton
Long Henry L. clerk, boards 14 Elm
Long Isaac M. (*Browning & Long*), ladies' furnishing goods,
    177 Essex, boards Essex House
Looby Catharine, widow, house Watson, near Beaver
Looby Jeremiah, laborer, boards 22 Beaver   [105 Mason
Looby Thomas, tanner and currier, Grove, near Milldam, house
Looney William, currier, house 60 Broad
Lord Andrew & D. marble and grave stone manufactures,
    Market Wharf, house 12 Odell square
Lord Andrew H. marble worker, 11 St. Peter, house 7 Central
Lord Augustus, clerk, boards 20 Norman
Lord Calvin, 1 and 2 Market House, house at South Danvers
Lord Charles H. shoemaker, house 52 Endicott
Lord Charles L. carpenter, house 195 Bridge
Lord Daniel (*A. & D. Lord*), house 195 Bridge
Lord Daniel A. tanner, house 5 North Pine   [24 Howard
Lord Daniel B. (*Russell & L.*), carpenters, 15 Forrester, house
Lord Daniel B. jr. gasfitter, 147 Essex, house 166 do.
Lord Daniel W. stonecutter, b. 15 Whittemore   [Whittemore
Lord Daniel W. marble worker, Market Wharf, house 15

Lord Elizabeth Miss, house 27 Pleasant
Lord Emeline, teacher, private school, house 27 Pleasant
Lord Enoch, house 180 Federal
Lord Ephraim, tailor, 249 Essex, house 20 Norman
Lord Ernest D. clerk, boards 9 Central
Lord Francis, tanner, house 7 Phelps court
Lord (*George C.*) & Fuller (*George A.*), architects, 243½ Essex,
    house 12 Odell square
Lord George E. master mariner, house 27 Pleasant
Lord George R. asst. clerk, Court House, house at Ipswich
Lord Henry C. currier, house 13 Crombie
Lord James & Son (*James A.*), tanner, rear 180 Federal, h.
    180 do.
Lord James A. (*James Lord & Son*), tanners, h. 188 Federal
Lord John B. carpenter, 144 Bridge, house 16 Federal
Lord Mary A. W. widow, house 27 Williams
Lord Michael, captain, house 173 Federal
Lord Nancy D. Mrs. boards 15 Buffum
Lord Nathaniel J. counsellor, house 6 Brown   [14 North
Lord Otis P. judge superior court, office 27 Washington, house
Lord Samuel A. master mariner, boards 25 Hardy
Lord William, house 102 North
Lord William S. (135 Pearl, B.), house 69 Mill
Lorene Phillip, shipkeeper, house 21 Carlton
Lorigan John, tanner, house 22 Rivèr
Lorigan Michael, currier, house 76 North
Loring Edward D. carriage maker, West pl. house 80 Summer
Loring George B. house 328 Essex
Loring Joshua, house 55 Federal
Lougee Joseph L. (*Haskell & L.*), 279 Essex, boards 325 do.
Loveday Frank, mariner, house 8 Essex
Lovejoy John, carpenter, 108 Essex, house 40 do.
Lovering Lydia Mrs. house 14 Federal
Lovett John L. coffinmaker, at H. G. Hubon's, h. 10 St. Peter
Lovett John T. machinist, boards 40 St. Peter
Low Aaron T. boots & shoes, 76 Boston, house 79 do.
Low Charles H. laborer, house 14 High
Low Cornelius B. morocco dresser, boards 79 Boston
Low George H. morocco dresser, boards 79 Boston
Low Hannah, house 17 Creek
Low Richard, cooper, house 9 Gedney court
Lowd Albert J. (*Mark Lowd & Son*), painter, house 4 Ash
Lowd David, tanner, house 12 Hathorne
Lowd Edward B. machinist, boards 9 Buffum
Lowd Joseph G. currier, boards 12 Hathorne
Lowd Mark & Son (*Albert J.*), painters, 8 North, h. 9 Buffum
Loud Noah, sparmaker, house 9 Mason
Low Daniel, jeweller, 207 Essex, boards 9 Gedney court
Lucas Sarah H. Mrs. house 5 Dean
Lucey Hannah, house 17 Odell square

14

Lucey Michael, laborer, house 95 Mason
Lucey Patrick, laborer, house rear 143 Boston
Lucey Patrick, currier, house 85 Mason
Lucey Timothy, shoefinisher, house 13 Williams
Lull John E. laborer, house 140 Bridge
Lummus William, morocco dresser, house 13 Aborn
Lundgren Ellen M. seamstress, house 84 Derby
Lundgren James F. carpenter, house 84 Derby
Luscomb Abial T. boards 84 Mill (U. S. N.)
Luscomb Charles P. boards 84 Mill (U. S. N.)
Luscomb George, shoemaker, house 3 Dow
Luscomb George W. cooper, house 39 Lafayette
Luscomb Hannah, widow, house 23 North
Luscomb Harriet A. teacher, boards 41 Lafayette
Luscomb Harriet N. house 24 Lafayette
Luscomb Henry, treas. S. I. P. A. house 84 Mill
Luscomb Henry R. carpenter, boards 84 Mill
Luscomb John C. captain, boards 42 Pleasant
Luscomb John G. jeweller, 143 Essex, house 24 Lafayette
Luscomb Joseph Warren, mariner, boards 4 Conant
Luscomb Joseph W. captain, house 4 Conant
Luscomb William, shoemaker, house 78 North
Luscomb William F. carpenter, boards 42 Pleasant   [Cedar
Luscomb Wm. H. sign and fancy painting, 4 Hamilton, h. 14
Lyford Francis W. farmer, house on the Neck
Lynch Andrew, laborer, house 123 Boston
Lynch Dennis, dry goods, 94 Derby, house 91 do.
Lynch Dennis, boards 92 Derby (U. S. N.)
Lynch James, saloon, 41 Derby, house foot of Daniels
Lynch John, laborer, house 15 Pond
Lynch John, laborer, house 143 North
Lynch John, laborer, house 28 Ward
Lynch John, laborer, boards 92 Derby
Lynch John jr. laborer, house 143 North
Lynch Joseph, currier, house rear 141 Boston
Lynch Mary Ann, widow, house 11 Charter
Lynch Michael, laborer, house 13 Charter
Lynch Patrick, umbrella maker, house 92 Derby
Lynch Patrick, tanner, house rear 89 North
Lynch Patrick, moulder, house 10 Herbert
Lynch William, umbrella maker, house 96 Derby
Lynch William, trunk maker, boards 7 Church
Lynde Sarah A. teacher, Higginson School, b. 6 Federal court
Lynn William C. turner, 5 Front, house 4 Winthrop
Lyons Charles, machinist, house 26 Winthrop
Lyons James, cooper, house 3 Daniels
Lyons James, Naumkeag mill, house foot of East Gardner
Lyons Jeremiah, laborer, house 3 Daniels
Lyons Timothy, grocer, 38 Charter, house 15 Liberty
Lyons Timothy, paper hanger, boards 3 Daniels'

MACK THOMAS, mason, house rear Adams
Mack William, physician, house 21 Chestnut
Mackenzie Margaret Mrs. house 172 Federal
Mackenzie Roderick A. tailor, 29 Washington, h. 172 Federal
Mackie John, upholsterer, 8 Central, house do.
Mackie John A. clerk, boards 8 Central
Mackintire Catharine Mrs. house 22 Crombie
Mackintire Hiram, cabinetmaker, house 14 Prescott
Mackintire Ingalls K. boots & shoes, 4 Norman, h. 62 Summer
Mackintire John, jeweller, 10 Central, house 22 Crombie
Mackintire Samuel, piano-fortes, 218 Essex, house 38 Summer
Macintire Samuel A. insur. agent, 27 Wash. house 9 Dearborn
Madden Patrick Mrs. widow, house 14 Congress
Madden Timothy, carver, house rear 38 St. Peter
Madigan John D. currier, house 24 Beaver   [h. 133 Boston
Madigan (*Patrick*) & Brennan (*Thomas*), curriers, Goodhue,
Magill Frank, laborer, house rear 19 Daniels
Maginess John, currier, house rear 56 Broad
Magoun Samuel B. carpenter, boards 29 Norman
Magoun Thomas, shipwright and calker, house 28 Derby
Magoun Thomas H. mariner, boards 28 Derby
Magoun Warren G. mariner, house 11 Warren
Maguire Bernard, grocer, 12 Front, house 19 Fowler
Mahan Mary N. widow, boards 1 English
Mahoney Andrew, at gas house, house 25 Northey
Mahoney Cornelius, shoemaker, house Lynch, corner Perkins
Mahoney Dennis, laborer, house 405 Essex
Mahoney James, laborer, house 30 Congress
Mahoney James jr. boards 30 Congress (U. S. N.)
Mahoney Jeremiah, leather dealer, house 12 Boston
Mahoney John, hostler, house 3 Milk
Mahoney John, laborer, house Tucker's wharf
Mahoney John C. house 13 Becket (Co. D, 24th Regt.)
Mahoney Matthew, laborer, house 11 Tucker's wharf
Mahoney Patrick, laborer, house 3 Parker's court
Mahoney Patrick, laborer, house 10 Silver
Mahoney Patrick, laborer, house foot Congress
Mahoney Patrick, painter, house 7 Upham
Mahoney Thomas, grocer, 110 Derby, house 11 Charter
Mahoney Timothy, laborer, house 168 Derby
Mahoney Timothy, laborer, house 20 Lemon
Maid Richard, laborer, house rear foot Pingree
Malady Martin, laborer, house rear 24 Congress
Malady Michael, laborer, house 26 Peabody
Mallon Andrew, farmer, house rear Adams
Mallon Henry, currier, boards 75 Mason
Malone Nicholas, laborer, house 8 Turner
Malone Nicholas jr. printer, 193 Essex, boards 8 Turner
Maloney Bridget, widow, house 42 Ward
Maloney Catharine, widow, house 123 Boston

Maloon Abigail Mrs. house 81 Boston
Maloon John W. tanner, house 81 Boston
Maloon Lucy M. nurse, boards John Warren's, Union place
Maloon William, tanner, house School, corner Tremont
Maloon William H. tanner, boards School corner Tremont
Mangan John, laborer, house 26 Mill
Mann Elizabeth N. private school, 190 Federal, boards 180 do.
Mann James B. grocer, 40 Boston, house 42 do.
Manning Charles H. house 9 Phelps' court
Manning Daniel A. Mrs. house 14 Albion
Manning Daniel C. (*Smith & M.*), livery stables, h. 62 Forrester
Manning James, proprietor Merchants' News Room, Asiatic
    building, house 4 Daniels
Manning John W. tin peddler, house 14 School
Manning Joseph, bootmaker, house 20 Mall
Manning Margaret, widow, house rear 143 Boston
Manning Michael, stonemason, house 58 Mason
Manning Nancy G. widow, house 61 Derby
Manning Otis T. mason, house 27 Warren
Manning Philip A. currier, boards 61 Derby
Manning Rebecca D. widow, house 33 Dearborn
Manning Richard, student, boards 9 Phelps' court
Manning Richard C. & Co. (*N. C. Robbins*), coal, wood, &c.
    189 Derby, house 71 Lafayette
Manning Robert, nursery of fruit trees, house 33 Dearborn
Manning Robert R. master mariner, house 4 Daniels   •
Manning Thomas B. clerk, house 17 Peabody
Manning Thomas D. laborer, house 3 Elm
Manning William H. carpenter, boards 61 Derby
Manning William S. morocco dresser, boards 13 Aborn [field)
Mansell Frank A. machinist, house Grove, near Irving (Spring-
Mansell John, rockblaster, house 18 Park
Mansfield Benjamin S. painter, 31 Endicott, house 2 Margin
Mansfield Charles, captain, house 11 Federal
Mansfield Charles A. mariner, boards 11 Federal
Mansfield Charles H. mason, boards 55 Mill
Mansfield Daniel H. merchant, house 8 Chestnut
Mansfield Freelove A. Miss, house 13 Crombie
Mansfield Henry, laborer, house 8 Hardy
Mansfield Henry T. house 73 Bridge
Mansfield Ira, mason, 57 Union, house 3 Lagrange
Mansfield Ira K. (*Henry J. Pratt & Co.*), druggist, 137 Essex,
    boards 3 Lagrange
Mansfield John Mrs. house 50 Mill
Mansfield John R. house 11 Nursery
Mansfield Joseph, painter, 9 Lafayette, house 21 Harbor
Mansfield Micajah B. counsellor, 226½ Essex, house 55 Mill
Mansfield Nathaniel B. Mrs. house 27 Broad
Mansfield Robert, shoemanuf. (Lynn), house 8 Federal
Mansfield William, constable and city messenger, h. 55 Mill

Mansfield William B. candle maker, house 50 Mill
Mansfield William R. D. carpenter, house 55 Mill
Marden Aaron, carpenter, house 112 Bridge
Marden Joseph, carpenter, house 5 Cross
Marden Lemuel B. carpenter, house 22 North
Margati Jose (Boston), house 10 Lynde
Margeson Christopher, boards 14 Elm
Markey Patrick, laborer, house 172 Derby
Markoe Nancy F. and Mary, house 39 Derby
Markoe Philip Mrs. house 39 Derby
Marks John L. salesman, 165 Derby, house 10 Winter
Marks Thomas H. captain, house 43 Forrester
Maroney Margaret and Mary, Misses, house 16 Elm
Maroney Thomas, laborer, house rear 4 Essex
Marren John, boot and shoemaker, 165 Essex, house 18 Northey
Marrs Catharine, widow, house 3 Parker's court
Marrs James, shoemaker, house Shillaber
Marrs James jr. shoemaker, boards Shillaber
Marsh P. R. Mrs. boards 136 Federal
Marshall Daniel, captain, house 4 North Pine
Marshall George H. morocco dresser, boards 4 North Pine
Marshall George H. shoemaker, boards 105 North
Marshall Hannah Mrs. upholsteress, house 2 Monroe
Marshall Henry E. saloon (B.), boards 10 Prince
Marshall Joseph, mason, house 17 Winthrop
Marshall Samuel, shoemaker, house 64 Boston
Marshall William, mariner, house 6 Prince
Marston Ann A. widow, house 14 Federal
Marston Asa, boards 7 Ash
Marston Daniel, house 7 Ash
Marston Henry, 212 Essex, boards 14 Federal
Marston Isabella T. house 15 Washington
Martin (*Christopher*) & Cunningham (*Lawrence*), boots and
    shoes, 145 Essex, house 8 Ward
Martin Edward Mrs. house 19 Lemon
Martin Henry, carpenter, house 25 Cedar
Martin John D. clerk, boards, 54 Bridge
Martin John N. Mrs. house 54 Bridge
Martin Joshua C. painter, boards foot Leach
Martin Lucy, house 100 Federal
Martin Oliver Mrs. house 7 English
Martin William P. currier, 1 Beach, house 159 Federal
Mason George, mariner, boards 30 Essex
Masury Priscilla, widow, house 9 Becket
Matthews James, coachman, house 17 Flint
Matthews James, expressman, 14 Washington, h. 76 North
Matthews James, laborer, house Phillips, near Grove
Matthews John E. clerk (B), boards 8 Ash
Matthews Sarah N. Mrs. nurse, house 8 Ash
Matthews Vincent, laborer, house 385 Essex

Maxfield Benjamin, laborer, house 84 Mill
Maxfield James, tanner, house 37 Boston
Maxfield Jesse Mrs. boarding, house 10 Prince
Maxfield Joseph H. house Porter's court
Maxfield Martha Mrs. house 28 Chestnut
May Calvin W. furniture, 274 Essex, house 30 Lynde
Maynes Wm. hats, caps, and furs, 35 Washington, h. 88 North
Maynes William R. clerk, 243 Essex, boards 88 North
Mayo Gardner, shoemaker, house 1 Woodbury's court
McAdams Patrick, laborer, house 9 Herbert
McBride Patrick, shoemaker, house 3 Warren court
McBride Peter, currier, house 15 River
McCabe Ann, widow, boards East Webb
McCaffrey Eliza Mrs. house Grafton, near Hanson
McCallum David, laborer, house 2 Dow
McCann Ann, widow, house 15 Lemon
McCannon Catharine, widow, boards 142 Derby
McCannon Susan Mrs. house 53 Warren
McCannon Thomas, currier, house 7 May
McCarn Daniel, clothing, house 26 Daniel
McCartney James Mrs. house 4 May
McCartney William, cabinetmaker, house 13 Saunders
McCarty Charles, currier, boards 14 River
McCarty Daniel, currier, house 9 Beaver
McCarty Dennis, currier, house 34 Beaver
McCarty Florence, currier, house rear Adams
McCarty Hannah, widow, house 123 Boston
McCarty Jeremiah, laborer, house 1 Friend
McCarty Joanna, widow, house 8 Perkins
McCarty John, tanner, house 18 Aborn
McCarty John Mrs. boards 24 Herbert
McCarty John, currier, house 435 Essex
McCarty John, currier, house 24 River
McCarty John, laborer, house rear 168 Derby
McCarty John, Naumkeag mill, boards 8 Perkins
McCarty Joseph, machinist, boards 10 Prince
McCarty Julia, widow, house 1 Friend
McCarty Margaret Mrs. house 20 Odell square
McCarty Margaret, widow, house So. Prospect, n. E. Gardner
McCarty Mary, widow, house 38 Ward
McCarty Michael, currier, house 2 Ives
McCarty Michael, boards 14 River
McCarty Michael, currier, boards 2 Ives
McCarty Michael, shoemaker, house Putnam, n. Hanson
McCarty Michael, currier, house 1 Friend
McCarty Michael, Naumkeag mill, house 8 Perkins
McCarty Michael jr. currier, house 14 River
McCarty Owen, laborer, house Harrod, near Phillips
McCarty Patrick J. (*Green & McCarty*), 123 Boston, h. do.
McCarty Thomas, laborer, house 129 Boston

McCary Daniel, laborer, house 28 Peabody
McCauley Terrence, laborer, house 28 Peabody
McCauley Thomas, laborer, house 2 High street court
McCausland George A. tanner, house 3 North Pine,
McCausland Martin L. currier, boards 116 Prospect
McClellan George H. clerk, boards 5 Gedney court
McCliggatt John, currier, house 405 Essex
McCloy Alexander, blacksmith, house 17 Union
McCloy Alexander jr. bookkeeper, 169 Derby, h. 4 Walnut
McCloy Charlotte A. widow, house 112 Essex
McCloy Isabella Mrs. house 14 Union
McCloy John, blacksmith, house 17 Union
McCloy John B. painter, boards 14 Union
McCloy Robert, provisions, house 14 Union
McCoard Thomas, dealer in live stock, house 146 Derby
McCormick Charles, laborer, boards 22 Congress
McCormick George, mariner, boards 22 Congress
McCormick John, currier, boards 10 Derby
McCormick John Mrs. house 77 Derby .
McCormick Mary, widow, house 10 Derby
McCormick William Mrs. widow, house 22 Congress
McCormick Patrick, operative, house rear 89 Derby
McCormick Thomas, mariner, boards 10 Derby
McCormick Richard, mariner, boards 10 Derby
McCormick Winnefred Mrs. house rear 10 Congress
McCruden Thomas, laborer, house rear 19 Daniels
McCue Michael, farmer, house foot of Dearborn   [Mason
McCurdy Thomas G. boot and shoe manuf. 144 Essex, h. 67
McDeavitt William, laborer, boards 38 Harbor
McDermott Patrick, laborer, house 20 Odell square
McDonald Andrew, currier, house Mason Hill
McDonald Catharine, widow, house 20 Walnut
McDonald John, currier, house 101 Mason
McDonald Michael, laborer, house 31 Derby
McDonald Michael, mariner, house 1 Bridge
McDonnell Catharine, widow, house rear 31 Derby
McDonnell David, laborer, house 77 Derby
McDonnell John, laborer, house 12 Pingree
McDonnell John, laborer, boards 77 Derby
McDonnell Margaret, widow, house 23 Carlton
McDonnell Michael, boilermaker, house 12 Pingree
McDonnell Philip, shoemaker, house rear 31 Derby
McDonnell Philip, machinist, boards 77 Derby
McDonough Edward, currier, house 11 Whittemore
McDonough William, blacksmith, house 10 Park
McDuffee Charles D. overseer Naumkeag mills, h. 4 Lagrange
McDuffie Augustus P. trader, house Ives, corner Orne
McDuffie Hugh, currier, boards 63 Broad
McFadden Albert, fisherman, boards 9 Allen
McFadden Daniel, fisherman, house 9 Allen

McFaden Lemuel, fisherman, boards 9 Allen
McFarland William Mrs. house 7 Harbor
McGarey Timothy, laborer, house foot of Park
McGarvey James, shoemaker, house 2 High street court
McGeary James, leather, house 65 Mason
McGee Cormick, currier, house 13 Gedney court
McGee Henry, currier, house 57 Broad
McGinley Sarah, widow, house Harbor cor. Congress
McGough James, machinist, house 99 Derby
McGlue Mary, widow, operative, house rear 7 Charter
McGlue Peter, blacksmith, 3 Laboratory, house 24 Mechanic
McGrain Christopher, printer, boards 41 Harbor
McGrain John, teamster, house 6 Park
McGrain Nicholas, laborer, house 89½ Derby
McGrain William, at R. C. Manning & Co.'s, h. 41 Harbor
McGrath David, boards foot of Tucker's Wharf (U. S. A.)
McGrath Dennis, laborer, boards foot of Tucker's Wharf
McGrath James, laborer, house 411 Essex
McGrath Joanna, widow, house foot of Tucker's Wharf
McGrath John, tanner, house 10 Lynn
McGrath Michael, laborer, house 9 Beaver
McGrath Patrick, laborer, house 6 Friend
McGrath Thomas, mariner house 6 Oliver
McGrath William, laborer, boards foot of Tucker's Wharf
McGraw James, laborer, house Mason Hill
McGregor Alexander, harness-maker, house 15 Carlton
McGuire Andrew, laborer, house 8 Park
McGuire Bernard, agent, N. E. P. Union, 12 Front, house 19
    Fowler
McGuire Bridget, widow, house 65 Mason
McGuire James, currier, house 40 Phelps court
McGuire John, shoemaker, City Scales
McGuire Patrick, laborer, house 9 Beaver
McGuire Peter, shoemaker, house 16 Vale
McGuire Thomas, tanner, house 411 Essex
McGuire Timothy, laborer, house 6 Tucker's Wharf
McGuire William, hostler, Essex House
McGuire William, laborer, house 142 Bridge
McIntee Mary, cook, Essex House, house rear 9½ St. Peter
McIntire Hannah, widow, house 13 Prince
McIntire Samuel J. teamster, house 4 Whittemore
McIntire William C. shoemaker, house 135 North
McIntire William E. carpenter, house 4 Whittemore
McIntyre Mary, tailoress, house 36 Norman
McIntyre Nathaniel, laborer, house 72 Mill
McKean William, shoe manufacturer, 30 Boston, h. 20 Fowler
McKeever Hugh, laborer, house 9 Creek
McKenner Charles, Naumkeag mill, boards 2 Pingree
McKenzie Henry, stone mason, board 21 Lafayette
McKenzie Reuben, Mrs. house 7 Williams

McKenzie Roderick H. mariner, boards 7 Williams
McKligett James, laborer, house 168 Derby
McLaughlin Mary Miss, confectionary, 76 Mill, house do.
McLaughlin Mary, widow, house 4 Prince
McLaughlin Michael, shoemaker, house 53 St. Peter
McLaughlin Michael, currier, house 76 North
McLaughlin Patrick, shoemaker, boards 4 Prince
McLaughlin Peter, shoemaker, house Prince
McLaughlin William, shoemaker, 141 Essex, h. 4 Prince
McLaughlin William J., Naumkeag mill, bds. ft. E. Gardner
McLoughlin Edward, currier, boards Watson cor. Beaver
McMahan Bridget, widow, house 28 Ward
McMahan Philip, weaver, house 14 Congress
McMann Ann, widow, house 12 Ward
McMann Susan, widow, house Harbor cor. Congress
McManners Ellen, widow, house 2 Pratt street court
McMullan John, master mariner, house 25 Essex
McMullan William Mrs. house 6 North
McMurphy Benjamin F. steam fitter, house 25 Pickman
McMurphy Ellen J. Mrs. house 6 Ash
McMurphy James F. boards 6 Ash
McNeal Daniel F. driver, H. R. R. house 7 Pleasant
McNeil Alexander, stevedore, house 1 Prescott
McNeil Malcolm, mariner, house Hanson, near Boston
McNiff James, mason, house 16 Vale
McNiff John, currier, house 57 Broad
McNulty James, laborer, house 21 High
McNulty Michael, gum copal worker, house 22 Becket
McShane Bernard, laborer, house 15 Lemon
McShane James, saloon, 48 Pleasant, boards 15 Lemon
McSweegen Peter, shoemaker, 144 Essex, h. 22 Beaver
Mead George E. shoemaker, house rear 89 North
Mead William E. fireman E. R. R. house 37 North
Mead William J. shoemaker, house rear 89 North
Meady Daniel F. confectioner, house 10 Carlton
Meady Louisa, widow, house 10 Carlton
Meara Sherman T. shoemaker, house 17 Carlton
Meek Aroline B. teacher, Phillips grammar school, b. 2 Curtis
Meek Henry, house 2 Curtis
Meek Henry M. clerk, boards 2 Curtis
Melcher Edward, carpenter, 83 North, house 32 Buffum
Melcher George B. painter, house 44 Buffum
Melcher George P. carpenter, boards 32 Buffum
Melcher John, carpenter, house 80 North
Melcher John E. carpenter, boards 32 Buffum
Melcher Levi L. mason, house 89 North
Melden Alvin, baker, boards 1 Carlton
Melden Eldret, painter, boards 1 Carlton
Melden George, laborer, house 1 Carlton
Melden William R. baker, boards 1 Carlton

15

Meliar James, currier, house 10 Ward
Melzard Thomas B. shoemaker, boards 6 Becket
Mercy Lewis, laborer, house 66 Harbor
Meredith Joseph, tanner, house 15 Albion
Merrill Augustus, clerk, 26 Front, house 45 Broad
Merrill Augustus, shoemaker, house 20 Crombie
Merrill Elizabeth K. Mrs. house 42 Broad
Merrill Jabez H. (*Butler, Davis & M.*), stonecutter, 18 Lafayette, house at Chelsea
Merrill James I., E. R. R. car shop, house 12 School street
Merrill John C. currier, boards 42 Broad
Merrill L. E. Miss, teacher of drawing, 243½ Essex, boards 33 Summer
Merrill William H. cooper, house 12 Liberty
Merritt Charles E. clerk, boards 35 Pleasant
Merritt David Mrs. house 94 Federal   [Wash. h. 26 Mason
Merritt David (*Merritt & Co.*), merchants and express line, 14
Merritt Henry (Boston), boards 113 Federal
Merritt Henry Mrs. house 113 Federal
Merritt William, supt. B. & M. R. R. house 35 Pleasant
Merritt William, jr. (Portland), boards 35 Pleasant
Messervy John, painter, house 2 Lagrange
Messervy Thomas K. mariner, house 91 Lafayette
Messervy William S. house 91 Lafayette   [Lead works
Metcalf Benjamin G. farmer, house Lafayette, near the F. R.
Metcalf Charles A. farmer, boards B. G. Metcalf's
Meyer William, shoemaker, house Tuttle court
Micklefield Rebecca B. house 20 Central
Milan James, boarding, house 129 Derby
Mildram Oren, house 6 Church
Mildram William H. tanner, boards 6 Church
Miles Thomas, laborer, house 24 Ward
Millea Lawrence, restorator, 2 Washington, house 79 Mason
Miller Arthur J. mariner, boards 31 Salem
Miller Charles H. merchant, 170 Essex, house 17 Pleasant
Miller Edward, mariner, house 12 Carlton
Miller Edward F. ship builder, house 31 Forrester
Miller Edward W. clerk, S. & S. D. H. R. R. boards 31 Forrester
Miller Ephraim F. British consular agent, house 66 Bridge
Miller Frederick L. boards 31 Salem (U. S. N.)
Miller James, boards 66 Bridge (Capt. 4th Vet. Cav.)·
Miller Lewis F. captain, house 31 Salem
Miller Mary Ann, widow, house 65 Essex
Miller Peter, laborer, house 34 Beaver ·
Millett Andrew J. currier, house 19 Winthrop
Millett Benjamin F. cooper, boards 69 Mason [17 Barton square
Millett Benjamin R. (*Currier & M.*), furniture, 261 Essex, h.
Millett Charles, captain, house 24 Pleasant
Millett Charles 2d, master mariner, house 5 Saunders
Millett Charles W. currier, boards 6 Curtis

Millett Daniel, house 49 Derby
Millett Edward A. clerk (100 Pearl, B.), house 4½ Northey
Millett George W. boards 6 Curtis (Cienfuegos)
Millett John H. boards 6 Curtis (Cal.)
Millett Joseph H. captain, house 4½ Northey
Millett Joseph H. jr. (100 Pearl, B.), house 4½ Northey
Millett Joseph Henry, grocer, 67 Derby, house 69 do.
Millett Louisa Mrs. house 69 North
Millett Martha, widow, house 6 Curtis
Millett Martha, widow, house 61 Summer
Millett Nathan H. master mariner, house 8 Curtis
Millett Needham C. house 8 Buffum
Mills Elizabeth H. dressmaker, boards 6 Pond
Mills James, grinder, house 110½ Derby
Mills Robert C. Rev. house 119 Federal
Mills Sarah Mrs. house 6 Pond   [Carpenter
Milton B. Sylvester S. fruits, &c. Wash. c. Essex, house 10
Milton Payson, shoemaker, house 3 March
Minehan Daniel, laborer, house 90 Derby
Minehan Francis, tanner, house rear Adams, Mason Hill
Minehan Thomas, currier, house 13 Congress
Miner John T. at Naumkeag mill, house 7 Daniels
Minor Albert H. Mrs. variety store, 18 Beckford, house do.
Minor Mary Mrs. Home for Aged Females
Mitchell Benjamin E. driver, H. R. R. house 2 Mason's court
Mitchell Catharine, widow, house foot Park
Mitchell Edward, currier, house rear 26 Beaver
Mitchell Edward, tinsmith, house 25 Beckford
Mitchell John, peddler, house 44 Peabody
Mitchell John, shoemaker, house 91 North
Mitchell Robert, 165 Derby, h. E. Gardner, c. S. Prospect
Mitchell Robert, mariner, boards 27 Charter
Mitchell Rucia A. widow, house 2 Mason's court
Mitchell William H. shoemaker, house Harrod, op. Phillips
Mitchell Winnifred, widow, house rear 28 North
Molan John, laborer, house Ward, Kelley's block
Moland George W. carpenter, house 23 Turner
Monaghan Catharine, widow, house 1 Pratt
Monaghan Daniel A. carpenter, boards 1 Pratt
Monaghan James, Naumkeag mill, house foot Perkins
Monaghan John P. painter, boards 1 Pratt
Monaghan Joseph H. boards 1 Pratt
Monarch Ebenezer, house 6 Vale
Monarch George H. blacksmith, boards 13 Skerry
Monies George T. shoemaker, house 2 Dow
Monies Michael D. carpenter, house Grove, near Cemetery
Monies William, butcher, foot Ives, house 6 Whittemore
Monies William A. laborer, house 12 Broad
Moody James S. overseer, Naumkeag mill, boards 38 Harbor
Moody Joseph, overseer, Naumkeag mill, boards 38 Harbor

Moody Lewis B. newspaper and periodical depot, 22 Wash. h.
    14 Odell sq.
Mooney Andrew, gardener, house top Hanson
Mooney Betsey, widow, boards 54 Buffum
Mooney Daniel, peddler, house 54 Buffum
Mooney John, gum copal worker, house 22 Becket
Mooney John, teamster, house Lynch, corner Perkins
Mooney John, blacksmith, boards rear Adams
Mooney (*John T.*) & Wadleigh (*C. E.*), stoves and tin ware,
    40 & 42 North, house 120 do.
Mooney Lawrence, at glue factory, boards Hanson .
Mooney Mary Ann, widow, house 172 Derby
Mooney Patrick, teamster, house rear Adams
Moore David, treasurer Gas Co. 188 Essex, house 18 Chestnut
Moore Dennison P. mariner, boards 13 Northey
Moore Edward, laborer, house rear Pingree
Moore George W. shoemaker, boards 6 Beach
Moore Harriet, widow, house 68 North
Moore Henry, student, boards 20 Fowler
Moore Henry, clerk, 10 Derby square, house 48 Charter
Moore Henry W. shoemaker, house 48 Charter
Moore Hiram W. carriage painter, rear 3 Cambridge, h. 6 do.
Moore James, carpenter, house 14 Whittemore
Moore Samuel, tailor, and Union Button Hole machine agent
    over 158 Essex, house do.
Moore Thomas, carpenter, boards 21 Lafayette
Moore William, boards 2 Beach
Moore William H. morocco dresser, house 173 Boston
Moran Catharine, widow, house 8 Perkins
Moran Jane, widow, house foot Hanson
Moran Matthew, laborer, house rear 8 English
Moran Michael, shoemaker, house 14 Ward
Moran Nathaniel, clerk, boards rear 8 English
Moran Samuel P. mariner, boards rear 8 English
Morant Philip, master mariner, house 17 Cedar
Moreland George W. carpenter, house 23 Turner
Morgan Charles, engineer, house 43 Boston
Morgan George S. Mrs. house Phillips' court
Morgan Henry W. shoemaker, boards 4 East Webb
Morgan Honora Mrs. house 17 River
Morgan John Mrs. house 1 North Pine
Morgan John, laborer, house 13 Lynn
Morgan John A. Mrs. house 62 Mill
Morgan Joseph S. mariner, boards 11 English
Morgan Lucy, widow, boards 22 North
Morgan Mary, widow, house 2 Palfrey court
Morgan Michael, currier, boards 17 River
Morgan Misses, house 358 Essex
Morgan Patrick Mrs. house 11 English
Morgan Thomas, marble worker, 14 Central, house do.

Moriarty Michael, laborer, house rear Adams, Mason Hill
Morrill Anna M. dressmaker, 86 Mill
Morrill Francis A. fruit and confectionery, 140 Essex, house do.
Morrill Joseph, farmer, house 3 Lynn road
Morrill Mary E. widow, house 105 North
Morris Charles P. house 10 March
Morris Joseph B. restaurant, 18 & 20 Derby sq. house 17 Mall
Morris Mercy, widow, house 10 March
Morrissy John, laborer, house rear foot Pingree
Morse Abigail H. Mrs. boards 7 Lynn
Morse Edward A. currier, house 28 High
Morse E. Henry, carpenter, house 3 Leach   [Warren
Morse George F. (*Hancock & Morse*) 39 Derby, house 23
Morse Hannah E. teacher Fowler street school
Morse John, tanner, house 55 Broad
Morse Lucius B. tanner, house 162 Federal
Morse Mary E. Mrs. house 91 Federal
Morse Nathan R. physician, house 13 Washington
Morse Payne, watchman, house 133 North
Morton Charles, clerk, 245 Essex, boards 114 Bridge
Morton Henry (*Buswell & M.*), boots and shoes, 196 Essex,
    house 114 Bridge
Morton Mary H. widow, house 131 Essex
Moseley Joseph, surveyor, Custom House, house 29 Beckford
Moseley Martha P. Mrs. house 97 Essex
Moses Aaron, mariner, house Webb, near East Webb
Moulton Daniel W. clerk, 178 Essex, boards 105 Federal
Moulton Frederick, mason, house 105 Federal
Moulton George F. currier, house 11 May
Moulton Jay H. Boston express, 10 Washington, h. 1 Everett
    corner Salem
Moulton John G. flour and grain, house 35 Salem
Moulton Joseph C. carpenter, boards 5 Mechanic
Moulton Joshua W. photographer, 214 Essex, house 116 Bridge
Moulton Nathaniel P. carpenter, house 5 Mechanic
Moulton Nelson H. & Brother (*Wm. C. C.*) fancy goods, 164
    Essex, boards 110 Essex
Moulton Stillman H. clerk, 164 Essex
Moulton William, fruit and confectionery, 18 Lafayette, house
    77 Mill
Moulton Wm. C. C. (*Nelson H. Moulton & Bro.*), h. 31 Church
Moyhan Humphrey, currier, house 12 Friend   •
Moynagan Dennis, laborer, house 15 Turner
Moynahan Cornelius, laborer, house 15 Turner
Moynihan John, laborer, house Mason Hill
Muchmore George H. express, house 8 Church
Muchmore Richard, express, house 8 Church   [Lagrange
Mudgett Daniel A. teamster, at the F. R. Lead Mills, house 5
Mudgett Eben P. blacksmith, house 1 Downing
Mudgett Samuel A. ale depot, Higginson sq. h. 16 Winthrop

Mugford Charles D. merchant, house 337 Essex
Mugford George Mrs. house 88 Federal
Muhlig James J. carpenter, house 50 Bridge
Muhlig Robert, tanner, foot Buffum, house 8 Barr
Mulcahey Edward, carpenter, house 25 Albion
Mulcahey James, wheelwright, house 8 Pratt
Mulcahey Maurice, laborer, house 17 Derby
Muldoon Felix, peddler, house 16 Elm
Mullen David, laborer, house 14 Lafayette
Mullen Edward, tailor, house 13 Ash
Mullen Ellen, widow, boards 435 Essex
Mullen James, laborer, house Nichols, corner Varney
Mullen John, master mariner, house 27 Essex
Mullen Mary A. cloak and dressmaker, house 50 Charter
Mullen Richard, tailor, 37 Wash., house 28 Union
Mullett George W. house 62 Summer
Mulrady Catharine, widow, house Mason, n. Mason Hill
Mulrady Stephen, plumber, house 36 Charter
Munday John, laborer, house 4 Daniels
Monroe Jeanette Mrs. nurse, house 25 North
Monroe Louisa, boarding, house 1 Perkins
Monroe Olive, widow, boards 13 Ward
Monroe Ruth, widow, house 3 Mechanic
Monroe Stephen N. (*Wiggin & Monroe*), provisions, 111 Essex,
    house 57 Endicott
Monroe William D. W. machinist, house 14 Osgood
Murphy Daniel, currier, house 29 Beaver
Murphy Daniel, laborer, house 23 Beaver
Murphy David, currier, house 7 High
Murphy David, laborer, house foot of Ives
Murphy David, laborer, house 130 North
Murphy Eliza M. Mrs. house 25 Summer
Murphy James, laborer, house 50 Derby
Murphy James, currier, house 123 Boston
Murphy James, currier, boards Prospect, n. Aborn
Murphy James E. engineer, house 15 Pond
Murphy Jeremiah, currier, house 76 North
Murphy John, laborer, house 4 Gerrish place
Murphy John, laborer, house Grove, near cemetery
Murphy John, coachman, house Harrod, opp. Phillips
Murphy John, currier, house Mason Hill
Murphy John, saloon, house 156 Derby
Murphy John, laborer, house 11 Tucker's Wharf
Murphy Mary, widow, house rear 28 North
Murphy Michael, gardener, house 407 Essex
Murphy Michael, engineer, house 13 Pond
Murphy Michael, currier, boards 50 Derby
Murphy Michael, currier, house 40 Phelps court
Murphy Nicholas, laborer, house Grove, near cemetery
Murphy Patrick, currier, house 39 Beaver

Murphy Patrick, currier, house 30 Varney
Murphy Patrick, laborer, house Grove, near cemetery
Murphy Peter Mrs. house Grove, above Mason
Murphy Richard, currier, house 77 Mason
Murphy Sarah, widow, house 30 Congress
Murphy Thomas, currier, boards Mason Hill
Murphy Timothy, laborer, house 130 North
Murphy William, currier, house Mason Hill
Murphy William, boards 11 Central
Murray Elverton H. musician, house 6 Downing
Murray Hugh, laborer, house foot of Pingree
Murray James, teamster, house 11 Gedney court
Murray John, laborer, house 6 Perkins
Murray Joseph T. clerk, house 72 North
Murray Michael, laborer, house 172 Derby
Murray Owen, currier, boards 63 Broad
Murray Timothy, laborer, house 152 Derby
Myers Catharine, widow, house 28 Peabody
Myers Daniel, laborer, house Felt, near foot Dearborn
Myers David, laborer, house 5 Park
Myers Patrick, laborer, house rear 1 Pingree
Myers Thomas, Naumkeag mill, house foot of Perkins

NAOS HENRY, laborer, house 58 Broad
Narbonne Sarah Mrs. house 71 Essex
Nash Mary E. teacher, N. S. boards 17 Margin
Nash Prince E. foreman shoe manuf. house 7 Botts court
Nash Warren, clerk, 9 Derby Square, boards 5 Botts court
Nason Alfred, fisherman, house 5 Gerrish place
Nason David, conductor L. R. R. house 10 Mason
Nason Peter A. clerk (B.), boards 10 Mason
Nason Samuel, farmer, house 15 Pond
Navey Mary, widow, house E. Gardner, near Harbor
Navey Thomas, laborer, house East Gardner, near Harbor
Nay Joshua, engineer, house 10 Park
Neagle Sarah, widow, house rear 8 Essex
Neal Alonzo N., Naumkeag mill, boards 1 Perkins
Neal Benjamin B. fire-brick maker, 10 Franklin, house 9 Cam-
    bridge
Neal George L. carpenter, boards 19 Hathorne
Neal Henry, coach-driver, house 12 Broad
Neal Isaac B. horseshoer, West Place, house at Lynn, bds.
    Washington House
Neal John H. Mrs. house 66 Washington
Neal Jonathan, mason, house 12 Broad
Neal Joseph, mason, house 19 Hathorne
Neal Patrick, laborer, house 16 Derby
Neal William H. Mrs. house 13 Chestnut
Neal Mrs. widow, house near foot of Pingree
Needham Charles H. clerk, boards 3 Elm

Needham George P. clerk, 1 and 2 Market House, boards 3 Elm
Needham James, cigar maker, house 3 Elm
Needham James F. clerk, 22 Central, boards 3 Elm
Needham J. S. fruit and confectionery, 272 Essex, house Lo-
    cust Dale, South Danvers
Neilson William, physician, 49 Washington, house 47 do.
Nelles Augustus C. baker, 72½ North, house 1 Mechanic
Nelson James S. produce, 26 Front, house 3 Cambridge
Nelson John F. mariner, house 71½ Bridge
Nelson Marquise (Charlestown), house 7 Cedar
Nelson Samuel F. shoemaker, house 21 Beckford
Nelson William H. captain, boards 68 Bridge
Neptune Felix, mariner, house Webb
Nesbett Margaret, widow, house 9 Herbert
Neville Ellen, widow, house 17 Derby
Neville Patrick, laborer, house Phillips near Grove
Neville Thomas, laborer, house rear 143 Boston
Neville William, laborer, house 14 Derby
Nevells Ellen Miss, house 20 Oliver
Newcomb Caleb, house 8 Cherry
Newcomb Caleb H. clerk at Provost Marshal's (Boston), house
    92 Federal
Newcomb Charles B. engineer, house 22 Salem
Newcomb Charles B. jr. turner, house 14 Conant
Newcomb David, house 82 Essex
Newcomb David B. & John, oysters, 24 & 26 Derby sq. house
    9 Walnut
Newcomb George, machinist, house 58 Mill
Newcomb George L. machinist, 18 Peabody, house 1 Cedar
Newcomb James Alfred, machinist, h. 26 Lafayette   [Howard
Newcomb John (*David B. & J.*), 24 & 26 Derby sq. house 20
Newcomb John D. Mrs. boards 5 Mall
Newcomb Lemuel W. shoemaker, house 28 Norman
Newell Charles O. boards 142½ Essex
Newell Joseph, sash, blind, and door manufacturer, 7 Front,
    house 38 Lafayette
Newell Lucinda T. vestmaker, boards 7 Lagrange
Newell Stillman, boarding house, 70 Harbor
Newell Thomas P. billiard hall, 153 Essex, house 30 Charter
Newhall Benjamin, engineer, house Grove, near Cemetery
Newhall Ezra F. (B.), house 9 Pleasant   [Harbor
Newhall Fidelia E. cashier at Jas. F. Almy & Co's. boards 20
Newhall Gilbert G. Mrs. house 9 Pleasant
Newhall James S. tanner, boards 94 Boston
Newhall John F. printer, 199 Essex, house 4 Harbor street ct.
Newhall Joseph M. Mrs. house 30 St. Peter
Newhall Rebecca, nurse, house 39 St. Peter
Newhall William, city crier, house 10 Church
Newport Sarah A. Mrs. house 1 Cedar court
Newton Albert, baker, boards 1 Mt. Vernon

Nichols Abby F. teacher, Epes school, boards 146 Federal
Nichols Abigail, variety store, 68 Boston, house do.
Nichols Abigail A. house 16 School
Nichols Andrew Mrs. house 34 Summer
Nichols Benjamin C. currier, boards 146 Federal
Nichols Charles S. secretary Salem M. F. I. Co. 42 Washington, house 6 Chestnut
Nichols Clement, mariner, house 5 Gedney court
Nichols Daniel F. house 146 Federal
Nichols David Augustus, grocer, 76 Derby, house 10 Elm
Nichols David, house 8 Proctor court
Nichols Elizabeth R. widow, house 104 Boston
Nichols George Mrs. house 80 Federal
Nichols George S. tanner, house 8 Carpenter
Nichols Hannah, house 10 Northey
Nichols Henry C. currier, boards 146 Federal
Nichols Isaiah, merchant, house 104 Boston
Nichols James, shoemaker, house Tremont, above Grove
Nichols James D. (36 Pearl, B.), house 9 Liberty
Nichols James W. hairdresser, boards Tremont above Grove
Nichols J. Henry, shipsmith (B.), house 10 Elm
Nichols John, shipsmith, 45 Union, house 10 Elm
Nichols John, house 16 Cambridge
Nichols John, tanner, boards 4 Botts court
Nichols John, printer, house 2 St. Peter's court
Nichols John H. auctioneer and insurance agent, 42 Washington, house 37 Chestnut
Nichols John R. house 14 Webb
Nichols John S. painter, boards 170 Bridge
Nichols Jonathan Mrs. house 104 Boston
Nichols Mary Jane and Abby Misses, house 105 Boston
Nichols Nathan (63 Hanover, B.), house 12 Chestnut
Nichols Samuel Mrs. house 112 Lafayette
Nichols Samuel B. shoemaker, house 4 Botts court
Nichols Stephen F. painter, at Beverly, house 9 Northey
Nichols Thomas, currier, 10 Goodhue, house 3 Boston
Nichols Thomas jr. tanner, house 400 Essex
Nichols Thomas B. clerk, 310 Essex, boards 3 Boston
Nichols William D. shoemaker, house rear 5 Becket
Nichols William F. grocer, 107 Boston, house 115 do.
Nichols William H. cooper, Brookhouse whf. house 12 Essex
Nichols William H. painter, Naumkeag mills, house r. 86 Mill
Nichols William H. 3d, clerk, boards 12 Essex
Nickerson Asa W. watches, clocks, and jewelry, 24 Washington, boards Essex House
Nicoll Ellen Miss, 14 Andrew
Niles Amos, mariner, house 35 Derby
Niles Ann, widow, house 35 Derby
Niles John, mariner, house 35 Derby
Nimblet Benjamin, tanner, house 6 Beaver

Nimblet Benj. F. currier, boards 6 Beaver
Nimblet Eliza and Sarah, Home for Aged Females
Noah George G. currier, Nichols, house 14 Albion
Noah Henry C. tanner, house 91 Boston
Noah Samuel, currier, house 420 Essex
Noah Samuel Mrs. house 103 Boston
Noble James A. clerk (B.), boards 67 Essex
Noble Joseph Mrs. house 13 Salem
Noble Richard S. Mrs. house 67 Essex
Nolan Bridget, widow, boards near foot of Pingree
Nolan Cornelius, currier, boards 24 Herbert
Nolan Dennis, laborer, house 24 Herbert
Nolan Frank, painter, boards 24 Herbert
Nolan James, currier, house 16 Aborn
Nolan Nicholas, tanner, house Grafton, near Hanson
Nolan Patrick, tanner, house 12 Friend
Nolan Thomas, laborer, boards 24 Herbert
Noonan Ellen, widow, house 5 Pratt st. court
Noonan James, laborer, house 2 Pratt
Noonan John, laborer, house rear 7 Charter
Noonan John, laborer, house 3 Tucker's Wharf
Noonan Patrick, laborer, house 41 Union
Norcross James A. carpenter, house 24 Hancock
Norcross Margaret A. widow, house 24 Hancock
Norcross Orlando W. carpenter, house 24 Hancock
Norfolk John R. engineer, at F. Peabody's, h. 65 Bridge
Norfolk Joseph, sailmaker, house 72 Derby
Norris Charles A. clothing, 189 Essex, house 6 Lagrange .
Norris Dolly Mrs. house 6 Lagrange
Norris Elizabeth K. house 4 Andover
Norris John, boards 156 Federal
Norris Walter Mrs. house 36 Endicott
Norris William E. shoemaker, house 18 Ward
Northend William D. counsellor, 24 Wash. h. 24 School
Northey Cynthia Mrs. house 395 Essex
Northey William, sec'y Salem Marine Ins. Co., Asiatic bd'g.,
    house 395 Essex
Norton George E. gasfitter, boards 3 Pleasant
Norton Patrick, farmer, house 61 Mason
Norwood Abraham T. building mover, boards 16 Becket
Norwood Alexander, weaver, house 5 Woodbury's court
Norwood Esther, widow, boards 9 Allen
Nourse Aaron, hats, caps & furs, 37 Wash. h. 35 Andrew
Nourse Abigail, nurse, house 80 North   [3 Federal
Nourse Ebenezer, fruit and confectionery, 41 Wash., house
Nourse George W. currier, boards 27 Andrew
Nourse William, 41 Wash. house 3 Federal
Nowell Phœbe A. nurse, house 21 Beckford
Noyes Enoch K. & Co. (*E. F. Baker*), grocers, 6 and 8
    Front, house Leach

Noyes Jane S. W. Mrs. variety store, 263 Essex, h. 371 do.
Nuttall Sarah A. Miss, house 108 Derby
Nutter Horace, blacksmith, house 14 Creek
Nutting Joseph G. cabinetmaker, house 11 Becket
Nutting Joseph H. mason, b. 11 Becket
Nutting Rachel, house 12 Beckford
Nye Abbie P. nurse, house rear 63 Essex
Nye John C. mason, house rear 63 Essex
Nye T. Wilson, painter, boards rear 63 Essex

OAKES THOMAS, sailmaker, 7 Derby whf. b. Essex House
Ober Andrew, carpenter, rear 44 Charter, house 8 Winthrop
Ober Samuel jr. clerk, 26 Washington, boards 14 Elm
Ober Sarah Miss, Home for Aged Females
O'Brien Daniel, carpenter, house Grafton, near Hanson
O'Brien Edward, currier, house rear 143 Boston
O'Brien Ellen, widow, boards 89 Derby
O'Brien James, laborer, house 8 Pratt
O'Brien James Mrs. house 4 Elm
O'Brien James 2d, laborer, house 8 Pratt
O'Brien John, laborer, house foot of Tucker's Wharf
O'Brien John, laborer, house 16 Turner
O'Brien Martin, butcher, house 110 Mason
O'Brien Mary, widow, house 5 Daniels
O'Brien Michael, laborer, house 151 Derby
O'Brien Stephen, laborer, house 89 Derby
O'Brien Thomas, laborer, house 16 Turner
O'Brien William, clerk, 20 Front, boards 8 Pratt
O'Callahan Timothy, gardener, house 9 St. Peter
O'Connell Bert, laborer, house 6 Allen
O'Connell Jeffry, shoemaker, house 29 Mill
O'Connell John, provisions, house Summit
O'Connell John, shoemaker, house 23 Prospect
O'Connell Patrick, coachman, 204 Essex, boards do.
O'Connell Timothy, boots and shoes, 299 Essex, h. 297 do.
O'Conner James, mechanic, boards 9 Prince
O'Conner Thomas, trader, house 9 Prince
O'Connor Bryan, laborer, house rear 10 Herbert
Odell Charles, clerk (Boston), house 58 Federal
Odell David, shoemaker, house 26 Ward
Odell Edward E. machinist, boards 16 Odell square
Odell James Mrs. house 16 Odell square
Odell James A. wines, &c. 23 Front, house 10 Crombie
Odell Lydia P. Mrs. house 5 Creek
Odell William H. city watchman, boards 13 Carlton
Odlin Mary, widow, nurse, house 25 Hardy
O'Donnell Cornelius, chair seater, house 14 Norman
O'Donnell Dennis, currier, house 432 Essex
O'Donnell Donald, agent Boston Pilot, house 150 Federal
O'Donnell James, currier, house 18 High

O'Donnell James, clerk, 20 Front, house 31 Forrester
O'Donnell James, house 23 Ward
O'Donnell John, printer, 199 Essex, house 14 Whittemore
O'Donnell Michael, house 436 Essex
O'Donnell Michael, laborer, house 10 Herbert
O'Donnell Morris, currier, house Adams, cor. Mason
O'Donnell Patrick, moulder, boards 23 Ward
O'Donnell Terrence, laborer, boards 5 Charter
O'Donnell William, grocer, 131 Derby, house 172 do.
O'Flaherty Catharine, Jane M. and Polly, h. 131 Bridge
O'Flaherty John, boilermaker, house 16 Ward
Ogden Benjamin, Naumkeag mill, house 17 Park
O'Hanlon Catharine, widow, house 28 Union
O'Hara James, currier, house 29 Beaver
O'Hara Michael, laborer, house 26 Ward
O'Hare James, laborer, house 81 Derby
O'Hare Stephen, gardener, house 32 Williams
O'Hare William W. machinist, boards 32 Williams
O'Hern John, shoemaker, house 26 Congress, west side
O'Herrin John, laborer, house foot Pingree
O'Keefe Ann Mrs. house rear 41 Derby
O'Keefe Jeremiah, currier, house 26 Beaver
O'Keefe Mary, widow, variety store, house 11 Charter
O'Keefe Patrick, shoemaker, house 64 Mason
Oldson Elizabeth Mrs. house 1 North Pine
Oldson Francis Mrs. house 26 Essex
Oldson Frank T. Mrs. house 9 Turner
Oldson John H. mariner, boards 24 Essex
O'Leary Daniel, currier, boards 20 Fowler
O'Leary Jeremiah, laborer, house 14 Flint
O'Leary Jeremiah, mason, house 21 High
O'Leary Timothy, tailor, house 26 Essex
O'Leary Timothy, currier, house Grove, corner Phillip
O'Leary Timothy, gardener, house 24 Lemon
Oliver Frederick, engineer, house 5 Skerry
Oliver Henry, laborer, house 27 Norman
Oliver Henry K. house 142 Federal
Oliver Samuel C. boards 24 Lynde
Oliver William W. house 36 Broad
Onan Joanna, widow, house 13 Congress
O'Neal Daniel, laborer, house 14 Congress
O'Neal Henry, Naumkeag mill, boards foot East Gardne
O'Neal James, currier, house 12 Beach
O'Neal Mary, widow, house 93 Derby
O'Neal Michael, house 62 Mason
O'Neal Michael, laborer, house rear 26 Peabody
O'Neal Patrick, Naumkeag mill, house near foot Pingree
O'Neil Bryan, laborer, boards 19 Daniels
O'Neil Cornelius, laborer, house Tucker's wharf
O'Neil James, Naumkeag mill, house 16 Cedar

O'Neil John, charcoal, house Tucker's wharf
O'Neil Thomas, laborer, house 2 Tucker's wharf
O'Neil William, machinist, house Congress, west side
O'Neil William, Naumkeag mill, house 18 Cedar
Ormsbee Samuel H. shoemaker, house 11 Beaver
Orne John jr. private teacher, house 4 Broad
Orne Sarah F. Mrs. house 318 Essex
O'Rourke James, currier, house 10 Beach
Osborn Charles P. tinsmith, house 14 Winter
Osborn David S. engineer, house 28 Dearborn
Osborn George F. morocco dresser, house 148 Federal
Osborn Horace, currier, boards 21 Pickman
Osborn Jane F. house 14 Winter
Osborn John, at laboratory, boards Orne, near Upham
Osborn Jonathan, sailmaker, house 21 Pickman
Osborn Jonathan jr. clerk, 181 Essex, house 13 Mt. Vernon
Osborn Joseph B. cooper, house 10 Turner
Osborn Josiah B. hairdresser, house 21 Church
Osborn Laban S. shoemaker, house Orne
Osborn Lydia Mrs. house 17 Turner
Osborn Samuel B. horticulturist, house Orne, near Upham
Osborn William E. printer, boards 2 Orne
Osborne Aaron, clerk, E. R. R. house 88 Mill   ·
Osborne Eben, shoecutter, boards 8 Hardy
Osborne Ezra Mrs. widow, house 88 Mill   ·
Osborne Henry, 191 Essex, boards Essex House
Osborne John B. shoes (Lynn) house 29 Union
Osborne Martha L. Miss, boards 12 Pickman
Osborne Nathan W. boards 17 Oliver (13th U. S. Regt.)
Osborne Orville O. clerk, boards 17 Oliver   [Oliver
Osborne Stephen, hat, cap, and fur store, 191 Essex, house 17
Osborne Stephen H. house 17 Oliver
Osborne William A. tanner and currier, house 17 Dean
Osgood Abby S., Mary S., and Susan E., Misses, h. 314 Essex
Osgood Benj. H. harness maker, 50 Washington, h. 31 Church
Osgood Charles, artist, house 14 Brown
Osgood Charles C. captain, house rear 26 Brown
Osgood Charles S. deputy col. Custom-house, 112 Derby, coun-
    sellor, 243½ Essex, boards 14 Brown ·
Osgood Elizabeth Miss, house 15 Norman
Osgood George E. harness maker, boards 31 Church
Osgood George P. house 33 Chestnut
Osgood Henry Mrs. house 131 Essex
Osgood John B. Mrs. house 45 Lafayette
Osgood John C. merchant, 25 Asiatic building, h. 3 Barton sq.
Osgood John W. Mrs. house 33 Chestnut
Osgood Joseph, captain, house 13 Summer
Osgood Joseph B. F. counsellor, 235 Essex, house 312 do.
Osgood Nathaniel Mrs. house 401 Essex
Osgood Nathaniel W. Mrs. house 175 Federal

Osgood Nathaniel W. tanner, Goodhue, house 404 Essex
Osgood Robert, clerk at W. P. Phillips', boards 14 Brown
Osgood Susan W. Miss, house 15 Norman
Osgood Thaddeus Mrs. house 97 Essex
O'Shea Bartholomew, laborer, house foot Ropes
O'Shea Cornelius, printer, house 11 Ropes
O'Shea Cornelius B. printer, boards foot Ropes
O'Shea John, currier, house rear 141 Boston
O'Shea Mary, widow, house rear 141 Boston
O'Shea Patrick, tanner, house rear Adams, Mason Hill
O'Shea Patrick, morocco dresser, boards 24 Beaver
O'Shea Timothy, currier, South Danvers, house 36 Beaver
O'Shea Timothy, laborer, house 24 Beaver
O'Shea Timothy A. blacksmith, boards foot Ropes
Otis George, building mover, boards 6 Webb
Ottignon Ann Jane, widow, house 133 North
Owen Catharine, widow, boards 21 Becket
Owen Eliza Ann Mrs. seamstress, house rear 22 Hardy

PACK FITZWILLIAM, currier, house Grove, cor. Irving
Page Isaac M. conductor, E. R. R. house 29 Endicott
Page James E. farmer, house foot Linden, rear 118 Lafayette
Page Jeremiah, president Salem Marine Insurance Co. Asiatic
    building, house 140 Federal
Page John G. farmer, house foot Linden, rear 118 Lafayette
Page John O. carpenter, Naumkeag mill, boards 59 Harbor
Page Sarah L. Mrs. house 84 Derby
Page Timothy E. carpenter, house 8 Broad
Paine Enoch, house 15 Chestnut
Paine John L. carpenter, house 8 Saunders
Palfray Charles W. (*Chapman & P.*), publisher "Salem Reg-
    ister," 193 Essex, house 47 Lafayette, corner Dow
Palfray Edward, trader, house 15 Lynde
Palfray Elizabeth Mrs. house 47 Lafayette
Palmer Abigail, widow, house 34 Phelps' court
Palmer Alice P. Mrs. house 8 Beckford
Palmer Charles Mrs. house 10 Oak
Palmer Charles R. Rev. house 14 Northey
Palmer Frances D. Mrs. house 151 Federal
Palmer George W. clerk, 151 Essex, boards 21 Buffum
Palmer Margaret P. widow, house rear 220 Essex
Palmer Richard, house 34 Phelps court
Palmer Sumner, Naumkeag mill, boards 70 Harbor   [Buffum
Palmer Theron, boots, shoes, and rubbers, 216 Essex, house 13
Palmer William H. clothing, 247 Essex, house 21 Buffum
Palmer William H. carpenter, boards 10 Oak
Palmer William H. H. clerk, 247 Essex, boards 21 Buffum
Palmer William L. clerk, 149 Essex, boards 151 Federal
Parker Charles, house 103 Essex
Parker George A. house 103 Essex

Parker George F. confectioner, 170 Essex, boards 20 Union
Parker Isaac, machinist, house 32 Lynde
Parker John, hairdresser, boards 59 Summer
Parker John B. treas. E. Railroad (B.), house 6 Federal
Parker John B. house 8 Lagrange
Parker Sophia, widow, Home for Aged Females —
Parker William B. merchant, house 22 Pleasant
Parker William B. Mrs. house 103 Essex
Parker —— Mrs. house 21 Saunders
Parkland Mary, widow, house foot Perkins
Parks Thomas C. boards 57 Washington
Parmelee Charles S. coachman, 212 Essex, house 20 Norman
Parshley Charles C. Lynn Express, 19 Central, house 26 Ward
Parshley (*David T.*) & Shaw (*John*), curriers, 35 Boston, house
    9 Fowler
Parshley Nathaniel H. shoemaker, house 14 Peabody
Parshley Sylvester, currier, boards 26 Ward
Parshley ——, moulder, boards 10 Prince
Parsons Augustus, lastmaker, boards 12 Turner
Parsons Cyrus, carpenter, boards 111 Boston
Parsons Eben O. tanner, boards 6 Oak
Parsons Frederick, laborer, house 12 Sewall
Parsons Frederick jr. farmer, house Orne, opposite Ives
Parsons George W. printer, "Observer" office, house 210
    Derby
Parsons Hannah, widow, house 16 Becket
Parsons John Mrs. house 6 Oak
Parsons John H. musician, house 3 Pleasant
Parsons (*John M.*) & Shackelford (*Wm.*), fish, and water for
    shipping, 64 Union, house at Gloucester
Parsons Jonathan (China), house 92 Essex
Parsons Jonathan Mrs. boards 72 Essex
Parsons Joseph M. boards 2½ Federal (Capt. U. S. A.)
Parsons William D. Mrs. house 39 St. Peter
Parsons William H. laborer, house 13 Prince
Patch John S. driver, boards 5 Margin
Patten James, boards 1 Sewall
Patten James M. clerk, boards 25 Harbor
Patten Margaret, widow, 39 Peabody
Patten Paul B. machinist, house 27 Endicott
Patten Samuel R. shoemaker, house Cross street court
Patterson Eliphalet S. blacksmith, house 39 Bridge
Patterson John, stonecutter, boards 25 Harbor
Patterson Nancy, widow, house 16 Crombie
Patterson Nathaniel, currier, house 12 Boston
Patterson Nicholas, currier, house Prospect
Paty Seth B. clerk, 156 Essex, boards 24 St. Peters
Pausi Adaline, widow, boards 66 Harbor
Payne James E. shoemaker, house 13 Allen
Payne Phebe, widow, house 59 Summer

Payson⸱ Edward H. cashier, First National Bank, 7 Central, house 121 Lafayette
Payson Joanna Mrs. house 27 Forrester
Peabody Alfred, merchant (114 State, B.), house 45 Summer
Peabody Brackley R. captain, ⸱house 4 Flint
Peabody Brackley R. 2d, 229 Derby, house rear 13 Ward
Peabody David R. clerk, house 12 Prescott   [Carlton
Peabody Edward C. jr. & Co. grocers, 115 and 117 Essex, h. 5
Peabody Francis, machinist, 196 Derby, house 136 Essex
Peabody George, merchant, house 7 Brown
Peabody George A. (Boston), house 7 Brown   [Beckford
Peabody George W. furniture repairer, 24 Federal, house 24
Peabody Henry A. driver, H. R. R. house 16 Lemon
Peabody Henry W. merchant (Boston), house 19 Chestnut
Peabody John P. embroideries and trimmings, 220 Essex, house 80 Summer
Peabody Oliver, carpenter, house 16 Flint
Peabody Oliver, blacksmith, house 8 Leach   [16 Flint
Peabody Rufus M. watchmaker and jeweller, 187 Essex, bds.
Peabody Ruth and Mary Misses, house 7 Aborn
Peabody Sally Mrs. nurse, house 30 St. Peters
Peabody Samuel E. merchant (40 State, B.), h. 31 Warren
Peabody William M. carpenter, boards 8 Leach
Peace William H. Mrs. house 36 Derby
Peach Benjamin Mrs. house 27 Harbor
Peach E. Franklin, shoemaker, house Ives court
Peach George S. restorator, 10 Lafayette, boards 14 High
Peach George W. painter, boards 3 Ward
Peach William jr. painter, house 7 Herbert
Pearson Benjamin, furniture, stoves, &c. 3 Franklin Building, house 15 Oliver
Pearson Charles H. student, boards 15 Oliver
Pearson Edward L. (B.), boards 15 Oliver
Pearson Horace W. 3 Franklin Building, boards 15 Oliver
Pearson Nathan Mrs. house 130 Boston
Pease Benjamin, shoemaker, at H. O. Flint's, h. 5 Pond
Pease George W. printer and publisher "Salem Observer," 226½ Essex, house 45 Federal
Pease (*Richard*) & Price (*Charles*), bakers, 13 High, h. 11 do.
Pease Samuel W. stoves and tinware, 125 Derby, house 75 Bridge
Peck Freeman S. clothing and furnishing store, 240 Essex, house 133 do.
Peck William F. clothing, 240 Essex, boards 133 do.
Peckham Charles, carpenter, boards 24 Essex
Peckham William H. weaver, house 20 Salem
Peele Elizabeth R. house 86 Federal
Peele Robert, 280½ Essex, house 86 Federal
Peele Robert jr. ship carpenter, house 22 Hardy
Peele William Mrs. house 10 Monroe

Peele William Mrs. house 12 Summer
Peirce Abigail, widow, boards 20 Becket
Peirce Antiss D. Mrs. house 12 Summer
Peirce Elizabeth P. teacher, private school, 135 Essex, bds. do.
Pierce Charles H. teamster, house 13 Carlton
Peirce Jonathan (B.), house 10 Summer
Peirce Mary A. widow, house 12 Broad
Peirce Nathan, stock and loan office, 161 Essex, h. 135 do.
Peirce Nathaniel D. shoemaker, house 20 Becket
Peirce Rebecca Miss, house 12 Summer
Peirce Samuel B. (B.), house 108 Federal
Peirson Abel L. Mrs. house 11 Barton square
Peirson Charles L. 48 Kilby (B.), boards 11 Barton square
Peirson Edward B. physician, house 13 Barton square
Peirson George H. blacksmith, West pl.
Peirson William, laborer, house 16 English
Peke John (Cal.), house 25 Daniels
Pendar Simon, trader, house 60 Endicott
Pender Edward, currier, house rear Adams, Mason Hill
Pender John, currier, house 13 Oak
Pendergast Joseph, shoe stiffener, boards 87 Mason
Pendergast Mary, widow, house 411 Essex
Pendergast Michael, currier, house 87 Mason
Pennell Mary Mrs. house 7 Cross
Pepper Charles H. confectioner, house 63 Dearborn
Pepper Charles H. (*Goss & Pepper*), photographer, 46 Wash.
    house 32 Dearborn
Pepper John S. shoemaker, house 16 St. Peter
Pepper John W. Mrs. confectioner, 44 Buffum, house do.
Pepper Thomas S. confectioner, house 6 Cross
Pepper Thomas S. confectioner, 71 Bridge, house 6 Saunders
Pepper Walter A. mariner, house 7½ Turner
Pepper Walter W. confectioner, boards 44 Buffum
Perigan Lucy, variety store, 5½ English, house do.
Perkins Aaron, house 34 Lafayette
Perkins Aaron, jr. clerk, boards 2 Pleasant st. avenue
Perkins Asa B. pilot, boards 4 Allen
Perkins Augustine S. merchant, house 82 Lafayette
Perkins Benjamin M. (*Perkins, Smith, & Co.*), tailor, 44 Wash.
    house 28 Pleasant
Perkins Charles, mason, boards 2 Pleasant street avenue
Perkins Charles W. (Boston), boards 5 Oliver
Perkins (*Daniel*), Smith (*Elliot F.*), & Co. (*B. M. Perkins*),
    merchant tailors, 44 Wash. house 15 Church
Perkins David, house 18 Lynde
Perkins Eben, boards 14 Saunders (U. S. A.)
Perkins Edward B. carpenter, 11 Cherry, house 9 do.
Perkins Elijah R. photographic artist, 241 Essex, h. 59 Warren
Perkins Emery J. (N. Y.), house 11 Williams
Perkins Frederick J. house 14 Saunders

Perkins George, bookkeeper, Mercantile National Bank, boards
    34 Lafayette
Perkins George A. physician, house 129 Essex
Perkins George E. clerk, 20 Front, boards 9 Norman
Perkins George H. (B.), boards 5 Oliver
Perkins Henry F. clerk (B.), boards 14 Winthrop
Perkins Henry C. mariner, boards 12 Mall
Perkins Henry W. carpenter, house 21 Hardy
Perkins Henry W. jr. cashier (Mt. Vernon National Bank, B.),
    house 27 St. Peter
Perkins Horace S. (B.), boards 5 Oliver
Perkins Isaac, carpenter, house 26 Cedar
Perkins Jeremiah S. superintendent burials, City Hall, house
    2 Pleasant street avenue
Perkins John Mrs. house 18 Winthrop
Perkins John, teacher, High School, boards 11 Washington
Perkins Jonathan C. counsellor, 243½ Essex, h. 130 Federal
Perkins Jonathan W. Mrs. house 14 Saunders
Perkins Joseph, pilot, house 4 Allen
Perkins Joseph jr. pilot, boards 4 Allen
Perkins Joseph A. watchmaker, 230 Essex, boards 2 Pleas-
    ant street avenue
Perkins Joseph S. currier, house 186 Federal
Perkins J. Warren, captain, house 21 North
Perkins Moses P. house 9 Norman
Perkins Nathaniel B. cashier Merchants' Bank, Asiatic build-
    ing, house 5 Oliver
Perkins Nathaniel B. 2d (1st National Bank, B.), h. 42 Charter
Perkins Rebecca D. house 25 Dearborn
Perkins Samuel W. clerk (B.), house 24 Hardy
Perkins Sophia Ann, house 11 Williams
Perkins Thomas, house 124 Federal
Perkins Thomas jr. merchant (Boston), house 300 Essex
Perkins Thomas B. house 14 Winthrop
Perkins Ward C. boards 15 Church
Perkins William A. pattern maker, Union, South Salem, house
    19 Briggs
Perley Edward L. bookbinder, house 2 Winter
Perley Jacob, morocco dresser (S. Danvers), house 179 Boston
Perley John, boots and shoes, 252 Essex, house 254 do.
Perley John E. watchman, house 164 Federal
Perley Jonathan, bookbinder, 194 Essex, h. 2 Winter [buryport
Perley R. M. & Co. wines, ales, &c. 135 Derby, house at New-
Perry Abbie L. house 21 Carlton
Perry Abbie W. cloakmaker, 188 Essex, boards 27 Brown
Perry Albert H. clock repairer, 144 Essex, house 25 Carlton
Perry Augusta, house 45 Derby
Perry Augustus, merchant, house 29 Warren
Perry Augustus H. gunsmith, boards 7 Curtis
Perry Francis L. blacksmith, Phillips' wharf, house 26 Carlton

Perry Francis L. boards 26 Carlton
Perry Henry W. shoemaker, 8 Central, house 5 Creek
Perry Horatio B. gunsmith, West place, house 7 Curtis
Perry Horatio Mrs. house 45 Derby
Perry Ittai, pilot, house 59 Derby
Perry Jefferson Mrs. house 27 Brown   [rear 101 Lafayette
Perry (*J. W.*) & Endicott (*W. C.*), counsellors, 182 Essex, h.
Perry Rebecca Mrs. variety store, 60 Boston, house do.
Perry William A. clerk, 225 Essex, boards 7 Curtis
Pervier Benjamin L. machinist, boards 47 Broad
Pervier Nancy K. house 47 Broad
Peters Frances Mrs. house 11 Prescott
Peterson Andrew G. currier, boards 3 Hardy
Peterson John, mariner, house 38 Derby, cor. Becket avenue
Peterson Joseph, police, house 163 Bridge
Peterson Priscilla Mrs. nurse, house 3 Hardy
Peterson Thomas S. house 10 Creek (U. S. N.)
Petry John C. captain, house 10 Broad
Pettee David C. watchman, house 5 Skerry
Pettingill George, farmer, house rear Grove, opposite Irving
Pettingill Eliza E. house 11 Woodbury's court
Pettingill Samuel W. carpenter, house 11 Woodbury's court
Pettingill Sarah, widow, house 108 North
Petty Caroline, widow, house 1 Daniels
Petty John, laborer, house 1 Daniels
Phalen Anna, widow, house 66 North
Phalen Edward A. clerk, boards 66 North
Phalen Thomas J. carpenter, boards North, near the line
Phalen William, railroad contractor, house North, near the line
Phelps Abby M. widow, house 130 Boston   [more
Phelps Charles, machine stitching 17¼ St. Peter, b. 6 Whitte-
Phelps Hannah Miss, house 160 Boston
Phelps Israel R. (*W. Phelps jr. & Co.*), house 6 Whittemore
Phelps John P. (*W. Phelps jr. & Co.*), house 19 Lynde
Phelps V. J. Mrs. dressmaker, house 10 Sewall
Phelps William jr. & Co. (*John P. & Israel R.*), sash and blind
    makers, 84 Federal, house 16 River
Phelps William, house 1 Federal
Pherson Albert W. machinist, house 33 Essex
Philbrick Charles J. clerk, 20 Front, house 4 Orne
Philbrick John, clerk, 6 Washington
Phillips Aurelia, bookseller, stationer, picture frames, &c. 9
    Central, boards 14 St. Peter
Phillips Charles A. boards 33 Warren
Phillips Edward B. tailor, house 9 Salem
Phillips Eliza Ann, widow, house 218 Essex
Phillips George Mrs. variety store, 38 St. Peter, house do.
Phillips Harry B. house 48 Charter
Phillips Henry B. foreman at F. Peabody, house 12 Liberty
Phillips John, at laboratory, house 64 North

Phillips John Mrs. boards 22 Andrew
Phillips Lemuel, shipwright, house 19 Turner
Phillips Marshall S. shoemaker, house 25 Harbor
Phillips Phineas W. machinist, house 48 Charter
Phillips Stephen C. Mrs. house 33 Warren
Phillips (*Stephen H.*) & Gillis (*James A.*), counsellors, 243½
    Essex (and 30 Court, B.), house 17 Chestnut
Phillips Willard P. merchant, Phillips' wharf, house 7 Chestnut
Phippen Ann, house 18 Norman
Phippen Arthur, clerk, 251 Essex, boards 92 Bridge
Phippen Benjamin F. cooper, house 25 Hardy
Phippen George B. clerk (74 State, B.), house 104 North
Phippen George D. cashier, Salem Nat. Bank, h. 92 Bridge
Phippen George P. shoemaker, boards 72 Mill
Phippen Hardy, house 38 Pleasant
Phippen John P. clerk (B.), boards 25 Hardy
Phippen Joseph E. cooper, house 59 Derby
Phippen Joseph H. house 18 Hathorne
Phippen Joshua, house 1 Northey
Phippen Joshua 2d, gasfitter, house 25 Hardy
Phippen J. Hardy, cashier, Mercantile Nat. Bank, h. 94 Bridge
Phippen Lucy Miss, Home for Aged Females
Phippen Mary A. house 8½ Allen
Phippen Mary E. house 10 Essex
Phippen Mary J. laundress, house 170 Bridge
Phippen Mary M. widow, house 25 Hardy
Phippen Nathaniel Mrs. house 25 Hardy
Phippen Nathaniel, cooper, house 25 Hardy
Phippen Rebecca, grocer, 10 Essex, house do.
Phippen Robert A. police, house Wittemore, corner Mechanic
Phippen Robert C. tanner, house 2 Laboratory
Phippen Susan Miss, house 14 Norman
Phippen William T. artist, house 4 Hardy
Phipps Eliza, widow, boards 29 Williams
Phipps Harriet, widow, house rear 72 Mill
Phipps John A. master mariner, house 25 Becket
Phipps John A. jr. master mariner, house 7 Hardy
Phipps Samuel Mrs. boards 30 Charter
Phipps Samuel, shoemaker, toll house, Salem turnpike
Phipps Thomas P. tanner, house 19 Dean
Pickering Benjamin F. shoemaker, house 25 Summer
Pickering Benjamin P. boards 27 Harbor
Pickering Jackson H. provisions, South Market, 37 Lafayette,
    house do.
Pickering James, currier, house 17 Cedar
Pickering John, broker (40 State, B.), house 18 Broad
Pickering John jr. clerk at C. A. Ropes', house 1 Newbury
Pickering William, wood, house 27 Harbor
Pickering William jr. wood, bark, lumber, and teaming, 17 Pea-
    body, house 18 Harbor

Pickman Francis W. house 15 Winter
Pickman H. D. student, boards 15 Winter
Pickman William D. merchant, 14 Asiatic building
Pickman William R. Rev. rector St. Peters' (Beverly), h. 15
    Winter
Pierce Ann Miss, boards 12 Pickman
Pierce Charles H. mariner, house 8 Dean
Pierce Ellen M. teacher, Phillips school
Pierce George W. clerk, boards 57 Bridge
Pierce Henry, teamster, house 13 Carlton
Pike Francis, upholsterer, house 9 Federal
Pike William B. house 18 Crombie
Pillsbury Lucy Mrs. house 14 Sewall
Pillsbury S. H. Miss, fancy goods, 284 Essex, house 14 Sewall
Pinel Philip P. Mrs. house 44 Federal
Pingree Annar, house 2 Ash
Pingree David Mrs. house 128 Essex
Pingree David, boards 128 Essex
Pingree Sarah R. widow, house 23 Becket
Pingree Thomas P. 3d, merchant, 172 Essex, h. at Wenham
Pinkham Charles H. apothecary, 288 Essex, house 2 Broad
Pinkham Ephraim G. morocco dresser, boards 160 Boston
Pinkham James E. house 364 Essex
Pinkham Lydia, widow, house 6 Cambridge
Pinnock Thomas, slater, 25 Peabody, house 5 Hancock
Piper John, machinist, house 37 Salem
Pitcher Joseph W. mariner, house 20 Derby   [Harbor
Pitcher Sarah E. Miss, machine stitching, 42 Lafayette, h. 21
Pitcher Washington, captain, house 21 Harbor
Pitman Augustus P. clerk, house 23 Oliver
Pitman Benjamin, house 11 Andover
Pitman Benjamin & George, curriers, 24 Boston, house 6 do.
Pitman George, currier, house 7 Lynn
Pitman Hannah Mrs. house 23 Oliver
Pitman Henry, currier, boards 421 Essex
Pitman Henry C. stevedore, house 178 Federal
Pitman John C. currier, house 13 Boston
Pitman John H. currier, house 57 Warren
Pitman John Mrs. house 23 Oliver
Pitman Michael Mrs. house 178 Federal
Pitman Nathaniel Mrs. house 418 Essex
Pitman Nathaniel jr. Mrs. house Salem turnpike
Pitman Samuel jr. currier, 2 Goodhue, house 4 Boston
Pitman Sophia, widow, house 327 Essex
Pitman William H. painter, house 8 River
Pitts Albert William, boards 18 Lemon (Co. I, 1st H. Art.)
Pitts Darling, teamster, 2 Lafayette, house 30 Winthrop
Pitts George H. shoemaker, house 3 Pond
Pitts Henry Mrs. house 3 Pond
Pitts James E. stone cutter, boards 30 Winthrop

Pitts Nathaniel, teamster, 5 Front, house 27 Winthrop
Pitts Thomas, teamster, house 18 Lemon
Pitts William A. carpenter, boards 30 Winthrop
Plander George E. boards 15 Curtis (U. S. N.)
Plander John G. provisions, 116 Derby, house 15 Curtis
Plouff Edward jr. tinsmith, house 3 Salem
Plouff John, tinsmith, boards 18 Mechanic
Plumer Mary N. teacher S. N. S. house at Newburyport
Plummer Abigail, widow, house 7 Margin
Plummer Albert, shoemaker, house 21 Northey
Plummer George H. house rear 21 Northey
Plummer James Mrs. house 14 Barton
Plummer John F. pilot, house rear 14 Barton
Plummer Moses Mrs. house 21 Northey
Plummer Moses J. shoemaker, house 13 Lemon
Plummer Rhoda Mrs. fancy goods, 248 Essex, house do.
Plummer Sarah Miss, dressmaker, boards 30 Lynde
Plummer William, tanner, house 101 North
Plummer William H. shoemaker, house 18 Conant
Plummer William H. teamster, house 16 Peabody
Poland Alvin J. joiner, boards 19 Northey
Pollock David, currier, boards 14 Prince
Pollock James, laborer, house 21 High
Pollock Matilda, teacher, Brown school, boards 11 Prince
Pollock Samuel, laborer, house 11 Prince
Pollock Thomas, laborer, house 14 Prince
Pomeroy Arad Mrs. house 14 Salem
Pond Harriet Mrs. milliner, 276 Essex, house 375 do.
Pond James S. dry goods, 29 Lafayette, house 2 Ward
Pond John C. mariner, boards 2 Ward
Poole Mary, widow, house 6 Norman
Pool Nathan Mrs. widow, house 1 Ward, corner Lafayette
Poor Alfred, copyist, house 117 Boston
Poor James jr. currier, house 47 Broad
Pope Benjamin C. teamster, house 7 Herbert
Pope Eleazer & Son (*Wm. A. Pope*), tanners, rear 87 Boston, house 98 do.
Pope Henry, physician, house 43 Boston
Pope Horatio G. clerk (Boston), house 61 Charter
Pope James, clerk (B.), boards 98 Boston
Pope Rebecca S. Mrs. nurse, house 7 Herbert
Pope Thomas S. house 155 Bridge
Pope William A. (*E. Pope & Son*), tanner, house 93 Boston
Porter Ann B. tailoress, house 6 Ash
Porter Benjamin F. ice dealer (Lynn), house 1 Summer
Porter Benj. P. tanner and currier, house rear 59 Warren
Porter Elijah Mrs. widow, house 40 Summer
Porter Frederick, provisions (*Roberts & Porter*), 19 St. Peter, house 150 North
Porter Hathorne Mrs. house 31 Norman

Porter John W. war claim agent, 243½ Essex, house at Danvers
Porter Margaret S. Mrs. house 38 St. Peter
Porter Martha A. thread store and watchspring skirts, 236 Essex, house 31 Norman
Porter Mary Mrs. house 6 Ash
Porter William H. clerk (B.), boards 40 Summer
Porter William R. constable, house 12 Carpenter
Porter William T. boards 12 Carpenter
Potter Daniel, deputy sheriff, 210 Essex, house 343 do.
Potter George W. sexton First Church. house 166 Bridge
Potter George W. mariner, boards 13 English
Potter James F. carpenter, Eastern railroad, house 9 Fowler
Potter Jesse F. master mariner, house 17 Turner
Potter Joseph, Boston Express, 34 Front, house 14 Mall
Potter Mary, widow, house 13 English
Potter Samuel A. messenger, 42 Washington, bds. 13 English
Potter. Sarah A. Miss, music teacher, boards 12 Mall
Poulson Lewis N. mariner, house 4 Elm
Pousland David N. boards 100 Lafayette (clerk, Boston and Philadelphia steamer)
Pousland Edward A. boards 64 Mill (U. S. N.)
Pousland George A. painter, 17 Peabody, house 10 Leach
Pousland George H. clerk (9 T wharf, B.), h. 100 Lafayette
Pousland George W. (9 T wharf, B.), house 100 Lafayette
Pousland John H. farmer, boards 64 Mill
Pousland Joseph, engineer, house 14 School
Pousland Thomas D. house 58 Charter
Pousland William, captain, house 102 Lafayette
Powell Nathaniel, currier, house 8 Essex
Power James, laborer, house near foot Pingree
Powers Charles H. master's mate, boards rear 22 Hardy
Powers Edward, currier, house rear Adams, Mason Hill
Powers Edward E. master's mate, boards rear 22 Hardy
Powers Eliza F. widow, house rear 22 Hardy
Powers James, tanner, house Grove, above Mason
Powers James, laborer, house 46 Phelps' court
Powers John, tanner, boards 46 Phelps' court
Powers John, shoe stiffenings, 55 Warren, house do.
Powers Stephen A. boatman, Custom House, h. r. 22 Hardy
Powers William F. mariner, boards rear 22 Hardy
Pownell Mary, widow, house 20 High
Pratt A. W. currier, boards 12 Oak
Pratt Caleb, tanner, house 7 Beach
Pratt Calvin L. currier, boards 12 Oak
Pratt C. Wesley, machine stitching, 17½ St. Peter, house 8 Ash
Pratt Edwin F. currier, boards 12 Oak
Pratt Elisha, currier, 71 Mason, house 12 Oak
Pratt George W. currier, house rear 12 Oak [house 4 Liberty
Pratt Henry J. & Co. (*Ira K. Mansfield*), druggists, 137 Essex,
Pratt John, house 60 Lafayette

Pratt John W. farmer, house rear 130 Lafayette
Pratt Joseph, machinist, boards 21 Lafayette
Pratt Lewis R. currier, house 9 Phelps' court
Pratt Lydia, widow, house 107 North
Pratt Relief Mrs. house 12 Union
Pratt Samuel, farmer, house rear 130 Lafayette
Pratt William, shoemaker, house Salem Turnpike
Pratt William A. boards Salem Turnpike (3d Co. Heavy Art.)
Pray Alamba H. door, sash, and blind maker, boards 8 Margin
Pray Isaac C. shoebinder, 7 Lafayette, house 1 Leach
Pray Isaac C. jr. shoebinder, 232 Derby
Pray Joseph S. farmer, boards 1 Leach
Prentiss Alexander, baker at Alms House, h. 2 Jeffrey court
Prescott David Mrs. house 14 Aborn
Preston Charles F. artist, 188 Essex, house at Beverly
Preston Francis P. clerk, boards 1 Mount Vernon
Preston John, baker, 53 Summer, house 1 Mount Vernon
Preston Jonathan, tinplate worker, 12 Central, h. 55 Summer
Preston Jonathan jr. tinsmith, 12 Central, house 171 Boston
Preston Joseph Mrs. house 67 Essex
Preston Richard, ropemaker, house 20 Osgood
Preston Sarah, widow, house 53 Summer
Preston William A. photographer, house 22 Norman
Price Catharine Mrs. house 150 Boston
Price Charles (*Pease & P.*), house 11 High
Price Charles H. & J. druggists and apothecaries, 226 Essex,
     Browne's block, house 81 Summer
Price Eben N. house 81 Summer
Price Henry A. baker, house 30 Endicott
Price Henry A. clerk, boards 11 High
Price John, house 10 Norman   [20 Chestnut
Price Joseph (*C. H. & J. Price*), druggist, 226 Essex, house
Price Richard (*Tudor & Co.* 20 Court, Boston), h. 330 Essex
Price Richard, baker, boards 11 High
Price William Mrs. house 30 Endicott
Prime B. Franklin, tanner, house 28 Dearborn
Prime David N. Mrs. widow, house 24 Vale
Prime James M. grocer, 115 North, house 113½ do.
Prime Joshua S. shoecutter, house 67 Buffum
Prime Samuel L. shoe manufacturer, house 4 Lagrange
Prime Thomas H. house 10 Margin
Prince Elizabeth, widow, house 16 Pickman
Prince George Mrs. house 20 Mall
Prince John, baker, house 27 Williams
Prince John jr. Mrs. house 26 Howard
Prince Nathaniel W. currier, house 6 Albion
Proctor Elizabeth M. Mrs. house 404 Essex
Proctor Geo. K. photographist, 208 Essex, house rear 250 do.
Proctor John, carpenter, house 14 Skerry
Proctor Mary A. Miss, house 51 Warren

Proctor Nicholas, engineer, house 12 Walter
Proctor Thomas E., Grove, near Mason, house at So. Danvers
Proctor William, shoemaker, house 21 Cedar
Pulsifer Charles A. painter, boards 9 Spring
Pulsifer Charles H. painter, 27 Front, h. Hanson, n. Boston
Pulsifer David & Co. painters, 25 Front, house 35 Lafayette
Pulsifer Edward B. clerk, 25 Front, boards 35 Lafayette
Pulsifer Joseph, painter, 230 Derby, house 20 Lynde   [do.
Pulsifer Nathaniel, painter and carpet manuf. 11 Spring, h. 9
Pulsifer Nathaniel Mrs. F. house 1 Parker's court
Pulsifer William H. boards 35 Lafayette (U. S. A.)
Punchard Jonathan P. gaiter boot manuf. 24 Winthrop, h. do.
Purbeck John H. painter, house 9 Mason
Purbeck William A. merchant tailor, 267 Essex, h. 33 Turner
Putnam Allen, assessor, City Hall, house 35 Warren
Putnam Amos P. carpenter, house 1 Oak   [ginson square
Putnam Caroline R. hairwork manuf. 183 Essex, house 5 Hig-
Putnam Charles A. engineer and surveyor, 251 Essex, h. 59 do.
Putnam Charles F. Mrs. house 1 Orange
Putnam David, house 242 Essex
Putnam Eben, house 226 Derby
Putnam Francis, florist, 6 Crombie, and Mason, house 59 Essex
Putnam Frederick W. supt. Essex Institute, boards 226 Derby
Putnam George F. (J. Putnam & Co.), house 392 Essex
Putnam Hannah P. house 242 Essex
Putnam Henry W. (12 Central wharf, B.), bds. 59 Essex
Putnam Jacob & Co. (G. F. Putnam), tanners and curriers, 65
    Boston, house 94 do.
Putnam James H. provisions, 319 Essex, house 151 North
Putnam James S. house 94 Boston
Putnam John F. captain, house 89 Federal
Putnam John M. mariner, house 12 Cedar
Putnam John P. painter, house 10 Andrew
Putnam Lucinda P. bookkeeper, 186 Essex, house at Danvers
Putnam Mary and Nancy, house 50 Broad
Putnam Mary Ann, house 10 Andrew
Putnam Nathan, wood and lumber, 157 Derby, h 2 Winthrop
Putnam Perley jr. mariner, boards 12 Andrew
Putnam Perley Z. M. P. Mrs. house 12 Andrew   [S. Danvers
Putnam Rebecca, cloak and dressmaker, 183 Essex, house at
Putnam Sarah, widow, house 81 Essex
Putnam William H. A. captain, house 24 Endicott
Putnam William S. mariner, house 81 Essex

QUARLES SAMUEL, house 4 Church
Quill Dennis, laborer, house 433 Essex
Quimby Ann Maria, music teacher, house 48 Federal
Quimby E. Hervey, physician, 46 Wash. house 13½ Church
Quimby Elisha, physician, house 48 Federal
Quimby Moses Y. Lead mills, h. Lafayette, opp. Lead works

Quimby S. Foster, physican, 48 Federal, house 5 River
Quinlan James Rev. house 22 Union
Quinlan Thomas, laborer, house 7 English
Quinn Daniel, Naumkeag mill, house 42 Harbor
Quinn James, laborer, boards 16 Elm
Quinn Patrick, currier, house 82 Mason
Quinn Patrick, house 30 Union
Quinn Patrick, tanner, house 4 Friend
Quinn Patrick, laborer, house 16 Elm   [Charter
Quinn (*Thomas*) & Kelley (*James*), tailors, 203 Essex, h. 22

RABB CHARLES V. farmer, house Phillips, above Grove
Radey William, mariner, house 140 North
Radford Benjamin F. shoemaker, house 25 Winthrop
Radford Benjamin F. clerk, 18 Washington, boards 56 Endicott
Radford Charles K. shoemaker, 11 Ward, house 10 Peabody
Radford George A. currier, boards 56 Endicott
Radford Harriet Miss, house 13 Pond
Radford John, shoemaker, house 56 Endicott
Rafter Michael Mrs. house 79 Mason
Ragan Dennis, laborer, house near foot Congress
Ragan Ellen, widow, house near foot Congress
Ragan Jeremiah, laborer, boards 12 Goodhue
Ramsdell Alexander, ropemaker, house 5 East Webb
Ramsdell Alonzo, shoecutter, boards 8 Hardy
Ramsdell Jacob, shoemaker, boards Shillaber
Ramsdell J. Alexander jr. Phillips' wharf, boards 5 East Webb
Ramsdell Joseph R. ropemaker, house East Webb
Ramsdell Peter A. shoemaker, boards East Webb
Ramsdell William F. laborer, house East Webb
Rand Augustus C. stonecutter, house 55 Lafayette
Rand Charles F. contractor, house 55 Lafayette
Randall Edward H. tinsmith, 29 Front, house 15 Hardy
Randall Samuel Mrs. house 28 Buffum
Rantoul Robert S. collector of customs and counsellor, house
    17 Winter
Ravel John A. shoemaker, house 39 Lafayette
Raymond Alfred A. blacksmith, house rear 27 Buffum
Raymond Thomas W. carpenter, boards 49 Mill
Rea Charles S teller Asiatic Bank, house 45 Wash.
Rea Edward H. tailor, house 8 Conant
Rea Samuel G. house 45 Washington
Read Andrew, laborer, house rear E. Webb
Read George, machinist, house 23 Andrew
Read George F. teacher, house 42 Buffum
Read John, house 87 Federal
Read John F. fruit and vegetables, 7, 8, and 9 Market House,
    house 13 North
Read Mary S. widow, house 33 Salem   [h. 12 Mason
Read Warren A. butter and cheese, 10 and 11 Market House,

Real Ellen M. widow, house 31 Hardy
Real John H. mariner, boards 31 Hardy
Real Joseph F. laborer, boards 31 Hardy
Reardon Joanna, widow, house 16 Turner
Reardon John, laborer, house 30 Peabody
Reardon John, laborer, house 160 Bridge
Reardon John, laborer, house 21 High
Reardon Patrick, laborer, house Phillips
Reardon Thomas, laborer, boards 160 Bridge
Redmond Bernard, house 6 Tucker's Wharf (U. S. A.)
Redmond Bridget, widow, house 100 Mason
Redmond John, laborer, house 95 Mason
Redmond John, currier, rear 41 North, house 10 Barr
Redmond John, currier, house 100 Mason
Redmond Miles, grocer, 12 Derby, house do.
Redmond William, laborer, house 2 High street court
Reed Benjamin A. carpenter, house 13 Williams
Reed Benjamin C. tailor (B.), house 216 Derby
Reed George W. carpenter, house 19 Central
Reed John, Washington House, 9 Higginson square
Reed Mary Mrs. nurse, house 408 Essex
Reed Milo, Naumkeag mill, house 53 Harbor
Reed Nathan J. shoemaker, house 11 Salem
Reed Nathaniel Mrs. house 90 Federal
Reed Richard, letter carrier, house 1 Whittemore
Reed Sarah, house 354 Essex
Reed Thomas, shoemaker, house 4 East Webb
Reed William, laborer, house Bryant, corner Buffum
Reaves Charles F. cigar maker, boards 1 Forrester
Reeves Edward, house 37 Pleasant
Reeves George, house 70 North
Reeves John, cooper, house 25 Cedar
Reeves Robert, ropemaker, house 37 Pleasant
Reeves (*Robert W.*) & Griffin (*H. B.*), fish oils, 13 Front, house
    37 Pleasant
Reeves William, grocer, 20 Essex, house 1 Forrester
Reith (*Wm. jr.*) & Co. millinery, 2 West Block, 188 Essex,
    house 14½ Church   •
Relihan Patrick, currier, house 141 Boston
Relihan Thomas J. Mrs. house 143 Boston
Relihan Thomas J. currier, boards 143 Boston
Remington Elisha, cabinetmaker, house 10 Carlton
Remon Elizabeth C. widow, house 27 Carlton
Remon John C. engineer, at car factory, house 26 Hardy
Remon Simon L. painter, house 29 Mill
Remond John, old wines, cordials, &c. 5 Higginson square
    house do.
Remond M. J. 188 Essex, house 5 Higginson square
Remonds John W. carpenter, boards 29 Brown
Rennard Frederick W. laborer, house 5 Woodbury's court

Newburyport Directory, Published by Sampson, Davenport, &
Co. (formerly Adams, Sampson, & Co.) 47 Congress St., Boston.

Rennard William J. boards 5 Woodbury's court
Reynolds Francis, currier, house Irving, near Harrod
Reynolds James, laborer, house rear 10 Congress
Reynolds James, farmer, boards 170 Federal
Reynolds John P. Mrs. house 13 Northey
Reynolds John P. boards 13 Northey (Capt. Invalid Corps)
Reynolds Moses C. & Co. (*D. B. Gardner jr.*), grocers, 20 Front, house 4 Barton square
Reynolds Thomas, laborer, house 8 Peabody
Reynolds Thomas, farmer, house 170 Federal
Rhoades George F., Naumkeag mill, house 110 Derby
Rhoades John W. carriage painter, 23 Endicott, h. 32 Andrew
Rhodes Amos H. engineer, Naumkeag mill, house 58 Harbor
Rhodes Crispus, house 16 School
Rhue Helen Mrs. house 161 Federal
Rial John F. rigger, boards 30 Mill
Rice Andrew J. shoemaker, 9½ St. Peter, boards 43 Bridge
Rice John, tailor, 29 North, house 22 River
Rice Sylvester, shoemaker, house 432 Essex
Rice William H. shoemaker, house 43 Bridge
Richards George S. Mrs. house 86 Boston
Richards John H. (*Henderson & Co.*), 150 Essex, h. 86 Boston
Richards John H. Naumkeag mill, boards 70 Harbor
Richards Lewis D. policeman, house 28 Vale
Richardson Albert P. clerk, Naumkeag Bank, boards 2 River
Richardson Alfred, currier, house rear Adams, Mason Hill
Richardson Alonzo, carpenter, house 26 Lafayette
Richardson Charles.Mrs. house 31 Broad
Richardson Charles M. (*Adams, Richardson, & Co.*), hardware, 215 Essex, house 31 Broad
Richardson Charles W. house 2 River
Richardson Emma, widow, house 27 Charter
Richardson Franklin A. carpenter, house 419 Essex
Richardson James, shoemaker, house Tremont, near Harrod
Richardson James H. morocco dresser, boards 126 Boston
Richardson Jeremiah Mrs. house 2 River
Richardson Jeremiah J. salesman, house 29 Norman
Richardson Mary A. widow, house near foot of Park
Richardson Samuel P. (15 Central, B.), boards 14 Elm
Richardson S. Pearce, clerk (33 Summer, B.), bds. 9 Crombie
Richardson William, hostler, boards 126 Boston
Richardson Wm. Harris (*J. W. Symonds & Co.*), boots & shoes, 221 Essex, house 6 Buffum
Richers Henry, captain, house rear 23 Cedar
Ricker Francis M. mason, boards 56 Endicott
Ricker Morrill, mason, house 56 Endicott
Ricker Oliver P. house 22 Winter
Ricker Richard, housemover, house Silver
Rideout Anna, widow, house 4 Bentley
Rideout Ruth, widow, house 1 Prospect

Roxbury Directory, Published by Sampson, Davenport, & Co.
(formerly Adams, Sampson, & Co.) **47 Congress St., Boston.**

Rider Joseph J. captain, house 183 Federal
Rider Joshua O. house 65 Lafayette
Riley Cornelius, laborer, house 10 Phelps' court
Riley Daniel, mariner, boards 21 Daniels
Riley Dennis, coachman, house 87 Mason
Riley James, laborer, house 21 Daniels
Riley James, shoe manuf. Bridge, cor. Wash. tanner and currier,
  Franklin near North, house 19 Upham
Riley James B. currier, boards 21 Daniels
Riley Jane, widow, boards foot of Daniels
Riley John, laborer, house rear 170 Derby
Riley John, shoemaker, boards 16 Congress
Riley John, shoemaker, boards 21 Daniels
Riley Margaret, widow, house rear 168 Derby
Riley Mary, widow, house 10 Odell square
Riley Matthew, laborer, house 86 Derby
Riley Owen, blacksmith, boards 148 Derby
Riley Philip, currier, house 51 Broad
Ring David, laborer, house 42 Peabody
Ring John, laborer, house 32 Union
Rinks John, watchman, house Harbor street court
Rinks John H. currier, boards 1 Harbor street court
Rinks Newell S. currier, boards Harbor street court
Roach David, currier, house Grove, near Mason
Roach Dennis, currier, house 8 Aborn
Roach John, laborer, house 30 Ward
Roach Julia, widow, house 10 Odell square
Roach Mary, widow, house 15 Ash
Roach Thomas, laborer, house 30 Ward
Roach Thomas, shoemaker, 196 Essex, house 15 Ash
Robbins Jesse, clerk, 38 Harbor
Robbins Nathaniel C. (*R. C. Manning & Co.*), coal, &c. 189
  Derby, house 2 Pickman   [Essex, bds. Essex House
Robbins Thomas A. livery stable, 167 Boston and rear 161
Roberts Adeline, teacher, boards 13 Cedar
Roberts Caroline C. tailoress, house Prospect, near Summit
Roberts Charles Mrs. house Prospect, near Summit
Roberts David, counsellor (Studio build. B.), house 21 Winter
Roberts David A. captain, house 24 Mechanic
Roberts Edward F. & J. W. fruit and confectionery, 209 Essex,
  and Washington, cor. Front, boards 2½ Federal
Roberts Ezekiel, house 13 Cedar
Roberts George Mrs. house 7 Elm
Roberts Hannah Mrs. house 24 Mechanic
Roberts Henry L. shoemaker, house 13 Prince
Roberts Henry O. boards 24 Mechanic
Roberts (*Jacob K.*) & Porter (*Frederick*), provisions, 19 St.
  Peter, house 77 Bridge
Roberts John, butcher, 116 Prospect, cor. Summit, house do.
Roberts John jr. laborer, house Summit, near Prospect

Roberts John H. clerk 230 Essex, boards 116 Prospect
Roberts John S. shoemaker, boards 7 Elm
Roberts John W. (*E. F. & J. W. Roberts*), house 12 Church
Roberts Joseph W. carpenter, 12 Herbert, house do.
Roberts Mary W. widow, house Prospect, near Summit
Roberts Phœbe, clerk, 54 Washington, boards 3 Jeffrey court
Roberts Porter F. counsellor, boards Mary W. Roberts
Roberts Stephen H. teamster, house 14 Winter
Roberts William, house 91 Federal
Roberts William P. mason, house 12 St. Peter
Robertson Stratton W. soap and candle manufac. rear 44 Boston,
    house 44 do.
Robertson William W. boards 44 Boston
Robinson Amasa C. shoecutter, house 15 Hathorne
Robinson Benjamin F. master mariner, house 10 Turner
Robinson Benjamin F. bookkeeper, 135 Derby, house 9 Carlton
Robinson Enos S. engineer, house 30 Mill
Robinson Henry, laborer, house 59 Derby
Robinson Lucy T. Miss, milliner, house 14 Crombie
Robinson Martha C. Mrs. house 23 Church
Robinson Peter A. mariner, house 9 High street court
Robinson Susan A. Miss, house 9 Elm
Robinson Sylvester C. house 138 Federal
Robinson S. E. Miss, boards 41 St. Peter
Robinson William, tinsmith, house rear 16 Congress
Robinson William W. engineer, E. R. R. house 32 Mill
Robson Matthew, currier, 69 Mason, boards 19 Boston
Robyshow Paul, ship carpenter, house E. Gardner, c. S. Prospect
Rock Mary, widow, boards 129 Derby
Rocke John, laborer, house 172 Derby
Rocke Thomas, currier, house 151 Derby
Rogers Albert, mariner, house 23 Harbor
Rogers Albert, laborer, house 6 North Pine
Rogers Arthur S. boards 204 Essex
Rogers Augustus D. counsellor, house 376 Essex
Rogers Benjamin F. butcher, 15 Herbert, house 70 Derby
Rogers Benj. F. jr. mariner, house 70 Derby
Rogers Charles D. mariner, house 3 North court
Rogers Edward S. house 376 Essex
Rogers John W. upholsterer, house 7 Winter
Rogers Joseph P. clerk, 14½ Front, house 17 Winthrop
Rogers Lucinda Mrs. house 17 Union
Rogers Martha Mrs. house 27 Turner
Rogers Matilda Mrs. house 140 Bridge
Rogers Nathaniel L. Mrs. house 376 Essex
Rogers Richard D. merchant (B.), house 136 Essex
Rogers Richard S. merchant, house 204 Essex
Rogers Russell, laborer, house 7 Fowler   [Union
Rogers Seabury F. confectionery, 170 & 172 Essex, house 20
Rogers Thomas, laborer, house 77 Derby

Rogers William H. cooper, boards 27 Turner
Roles Samuel jr. dyer, 7 Franklin, house 12 Mechanic
Rolfe Edward jr. tinsmith, 29 Front, house 31 Turner
Rollins George W. S. carver, boards 21 Lafayette
Rollins John B. machinist, house rear 86 Mill
Rollins Sarah J. Mrs. boarding house, 21 Lafayette
Ronan James, at R. C. Manning & Co.'s, house 7 Ropes
Ronan Joanna, widow, house rear 30 Congress
Ronan Mary, boards Thorndike
Ronan William H. mariner, house rear 30 Congress
Ropes Abigail W. Miss, boards 28 Williams
Ropes Andrew, mariner, boards 30 Essex
Ropes Augustus, boards 106 Derby
Ropes Benjamin, shoemaker, boards 78 Mill
Ropes Benjamin M. house 106 Derby
Ropes Charles A. flour and grain, 165 Derby, h. ft. Dearborn
Ropes Elizabeth Mrs. house 7 Becket
Ropes Fanny, widow, house 18 Williams
Ropes George, merchant, 22 Asiatic building, b. 33 Summer
Ropes George N. Mrs. house 106 Derby   [Dearborn
Ropes James, asst. register of probate and insolvency, house 26
Ropes John C. machinist, 19 Front, house 17 Harbor
Ropes John T. stoves, &c. 17 and 19 Front, h. 7 Munroe
Ropes Jonathan, shoemaker, house 78 Mill
Ropes Joseph H. house 106 Derby
Ropes Lucy Jane Mrs. dressmaker, house 80 Mill
Ropes Maria, boards 42 Chestnut
Ropes Mary Mrs. house 28 Williams
Ropes Mary Mrs. widow, house 78 Mill
Ropes Mary P. widow, house 106 Derby
Ropes Rachel, widow of William, house 6 Andrew
Ropes Samuel Mrs. house 64 Summer
Ropes Sarah G. house 379 Essex   [Pine
Ropes Timothy, crockery, glass, and hardware, 214 Essex, h. 1
Ropes William, shoemaker, boards 78 Mill
Ropes William Mrs. house 6 Andrew
Ropes William jr. tinsmith, 19 Front, boards 7 Monroe
Rose Hannah S. house 5 Ash
Rose Martha A. saleswoman, 190 Essex, house 5 Ash
Rose Sarah H. Mrs. house 19 Washington
Ross Ann C. Mrs. house 19 Williams
Ross Henry, shoemaker, house 4 Endicott
Ross James, machinist, Naumkeag, house 19 Harbor
Ross James D. tanner, house 8 Beckford
Ross John P. trader, boards 38 Broad
Ross Joseph, tanner house 8 Beckford
Ross Nathaniel, hairdresser, 10 Boston, house 2 Beach
Ross Samuel, shoemaker, boards 19 Harbor
Ross William S. trader, house 38 Broad
Roundy Charles, captain, house 47 Lafayette

144   SALEM [R] DIRECTORY.

Rourke Daniel, shoemaker, house Lynch, corner Perkins
Roundy Harry, house 384 Essex (China)
Rourke Thomas, laborer, house Ward, near Peabody
Rourke Thomas, grocer, house 17 Salem
Rowe George E. shoemaker, boards 30 Buffum
Rowe Joseph S. hairdresser, 35 Washington, house 5 Margin
Rowe Mary C. widow, boards 30 Buffum
Rowell Benjamin, painter, 4 Sewall, house 11 Upham
Rowell Edward, cooper, Webb's wharf, house on the Neck
Rowell Edward, mariner, boards 24 Carlton
Rowell Frederick, cigarmaker, house 24 Carlton
Rowell Frederick jr. cigar manuf. 130 Derby, h. 24 Carlton
Rowell Joseph, captain, house 68 Bridge
Rowell Sydney B. butcher, house 118 Derby
Rowell S. B. Mrs. milliner, 31 Lafayette, house do.
Rowell Thomas A. carpenter, house 14 Central
Rowell Thomas P. house 31 Lafayette
Rowley Lydia L. widow, house 6 Pratt
Rowley Robert, currier, house Buffum, near School
Ruber Charles, laborer, house 66 Harbor
Ruee Benjamin B. cooper, house 61 Derby
Ruee Helen Mrs. house 161 Federal
Ruee Henry A. carpenter, house 10 Howard
Ruee Philip B. 10 Lafayette, boards 10 Howard
Ruee Thomas J. kegmaker, boards 61 Derby
Ruff Caroline A. Mrs. house 66 Federal
Ruliff James B. mariner, house rear 131 North
Rupp Charles A. mariner, boards 164 Federal
Rupp Frederick, currier, house 17 Hathorne
Rush Francis, currier, house 27 Beaver
Russ John V. W. mariner, house 7 Turner
Russell Annabiah, bookkeeper, 222 Essex, boards 2 Winthrop
Russell Benjamin Mrs. house 11 Pickman
Russell Benj. W. bookkeeper, Salem Nat. Bank, h. 11 Pickman
Russell Christina, widow, house 43 Broad
Russell Elizabeth C. teacher, house 11 Pickman
Russell Ephraim, house 61 Charter
Russell Francis T. carpenter, house 4 Botts' court
Russell George, clerk, E. R. R. depot (B.), house 5 Becket
Russell John B. boards 43 Broad
Russell John L. Rev. house 22 Lafayette   [h. 53 Essex
Russell (John W.) & Lord (Daniel B.), carpenters, 15 Forrester,
Russell John H. laborer, house 8 Webb
Russell Joseph W. mariner, boards 5 Mall
Russell Mary A. teacher private school, Pleasant, h. 121 Essex
Russell Mary U. widow, house foot Pingree
Russell Martin V. B. shoemaker, boards head North court
Russell Priscilla, house 121 Essex
Russell Samuel H. house 10 St. Peter
Russell Sarah Orne, house 55 Washington

Russell Susan Mrs. nurse, house 5 Mall
Russell Thomas B. manuf. patent office models, h. 354 Essex
Russell William, job wagon, house 29 Norman
Rust Francis A. P. house 15 Briggs
Rust John O. clerk, 198 Essex, house 121 do.
Rust N. P. Mrs. house 15 Briggs
Rust Susan, widow, house 121 Essex
Ruth James, carpenter, house 24 Herbert
Ruth John, currier, boards 24 Herbert
Ruth Richard, clerk, 6 Washington, boards 5 Pine
Rutherford Henry, E. R. R. house 6 Broad
Ryan Edward, currier, house 8 Aborn
Ryan Ellen, widow, house 10 Congress
Ryan James, currier, house 87½ North
Ryan James, laborer, house 11 Tucker's wharf
Ryan James, gardener, house 8 Cabot
Ryan James B. tanner, house Putnam
Ryan Joseph, currier, house 9 Beaver
Ryan Kenneday, currier, house 13 Flint
Ryan Michael, gardener, house 123 Boston
Ryan Michael, laborer, house 12 River
Ryan Patrick, tailor, house 15 Lafayette
Ryar Frederick, boards 30 Mill

SADLER HARRIET M. dressmaker, house 7 Pl
Sadler Joseph D. fruit, &c. 13 Church, house 7 Pleasant
Safford Daniel E. counsellor, 251 Essex, house at Hamilton
Safford Elizabeth E. house 33 Essex
Safford Harriet M. music teacher, house 12 Laboratory
Safford Harriet P. and Martha O. house 152 Boston
Safford James O. house 19 Brown
Safford John B. boards 3 Harbor (engineer U. S. N.)
Safford Joseph H. clerk, house 41 Warren
Safford Joshua, house 78 Essex
Safford Joshua F. captain, house 12 Laboratory
Salem Leg Co. 22 High
Saltonstall Annie E. & Caroline, house 39 Chestnut
Saltonstall Nathaniel Mrs. house 44 Chestnut
Saltonstall William G. house 43 Chestnut
Sampson Edward, captain, house 50 Bridge
Sanborn Benjamin B. carpenter, house 6 Bentley
Sanborn David A. engineer, boards 17 Harbor
Sanborn Edwin F. clerk, 226 Essex, house Orne, near Upham
Sanborn Eliza M. seamstress, house 33 Brown
Sanborn Franklin T. (*G. & F. T. Sanborn*), house 7 Harbor
Sanborn George & F. T. coal and wood, 115 Derby, h. 3 Turner
Sanborn George O. carpenter, boards 29 Union
Sanborn Hiram, cooper, house 17 Carlton
Sanborn James A. currier, rear 11 Mason, h. Orne, n. Upham
Sanborn Joseph W. tanner, house 19 School

Sanborn Mark, hair dealer, house 15 Buffum
Sanborn Mark, clerk, 124 Essex, boards 19 School
Sanborn Mary Ann, widow, house 5 Allen
Sanborn Theophilus Mrs. house 5 Becket
Sanders Charles, house 292 Essex
Sanders George T. Mrs., house 292 Essex
Sanders Thomas, house 292 Essex
Sanderson John Mrs. boards 122 Federal
Sanderson John A. carpenter, boards 122 Federal
Sanford Samuel, wood sawyer, boards 61 Derby
Sargent Milton, stonecutter, boards 1 Perkins   [Peter's
Saroni E. Mrs. children's clothing, 154 Essex, boards 24 St.
Saul Easton, carpenter, foot of Friend, house 12 Phelps' court
Saul John, house 4 Essex
Saul John F. carpenter, house 12 Phelps' court
Saul Joseph (Boston), house 1 Lagrange
Saul Thomas, master mariner, house 7 Mount Vernon
Saunders Ambrose S. C. boards 117 Federal
Saunders Charles, shoecutter, house 31 Turner
Saunders Charles F. printer, boards 31 Turner
Saunders Charles H. mariner, house 5 Cedar
Saunders Charles R. P. carpenter, house rear 36 Charter
Saunders David E. (5 & 6 Charlestown st. B.), house 8 Winter
Saunders David E. jr. (B.), boards 8 Winter
Saunders Delia Miss, house 6 Mill
Saunders Elizabeth, widow, house 35 Buffum
Saunders George A., Lawrence Ex. 10 Washington
Saunders George M. mariner, house 7 Botts' court
Saunders James A. (*Chandler & Co.*), 4 Washington, house
    6 Prescott
Saunders Jeremiah, currier, house 47 Beaver
Saunders John J. cabinetmaker, 4 Lafayette, boards 8 Winter
Saunders Manassa, machinist, house 72 Summer
Saunders Margaret, nurse, house 65 North
Saunders Mary A. Mrs. house 5 Cedar
Saunders Philip H. carpenter, house Prospect, near Summit
Saunders Robert J. veterinary surgeon, house 7 Buffum
Saunders Susan N. widow, house 85 Derby
Saunders Thomas M. captain, house 14 Andrew
Saunders William, veterinary surgeon, house 5 Buffum
Savage Henry Mrs. house 10 Cedar
Savage Mary H. and Ann, house 35 Broad
Savory (*Benjamin*) & Co. (*T. T. Savory*), Salem and Boston
    Express, 7 Washington, house 30 Brown
Savory Mary, dressmaker, house 21 Beckford
Savory Tristram T. (*Savory & Co.*), 7 Wash. b. 30 Brown
Savory William T. master mariner, house 109 Essex
Sawyer Caleb, painter, house 5 Woodbury's court
Sawyer E. Mrs. boards 12 St. Peter
Sawyer George, counsellor, house 16 Albion

Albany Directory, Published by Sampson, Davenport, & Co.
(formerly Adams, Sampson, & Co.) **47 Congress St., Boston.**

Sawyer Mary Mrs. house 5 Woodbury's court
Sawyer Nathaniel, car builder, house 26 Charter
Sawyer (*Thos. H.*) & Tilton (*Benjamin T.*), provisions, 9 Derby square, house at S. Danvers
Scanlan Daniel, laborer, boards 140 Bridge
Scanlan Joanna, widow, house 140 Bridge
Scanlan Mary, widow, house 31 North
Scanlan Patrick, currier, house Mason Hill
Scanlon Patrick, waiter, house 3 Tucker's wharf
Scobie Catharine, house 6 Oliver
Scobie Mary Jane, house 1 Rust
Scott Abijah D. shoemaker, house 3 Ward
Scott Benj. jr. machinist, boards 6 Norman
Scott Sias, pop corn balls, house 11 Herbert
Scribner Mary A. widow, house 6 Norman
Scriggins Joshua, laborer, house 16 Williams
Scripture James O. Rev. rector St. Peter's church, h. 14 Church
Sculley James, shoe stiffenings, boards 44 Phelps' court
Sculley Mary, widow, house 44 Phelps' court
Sculley Patrick, currier, boards 44 Phelps' court
Sculley Thomas, laborer, house 3 Tucker's wharf
Scully Patrick, laborer, house 24 Ward
Searl Frank, clerk (B.), boards 147 Boston
Searl George, painter, house 147 Boston
Searl Joseph, tanner, house 147 Boston
Searl Joseph jr. tanner, boards 147 Boston
Seaver Daniel A., Naumkeag mill, boards 14 Daniels
Seaver Rachel Mrs. house 14 Daniels
Seaver Joseph H. Rev. boards 14 Daniels
Seccomb Ebenezer, treasurer Seccomb Oil Manufacturing Co. foot of Harbor (and Broad, cor. Milk, B.), h. 26 Andrew
Segee Mary, widow, boards 168 Bridge
Selby William, laborer, house 14 Hardy
Semons Edward, machinist, 142 Essex, boards 10 Dearborn
Semons Francis A. cigarmaker, house 8 Walnut
Semons Wm. C. cigarmaker, house 11 Herbert
Sennott John, Naumkeag mill, boards 2 Pingree
Senter Charles (Lynn), house 14½ Andrew
Servey Wm. T. umbrella manufacturer, 310 Essex, house do.
Sewall Charles, counsellor, 214 Essex, house 23 Forrester
Sexton Catharine, widow, boards 98 Derby
Shackelford William (*Parsons & Shackelford*), fish, 64 Union, house at Gloucester
Shanley Ellen, widow, house 5 May
Shanley William, currier, house 5 May
Shannon Isaac W. house Walter, near Orne
Shapleigh Henry S. express messenger, house 2 Mason
Sharkey Charles, laborer, house foot of Tucker's wharf
Shatswell James, clerk, Register of Deeds, b. 28 Andrew
Shatswell Joseph, merchant, 23 Front, house 80 Lafayette

Shatswell J. Augustus, millinery, 169 Essex, h. Pickman place
Shatswell Moses, shoemaker, 28 Andrew, house 30 do.
Shaw Ann, widow, house 7 Prince
Shaw (*Aaron*) & Winson (*John*), furniture, crockery, and glass,
    8 Lafayette, house 7 Prince
Shaw Bartholomew, laborer, house 17 Lemon
Shaw Brown Emerson (*H. Shaw & Son*), gilder, 283 Essex,
    house 144 Federal
Shaw Catharine, teacher, St. Mary's school, boards 19 Lemon
Shaw Jacob N. house 11 Central   [13 Fowler
Shaw John H. (*Parshley & Shaw*), currier, 35 Boston, house
Shaw Jonathan A. shoemaker, house 6 Prince
Shaw Margaret A. nurse, house 158 Boston
Shaw Mary A. assistant teacher, St. Mary's school, b. 28 Union
Shaw Timothy R. gardener, house 28 Union
Shaw Xenophon H. & Son (*Brown E.*), gilders, 283 Essex, h.
    144 Federal
Shay Patrick, tanner, house rear 123 Boston
Shea Daniel, currier, house 14 Friend
Shea Dennis, tailor, house 140 Derby
Shea John, laborer, house 86 Derby
Shea Julia, widow, boards 140 Derby
Shea Mary, widow, house 8 Turner
Shea Nicholas, teamster, house 13 Oak
Shea Richard, laborer, house 8 Lagrange
Shea Susan, widow, house 8 Turner
Shea Thomas, laborer, house 14 Friend
Shea Thomas, machinist, boards 86 Derby
Shea William, shoemaker, house 202 Derby
Shearman George F. 18 Derby square, house 13 Warren
Shearman James L. house 23 Cedar
Shearman William, boards 23 Cedar
Sheehan Abby, widow, house 28 Peabody
Sheehan James, currier, house 10 High street court
Sheehan John J. printer, Statesman Office, house r. 133 Boston
Sheehan Maurice, laborer, house 10 Pingree
Sheehan William, laborer, house 22 Pingree
Sheils Thomas, laborer, house 9 Herbert
Sheldon Augustus, shoemaker, boards 90 Federal
Sheldon Eliab Mrs. house 90 Federal
Sheldon Joseph B. clerk, 221 Derby, boards 90 Federal
Sheldon Mary N. Miss, tailoress, house 5 Upham
Shepard Charles J. clerk, 243 Essex, boards 8 Williams
Shepard Elizabeth and Betsey, Misses, house 47 Summer
Shepard Elizabeth T. Mrs. house 25 Brown
Shepard Francis F. clerk, 7 Washington, boards 8 Williams
Shepard Henry F. merchant, house 302 Essex
Shepard Israel D. Mrs. house 8 Williams
Shepard John B. & S. D. dry goods, 173 Essex (Pickman pl.),
    house 63 Lafayette

Providence Directory, Published by Sampson, Davenport, & Co.
(formerly Adams, Sampson, & Co.) **47 Congress St., Boston.**

Shepard Luther D. (*Bowdoin & Shepard*), dentist, 208 Essex. boards 33 Summer
Shepard Mary L. principal Higginson school
Shepard Michael W. house 135 Federal
Shepard Samuel (*Nichols & S.*), tanner, Nichols, h. 173 Federal
Shepard Samuel D. (*J. B. & S. D. Shepard*), h 61 Lafayette
Sheppard Samuel, upholsterer, 298 Essex, house 9 Lynn
Sheppard Samuel A. D. clerk, 226 Essex, boards 9 Lynn
Sheridan Elizabeth Mrs. house 3 Gerrish place
Sheridan Francis, grocer, 391 Essex, house 19 Fowler
Sheridan James, tanner, house 8 North Pine
Sheridan John, shoemaker, 10 Lafayette, house 21 Fowler
Sheridan Patrick, tanner, house 7 May
Sheridan Philip, laborer, house 8 North Pine
Sheridan Philip jr. clerk, boards 8 North Pine
Sheriden Charles, currier, house 7 May
Sheriden Thomas, mariner, boards 3 Gerrish place
Sherry Hannah C. seamstress, boards 14 Walnut
Shillaber Sally, thread and hosiery, 253 Essex, house 6 Lynde
Shinkwin William, currier, house 407 Essex
Shirley Caroline Mrs. house 15 Salem
Shirley Jonathan, mariner, house 32 Salem
Shirley William H. shoemaker, 62 Derby, house 14 Carlton
Short Charles, house 31 Bridge
Short Charles H. clerk, 179 Essex, boards 6 Northey
Short James Mrs. house 6 Northey
Shortell Charles, master mariner, house rear 8 English
Shortell James, house 6 Turner
Shortell Mary A. widow, house 172 Derby
Shortell Michael, shoemaker, house 16 March
Shorter Royal M. stove setter, house 11 Osgood   [Peter
Shoules Charles J. blacksmith, Jeffrey court, house rear 38 St.
Shove George H. currier, house rear 9 Albion
Shreve Benjamin, jeweller (B.), house 128 Federal
Shreve Isaac Mrs. house 22 Dearborn
Shreve O. B. physician, boards 128 Federal
Shreve Samuel V. grocer, 225 Derby, house 224 do.
Shreve William P. salesman (B.), boards 224 Derby
Sibley Ann, variety store, 9 Winter, house do.
Sibley George, shoe manufacturer, 21 Central, boards 1 Park
Sibley George V. shoe manuf. 21 Central, house 1 Park
Sibley John S. Mrs. house 12 Hancock
Sibley Joseph Mrs. house 54 Mill
Sibley Joseph A. fireman E. R. R. house Union place
Sibley Moses H. tailor, 41½ Washington, house 6 Pond
Sibley William H. carpenter, house 3 Warner
Silsbee Benjamin H. merchant, president Merchants' National Bank, 32 Washington, house 2 Oliver   [corner Flint
Silsbee George Z. merchant, 14 Asiatic building, house Warren,
Silsbee John B. merchant, 22 Asiatic building, h. 27 Chestnut

Silsbee John H. merchant, 14 Asiatic building, h. 380 Essex
Silsbee Peter J. painter, house 77 Derby
Silsbee William, boards 380 Essex
Silsbee Zachariah F. merchant, house 11 Pleasant
Silver Augustus, tanner, house 19 Saunders
Silver Eliza, widow, house 8 High
Silver Eliza Mrs. house 384 Essex
Silver Joseph M. hairdresser, boards 8 High
Silver Peter, captain, house 18 Brown
Silver Thomas H. hairdresser, 6 Washington, house 8 High
Silver William, captain, house 98 Lafayette
Simes John D. Mrs. house 131 Essex
Simonds John H. shoe stiffener, house 6 Phelps' court
Simmons Martha, widow, house 10 Winthrop
Simon Francis B. express, house 32 Charter
Simon Joseph H. tel. op. (B.), boards 32 Charter
Simon Stephen Augustus, confectioner, 160 Essex, house do.
Simonds Edward A. (S. C. & E. A. Simonds), h. 101 Bridge
Simonds George W. clerk (Hide and Leather Bank, B.), bds.
    101 Bridge
Simonds Nathaniel G. clerk, boards 4 Winter
Simonds Samuel Mrs. house 101 Bridge
Simonds Samuel C. & E. A. crockery, hardware, paints, and
    oils, 32 Front, house 4 Winter
Simonds Susan A. house 57 Washington
Simonds William H. painter, 76 Derby, house 17 Hardy
Simonds William H. jr. clerk, Salem Sav. Bank, b. 17 Hardy
Simons William, laborer, house South Prospect, cor. Pingree
Simpson John, oil factory, house foot Pingree
Sinclair David, house 15 Essex (Co. B. 24th Regt.)
Sinclair Edward M. clerk, at Gayle & Co's, boards 15 Essex
Sinclair John, sailmaker, boards 15 Essex
Sinclair John Gasper, laborer, house 15 Essex
Skay Robert, stonecutter, house rear 17 Lafayette
Skay William B. stonecutter, boards rear 17 Lafayette
Skerry Edward S. painter, house 18 English
Skerry Francis Mrs. house 3 Lynn
Skerry Francis H. clerk, 180 Essex, boards 3 Lynn
Skerry Henry F. fancy goods, 180 Essex, house 3 Lynn
Skerry Robert, painter, house 17 Federal
Skinner Charles E. policeman, house 6 Cross
Skinner Emery B. cigar maker, boards 62 Federal
Skinner James N. (S. S. Skinner & Co.), 4 St. Peter, house 9
    Lemon
Skinner John B. tobacconist, boards 62 Federal
Skinner Phillip G. tobacconist, house 14 St. Peter
Skinner Richard, tobacconist, 64 Federal, house 62 do.
Skinner Richard jr. city marshal, 11 Front, house 16 Andrew
Skinner Richard W. clerk, 24 Front, boards 16 Andrew
Skinner Samuel S. Mrs. house 6 Cross

Skinner Stephen S. & Co. (*James N. Skinner*), cigar manu-
facturer, 4 St. Peter, house 8 Northey
Slattery James, tanner, house 93 Mason
Sleeper Hezekiah, gardener, house 34 Endicott
Slocum Ebenezer Mrs. house 4 Hardy
Slocum Sarah B. Miss, house 19 Andrew
Sloper William, currier, boards 5 Mason
Slueman Andrew (138 Devonshire, B.), house 2 Harrison av.
Slueman Benjamin H. expressman, house 17 Cambridge
Slueman Charles A. (B.), boards 2 Harrison avenue
Small Mary J. boarding house, 11 Washington
Small William F. gas and steam pipe and gas fixtures, 273
Essex, house 9 Washington
Small William M. carpenter, house 63 Essex
Smalley Roland, stevedore, Phillips' wharf, house 7 Daniels
Smiley James, currier, house 129 Boston
Smith Aaron, carpenter, 3 Howard, house do.
Smith Ann, widow, house foot Congress, west side
Smith A. Augustus (*G. M. Whipple & A. A. Smith*), books and
stationery, 243 Essex, house 4 Linden
Smith Addison, carpenter, house 10 Whittemore
Smith Agnes, house 36 Summer
Smith Albert P. machinist, boards Pleasant, n. H. R. R. stable
Smith Amos F. carpenter, house 13 Gardner court
Smith Augustus A. carpenter, boards 20 Winthrop
Smith Benjamin C. carpenter, house 44 Forrester
Smith Caleb, house 12 Lynde
Smith Caleb A. house 145 North
Smith Catharine Mrs. nurse, house 18 Derby
Smith Charles Mrs. widow, house 100 North
Smith Charles, laborer, boards 2 Pingree
Smith Charles, clerk, 179 Essex, boards 166 do.
Smith Charles F. cooper, boards 12 Congress
Smith Charles H. shoemaker, house 9 Spring
Smith Charles W. mariner, boards 24 Vale
Smith Dana Z. road master E. R. R. house 39 Endicott
Smith Daniel T. watchmaker, 262 Essex, h. 75 Summer
Smith David N. shoemaker, house rear 18 Beckford
Smith Edward, tailor, 29 Washington, house 28 Church
Smith Edward A. watchmaker, 262 Essex, house 15 Crombie
Smith Edward A. 2d, bookkeeper, 26 Washington, boards 14
Federal
Smith Edward P. restorator, 25 Front, house 14 Prescott
Smith Edward M. laborer, house rear Adams, Mason Hill
Smith Elliot F. (*Perkins, Smith, & Co.*), tailors, 44 Washington,
boards 54 Mill
Smith Francis E. (B.), house 36 Barr
Smith George C. carpenter, house 2 North court
Smith George H. house 2 Federal
Smith George M. clerk, boards 24 Phelps' court

Smith George P. Mrs. house 45 Lafayette [Essex, R. R. depot
Smith Gorham, joint supt. Essex R. R. in Salem, house over
Smith G. Emery, student, boards 6 Webb
Smith Harley P. moulder, house 23 Harbor
Smith Henry, inventor, boards Essex House
Smith Henry B. house 37 St. Peter
Smith Henry W. Mrs. house 22 School
Smith James, captain, house 1 Prescott
Smith James Mrs. house 27 Liberty
Smith James 'A. carpenter, 10 Walnut, house 11 do.
Smith James A. jr. carpenter, boards 11 Walnut
Smith James E. hostler, boards 24 Vale
Smith James H. mariner, house 16 Derby
Smith James S. harness maker, house 1 Parker's court
Smith (*J. Ford*) & Chamberlain (*B. M.*), manufacturing jew-
    ellers, 207 Essex, house 24 Mason
Smith Jesse, watchmaker, 262 Essex, house 36 Summer
Smith Jesse R. salesman (B.), boards 36 Summer
Smith John, cigarmaker, house 4 Blaney
Smith John, tanner, house 25 Albion
Smith John F. expressman, boards 24 Vale
Smith John H. brass finisher, house 61 Bridge   [Harbor
Smith John R. iron founder and machinist, Union, house 29
Smith Joseph, at laboratory, house 10 Dearborn
Smith (*Joseph*) & Manning (*D. C.*), livery stable, 212 Essex,
    9 Hamilton, and 47 Washington, house 3 Hamilton
Smith Joseph A. cabinetmaker, house 26 Winthrop
Smith Julia A. widow, house 6 Webb
Smith Lawrence P. boards 3 Hamilton
Smith Lorenzo A. foreman Oil Co. house 50 North
Smith Lorenzo D. clerk, boards 18 Derby
Smith Lucy A. teacher, house 3 Howard
Smith Lydia J. Mrs. nurse, house 24 Vale   [over depot
Smith Lyman A. ticket and freight agent, S. & L. R. R. boards
Smith Martha A. house 6 Prince
Smith Mary, widow, house 28 Congress
Smith Mary Mrs. house 29 Mill
Smith Mary A. L. Mrs. house 22 School
Smith Margaret B. Miss, variety store, 43 Essex, h. 20 Salem
Smith Mary E. and Sarah E. Misses, house 15 Norman
Smith Mary F. widow, house 9 Winter
Smith Mehitable, tailoress, house 148 Federal
Smith Mehitable, house 29 Pleasant
Smith Moses A. at Dye House, boards 2 Jeffrey court
Smith Nathan Mrs. house 29 Forrester
Smith Nehemiah A. (B.), boards 29 Pleasant
Smith Oliver C. machinist, house 29 Charter   [Mill
Smith Robert (*Babcock & S.*), hairdresser, 199 Essex, boards 50
Smith Robert B. captain, house 34 Buffum
Smith Samuel H. jeweller, 207 Essex, boards 24 Mason

Smith Sarah, teacher, house 8 Cambridge
Smith Sarah J. widow, house 14 Peabody
Smith Sarah J. widow, house 14 Federal
Smith Solomon J. at 208 Essex, house at Beverly
Smith Sterry, iron founder and machinist, East Gardiner, corner
    South Prospect, house 14 Harbor
Smith Thomas, teamster, house 12 Congress
Smith Thomas, currier, house Grove, corner Tremont
Smith Walter, currier, house 77 Mason
Smith William, oysters, house 21 Beckford
Smith William, clerk, house rear 21 Becket
Smith William, laborer, house 22½ Beckford
Smith William B. merchant, house 52 Bridge
Smith William F. mechanic, boards 21 Lafayette
Smith William H., Naumkeag mill, house Pingree, n. Harbor
Smith William R. cigarmaker, house foot of Ropes
Smith ——— (Lynn), house 15 Federal
Smothers Olive, seamstress, house 14 Norman
Snell Nicholas T. captain, house 17 Brown
Snell R. T. weaver, boards 38 Harbor
Snelling John, cooper, house Porter court
Snellings Samuel, teamster, house 2 Endicott
Snow Mehitable P. private school, 13 Beckford, boards 2 do.
Snow Nathaniel, currier, house 60 Mason
Snow Nathaniel Mrs. house 2 Beckford
Solaris George A. fireman, E. R. R. house 14 Upham
Soley Hannah, widow, house 14 English
Soley Nathaniel Mrs. house 14 English
Soley Nathaniel S. carpenter, boards 3 E. Webb
South (*George I.*) & Howard (*Frederick P.*), boot and shoe
    manufacturers, 19 Lafayette, house 1 Salem
South Isaiah & Co. (*Wm. D. Wright & S. F. Bicknell*), grocers
    and provisions, 33 Lafayette, house 12 Harbor
Southward George, portrait painter, Bank building, Central
Southward George F. machinist, boards 24 Barr
Southward Roderick, laborer, house 23 Turner
Southward Richard Mrs. house 24 Barr
Southwick Daniel, tanner, house 16 Boston
Southwick Edward, tanner, house 16 Boston
Southwick Eldridge M. gum copal worker, boards 48 Derby
Southwick Eliza Mrs. nurse, house 40 Broad
Southwick John, shoemaker, house 66 Mill
Southwick John T. shoemaker, boards 1 Perkins
Southwick Samuel G. clerk, boards 44 Pleasant
Spalding Josiah, merchant, house 106 Bridge
Spaulding Willard Rev. house 15 Pleasant
Spence George Mrs. house 391½ Essex
Spencer Edward P. peddler, house 3 Melcher court
Spencer William, tailor, house 15 Creek
Spiller Clara W. 5 Franklin building, boards 25 Daniels

Spiller John H. wool puller, house 3 Ord
Spiller John P. wheelwright, house 25 Daniels
Spiller Lura S. bookkeeper, 5 Franklin building, bds. 25 Daniels
Spiller Richard O. grocer, 162 Boston, house South Danvers
Spinney William O. physician, house 28 Charter
Spring James, cabinetmaker, boards 1 Sewall
Spring Patrick, at Gum Copal Works, boards 89½ Derby
Stacey Samuel E. (*James F. Almy & Co.*), 188 Essex, boards
    11 Wash.   \
Stacy Elizabeth L. Mrs. house 57 Summer
Stacy Mary, widow, house 45 Broad
Stacy Nancy Miss, house 17 Union
Stafford Nellie E. clairvoyant, 157 Essex
Stamper Frederick W. shoemaker, house 8 Prince
Stamper William F. shoemaker, boards 8 Prince   [North
Staniford Charles, assistant superintendent of burials, house 26
Staniford Daniel, printer, 183 Essex, boards 26 North
Staniford David P. expressman, house 142 North
Staniford John F. machinist, house 108 Bridge
Staniford Love R. Mrs. house 108 Bridge
Staniford Sarah C. Mrs. house 88 Bridge
Staniford, see Stentiford
Stanley Abraham J. gasfitter, 147 Essex, house 3 Pleasant
Stanley Edward Mrs. house 5 Daniels
Stanley Elizabeth Mrs. house 20 Andrew
Stanley James G. conductor, H. R. R. boards 5 Spring
Stanley John Mrs. house 5 Spring
Stanley John W. tailor at Beverly, house 18 Andrew
Stanley Margaret G. teacher, Hacker school, boards 5 Spring
Stanley Mary E. teacher, ·Browne school, boards 18 Andrew
Stanley Thankful Mrs. boarding, house 3 Pleasant
Stanley Thomas, laborer, house 4 Woodbury's court
Stanley Thomas, tanner, house 148 Boston
Stanton Charles, painter, house 9 Margin
Stanton John, farmer, house Orne
Stanton John, laborer, house rear 42 Ward
Stanton Julia, widow, house 20 High
Stanton Lucy, tailoress, house Orne
Stanton Michael, morocco dresser, house 42 Harbor
Stanton Thomas, stove worker, 29 Front, house rear 4 Ward
Stanton Thomas, tinsmith, house
Stanwood William Henry, machine stitching, r. 72 Mill, h. do.
Staples George Mrs. house 10 Church
Staples Lewis E. provisions, 69 Bridge, house 67 do.
Staples Mrs. widow, house 28 Norman
Staples Nancy, widow, cook, Salem jail, boards do.
Stapleton Paul, currier, house foot Pingree   [Lafayette
Staten Edward H. gas and steam fixtures, 147 Essex, house 59
Staten George, blacksmith, house 18 Pickman
Stearns Augustus, shoemaker, 60 Derby, house 56 do.

Stedman Joseph T. painter, house 22 Williams   [Federal
Stedman Samuel L. (*Hodgdon & S.*), tailors, 39 Wash. h. 165
Steel James T. machinist, boards 9 Linden
Steele Deborah and Maria A. Misses, house 14 Elm
Steele Mira G. saleswoman, 170 Essex, house 1 St. Peter
Steele Walter S. clerk, 20 Front, boards 9 Linden
Steele William J. currier, house Mason street Hill
Stentiford Charles H. painter, house 33 Barr, near School
Stentiford Charles H. jr. clerk, boards 33 Barr
Stephenson Elizabeth Mrs. variety store, 60 Essex, house do.
Stephenson John H. boards 60 Essex
Stetson James, shoemaker, 31 North, house 2 Melcher court
Stevens Alvin D. agent (B.), house 3 Phelps' court
Stevens Caroline, teacher, house 20 Winthrop
Stevens Charles B. captain, house 10 Liberty
Stevens Charles K. house 147 Bridge
Stevens Daniel Webster, boards 14 Broad
Stevens Edward P. baker, house 289 Essex
Stevens Eunice, house 6 Howard
Stevens George O. currier, boards Pope's court
Stevens Henry, laborer, house 15 Cambridge
Stevens Israel, tanner, house 20 Winthrop
Stevens John, house 17 Andrew
Stevens Robert, laborer, house 13 Phelps' court
Stevens Samuel A. gasfitter, boards 17 Andrew
Stevens Sarah B. Mrs. house 10 Andrew
Stevens Solomon, tanner, house Pope's court
Stevens Timothy J. Mrs. house 20 Winthrop
Stevens William, grocer, 13 Derby square, house 76 Summer
Stevenson Robert, shoemaker, boards 7 Turner
Stewart James, laborer, house rear 142 Bridge
Stewart Joseph, recruiting agent, boards 11 Washington
Stewart J. W. physician, 157 Essex, house do.
Stewart Lattanius, hairdresser, 6 Washington, h. High st. ct.
Stickney Charles W. shoemaker, boards 27 Williams
Stickney Charles T. carpenter, house 29 Forrester
Stickney Hannah, widow, house 163 Boston
Stickney John H. hostler, 212 Essex, house 7 Herbert
Stickney Joseph, calker and graver, house 8 Turner
Stickney Joseph, house East Webb
Stickney Joseph A. confectioner, boards East Webb
Stickney Martha Mrs. house 8 North court
Stickney Matthew A. house 119 Boston
Stickney Rebecca C. Miss, boards 100 Federal
Stickney Walter J. clerk, boards 29 Forrester
Stickney William W. shoemaker, 150 Essex, house 19 Andrew
Stiles Charles D. job wagon, house 12 Hancock
Stiles Dean, carpenter, 16 Endicott, house 53 do.
Still Thomas, bootmaker, 216 Essex, house 29 Cedar
Stillman Amos, fireman, boards 168 Bridge

Stillman Samuel, shoemaker, house 168 Bridge
Stimpson James B. currier, rear 43 Boston, house 192 Federal
Stimpson James C. tanner, 43 Boston, house 41 Warren
Stimpson Thomas M. counsellor, 194 Essex, h. at So. Danvers
Stocker Charles H. clerk, 228 Essex, boards 54 Endicott
Stocker John W. coach and chaise maker, rear 66 Washington, house 54 Endicott
Stocker Mary Miss, house 16 Federal
Stoddard Benjamin F. boards 39 Harbor (Co. C, 24th Regt.)
Stoddard Daniel, house 51 Lafayette
Stoddard George, machinist, boards 110½ Derby
Stoddard Mary A. Mrs. house 39 Harbor
Stoddard Mary B. widow, house 120 Federal
Stoddard Warren, machinist, boards 39 Harbor
Stodder Simon, captain, house 104 North
Stone Benjamin, mason, house 21 Williams
Stone Benjamin W. & Bros. (*Wm. jr. & Jos. W.*), merchants, 12 Asiatic building, house 23 Chestnut
Stone Charles, tanner, boards 12 Beaver
Stone Ebenezer, brickmaker, house Liberty Hill road, n. North
Stone Ebenezer jr. currier, house 16 Flint
Stone Esther P. Miss, house 8 Ash
Stone George, mason, house 4 Beaver
Stone George B. mason, house rear 14 Webb
Stone George L. currier, boards 12 Beaver
Stone Henry R. clerk (B.), house 18 Summer
Stone H. Osgood, physician, 19 Washington, house 23 Chestnut
Stone Irving (*Chandler & Co.*), periodicals, &c. 4 Wash. house 8 Lynde
Stone Isaac, carpenter, house 15 Dean
Stone James, mason, house 27 Warren
Stone James jr. M. D. house 40 Broad
Stone John H. Mrs. house 18 Summer
Stone Joseph W. (*B. W. Stone & Bros.*), 12 Asiatic building, house 23 Chestnut
Stone Lucinda, house 375 Essex
Stone Lydia, fancy goods, agent Employ. Soc. 366 Essex, bds. 27 Norman
Stone Mary, widow, house 109 Boston
Stone Mary H. widow, house 345 Essex
Stone Priscilla, widow, house 7 Margin
Stone Robert, house 23 Chestnut
Stone Sally, widow, house 27 Norman
Stone Stephen H. engineer, house 1 High
Stone Thomas, tinsmith, boards 10 Prince
Stone William, house 12 Beaver (Cal.)
Stone William jr. (*B. W. Stone & Bros.*), 12 Asiatic building, house 23 Chestnut   •
Stone William R. currier, house 12 Beaver
Stone ——, widow, house 10 Odell square

Roxbury Directory, Published by Sampson, Davenport, & Co.
(formerly Adams, Sampson, & Co.) **47 Congress St., Boston.**

Story Augustus, pres. Holyoke M. F. Ins. Co. 27 Washington, house 98 Bridge
Story Francis B. variety store, 148 Essex, house 8 Williams
Story William, captain, house 98 Bridge
Story William S. bootmaker, Ward, near Peabody, house Hardy
Stout John B. tanner, house 103 North
Stover Charles B. freight agent, E. R. R. house 12 Mill
Stover Nathaniel F. Mrs. house 12 English
Stowe Volney C. baker, head of Phillips' wharf, h. 21 Essex
Stowers Mary C. Mrs. house 315 Essex
Stowers Nathaniel, chair painter, house 21 Forrester
Straw Benj. wood mouldings, 5 Front, house 15 Winthrop
Straw Benjamin F. boards 15 Winthrop
Straw Isaiah, house 13 Barr
Streeter Gilbert L. teller First National Bank, house 80 Bridge
Streeter Sarah L. Mrs. house 80 Bridge
Striley Jacob, fisherman, house rear 13 Osgood
Striley Jacob jr. shoemaker, house 13 Osgood
Strout Samuel, mariner, boards 27 Carlton
Sullivan Bridget, widow, house rear 26 Peabody
Sullivan Daniel, laborer, house 98 Derby
Sullivan Daniel, laborer, house 5 Palfrey court
Sullivan Daniel, tanner, house Putnam, near Hanson
Sullivan Dennis, laborer, house Becket avenue·
Sullivan Ellen, widow, house 28 Congress
Sullivan Henry, laborer, house near foot Pingree
Sullivan Honora, widow, house 7 Church
Sullivan James, shoemaker, boards 42 Peabody
Sullivan James, laborer, house foot of Ives
Sullivan Jeremiah, laborer, house 38 Ward
Sullivan John, laborer, house 8 Pratt
Sullivan John, teamster at R. C. Manning & Co.'s, house Pingree, near Harbor
Sullivan John, laborer, house rear Adams, Mason Hill
Sullivan John, laborer, house 42 Peabody
Sullivan John, tanner, house near Adams, Mason Hill
Sullivan Joseph, laborer, house North, corner Bridge
Sullivan Margaret, widow, house 20 Odell square
Sullivan Margaret, widow, house 23 Prospect
Sullivan Michael, laborer, house 3 Gerrish place
Sullivan Michael, laborer, house 2 High street court
Sullivan Owen, laborer, house 57 Mill
Sullivan Patrick, currier, house 62 Mason
Sullivan Thomas Mrs. house 44 Peabody
Sullivan Thomas, laborer, house rear 8 Essex
Sullivan Timothy, laborer, house 7 Charter
Sullivan Timothy, laborer, h. Congress, west side, n. Harbor
Sullivan Timothy, laborer, house 9 Park
Sullivan Timothy, currier, house 23 Prospect

Summers William Mrs. house 92 Essex
Summers William H. clerk, house 92 Essex
Sumner (*Harrison G.*) & Carter (*John A.*), teamsters, 130
   Derby, house 23 Daniels
Sumner John A. morocco dresser, house 3 Ord
Sutton William, president First National Bank, 7 Central, house
   at South Danvers
Swan Charles H. civil engineer, office of Salem Water Com.
   boards 2½ Federal
Swan Miranda Miss, milliner, 293 Essex, house do.
Swan Joseph W. Mrs. house 16 Mechanic
Swasey Abigail, widow, house 30 St. Peter
Swasey Connor B. dentist, 208 Essex, house 28 Lafayette
Swasey Elizabeth R. widow, house 10 Daniels
Swasey John H. morocco dresser, house 177 Boston
Swasey Joseph, painter, 21 Dean, house 30 St. Peter
Swasey Lewis G. currier, house 59 Warren
Swasey L. A. Mrs. printer, 141 Essex, house 10 Federal
Swasey William M. boot and shoe machine stitching, St. Peter's
   court, house 103 Lafayette
Sweeney Daniel, laborer, house 152 Derby
Sweeney Dennis, currier, house 5 Charter
Sweeney Dennis, currier, house 9 Beaver
Sweeney John, laborer, house rear Adams, Mason Hill
Sweeney Morgan, currier, house 81 Mason
Sweeney Patrick, laborer, 26 Beckford
Sweeney Terrence, currier, house rear Adams, Mason Hill
Sweeney William, ropemaker, house 7 English
Sweeney William, laborer, house 18 Lemon
Sweetser Benjamin F. shoe cutter, boards 15 Fowler   ·
Sweetser Ephraim & Co. (*E. H. Sweetser*), boots and shoes,
   239 Essex, house 15 Fowler
Sweetser Ephraim H. (*E. Sweetser & Co.*), boards 15 Fowler
Sweetser Mary E. Miss, boards 63 Lafayette
Swift John, currier, house 5 North Pine
Symonds Abigail Miss, house 132 Boston
Symonds Benjamin, tanner and currier, house 99 North
Symonds Benjamin P. clerk, 9·Derby square, house Ives court
Symonds Benjamin R. grocer, 72·Federal, house 14 Barr
Symonds Benjamin R. boards rear 26 Brown
Symonds Calvin, house 91 North
Symonds Caroline J. teacher, house 68 Buffum
Symonds Charles A. boards rear 26 Brown
Symonds Charles B. currier, house 99 North
Symonds Charles E. treasurer, Salem Savings Bank, house
   90 North
Symonds Dean C. clerk, 29 Front, house 57 Mill
Symonds Eben, shoemaker, house 51 North
Symonds Edward, shoemaker, house 58 North
Symonds Edward jr. clerk, 74 North, house 77 do.

Taunton Directory, Published by Sampson, Davenport, & Co.
(formerly Adams, Sampson, & Co.) **47 Congress St., Boston.**

Symonds Edward A. bookkeeper, 4 Franklin Building, boards 9 Federal
Symonds Edward B. Mrs. house 9 Federal
Symonds Eliza and Pauline. Misses, house 132 Boston
Symonds Eliza G. house 98 Federal
Symonds Eliza M. cloak and mantilla maker, boards 98 Federal
Symonds Eliza S. teacher, boards 14 Barr
Symonds Ephraim G. varieties, house School, corner North
Symonds Ephraim Mrs. house 18 Mechanic
Symonds Hannah, Louisa and Martha, Misses, h. 13 Daniels
Symonds Hannah, widow, house 77 North
Symonds J. Shove, house 67 Buffum (Louisiana)
Symonds John D. mariner, house 47 North
Symonds Joseph, grocer, 109 North, house 14 Barr
Symonds Joseph P. engineer, house 65 Buffum
Symonds (*Joseph W.*) & Co. (*Wm. Harris Richardson*), boots and shoes, 221 Essex, house 46 Federal
Symonds Lemuel W. baker, 72½ North, boards 3 Mechanic
Symonds Mary, widow, house 122 Federal
Symonds Nathaniel A. carpenter, boards 18 Mechanic
Symonds Nathaniel D. house 50 North
Symonds Nathaniel G. treas. Salem and South Danvers Oil Co., Mason, house 49 Buffum   [house 132 Boston
Symonds Pauline Miss, milliner and fancy goods, 184 Essex,
Symonds Proctor, shoemaker, house 35 North
Symonds Samuel, grocer, 49 North, house 7 Buffum
Symonds Samuel C. tinsmith, boards 47 North
Symonds Stephen G. painter, house Barr, beyond School
Symonds Stillman G. bookkeeper, National Exchange Bank, boards 9 Buffum
Symonds Thomas, grocer, 74 North, house 7 Dearborn
Symonds Thomas S. clerk, 72 Federal, house 95 North
Symonds Timothy, shoemaker, house 91 North
Symonds T. Putnam, merchant (Central whf. B.), h. 65 North
Symonds William A. shoemaker, house 68 Buffum
Symonds William H. shoemaker, house 149 North
Symonds William H. mason, boards 50 North

TABOUR WILLIAM, cigar manuf. 162 Essex and 7 North, house do.
Taft Russell H. cabinetmaker, house 7 Mall
Tait Bacon C. coachman, 212 Essex, boards 21 Lafayette
Tanch Dennis E. carpenter, house 41 St. Peter
Tanch John, carpenter, house 41 St. Peter
Taney Bridget, widow, house Watson, corner Beaver
Taney Dominick, currier, house Watson, corner Beaver
Tapley Charles, house 9 Andrew
Tarbox Henry H. teamster, boards 89 North
Tarbox William, shoemaker, house 89 North
Tarr Benjamin, oysters, house 9 Allen

Tate Charles L. machinist, boards 3 Ash
Tate Sophia Mrs. house 3 Ash
Tay Henry, house 10 Beckford (Buenos Ayres)
Taylor Catharine A. widow, house 6 Broad
Taylor Charles H. book agent, house 63 Essex
Taylor George P. photographer, 188 Essex, boards 6 Broad
Taylor Margaret S. house 18 Chestnut
Taylor Matilda P. Miss, teacher, house 18 Chestnut
Taylor Thomas, confectioner, boards 73 Mason
Taylor Thomas A. carpenter, boards 28 High
Taylor William H. boots and shoes, 3 Central, house 18 Cedar
Tayte Anthony B. teacher mathematics, house 4 Peabody
Tayte Martin L. shoemaker, boards 4 Peabody
Tayte William George, printer, 193 Essex, boards 4 Peabody
Teague Amos G. police, house 82 Mill
Teague Charles C. shoemaker, house 4 School
Teague Charles H. carpenter, house 1 Turner
Teague Joseph B. clerk, house 59 Broad
Teague Phebe S. Mrs. house 101 North
Teague Robert, at Laboratory, house 19 Upham
Teague Sarah, widow, house 18 Webb
Teague Thomas A. carpenter, house 26 Essex
Teague William, saloon, 138 Derby, house 132 do.
Teague William H. H. shoemaker, boards 82 Mill
Teal George C. tanner, boards 35 Lafayette
Tedder John, mariner, house 20 Congress
Tenney Charles H. conductor, E. R. R. house 114½ Bridge
Tenney Isabella C. teacher Nomal School
Tenney J. S. Mrs. house 19 Pleasant
Teste Mary P. nurse, house 5 Creek
Tevnan John, Naumkeag mill, house rear 42 Harbor
Thain Edward, shoemaker, 60 Derby, boards 1 Pingree
Thayer Edward S. clerk Seccomb Oil Manuf. Co. house
    8 Curtis
Thayer Eliza & Harriet, house 8 North court
Thayer Mary J. teacher, boards 34 Broad
Thayer Nancy, dressmaker, house 34 Broad
Thayer Oliver & Co. lumber wharf, 190 and 199 Derby, house
    29 Broad
Thayer Rebecca Mrs. house 34 Broad
Thayer Sarah, house 34 Broad
Thayer Stephen, collector, house 34 Broad
Thayer William O. clerk (B.), boards 22 Liberty
Thomas Charles S. carpenter, house 72 Summer
Thomas Clarissa, widow, house foot Ives
Thomas Edward, sawyer, house Barr, beyond School
Thomas George E. carpenter, boards 72 Summer
Thomas George F. tanner, boards foot of Ives   ·
Thomas George W. boards 2 Jeffrey court
Thomas Nancy, widow, house Orne, near Upham

Thomas Richard, fishdealer, house 30 Phelps' court
Thomas Richard H. jr. dyer, house 1 Melcher's court
Thomas Robert, hairdresser, house 20 Crombie
Thomas Samuel W. shoemaker, house 64½ North
Thomas Sarah Mrs. house rear 89 North
Thomas Stephen W. carpenter, house Grove, corner Phillips
Thomas Stephen W. jr. carpenter, boards Grove, cor. Phillips
Thomas Wesley J. blacksmith, house 5 Pond
Thompson Edward, laborer, house 23 North
Thompson George J. baker, 28 Broad, house do.
Thompson Henry Mrs. house 30 Broad
Thompson Matilda, nurse, house 90 Federal
Thompson Orrin F. clerk, 167 Essex, house 30 Broad
Thompson W. F. Mrs. millinery and dressmaking, 3 North,
   house do.
Thomson Joseph A. house 11 Salem
Thorndike Charles F. clerk 173 Essex, boards 1 Prospect
Thorndike Charles J. boards 4 Brown
Thorndike Larkin Mrs. house 4 Brown
Thorndike Lydia A. saleswoman, 186 Essex, bds. 1 Prospect
Thorndike William D. currier, Hanson, house Prospect
Thorner John C. shoemaker, house 162 Bridge
Thorner Sarah Mrs. boards 15 Beckford
Thrasher David, farmer, house Lafayette, n. F. R. Lead Mills
Thurston Henry W. (*Henderson & T.*), 38 Washington, house
   6 Howard
Thyng (*J. Warren*) & Babbidge (*Wm. A.*), publishers Salem
   Witch, 182 Essex, house 3 Federal
Tibbets Eben, captain, house 12 Mall
Tibbets Elizabeth, variety store, 9 Winter, house do.
Tibbets Henry, house 24 Liberty
Tibbets Henry H. painter, 139 Derby, house 9 Curtis
Tibbets Sarah H. Miss, boards 24 Liberty
Tibbets William R. clerk, boards 24 Liberty
Tibbetts Andrew J. baker, 46 Pleasant
Tibbetts Andrew R. shoemaker, house 46 Charter
Tibbetts Ann, widow, boards 28 Howard
Tibbetts Charles H. mariner, house 12 Andrew
Tibbetts Edwin C. peddler, house 4 Mason
Tibbetts Russell S. restorator, 54 Washington, h. 3 Jeffrey court
Tierney Catherine, house 10 Herbert
Tierney James, laborer, house Grove, near Cemetery
Tierney James, currier, house 23 Fowler
Tierney Patrick, currier, house 13 Flint
Tilton Benjamin T. (*Sawyer & T.*), provisions, 9 Derby square,
   boards Essex House   [South Danvers
Tilton E. G. Mrs. dress and cloak maker, 251 Essex, house at
Tilton John P. clerk, 210 Essex, boards 24 St. Peter
Tilton Samuel D. carpenter, house 13 Andrew
Timmins Gerritt J. morocco finisher, boards 1 Silver

Timmins Patrick, tanner, house 1 Silver
Tirrell Michael, laborer, house 36 Ward
Tirrell Rebecca, widow, house 62 Mill
Tirrell Zibeon, shoemaker, house 16 Central
Tivnan John, Naumkeag mill, house 42 Harbor
Tivnan Michael, peddler, house rear Congress
Tivnan Michael, Naumkeag mill, boards 11 Congress
Tivnan Peter, umbrella maker, 244 Essex, house 11 Congress
Tobin John, laborer, house 4 Perkins
Tobin John, carpenter, house Watson, near Beaver
Tobin Michael, switchman, E. R. R. 31 Mill
Todd Charles P. hair spinner, house 11 March
Todd Jeremiah, city express, house 39 Summer
Todd John E. A. captain, house 2 Cherry
Todd Mary E. house 17 March
Todd Nathaniel M. salesman (B.), house 2 Cherry
Todd Rebecca Mrs. house 21 Creek
Tolen Neal, laborer, house foot Pingree
Tolman Sardis, shoemaker, house 27 Norman
Toohey John, laborer, house 9 Prince
Toole Christopher, blacksmith, house 148 Boston
Toomey John P. currier, house Hanson
Torr Joseph Henry, mariner, house 4 Becket
Torr Sally, widow, house 4 Becket
Torrey Francis, mariner, house 42 Essex
Touret Benjamin A. soda manuf. (B.), house 165 Bridge
Touts Walter, laborer, house 13 Gedney court
Towle Abraham, carpenter, Webster, house 36 Pleasant
Towle Albert L. carpenter, boards Pleasant, r. H. R. R. stables
Towne Charles H. sec'ry Salem Sav. Bank, Asiatic building, h.
    Holley, corner Linden
Towne Eliza Miss, house 2 Phelps' court
Towne Henry Mrs. house 49 Broad
Towne John, shoemaker, 60 Derby, house 28 Essex
Towne John C. teller Naumkeag National Bank, h. 17 Buffum
Towne Joseph, bookkeeper. 10 Washington, house 17 Buffum
Towne Joseph H. cashier Naumkeag National Bank, house 19
    Buffum
Townes Samuel, salt fish, 8 Derby wharf, house 7 Federal
Townes Ann Mrs. nurse, house 7 Federal
Townes Susan, widow, boards 100 Derby
Townes William, mariner, house 9 Federal
Townsend Catharine G. house 120 Bridge
Townsend Penn Mrs. house 23 Andrew
Townsend William, farmer, at Almshouse, boards do.
Tozier Amanda, widow, house 16 English
Tracy Hannah H. Mrs. house 31 Broad
Tracy Joseph, hostler, house 43 Bridge
Tracy Patrick, laborer, house Grove, near Irving
Tracy William, currier, house Varney, near Hanson

Albany Directory, Published by Sampson, Davenport, & Co.
(formerly Adams, Sampson, & Co.) **47 Congress St., Boston.**

Traill Horace S. printer, Salem Observer office, h. 18 Winthrop
Trainer Thomas, tanner, house 3 Palfrey court   [Boston
Trask Amos, dealer in ancient and modern curiosities, house 126
Trask Benjamin Mrs. house 17 Harbor
Trask Eben P. letter carrier, house 51 St. Peter
Trask Henry A. shoemaker, boards 63 Broad
Trask Israel, shoemaker, house 14 Allen
Trask James, grocer, 47 St. Peter. house 22 Howard
Trask James E. painter, boards 22 Howard
Trask John Mrs. house 24 Becket
Trask Mary Mrs. house 6 Phelps' court
Trask Moses A. teamster, house foot North court
Trask Thomas Mrs. house 129½ Essex
Trask William Mrs. house head North court
Trayers William, currier, house 13 River
Treadwell Frances A. assistant teacher, Bridge street primary
    school, house 1 Southwick
Treadwell Nathaniel R. currier, 11 Franklin, house 18 Barr
Treadwell Thomas, cabinetmaker, house Southwick
Treadwell Thomas J. cabinetmaker, boards Southwick
Trefren James, sewing machines and findings, 4 Franklin build-
    ing, house 20 Pleasant
Trefren Josiah J. clerk, 4 Franklin building, b. 20 Pleasant
Trescott James, shoemaker, house 13 Allen
Trescott James, shoemaker, house 28 Essex
Trofatter John H. agent, house 9 Upham
Trofatter Robert Mrs. house 18 Albion
Trofatter Samuel J. shoe stiffening manuf. r. 10 Beaver, h. 10 do.
Trofatter Sarah K. house 371 Essex
Trofatter William N. in planing mill, boards 18 Albion
True Abraham Mrs. house 12 Brown
True Joseph, house 5 High
Trull Frederick, shoemaker, 196 Essex, boards 13 Ward
Trull Frederick A. painter, boards 13 Ward
Trull Nathaniel W. mariner, boards 13 Ward
Trumbull Charles H. Mrs. house 6 Hardy
Trumbull Edward H. Mrs. house 18 Winter
Trumbull Margaret L. widow, house 6 Hardy
Tuck George C. currier, house rear 18 Beckford
Tucker Charles, currier, boards 36 Endicott
Tucker Edgar R. farmer, boards 14 Aborn
Tucker Edward, fisherman, house 4 Bridge
Tucker Henry G. lobsterman, boards 4 Bridge
Tucker Jewett C. farmer, house 14 Aborn
Tucker Jonathan, house 29 Andrew
Tucker Lucy C. Mrs. house 25 Turner
Tucker Mary, widow, boards 10 Beaver
Tucker Patrick, boards 105 Derby
Tucker Samuel, lobsterman, house 4 Bridge
Tucker Samuel A. tanner and currier, house 10 Barr

Tucker Sophia M. widow, house 13 Norman
Tucker Theodore E. at Naumkeag mills, boards 25 Turner
Tucker William W. farmer, boards 14 Aborn
Tucker ——— widow, house 2 Palfrey court
Tuckerman J. Francis (14 Court, B.), house 41 Chestnut
Tudbury William, peddler, house 24 North
Tufts Amos, pres't. Secomb Oil Manuf. Co. h. at Charlestown
Tufts Horace Mrs. house 5 Elm
Tufts Mary P. widow, house 150 Boston
Tufts Samuel C. Mrs. house 56 North
Tufts Sarah Mrs. house 15 High street court
Tufts William, mariner, house 5 Elm
Tufts William Mrs. house 4 Cherry
Tullock Clarissa A. nurse, house 1 Aborn
Turell Benjamin F. baker and confectioner, 15 Central, b. do.
Turner Calvin, tanner, 4 Goodhue, house 66 Boston
Turner Charles W. tanner, house 69 Boston
Turner Edward, clerk, 166 Derby, boards 20 Ward
Turner George Mrs. house 20 Ward
Turner James H. measurer of leather, house 66 Boston
Turner James H. jr. measurer of leather, boards 66 Boston
Turner Leverett, carpenter, boards 20 Ward
Tuttle Ebenezer, currier, house 11 Boston
Tuttle Eunice E. house 11 River
Tuttle Francis R. currier, boards 83 Boston
Tuttle Francis W. dry goods, 167 Essex, house 6 Hathorne
Tuttle Henry A. painter, house 165 Federal
Tuttle Henry C. Mrs. house 165 Federal
Tuttle Henry G. provisions, 36 Boston, house 83 do.
Tuttle Hiram A. carriage trimmer, West place, house 23
    Federal   [Federal], house 183 do.
Tuttle John, harness maker, 36 Boston, and livery stable, 191
Tuttle Joseph F. carder, boards 38 Harbor
Tuttle Mary E. widow, house 16 Oliver
Tuttle Nathaniel, currier, and tanner, 21 Boston, [h. 19 do.
Tuttle William W. clerk, boards 83 Boston   [Cambridge
Twombly E. A. Mrs. fancy goods, 242 Essex, boards 13
Tyler Alfred, shoemaker, house 2 Downing
Tyler Edward, driver bread cart, house 9 Upham
Tyler Franklin, morocco dresser, house 144 Boston
Tyler Harriet M. principal Browne primary sch. b. 7 Cherry
Tyler Moses C. shoemaker, house 6 Nursery
Tyler Sarah A. Mrs. house 7 Cherry

UPHAM BENJAMIN N. chemist, at Laboratory, house rear
    70 North
Upham Charles W. house 313 Essex
Upham Franklin, confectioner, house 16 Cedar
Upham Joshua, chemist, Laboratory, house rear 70 North
Upham Joshua W. confectioner, house 70 North

Upham O. W. H. boards 313 Essex
Upham Warren, confectioner, house 70 North
Upham William P. counsellor, 224 Essex, boards 313 do.
Upton Anna M. teacher, 59 Essex, house do.
Upton Benjamin Mrs. house 31 Pleasant
Upton Charles H. mariner, house 14 Skerry
Upton Charles Mrs. house 26 Winter
Upton Daniel (B.), boards 31 Pleasant
Upton Eben, musician, house 31 Barr
Upton Eben Mrs. house 89 North
Upton Edmund Mrs. house 5 Saunders
Upton Edmund A. master mariner, boards 5 Saunders
Upton Edward, currier, house 8 Monroe
Upton Edwin, merchant, 63 Union, boards Essex House
Upton Ezra, provision dealer, 2 Mill, house 4 do.
Upton Francis, music teacher, house 31 Pleasant
Upton George, merchant, 63 Union, house 8 Liberty
Upton George L. carpenter, boards 25 Saunders
Upton George W. clerk, 2 Mill, house 4 do.
Upton Henry, toll keeper, Beverly bridge, boards 5 Saunders
Upton Henry O. leader of Upton's Quadrille Band, 46 Washington, house 12 Lemon
Upton Henry P. merchant, 3 Commercial (B.), h. 69 Essex
Upton Horace G. tanner and currier, house 39 Bridge
Upton James, merchant (B.), house 100 Bridge
Upton Joseph, captain, house 5 Saunders
Upton Moses T. carpenter, 7 Walnut, house 2 Curtis
Upton Paul, captain, house 3 Hamilton
Upton Stephen, captain, house 124 Bridge
Upton Warren A. tinsmith, house 12 School
Upton William B. clerk, boards 4 Mill
Upton William F. captain, house 5 Arabella
Upton William M. cooper, house 23 Hardy

VALENTINE ELMER, insurance agent, house 4 Ash
Vanderford Benjamin F. engineer, house 19 Creek
Vanderford Elizabeth Mrs. house 3 Howard
Varney Daniel (*W., D. & S. Varney*), house 71 Boston
Varney D. Augustus, shoe dealer (B.), boards 24 Pleasant
Varney George W. currier, boards 78 Boston
Varney Henry, tanner, Goodhue, rear 82 Boston, b. 100 do.
Varney John F. currier, boards 78 Boston
Varney Solomon (*W., D. & S. Varney*), house 100 Boston
Varney W., D. & S. (*William, Daniel, & Solomon*), tanners, r.
    48 Boston, and curriers, 82 do.
Varney William (*W., D. & S. Varney*), house 78 Boston
Veno Felix, mariner, boards rear 30 Congress
Vent Eben N. watchman, house 78 Mill
Vent James H. currier, boards 14 Winter
Vent James M. Mrs. house 14 Winter

Charlestown Directory, Published by Sampson, Davenport, &
Co. (formerly Adams, Sampson, & Co.) 47 Congress St., Boston.

Vent Sarah, house 78 Mill
Verry Albert, musician, house 77 Mill
Very Abraham, house 30 Hathorne
Very Abraham A. mariner, house 30 Hathorne
Very Edwin, clerk, 210 Essex, house 7 Dearborn
Very Ephraim P. cook, house 168 Bridge
Very Frances E. private school, 95 Federal, house 154 do.
Very Harriet, house 1 Hardy
Very John C. Mrs. house 14 English
Very John F. house 69 North
Very Jones Rev. house 154 Federal
Very Joseph Mrs. widow, house 3 Boston
Very Lydia Mrs. house 154 Federal
Very Lydia L. A. teacher, house 154 Federal
Very Martha, widow, house 22 Boston
Very Martha N. Mrs. teacher, private school, 73 Federal, h. do.
Very Nathaniel, shipsmith, house 11 Turner
Very Nathaniel jr. cabinetmaker, 274 Essex, house 45½ North
Very Nathaniel A. chemist, Laboratory, house 19 Mason
Very Nathaniel O. clerk, 113 Derby, house 67½ Essex
Very Samuel, gum copal works, house 57 Bridge
Very Samuel A. grocer, 22 Boston, house do.
Viannah Francis J. house 16 Curtis (U. S. N.)
Viannah Frank, shoemaker, boards foot Northey
Viannah Sarah A. widow, house foot Northey
Victorato Constantine, bowling and billiard saloon, rear 14½
    Front, house 9 Lagrange
Vincent Letitia P. Mrs. tailoress, house 41 Essex
Vivuan Wilmot W. carpenter, house 14 Saunders
Vollor Mary E. house 18 Phelps' court
Vollor Nathan P. house 7 Herbert
Voorhees Lewis D. D. captain, house 79 Bridge
Vose George L. (12 Water, B.), house 12 Crombie

WADLEIGH ANN W. house 93 Federal   [bds. 120 do.
Wadleigh Curtis E. (*Mooney & W.*), stoves, &c., 40 & 42 North
Wadleigh Elizabeth S. dressmaker, house 93 Federal
Walcott Samuel B. Mrs. house 77 Lafayette
Walcott Samuel P. farmer, house 77 Lafayette
Walden Joseph F. currier, 48 Boston, house 176 Federal
Walden Nancy P. widow, house 49 St. Peter
Walden Wm. W. P. currier, house 7 Grove
Waldo Mary Miss, house 134 Federal
Waldron Sarah A. nurse, boards 1 Harbor
Walker Abbott, merchant, house 335 Essex
Walker Abbott jr. boards 335 Essex
Walker Crocker L. regulator (B.), boards 57 Endicott
Walker George E. shoemaker, 144 Essex, house 4 Endicott
Walker George S. gents' furnishing goods, 228 Essex, boards
    33 Summer

Walker Mary Mrs. tailoress, house 15 High street court
Walker Parker D. carpenter, 7 Boston, house 57 Endicott
Walker Parker L. at Mason & Hamlin's (B.), organist South
 Church, boards 57 Endicott
Walker William, tanner, 15 May
Wallace Patrick, tanner, house Irving, above Grove
Wallis Jane, widow, house near foot Park
Wallis Joseph, cabinetmaker and furniture dealer, 213 Essex,
 house 28 Lafayette
Wallis Rebecca Mrs. house 4 Northey
Wallis William, house 15 Beckford
Walsh John J. shoemaker, house 14 March
Walsh Patrick, cutter, 3 West's block, boards 14 Elm
Walsh Patrick, shoemaker, house 7 Ward
Walsh Robert Mrs. house 63 Broad
Walsh William F. shoemaker, house 14 March
Walton Benj. T. bone dealer, foot Ord, house 3 do.
Walton Eben N. printer, 193 Essex, house 6 Herbert
Walton Edward A. laborer, boards 9 Aborn
Walton George M. carpenter, house rear 9 Aborn
Walton Joseph, cigarbox maker, 147 Boston, house 145 do.
Walton Joseph A. carpenter, house 30 Derby
Walton Joseph H. carpenter, house 30 Derby
Walton Joseph H. carpenter, house 145 Boston
Walton Josiah, blacksmith, 131 Boston, house 9 Aborn
Walton Josiah Mrs. house 8 Beaver
Walton Thomas W. blacksmith, house 4 Ord
Walton Timothy, bone dealer, foot Ord, house 161 Boston
Walton William A. clerk, house 1 Prospect
Walton William J. shoedealer, Danvers, house rear 9 Aborn
Walwork Thomas (*A. S. Dudley & Co.*), dentist, 224 Essex,
 boards 29 Brown
Walwork Sara E. milliner, 5 Central, boards 29 Brown
Ward Alfred A. provisions, 5 & 6 City market, house at South
 Danvers
Ward Andrew A. Mrs. house 12 Elm
Ward Andrew R. Mrs. house 123 Federal
Ward Charles, merchant, house 2 Botts' court
Ward Eliza Mrs. house 15 Brown
Ward E. W. Miss, teacher, house 34 Chestnut
Ward Frances L. widow, house 19 Herbert
Ward James, laborer, house 21 Salem
Ward James, captain, house 61 Bridge
Ward James L. grocer, 61 Bridge, house do.
Ward John, blacksmith, house 16 Congress   [14 Broad
Ward Jonathan O. provisions, 15 and 16 Market House, house
Ward Louisa H. Mrs. cloak and dressmaker, 157 Essex, house
 20 Andrew
Ward L. Pierson, captain, house 4 Federal
Ward Malvina T. Mrs. house 34 Chestnut

Ward Mary, widow, house 396 Essex
Ward Mehitable Miss, house 34 Summer
Ward Richard, laborer, house 129 Derby
Ward Sarah A. millinery, 278 Essex, house 54 Mill
Ward Winsor M. carpenter, boards 23 Warren
Wardwell John, carpenter, house 11 Hathorne
Wardwell John S. watchman, house 20 Hathorne
Wardwell Nathaniel A. Mrs. house 42 Phelps' court
Ware Alfred F. farmer, house Salem turnpike
Ware Erastus D. farmer, house Salem turnpike
Ware Horace, farmer, house Salem turnpike
Ware Horace C. farmer, house Salem turnpike
Warner Clarence A. currier, boards 164 Boston
Warner Edward L. baker, house 6 Oak
Warner Elizabeth G. widow, house 99 Bridge
Warner Ellen, widow, house 68 Essex
Warner Frank B. clerk, boards 164 Boston
Warner John V. cooper, boards 6 Oak
Warner Joseph A. carpenter, house 164 Boston
Warren Edward J. currier, boards 4 Union place
Warren George H. carpenter, house 42 Pleasant
Warren John, at the Laboratory, house 4 Union place
Warren Levi F. principal Epes school, house 36 Endicott
Washington John S. stove worker, 29 Front, house 16 Porter
Waters Andrew S. copper founder, 6 Franklin, house 54 North
Waters Andrew S. jr. coppersmith, house 67½ Mason
Waters Charles R. house 10 Pleasant
Waters Eben, coppersmith, boards 54 Mason
Waters Edward, mariner, house 6 Mill
Waters Edward Stanley, teacher private school, h. 8 Pleasant
Waters Henry F. house 10 Pleasant
Waters James D. merchant, house 8 Pleasant
Waters John, carpenter, house 2 Essex
Waters John jr. bark measurer, house 5 Franklin
Waters John G. Mrs. house 14 Cambridge
Waters Joseph G. judge Police Court, house 10 Pleasant
Waters Lucy B. Mrs. dressmaker, house rear 106 Essex
Waters Mary, widow, boards 91 Derby
Waters Thomas S. machine sewing, 31 Endicott, h. 4 Buffum
Waters William C. public storekeeper, Custom-house, house at
    Beverly
Waters William D. merchant, house 6 Pleasant
Waters William F. clerk, 222 Essex, boards 106 do.
Watson Daniel P. enamelled leather manuf. house 39 Boston
Watson Elizabeth R. milliner, house 412 Essex
Watson Fenton, saddler, 414 Essex, house 412 do.
Watson Jane N. widow, house 5 Elm
Watson Lucy F. teacher, house 412 Essex
Watson Mary, house 412 Essex
Watson Mary S. widow, boards 16 Allen

Lowell Directory, Published by Sampson, Davenport, & Co.
(formerly Adams, Sampson, & Co.) **47 Congress St., Boston.**

Watson Norris E. city watch, house 5 Elm
Watson Otis, saddler, house 412 Essex
Watson Thomas R. conchman, 212 Essex, house rear do.
Watts Charles, baker, 53 Derby, house 55 do.
Watts Charles E. mariner, boards 55 Derby
Watts Richard, mariner, boards 25 Daniels
Way Oliver D. clerk (B.), boards 100 Boston
Webb Albert H., Salem Car Co., boards 8 Andrew
Webb Allen P. supt. Salem Car Co., house 8 Andrew
Webb Benjamin, merchant, Webb's wharf, boards 17 Turner
Webb Benjamin jr. chemist, 54 Essex, house 52 do.
Webb Elizabeth Mrs. house 106 Essex
Webb Francis R. master mariner, boards 80 Lafayette
Webb George F. mariner, boards rear 22 Hardy
Webb Hannah, boards 5 Northey
Webb Hannah Miss, house 14 Carlton
Webb Henry, mason, house rear 22 Hardy
Webb Henry jr. clerk, Essex House, boards do.
Webb John K. merchant tailor, 139 Essex, house 110 do.
Webb John T. clerk, 240 Essex, boards 110 do.
Webb Joseph Mrs. house 27 Brown
Webb Joseph B. merchant, Webb's wharf, house 17 Turner
Webb Joseph H. cashier, Nat. Exchange Bank, h. 65 Federal
Webb Margaret E. teacher, Phillips' school, house 4 Curtis
Webb Mary E. teacher, Norman school, house 27 Brown
Webb Sarah Miss, house 31 Turner   [boards 7 Central
Webb Sarah E. Miss, operator, Am. Telegraph, Asiatic Bld'g,
Webb Stephen, clerk, Internal Rev. office, 175 Essex. h. 81 do.
Webb Stephen P. city clerk, City Hall, house 314½ Essex
Webb Thomas Mrs. house 7 Central
Webb William, boards 4 Curtis
Webb William, apothecary, 54 Essex, house 52 do.
Webb William jr. apothecary, 159½ Essex, house 8 St. Peter
Webb William jr. Mrs. house 4 Curtis
Webb William T. laborer, house 8 Webb
Webber Edward A. machine stitching, 22 Winthrop
Webber Edwin A. boards 25 North
Webber Ira J. grocer, 58 Washington, house 11 Barr
Webber Martha C. widow, boards 11 Barr
Webber Mary, widow, house 49 Mill
Webber Moses, currier, house near foot Laboratory
Webber Moses W., Naumkeag mill, house rear 86 Mill
Webber William G. clerk, Jas. F. Almy & Co's b. 2½ Federal
Webster Elizabeth, widow, house 7 Northey
Webster Gilman, shoecutter, house 16 Winthrop
Webster John, treasurer Newmarket Manufacturing Co. and
　　pres. National Exchange Bank, house 75 Lafayette
Webster John C. grocer, Franklin building, Essex, cor. New-
　　bury, house 7 Northey
Webster Louisa S. F. Mrs. house 28 Beckford

Lynn Directory, Published by Sampson, Davenport, & Co. (for-
19   merly Adams, Sampson, & Co.) 47 Congress St., Boston.

Weeden Anna, widow, boards 3 North court
Weeks Alonzo P. clerk, Mercantile National Bank, b. 6 Cross
Weeks Betsey, widow, house 8 Dearborn
Weeks Dudley Mrs. dressmaker, house 9 Mason
Weeks Gilbert, Naumkeag mill, boards 38 Harbor
Weeks William, carpenter, house 8 Dearborn
Weeks William, gardener, house 8 Leach
Weeks William R. clerk (Boston), boards 8 Leach
Weir Daniel P. blacksmith, Endicott, c. Mill, h. 27 Endicott
Welch Aaron, farmer, house Neck
Welch Ann, widow, house 152 Derby
Welch Catharine, widow, house 13 English
Welch Charles L. master mariner, house 2 Becket
Welch Charles O. farmer, boards Aaron Welch's
Welch David, mariner, boards 10 Perkins
Welch Eliza A. dressmaker, house 2 Becket
Welch James, painter, house 22 Charter
Welch James, Naumkeag mill, boards 59 Harbor
Welch James, laborer, house Grove, corner Tremont
Welch John, blacksmith, boards 5 N. Pine
Welch John, laborer, house 92 Derby
Welch John, laborer, house 10 Perkins
Welch John, laborer, house 21 Ward
Welch John, laborer, house 36 Ward
Welch John, operative, boards 91 Derby
Welch John, Naumkeag mill, house 49 Harbor
Welch John A. laborer, boards 13 English
Welch Lawrence, jr. carder, boards 91 Derby
Welch Lawrence, laborer, boards 1 Ward
Welch Lawrence, laborer, house 91 Derby
Welch Mary, widow, house 6 Vale
Welch Mary, widow, boards 14 Ward
Welch Maurice, Naumkeag mill, boards 59 Harbor
Welch Michael, laborer, house 19 Daniels
Welch Michael, laborer, house 1 High street court
Welch Michael, carder, boards 91 Derby
Welch Patrick, house 14 Ward
Welch Patrick, currier, house Odell square
Welch Patrick, shoemaker, house 9 Prince
Welch Patrick F. cutter, boards 14 Elm
Welch Thomas, in picker room, boards 91 Derby
Welch Walter, laborer, house 9 Ropes
Welch Walter, laborer, house rear 42 Ward
Welch William, laborer, house 26 Mill   [1 Ward
Welch William E. provisions, 22 Central, corner Front, house
Welch Wm. L. clerk (Newbern, N. C.), b. at Aaron Welch's
Weldon John, laborer, house 13 High street court
Wellman George O. at oil factory, house 4 School
Wellman Nancy, clerk, boards 24 Turner
Wellman Samuel, mariner, house 8 Prescott

Manchester (N. H.) Directory, Published by Sampson, Davenport. & Co. (formerly Adams, Sampson, & Co.) 47 Congress St., Boston.

Wellman Timothy, painter, house 4 Botts' court
Wells Abbie G. Miss, house 24 Endicott
Wells Charles A. clerk, boards 22 Hardy
Wells Charles H. apothecary (Gloucester), boards 22 Hardy
Wells George A. boards 22 Hardy (Alexandria)
Wells George W. L. machinist, house 7 Spring
Wells James, watchman, house 13 Pickman
Wells John, gum copal worker, house 22 Hardy
Wells Lucius, house 22 Liberty
Wells William G. clerk (201 State, B.), boards 22 Liberty
Wendell Rufus Rev. house 6 Cross
Wentworth Charles A. shoemaker, boards 17 Essex
Wentworth Eliza E. widow, house 13 English
Wentworth John, laborer, house 17 Essex
Wentworth John H. laborer, boards 17 Essex
Wentworth William F. mariner, boards 17 Essex
Wentzell David, farmer, house Orne
West Benjamin A. merchant, 218 Derby, house 74 Lafayette
West Betsey, widow, house 120 Lafayette
West Elizabeth, widow, house 68 Essex
West George Mrs. house 57 Forrester
West George, currier, house rear 53 Warren
West George W. farmer, 120 Lafayette
West Rebecca Mrs. house 57 Lafayette
West Richard, boards 33 Summer
West Samuel, merchant, 218 Derby, house 77 Lafayette
West William, printer, house 62 North
West William H. Lead mill, h. r. Lafayette, opp. Lynn road
Weston Charles & Sons (*Thomas F., Charles H., and John W.
Weston*), tanners and curriers, May, house 30 Boston
Weston Charles H. (*Charles Weston & Sons*), boards 30 Boston
Weston Edward Mrs. house 7 Williams
Weston Eliza Mrs. house 3 Hardy
Weston John W. machinist, rear 11 Boston, boards 30 do.
Weston Nathaniel jr. house 9 Brown   [46 Essex
Weston Phineas R. paper and paper stock, 166 Derby, house
Weston Samuel C. sewing machines, 113 Essex, h. 17 Union
Weston Thomas F. (*C. Weston & Sons*), house 30 Boston
Wetherbee David, farmer, house 28 Williams   [10 Church
Wetherell Pliny (*Clapp & W.*), bleachers, 3 Sewall, house rear
Whalan Michael, currier, house 24 Prospect
Whaley Timothy, laborer, house 20 Carlton
Whartey Patrick, laborer, house 89 North
Whartey Peter, currier, house 87½ North
Whearty Patrick, currier, boards 61 Mason
Whearty Thomas, tanner, boards 61 Mason
Whearty Thomas jr. currier, boards 61 Mason
Wheatland George, counsellor, 194 Essex, house 374 do.
Wheatland George jr. counsellor, boards 374 Essex
Wheatland Henry, physician, house 21 Chestnut

Wheatland Martha G. house 136 Federal
Wheatland Richard, captain, house 358 Essex
Wheatland Simeon J. porter, 179 Essex, house foot Northey
Wheatland Stephen G. counsellor, 194 Essex, house 374 do.
Wheatland William R. tanner, house 358 Essex
Wheeler Asa Mrs. house 20 Lynde
Wheeler Benjamin S. provisions, 1, 2, 3, and 4 Market House,
    house at South Danvers
Wheeler John H. shoemaker, house 66 North
Wheeler Joseph, artist, boards 29 Union
Wheeler Michael Mrs. house 19 Daniels
Wheeler Michael S. Mrs. house 165 Bridge
Wheeler Samuel B. boards 165 Bridge
Wheeler Susan and Abby, tailoresses, house 165 Bridge
Whiley Rebecca, boarding, house 32 Derby
Whipple Albert (*S. Whipple & Brother*), house 45 Essex
Whipple George M. & A. A. Smith, books and stationery, 243
    Essex, house 2 Andover
Whipple Henry, charts, 243 Essex, house 2 Andover
Whipple John H. sailmaker, Phillips' whf. house 4 Arabella
Whipple J. Lovett Mrs. house 47 Essex
Whipple Stephen & Bro. (*Albert Whipple*), gum copal works,
    rear 35 Turner, house 12 Hardy
Whipple Stephen L. clerk (B.), boards 12 Hardy   [Andover
Whipple William H. bookkeeper, Mer. National Bank, house 2
Whirling Edward, fireman, house 164 Bridge
Whitaker William, boards 1 Rust
Whitcomb Jared P. grocer, 108 Boston, house 10 do.
White Andrew, laborer, house 26 Ward
White Benjamin R. mason, St. Peter's court, h. 68 Washington
White Benjamin R. (*S. & B. R.*), 66 Washington
White Charles H. tripe dealer, boards 116 Prospect
White Christopher, mason, house 10 River
White Elizabeth A. Mrs. 17 March
White Francis P. currier, boards 118 Lafayette
White Franklin & Co. grocers, 52 Harbor, house 29 do.
White George F. Mrs. house 13 Cedar
White Helen A. teacher, boards 13 Cedar
White James, house 10 River
White John, gardener, house 118 Lafayette
White John, currier, house 6 Pratt
White John, photographist, 224 Essex, house 73 North
White Mary Ann, widow, boards 15 Allen
White Sarah E. seamstress, house 15 Allen [ton, boards 68 do.
White S. & B. R. hay, lime and country produce, 66 Washing-
White Thomas, currier, house Pope's court
White William, restaurant, 6 Washington, house 27 Norman
White William, laborer, house 14 Congress
White Winslow, carpenter, house 50 Harbor
Whitehouse Martha J. Mrs. house 22 Lemon

Roxbury Directory, Published by Sampson, Davenport, & Co.
(formerly Adams, Sampson, & Co.) **47 Congress St., Boston.**

Whitford Mary, tailoress, house 8 Church
Whitmore Anna, teacher, house 73 Bridge
Whitmore Benjamin, house 13 Pickman
Whitmore Sarah, widow, house 4 Woodbury court
Whitmore Stephen, house 73 Bridge
Whitmore William W. (B.), house 67½ Essex
Whitney Abram, shoemaker, boards 1 Salem
Whitney Richard S. carriage trimmer and harnessmaker, 11
    Church, house 43 Lafayette
Whitney William W. laborer, house 8 Webb
Whittemore Samuel, house 23 Summer
Whitten William, cigarmaker, house Peabody, corner Ward
Wiggin Abigail Mrs. house 1 Federal
Wiggin Asa A. cabinetmaker, house 9 Skerry
Wiggin Benjamin T. painter, house rear 89 North
Wiggin Edward P. clerk (B.), boards 8 Leach
Wiggin George F. house 18 English   [house 28 Howard
Wiggin (*Levi*) & Munroe (*Stephen N.*), provisions, 11 Essex,
Wiggin (*Nathaniel*) & Clark (*Charles S.*), wood, coal, &c., 29
    Peabody, house 48 Endicott
Wiggin Pierce L. Mrs. house 9 Daniels
Wiggin Sarah B. and Mary E. seamstresses, house 1 Federal
Wiggin Thomas Mrs. house 9 Elm
Wiggin Thomas H. assistant Postmaster, house 9 Elm
Wiihr Lorrence W. variety store, 52 Endicott, house do.
Wildes George D. Rev. house Lynde, corner Washington
Wiley George H. shoemaker, house 13 Lemon
Wiley John G. carpenter, house 37 Salem
Wiley Margie D. widow, house 7 Oliver
Wiley Moses, mariner, house 37 Salem
Wilkens James, mariner, boards 5 Northey
Wilkins Albert, tanner, 50 Boston, house 157 Federal
Wilkins Albert jr. currier, house 9 May   [15 Williams
Wilkins Charles, blacksmith and horseshoer, 28 Liberty, house
Wilkins Charles F. expressman, h. 16 Church
Wilkins Charles R. master mariner, house 97 Essex
Wilkins Hezekiah, house 6 Bentley
Wilkins Hezekiah jr. watchman, Naumkeag Co. h. 1 Barton
Wilkins John G. house 92 Boston
Wilkins John H. tanner, rear 50 Boston, house 92 do.
Wilkins Joseph A. tanner, boards 157 Federal
Wilkins Michael C. baker, house 131 North
Wilkins Rufus P. painter, house 92 Boston
Willard Frederick, laborer, house 43 Union
Willey George M. laborer, boards 22 Derby
Willey Mark L. shoemaker, house 22 Derby
Willey Mark L. jr. boards 22 Derby
Willey William, captain, house 30 Pleasant
Williams Abraham, laborer, house 53 Forrester
Williams Andrew A. hairdresser, 6 Wash. house 38 Salem

Salem Directory, Published by Sampson, Davenport, & Co.
(formerly Adams, Sampson, & Co.) 47 Congress St., Boston.

Williams Charles, tanner, house 20 Vale
Williams Charles C. mariner, boards 15 Becket
Williams Charles F. Mrs. house 5 Monroe
Williams Eli C. miller, boards 49 Mill
Williams Emma Mrs. Seaman's Orphan Soc. 7 Carpenter
Williams George, laborer, house 22 Cedar
Williams George W. (6 Commercial whf. B.), boards 5 Monroe
Williams Henry, shoemaker, house rear 95 Boston
Williams Henry, varnisher, house foot of Lemon
Williams Henry L. merchant, house 342 Essex
Williams Horace P. at Salem Leg Co's. boards 33 Summer
Williams James S. boards 5 Monroe
Williams John jr. freightman, house 15 Becket
Williams John H. mariner, boards 15 Becket
Williams John S. Mrs. house 3 Federal court
Williams John S. clerk, 26 S. Market (B.), bds. 3 Federal ct.
Williams Julia A. widow, house 20 Vale
Williams Mary A. Mrs. washerwoman, house 22 Cedar
Williams Nathaniel D. miller, house 14 Goodhue
Williams Samuel G. cooper, boards 36 Salem
Williams Thomas, cabinetmaker, house 48 Charter
Williams Thomas Mrs. house 36 Salem
Williams Thomas F. laborer, house 10 Porter
Williams Thomas Jefferson, shoemaker, boards 89 North
Williams Urban R. currier, rear 44 Boston, house Summit
Williams William A. (U. S. engineer) Custom House, boards
    Essex House
Williamson Thomas H. cooper, house 1 Blaney
Willis George D. painter, house 15 Dean
Willis John Mrs. house 16 Oliver
Willis John G. com. mer. (N. Y.), house 26 St. Peter
Willis William H. tailor, 185 Essex, boards 16 Oliver
Williston Samuel S. sawfiler, 60 Charter, house do.
Willoughby Charles D. machinist, house 24 Barr
Willson Edmund B. Rev. house 5 Barton square
Wilson Asa A. machinist, boards 10 Carpenter
Wilson Edward, tailor, 249 Essex, boards 7 Phelps' court
Wilson Frank B. bookkeeper, 12 Derby wharf, house at Mar-
    blehead
Wilson Frederick, currier, house 1 Ward
Wilson George, clerk, 30 Front, boards 10 Broad
Wilson George A. shoemaker, boards 2 Dow
Wilson George W. currier, house 216 Derby
Wilson Hugh, gardener, house 6 Hamilton, near Essex
Wilson Jabez, blacking manuf., house 14 High street court
Wilson Jacob, lobster dealer, house 32 Bridge
Wilson Jacob H. mariner, house 10 Barton
Wilson James, laborer, house 216 Derby
Wilson Mary, widow, house 3 Melcher's court
Wilson Mary, widow, house 10 Broad

Wilson Mary B. milliner, 250 Essex, house at S. Danvers
Wilson Oliver, at F. R. L. mills, h. Lafayette, n.F. R. L. mills
Wilson William H. Mrs. house 12 Cedar
Winberry Thomas, provisions, 7¼ Boston, house do.
Winchester Isaac, stairbuilder, house 6 Winthrop
Winchester Jacob, house 97 Boston
Winchester Silas Mrs. boards 97 Bridge
Winkley Enoch, boards 2 Williams
Winn Daniel D. Rev. house 56 Lafayette
Winn George H. Front, corner Washington, house 6 Everett
Winn John K. house 74 Essex
Winn Joseph, house 121 Federal
Winn Mary, widow, house 56 Lafayette
Winn Silas B. brewer, Front, cor. Washington, h. 5 Margin
Winson John (*Shaw & W.*), crockery, glass, &c. 8 Lafayette,
    house 24 North
Winters Mary Mrs. house 2 Pingree, near Harbor
Wippich John, coffinmaker, at H. G. Hubon's, h. 6 Church
Wise George H. Mrs. confectioner, 271 Essex, house 265 do.
Wise John, shoemaker, house 60 Broad
Wise Mary D. boardinghouse, 67 Harbor
Wise Thomas, clerk, boards 67 Harbor
Wise William H. Naumkeag mill, house 9 Ward
Wittenhagen John, mariner, house 16 Derby
Wogan James, coachman, house rear 22 Charter
Wood Catharine, widow, house 25 Summer
Wood George, shoemaker, house 78 North
Wood James, painter, house 49 Washington
Wood James S. coffinmaker, at H. G. Hubon's, h. 47 Wash.
Wood Leonard S. at Laboratory, house 120 North
Wood Patrick, laborer, house foot Pingree
Wood William P. watchman, house 15 Crombie
Woodberry Emily, widow, house 22 Lynde
Woodbury Charles, mason, house 7 Woodbury's court
Woodbury Edmund, wheelwright, house 26 Liberty
Woodbury Eliza A. widow, house 60 North   [males
Woodbury Elizabeth and Margaret Misses, Home for Aged Fe-
Woodbury Ezra, carpenter, 126 Bridge, house 15 Northey
Woodbury Ezra L. clerk, boards 15 Northey
Woodbury George H. mason, house 18 Whittemore
Woodbury Harriet, widow, house 36 Norman
Woodbury Isaiah Mrs. house 14 Northey
Woodbury James, tanner, house 18 Whittemore
Woodbury Susan A. L. Mrs. house 15 Northey
Woodman Edwin W. driver bakecart, house 1 Phelps' court
Woodman George S. associate superintendent Salem Leg Co.
    High street, house 1 Holly
Woodman Henry F. principal Hacker School, b. Essex House
Woods Dominic, Naumkeag mill, boards 16 Congress
Woods Ephraim, horticulturist, house 122 North

Woods James, Naumkeag mill, boards 16 Congress
Woods Margaret, widow, house 16 Congress
Woodward E. S. milliner, 252½ Essex, boards 23 Harbor
Woodworth Albert, mariner, boards 32 Derby
Wooster Edward B. clerk, 181 Essex, boards 11 Washington
Worcester Elizabeth, widow, house 7 Dean
Worcester Frank, shoemaker, house 47 Broad
Worcester Jonathan F. house 31 Pleasant
Worcester Samuel M. Rev. D. D. house 6 Carpenter
Works John C., Essex Railroad, house 6 Northey
Wormell Catharine, widow, house 49 Derby
Worthen Henry G. carpenter, house 122 Boston
Wright Ann Mrs. house rear 14 Central
Wright Charles W. mariner, house 15 Daniels
Wright David Mrs. house Porter court
Wright David A. clerk, house Porter court
Wright John, shoemaker, house 44 Broad
Wright John, shoemaker, house 10 English
Wright Lois R. teacher, High School, boards 5 Barton square
Wright Nathaniel, shoemaker, house 1 Salem
Wright Peter E. Mrs. house 5 Saunders   [12 Harbor
Wright William D. (*I. South & Co.*), grocer, 33 Lafayette, h.
Wrin John, laborer, house 32 Union
Wruck F. A. watchmaker, 262 Essex, boards 13 Margin
Wyman Charles, blacksmith, boards 21 Lafayette
Wyman Isaac C. counsellor (B.), h. Lafayette, n. Marbl. line
Wyman Matilda F. Mrs. house 21 Mall
Wyman Theodore A. carpenter, house 29 Williams

YESINSKI EDWARD A. tobacconist, boards 21 Lafayette
York Benjamin F. mariner, boards 6 Perkins
York Daniel R. laborer, house 6 Perkins
York Edward W. house South Salem
Young Aaron C. carpenter, house foot of Lemon
Young Eunice, widow, house 24 Barr
Young Stephen, mason, boards 10 Leach
Young William A. mariner, house 10 Lagrange

New England Directory, Published by Sampson, Davenport, &
Co. (formerly Adams, Sampson, & Co.) 47 Congress St., Boston.

BUSINESS DIRECTORY

CITY OF SALEM.

Accordeon, (*Repairing and Tuning.*)
FOGG JULIAN A. & CO. 237 Essex

Agricultural Tools.
ADAMS, RICHARDSON & CO. 215 Essex [see adv. dept. p. 5]
HALE HENRY, 228 Essex [see adv. dept. p. 4]

Apothecaries.
Barton Gardner, 124 Essex
Brooks W. A. 33½ Lafayette
Chamberlain J. W. 1 Boston
EMERTON JAMES, 119 Essex [see adv. dept. p. 7]
FARRINGTON GEORGE P. 310 Essex, cor. North [see adv. dept. p. 19]
Pinkham Chas. H. 288 Essex
Pratt Henry J. & Co. 137 Essex
PRICE C. H. & J. 226 Essex, Browne's block [see adv. inside front cover]
Webb Wm. 54 Essex
WEBB WM. JR. 159½ Essex [see adv. front colored page]

Architects.
Emmerton & Foster, 26 Asiatic bldg
LORD & FULLER, 243½ Essex [see adv. dept. p. 47]

Artificial Limbs.
SALEM LEG CO. 22 High [see adv. back cover]

Artist's Materials.
BROOKS D. B. & Bro. 201 Essex

Auctioneers.
ARCHER WM. jr. 34 Front and 18 Wash. [see adv. dept. p. 2]
Colman Benj. 7½ Washington
NICHOLS JOHN H. 42 Washington [see miscellaneous dept. page 205]

Bakers.
Eaton N. J. 29 Brown
Gardner Simon, 24 Turner
Goss, Frye & Co. 87 North
Hathaway E. 72 Washington
Hathaway John, 416 Essex
Jelly Charles H. 10 Cedar

NELLES A. C. 72½ North [see adv. dept. p. 87]
Pease & Price, 13 High
Preston John, 53½ Summer
ROGERS S. F. 170 and 172 Essex [see adv. dept. p. 87]
Stowe V. C. head Phillips' wharf
Thompson George J. 28 Broad
Tibbetts A. J. 46 Pleasant
Watts Charles, 53 Derby

Baths.
Gardner Edward E. 148 Bridge

Billiard Hall.
CLYNES F. H. 4 Derby sq. [see adv. dept. p. 45] '

Blacksmiths.
AGGE JACOB, 20 Peabody [see adv. dept. p. 42]
ANDREWS GILMAN, 27 Beach [see adv. dept. p. 44]
Church Samuel, 3 Laboratory
Cox & Averill, Bridge, cor. North
Curtis Benjamin, 8 Sewall
Goodhue J. B. 3 Cambridge
NICHOLS JOHN, 45 Union [*ship-smith*] [see adv. dept. p. 42]
Peirson George H. West place
Perry Francis L. Phillips' wharf
SHOULES CHARLES J. Jeffrey ct. [see adv. dept. p. 44]
Walton Josiah, 131 Boston
Weir Daniel P. Endicott, cor. Mill
Wilkins Charles, 28 Liberty

Blank Book Manufacturer.
PERLEY J. 194 Essex [see adv. dept. p. 7]

Bleachers. (*Bonnet.*)
Clapp & Wetherell, 8 Sewall

Boarding Houses.
Anketell Edward, 176 Derby
Button Prentiss, 59 to 64 Harbor
Dorman Joseph Mrs. 24 St. Peter
Doyle Thomas, 33 Summer
Gallagher Thomas A. Mrs. 7 Church
Kimball Dorcas, 23 North

Knapp William H. 1 Sewall
Milan James, 129 Derby
Prentiss Alexander, 2 Jeffrey court
Reed John, 9 Higginson square.
Rollins Sarah J. 21 Lafayette
Stanley T. 3 Pleasant
Whiley Rebecca, 32 Derby

Boat Builders and Spar Makers.
Becket & Fellows, Salem Marine Railway
Leech William, 205 Derby

Boats, &c.
Hatch L. B. 113 Derby

Bone Dealer.
WALTON TIMOTHY, foot of Ord [see adv. dept. p. 23]

Bookbinders.
Ives Henry P. 232 Essex
PERLEY JONA. 194 Essex [see adv. dept. p. 7]

Books, Periodicals, & Stationery.
BROOKS D. B. & BRO. 201 Essex [see adv. 2d back colored page]
Chandler & Co. 4 Washington
Ives Henry P. 232 Essex
Ives J. S. 281 Essex
Moody L. B. 22 Washington
PHILLIPS A. MRS. 9 Central [see adv. dept. p. 9]
WHIPPLE GEO. M. & A. A. SMITH, 243 Essex [see adv. front colored page]
WHIPPLE HEN'Y, 243 Essex [charts]

Boot & Shoe Dealers.
BENNETT ABRAHAM, 159 Essex [see adv. dept. p. 7]
BOSSON & GLOVER, 10 Lafayette [see adv. dept. p. 15]
BOTT THOMAS, 46 Derby [see adv. dept. p. 17]
Buswell & Morton, 196 Essex
Chapman William H. 246 Essex
Flint Harrison O. 210 Essex
LOW AARON T. 76 Boston [see adv. dept. p. 18]
Mackintire I. K. 4 Norman
MARTIN & CUNNINGHAM, 145 Essex [see adv. dept. p. 17]
O'CONNELL TIMOTHY, 299 Essex [see adv. dept. p. 15]
PALMER THERON, 216 Essex [see adv. dept. p. 17]
Perley John, 252 Essex
SOUTH & HOWARD, 19 Lafayette [see adv. dept. p. 15]
Sweetser Ephraim & Co. 239 Essex
SYMONDS J. W. & CO. 221 Essex [see adv. dept. p. 15]
Taylor William H. 3 Central

Boot and Shoe Makers.
Armstrong Thomas, 39 Federal
Barnes Joseph, rear 201 Essex
Bartlett H. S. 5 North
BOTT THOMAS, 46 Derby [see adv. dept. p. 17]

CARTY J. H. on Union Bridge [see adv. dept. p. 19]
Collins Thomas, 85 Derby
Darcy John, Aborn, near Boston
Dodge William M. 3 Lemon
Donovan Michael, rear 168 Derby
Friend Joel, Aborn, near Boston
Gallison Joseph E. rear 89 Essex
Hay J. A. 81 Bridge
Henderson S. 37 Brown
Jordan Michael, 34 Union
Kimball Alfred M. 23 North
Lake George C. 150 Essex
Law George D. 12 Norman
LOW AARON T. 76 Boston [see adv. dept. p. 18]
Marren John, 165 Essex
MARTIN & CUNNINGHAM, 145 Essex [see adv. dept. p. 17]
McGuire John, at City Scales
O'CONNELL TIMOTHY, 299 Essex [see adv. dept. p. 15]
Perry H. W. 6 Central
Proctor William, Cedar, cor. Cabot
Rice Andrew J. 9½ St. Peter
Shatswell Moses, 28 Andrew
SOUTH & HOWARD, 19 Lafayette [see adv. dept. p. 15]
Stetson J. 31 North
Taylor William H. 3 Central

Boot & Shoe Manufacturers.
DRIVER STEPHEN, 84½ Front [see adv. dept. p. 16]
Riley James, Bridge, cor. Washington
Larabee Somers, 37 North
Lake Harrison H. 150 Essex [heeler]
Lake Geo. C. 150 Essex
Punchard J. P. 24 Winthrop [gaiter boots]
SIBLEY GEORGE, 21 Central [see adv. dept. p. 17]
Sibley George V. 21 Central
McCurdy Thomas G. 144 Essex
SALEM BOOT AND SHOE CO. Robert Chase, Supt.; Jona. A. Kenny, Treas. [see adv. dept. p. 16]

Boot & Shoe Stock.
(Soles, Stiffenings, Heels, &c.)
COLLIER JOHN H. 15 Lafayette [see adv. dept. p. 18]
Cusick Patrick, rear 4 Warren court
Gardiner John, 137 Boston
Green & McCarty, 123 Boston
HENDERSON & CO. 150 Essex [see adv. dept. p. 18]
Powers John, rear 55 Warren

Box Manufacturers.
(See Paper Box Manufacturers.)

Brass Founder and Finisher.
Waters A. S. 6 Franklin

Brewers.
WINN S. B. Front, cor. Washington [cellar] [see adv. dept. p. 9]

Brick Maker.
Neal Benj. B. 10 Franklin [fire]

Brokers.

(*Real Estate and Stock.*)

ARCHER WM. jr. 34 Front and 18 Washington [see adv. dept. p. 2]
NICHOLS JOHN H. [*stock*] 42 Washington [see miscellaneous department p. 205]
PEIRCE N. [*stock*] 161 Essex [see adv. dept. p. 60]

Butter and Cheese.

NELSON J. S. 26 Front [see adv. dept. p. 24]

Button Holes.

MOORE SAMUEL, 158 Essex [see adv. dept. p. 6]

Cabinet Makers.

Fellows Israel, 205 Essex
HUBON HENRY G. 59 Washington [*coffins*] [see adv. dept. p. 40]
Saunders John J. 4 Lafayette
Very Nathaniel jr. 274 Essex
WALLIS JOSEPH, 218 Essex [see adv. dept. p. 89]

Candle Manufacturer.

ROBERTSON S. W. rear 44 Boston [see adv. dept. p. 27]

Car Builders.

Salem Car Co. 49 Bridge

Carpenters and Builders.

Balcomb H. W. Phillips, near Grove
Barker Jacob, 89 North
Blake A. S. 29 Liberty
Blinn Geo. H. 40 Bridge
BROWN GEO. A. & C. A. 158 Derby [see adv. dept. p. 47]
Brown James M. Bridge, opposite St. Peter
Coffin C. South Railway [*ship*]
Copeland R. M. 8 North
Danforth S. G. 31 Endicott
DAY ALBERT, 16 Lafayette [see adv. dept. p. 48]
Dennis D. r. 17 Lafayette
Edwards John S. North
ELWELL CHARLES B. 98 Peabody [see adv. dept. p. 46]
Fairfield James, jr. head Derby wf.
FULLER E. P. 11 Beckford [see adv. dept. p. 46]
Gardner Wm. F. 32 Norman
Gifford T. J. & Co. rear Carpenter
Goldthwait & Day, 221 Derby
HAMOND WM. C. 113 Derby [*ship*] [see adv. dept. p. 52]
Harris D. M. 41 North
Hawes Wm. Prospect
Honeycomb Thomas P. 27 North
Honeycomb Wm. H. 14 Cross
Honeycomb S. R. 21 Margin
Hood David B. foot of Turner
Lord J. B. 144 Bridge
Lovejoy John, 108 Essex
Melcher Edward, 63 North
Ober Andrew, r. 54 Charter

Perkins E. B. 11 Cherry
Roberts Joseph W. 12 Herbert
Russell & Lord, 15 Forrester
Saul Easton, foot of Friend
Smith Aaron, jr. 3 Howard
SMITH JAS. A. 10 Walnut [see adv. dept. p. 48]
Stiles Dean, 16 Endicott
Towle Abraham, Webster
Upton Moses T. 7 Walnut
Walker P. D. 7 Boston
Woodbury Ezra, 126 Bridge

Carpetings.

DAMON S. H. [second hand] 5 Liberty [see adv. dept. p. 6]
DOWNING THOS. W. & Co. 179 Essex [see adv. dept. p. 10]
GOLDTHWAIT WILLARD, 151 Essex [see adv. dept. p. 11]
Ide Edwin R. 220 Essex
Pulsifer N. 11 Spring [*painted*]

Carpet Makers.

Daland Joanna, 12 Beckford
Pulsifer Nathaniel [oil cloth] 9 Spring

Carriage Builders.

ADAMS PETER F. 28 Endicott [see adv. dept. p. 44]
ANDREWS GILMAN, 27 Beach [see adv. dept. p. 44]
Batchelder Joseph, 35 North
Dodge J. W. 29 & 31 Liberty
LATIONS J. P. Jeffrey court [see adv. dept. p. 44]
Loring Edward D., West place
SHOULES C. J., Jeffrey court [see adv. dept. p. 44]
Stocker John W. r. 66 Washington
Tuttle Hiram A. [trimmer] West pl.

Carriage Dealer.

Chase William, 206 Essex

Carriage Repository.

ROBBINS THOS. A. r. 161 Essex [see adv. dept. p. 21]

Carriage Springs.

SHOULES CHARLES J., Jeffrey ct. [see adv. dept. p. 44]

Charcoal.

MANNING R. C. & Co. 188 Derby [see adv. dept. p. 55]

Chasers. (*Gold and Silver.*)

FOGG JULIAN A. & CO. 287 Essex [see card on front colored page]

Cigar Makers.

BATTIS & BROWN, 80 Front [see adv. dept. p. 24]
BOWELL FREDERICK, jr. 130 Derby [see adv. dept. p. 23]
Skinner R. 64 Federal
Skinner S. S. & Co. 4 St. Peter
TABOUR WM. 162 Essex and 7 North [see adv. dept. p. 24]

Cigar Box Manufacturer.

Walton Joseph, 147 Boston

Civil Engineer.

Putnam Charles A. 251 Essex

Claim Agent.

Porter John W. 243½ Essex

Clergymen.

Atwood Edward S. 81 Summer
Beane Samuel C. 9 Williams
Briggs G. W. 9 Summer
Cook Wm. 44 Charter
Crowell Lomnus, 2 Harbor st. court
Daly Wm. J. 152 Federal
Emerson Brown, 377 Essex
Felt Joseph B. 17 Norman
Hartney Michael, 22 Union
Haskell Augustus M. 5 Carpenter
Jewett Geo. B. 50 Federal
Johnson S. jr. 2 Chestnut
Mills R. C. 119 Federal
Palmer Chas. Ray, 14 Northey
Pickman Wm. R. 15 Winter
Quinban James [asst.] 22 Union
Russell John L. 22 Lafayette
Spaulding W. 15 Pleasant
Very Jones, 154 Federal
Wildes Geo. D. Lynde, cor. Washington
Wilson E. B. 5 Barton so.
Winn Daniel D. 56 Lafayette
Worcester S. M. 6 Carpenter

Cloaks and Mantillas.

ALMY JAMES F. & Co. 188 Essex
[see card on front cover]
ARCHER A. J. & Co. 181 Essex [see
adv. dept. p. 12]
BLACK & Co. 149 Essex [see adv.
dept. p. 14]
SHEPARD J. B. & S. D. 178 Essex
[see adv. dept. p. 11]
Symonds Eliza M. 98 Federal

Clothing & Furnishing Goods.

Ashton Wm. B. 225 Essex
BENNETT ABRAHAM, 159 Essex
[see adv. dept. p. 7]
BROWN WM. P. 198 Essex [see adv.
dept. p. 1]
BURBECK W. H. 249 Essex [see adv.
dept. p. 2]
Carpenter D. P. 211 Essex
Chamberlain Samuel, 282 Essex
Cross J. S. 219 Essex
DAMON S. H. [second hand] 5 Liber-
ty [see adv. dept. p. 8]
Jones S. G. 186 Essex
Lefavour Thos. H. 197 Essex
MACKENZIE R. A. 287 Essex [see
adv. dept. p. 3]
Norris Chas. H. 189 Essex, c. Central
PALMER WM. H. 247 Essex [see adv.
dept. p. 4]
Peck F. S. 240 Essex
Perkins, Smith, & Co. 44 Washington
Quinn & Kelley, 203 Essex
Saroni E. Mrs. [children's] 154 Essex

Coach Office.

18 Central street

Coal and Wood.

(See Wood and Bark.)
BROOKS A. T. 117 Derby [see adv.
dept. p. 22]
Clark Patrick, 169 Derby
Dodge J. L. 17 Lafayette [bark]
Grover J. Hunt's wharf
HATCH L. B. 118 Derby [bark] [see
adv. dept. p. 54]
MANNING R. C. & Co. 189 Derby
[see adv. dept. p. 55]
PHILLIPS W. P. Phillips' wharf [see
adv. back colored page]
Sanborn G. & F. T. 115 Derby
WIGGIN & CLARK, 29 Peabody [see
adv. dept. p. 52]

Coffin Warehouses.

BUFFUM CHAS. S. 43 Washington
[see adv. dept. p. 41]
HUBON HENRY G. 56 Wash. [see
adv. dept. p. 40]

Commission Merchants.

ARCHER WM. 18 Washington and 34
Front [see adv. dept. p. 2]
GAYLE & CO. Phillips' wharf [see
adv. dept. p. 22]
JONES J. S. & Co. Pierce's wharf [see
adv. dept. p. 22]
NELSON J. S. 26 Front [see adv. dept.
p. 24]
PHILLIPS W. P., Phillips' wharf [see
adv. back colored page]

Confectioners.

Needham J. S. 272 Essex
Pepper Thos. S. 71 Bridge
ROBERTS E. F. & J. W. 209 Essex
[see adv. dept. p. 28]
ROGERS S. F. 170 and 172 Essex [see
adv. dept. p. 37]
SIMON STEPHEN A. 160 Essex [see
adv. dept. p. 18]
Wise G. H. Mrs. 271 Essex

Consul, (British.)

Miller E. F. 112 Derby

Coopers.

BATTIS JOHN, 147 Derby [see adv.
dept. p. 35]
Farley Henry, 10 Hancock
FLORENCE T. T. 22 Cedar [see adv.
dept. p. 35]
Getchell Benj. W. head Phillips' whf.
Nichols Wm. H. Brookhouse wharf
ROWELL EDWARD, Webb's wharf
[see adv. dept. p. 35]

Cordage.

CHISHOLM JOS. 66 Mill [manilla]
[see adv. dept. p. 18]

Corsets.

FOLLETTE L. B. 186 Essex [see adv.
dept. p. 10]
PORTER M. A. 286 Essex [see adv.
dept. p. 12]
Twombly E. A. 242 Essex

Counsellors.

ABBOTT A. A. 24 Washington [see card on p.opp. 8. Danvers Directory]
Almon A. B. 27 Norman
Bancroft S. C. 27 Washington
Chever George F. 11 Hardy
Choate Geo. F. Court House
Cogswell Wm. 214 Essex
Flint Geo. F. 194 Essex
Gillis James A. 243½ Essex
Holden Nathaniel J. 218 Essex
Huntington A. Court House
Ives & Lincoln, 27 Washington
Kimball Charles, 226½ Essex
Kimball Charles A. 226½ Essex
Kimball D. B. 24 Washington
Lincoln Solomon, jr. 27 Washington
Lord Geo. R. 236½ Essex
Lord Nathaniel J. 6 Brown
Mansfield Micajah B. 226½ Essex
Northend Wm. D. 24 Washington
Osgood Chas. S. 243½ Essex
Osgood J. B. F. 235 Essex
Perkins J. C. 243½ Essex
Perry & Endicott, 182 Essex
Phillips Stephen B. 243½ Essex
Phillips & Gillis, 243½ Essex
Porter John W. 243½ Essex
Rantoul R. S. 251 Essex
Safford Daniel E. 251 Essex
Sewall Charles, 214 Essex
Stimpson T. M. 194 Essex
Story Augustus, 27 Washington
Upham Wm. P. 224 Essex
Waters Jos. G., Police Ct. room
Webb Stephen P. City Hall
Wheatland Geo. 194 Essex
Wheatland S. G. 194 Essex

Crockery, Glass, & China Ware.

Bowditch Wm. A. 227 Essex
Glazier Ezra & Son, 28 Central
Peele Robert, 282 Essex
Ropes Timothy, 214 Essex
SHAW & WINSON, 6 Lafayette [see adv. dept. p. 1]
SIMONDS S. C. & E. A. 32 Front [see adv. dept. page 25]

Curled Hair Factory.

English Wm. G. r. 40 Bridge

Carriers.

(See Leather Dressers, &c.)

Andrews Gilman A. 27 Beach
Austin Wm. r. May street court
Bott James, rear 27 Boston
Bott Wm. rear 27 Boston
Braden James, 47 Boston
Bruce Geo. W. 68 Boston
Carleton Frazier, 14 Franklin
Conrey James H. foot of Buffum
Conway J. H. r. 68 Mason
Culliton John, r. 91 Mason
Dalton Joseph A. 61 Mason
Dugan James, r. 95 Mason
Egan Martin, foot of Buffum
Evans A. A. & Sons, r. 9 Mason
Fanning James, r. 46 Boston

Frye Daniel Grove, opp. Goodhue
Gibney John, 11 Beach
Harrington Charles, Boston
Harrington L. B. 428 Essex
Haskell Daniel C. 78 Mason
Horton Nathaniel, foot of Buffum
Huse John, 59 Boston
Looby Thos. Grove, n. Milldam
Madigan & Brennan, Goodhue
Martin Wm. P. foot of Dean
McCarty M., Buffum, n. Mason
Nichols Thomas, 10 Goodhue
Noah George G., Nichols
Parshley & Shaw, 35 Boston
Perkins Joseph S. 59 Boston
Pitman B. & G. 24 Boston
Pitman S. jr. 2 Goodhue, n. Boston
Pratt Elisha, 71 Mason
Proctor Thomas E., Grove, near Mason
Putnam Jacob & Co. 68 Boston
Redmon John, r. 41 North
Riley James, Franklin, n. North
Robson Matthew, 69 Mason
Sanborn & Brown, r. 11 Mason
Stimpson James B. r. 43 Boston
Thorndike Wm. D. Hanson
Treadwell Nathaniel R. 11 Franklin
Tuttle Nathaniel, 21 Boston
Varney W., D. & S. 82 Boston
Walden Joseph F. 48 Boston
Weston Charles & Sons, May
Williams U. R. r. 44 Boston

Curriers' Tables and Tools.

GRANT JOSHUA B. 51 Boston [see adv. dept. p. 35].

Dentists.

Batchelder J. H. 20 Washington
Bates Wm. M. 46 Washington
BOWDOIN & SHEPARD, 208 Essex, (Residence 57 Washington)
Currier Geo. H. 22 Washington
DUDLEY A. S. & CO. 224 Essex [see adv. on back cover]
Farnum Joseph jr. 22 Washington
Fisk Joseph E. 11 Washington

Dining Saloons.

Abbott J. H. 12 Market sq.
HOLBROOK J. 5 Derby sq. [see adv. dept. p. 29]
MORRIS JOSEPH B. 18 and 20 Derby sq. [see adv. dept. p. 30]
ROGERS S. F. 170 and 172 Essex [see adv. dept. p. 37]
Smith Edward P. 25 Front
TIBBETTS R. S. 54 Washington [see adv. dept. p. 36]

Distiller.

Hodges Samuel R. 17 Elm

Drain Pipe.

FLINT SIMEON, 221 Derby [see adv. dept. p. 49]
GOSS F. P. 7 St. Peter [see adv. dept. p. 19]
WHITE B. R. St. Peter ct. [see adv. dept. p. 19]

Dressmakers.

Atkins Mary A. Walter, cor. Dodge
Bartlett M. W. Mrs. 24 Liberty
Boden Lucy A. 100 Derby
Breed Rebecca, 57 Summer
Brown Calvin Mrs. 4 Endicott
Byrne Julia, 86 Derby
Coombs Elizabeth, 51 North
Chew Anna J. 150 Essex
Davis H. L. 155 Essex
Dewing Dolly, 16 Central
Dimond Abigail, Botts Court
Docknam M. A. 397 Essex
Flannigan Maria, 40 Union
Ford Mary L. 18 Fowler
Gardner Martha, 59 Mill
Hewett D. R. Mrs. 168 Essex
Jelly M. H. 12 Winthrop
Lee Olive C. Mrs. 8 Phillips
Laskey Mary E. 182 Essex
Mills Elizabeth H. 6 Pond
Morrill Anna M. 86 Mill
Mullen Mary A. 50 Charter (cloak)
Phelps V. J. Mrs. 10 Sewall
Plummer Sarah, 30 Lynde
Ropes L. J. 80 Mill
Sadler Harriet M. 7 Pleasant
Savory Mary, 21 Beckford
Thayer Nancy, 30 Broad
Ward Louisa H. 157 Essex
Waters Lucy B. Mrs. r. 106 Essex
Weeks Dudley Mrs. 9 Mason

Druggists.

(See Apothecaries.)

Dry Goods.

(See Laces, Hosiery, Gloves, etc.)

ALMY JAMES F. & CO. 169 Essex
[see adv. on front cover]
ARCHER AUGUSTUS J. & Co. 181
Essex [see adv. dept. p. 12]
Batchelder Anna, 202 Essex
BLACK & Co. 149 Essex [see adv.
dept. p. 14]
Bray Ann R. 76 Federal
BROWNING & LONG, 177 Essex
[see adv. dept. p. 13]
Daniels Geo. P. & Wm. K. 190 Essex
Dix Asa C. 245 Essex
DOWNING THOS. W. & Co. 179 Es-
sex [see adv. dept. p. 10]
Gavett Wm. R. 192 Essex
Hill W. & R. 277 Essex
Huntoon F. W. L. 222 Essex
Ide Edwin R. 229 Essex
Lynch D. 94 Derby
Pond J. S. 29 Lafayette
SHEPARD J. B. & S. D. 173 Essex
[see adv. dept. p. 11]
Shillaber S. 253 Essex
Tuttle Francis W. 167 Essex

Dyer.

ROLES SAMUEL jr. 7 Franklin [see
adv. dept. p. 11]

Engravers.

FOGG JULIAN A. & Co. 287 Essex
[see adv. front colored page]

Essences and Extracts.

FLINT & GOLDTHWAIT, 4 Cambridge [see adv. dept. p. 56]

Expresses.

Andrews' (Essex), 17 Market sq.
Burnhams' (Lynn), 13 Central
Canney & Co. (New Hampshire), 7
Washington
Davis's (Boston), 6 Washington
Dow's (Manchester), 17 Market sq.
Eastern Express Co. (Maine), 7 Wash-
ington
Gillett & Co. (Newburyport and Row-
ley), 7 Washington
Gould's (North Danvers), 7 Washing-
ton
Haraden (Boston), basement Asiatic
Building
Jackson & Co.'s (Portsmouth), 7 Wash-
ington
Janes' (Topsfield), 17 Market Square
Littlefield's (South Danvers), 7 Wash-
ington
Lummus's (Wenham), 17 Market sq.
Marshall's (Manchester and Essex), 7
Washington
Merritt & Co.'s (Boston), 14 Washing-
ton
MOULTON'S (Boston), 10 Washing-
ton [see adv. on front cover]
Muchmore's (City), 8 Church
Page's (Gloucester), 7 Washington
Parshley's (Lynn), 15 Central
Parsons' (Rockport), 7 Washington
Potter's (Boston), 34 Front
Sargent's (Lowell), 14 Washington
Saunders (Lawrence), 10 Washington
SAVORY & Co.'s (Eastern, Boston
and Southern), 7 Washington [see
adv. on back cover]
Simons' (Boston), 27 Front
Stone's (Beverly), 18 Central
Thompson's (Marblehead), 14 Wash-
ington
Webber's (South Danvers), 13 Central
Willet's (Ipswich), 14 Washington
Wilson's (Ipswich), 7 Washington

Fancy Goods.

Combs, Toys, &c, &c.

Allen Laura W. 368 Essex
Davis H. L. 155 Essex
Dressor A. & Co. 152 Essex
Moulton Nelson H. & Brother, 164 Es-
sex
Pillsbury S. H. Mrs. 284 Essex
Plumer R. Mrs. 246 Essex
PORTER M. A. 286 Essex [see adv.
dept. p. 12]
SKERRY HENRY F. 160 Essex [see
adv. dept. p. 80]
SMITH & CHAMBERLAIN, 207 Es-
sex [see adv.dept. p. 8]
Stone Lydia, 366 Essex
SYMONDS PAULINE Miss, 184 Es-
sex [see adv. dept. p. 13]
Twombly E. A. Mrs. 242 Essex
WEBB WM. jr. 159½ Essex [see adv.
on front colored page]

Fertilizers.

WALTON TIMOTHY, foot of Ord [see adv. dept. p. 23]

Fish.

COLLINS CHAS. H. 80 Derby [see adv. dept. p. 30]
Cook Geo. T. North, near the bridge
DOWBRIDGE A. jr. 21 Front [see adv. dept. p. 29]
Floyd Samuel P. 56 Bridge
Parsons & Shackelford, 64 Union
TOWNES SAMUEL, 8 and 9 Derby wharf [see adv. dept. p. 29]
TUCKER HENRY G. 4 Bridge [see adv. dept. p. 30]
West B. A. 218 Derby [dry]

Flour and Grain.

Beckford Josiah, Grove, and 48 Mill
BROOKS A. T. 117 Derby [see adv. dept. p. 22]
Bowker Brothers, 227 and 229 Derby
Clark J. W. 8 Lafayette
GAYLE & Co. Phillips wharf see adv. dept. p. 22]
JONES J. S. & Co. Pierce's wharf [see adv. dept. p. 22]
Hanson J. V. & J. 1 Front
NELSON J. S. 26 Front [see adv. dept. p. 24]
NOYES E. K. & Co. 6 Front [see adv. dept. p. 23]
ROPES CHARLES A. 165 Derby [see adv. dept. p. 26]

Florists.

Lamson Frederick, 4 Northey
Putnam F. 6 Crombie, and Mason

Fruit, &c.

Knight Foster, 48 North
Milton B. Sylvester S., Washington, c. Essex
Morrill F. A. 140 Essex
Moulton Wm. 18 Lafayette
Needham J. S. 272 Essex
Nourse Ebenezer, 41 Washington
Read J. F. 7 and 9 City Market
ROBERTS E. F. & J. W. 209 Essex, and Front, cor. Washington [see adv. dept. p. 28]
ROGERS S. F. 170 and 172 Essex [see adv. dept. p. 37]
TIBBETTS R. S. 64 Washington [see adv. dept. p. 36]

Furnaces and Ranges.

Frothingham T. H. & Co. 31 Front
ROPES J. T. 17 and 19 Front [see adv. dept. p. 2]

Furniture and Feathers.

(See Cabinet Makers.)

CURRIER & MILLETT, 261 Essex [see adv. dept. p. 38]
DAMON S. H. [second hand] 5 Liberty [see adv. dept. p. 8]
Glazier Ezra & Son, 23 Central
Haskell & Lougee, 279 Essex

Haynes P. J. 10 Front
HENDERSON & THURSTON, Washington, c. Essex [see adv. dept. p. 38]
May Calvin W. 274 Essex
Pearson George W. 3 Franklin Bldg.
SHAW & WINSON, 8 Lafayette [see adv. dept. p. 1]
WALLIS JOSEPH, 213 Essex [see adv. dept. p. 39]

Furrier.

OSBORN STEPHEN, 191 Essex [see adv. dept. p. 4]

Fur Sewer.

Cole Catharine, 10 Northey

Gas & Steam Pipes & Fixtures.

SMALL WM. F. 273 Essex [see adv. dept. p. 20]
STATEN EDWARD H. 147 Essex [see adv. front colored page]

Gas Stoves.

STATEN EDWARD H. 147 Essex [see adv. front colored page]

Gents' Furnishing Goods.

PALMER WM. H. 247 Essex [see adv. dept. p. 4]
WALKER GEO. S. 228 Essex [see adv. back cover]

Glue Manufacturer.

ANDERSON J. M. Salem Turnpike [see adv. dept. p. 36]

Government Securities.

PEIRCE N. 161 Essex [see adv. dept. p. 60]

Grain Mills.

Beckford Josiah, Grove and 41 Mill
Hanson J. V. & J. 1 and 3 Front

Granite.

BLETHEN T. G. 25 Peabody [see adv. dept. p. 50]
BUTLER, DAVIS & MERRILL, 18 Lafayette [see adv. dept. p. 48]

Drapery.

Allen J. F. Dean street

Grocers.

ALDRICH MOSES, 55 Harbor [see adv. dept. p. 34]
Arnold Peter, 137 Derby
Bartlett Alexander, 82 Derby
Barton William C. 8 Brown
Brooks Luke jr. 178 Derby
BROOKS N. H. 178 Derby [see adv. dept. p. 34]
Brown Daniel, 16 Mill
CALEF JOHN, 26 Washington [see business card top front cover]
CHAMBERLAIN, HARRIS & Co. 24 Front, cor. Derby sq. [see adv. dept. p. 27]
Chandler John, 106 Federal
Cronan Michael, 2 and 3 Norman

Emerson N. 134 Boston
FOSTER I. P. 109 Derby [see adv.
    dept. p. 34]
Foster I. P. jr. 76 and 109 Derby
Friend F. 33 Bridge
Glidden Joseph H. 18 Boston
GOODHUE W. P. 44 Derby [whole-
    sale and retail] [see adv. dept. p. 25]
Gray William B. 15 English
GWINN T. W. 410 Essex [see adv.
    dept. p. 28]
Hale Pemberton, 27 Sumner
Hall Alvan, 195 Essex
Harris I. P. 6 St. Peter
HODGKINS GEORGE L. 40 Pleasant
    [see adv. dept. p. 33]
Lindsey & Durgin, 25 Lafayette
Lyon Timothy, 38 Charter
Maguire Bernard, 12 Front
Mahoney Thomas, 110 Derby
Mann James B. 40 Boston
MILLETT JOSEPH HENRY, 67 Der-
    by [see adv. dept. p. 24]
NICHOLS DAVID A. 76 Derby, cor.
    Hardy [see adv. dept. p. 33]
Nichols William F. 107 Boston
NOYES ENOCH K. & Co. 6 and 8
    Front [see adv. dept. p. 23]
O'Donnell William, 131 Derby
PEABODY E. C. jr. & Co. 115 and
    117 Essex [see adv. dept. p. 26]
Phippen Rebecca, 10 Essex
Prime James M. 115 North
Redmond Miles, 12 Derby
Reeves William, 20 Essex
REYNOLDS M. C. & Co. 20 Front
    [see adv. dept. p. 26]
Salem Independent Protective Asso-
    ciation, 37 Endicott
Shreeve Samuel V. 225 Derby
Spiller Richard O. 162 Boston
Stevens William, 13 Derby square
Symonds B. R. 72 Federal
Symonds Joseph, 109 North
Symonds Samuel, 49 North
Symonds Thomas, 74 North
Trask James, 47 St. Peter
Very Samuel A. 22 Boston
Ward James L. 61 Bridge
WEBBER IRA J. 58 Washington [see
    adv. dept. p. 27]
Webster J. C., Essex, cor. Newbury
Whitcombe Jared P. 108 Boston
White Franklin & Co. 52 Harbor

Ground Bone.

WALTON T. foot of Ord [see adv.
    dept. p. 23]

Gum Copal Works.

Whipple Stephen & Brother, rear 35
    Turner

Gunsmith.

Perry H. B. West Place

Guns and Fishing Tackle.

ADAMS, RICHARDSON & Co. 215
    Essex [see adv. dept. p. 5]

**Gymnasium and Shooting Gal-
    lery.**
Littlefield E. L. rear 161 Essex

Hairdressers.

Babcock & Smith, 199 Essex
Cassell John M. 9 Washington
Full Joseph F. 22 Washington
Gillespie J. W. & J. A. Higginson sq.
Haskins Jason A., Higginson sq.
Osborn Josiah B. 4 Central
Ross Nathaniel, 10 Boston
Rowe J. S. 35 Washington, cor. Essex
Williams A. A. 5 Arrington's Block

Hairwork, Wigs, &c.

Babcock Cecilia, 186 Essex
Putnam C. R. 163 Essex
SKERRY HENRY F. 190 Essex [see
    adv. opp. S. Danvers Directory]

Hardware and Cutlery.

ADAMS, RICHARDSON & Co. 215
    Essex [see adv. dept. p. 5]
Chase Wm. 306 Essex
HALE HENRY, 223 Essex [see adv.
    dept. p. 4]
Peele Robert, 282 Essex
Ropes Timothy, 214 Essex
SIMONDS S. C. & E. A. 32 Front
    [see adv. dept. p. 25]

Harness Makers.

Bennett G. W. 321 Essex
Coombs F. 81 North
Cunningham John, 17 Daniels
Dayton Isaac, 135 Boston
Osgood Benjamin H. 50 Washington
Tuttle H. A. West Place
Tuttle John, 36 Boston
Watson Fenton, 414 Essex
WHITNEY RICHARD S. 11 Church
    [see adv. dept.]

Hats, Caps, Furs, &c.

Driscoll Cornelius, 128 Derby
Hood Asa, 178 Essex
Kimball William, 217 Essex
Maynes William, 35 Washington
Nourse Aaron, 37 Washington
OSBORN STEPHEN, 191 Essex [see
    adv. dept. p. 4]

Hay. (Bundle.)

HATCH L. B. 113 Derby [see adv.
    dept. p. 54]
JEWETT D. H. 205 Derby [see adv.
    dept. p. 54]
MANNING R. C. & Co. 189 Derby
    [see adv. dept. p. 55]
White S. & B. R. 66 Washington
WIGGIN & CLARK, 29 Peabody [see
    adv. dept. p. 52]

Hoop Skirts.

FOLLETTE L. B. 166 Essex [see adv.
    dept. p. 10]
PORTER M. A. 236 Essex [see adv.
    dept. p. 12]

Horse Shoers.

CLARK JAMES, West Place [see adv. dept. p. 45
Harding David, r. 26 Front
HARTIGAN PATRICK, Jeffrey court [see adv. dept. p. 43]
McGlue Peter, 3 Laboratory
Wilkins Charles, 28 Liberty.

Hosiery, Gloves, &c.

BROWNING & LONG, 177 Essex [see ad. dept. p. 13]
FOLLETTE L. B. 186 Essex [see adv. dept. p. 10]
PEABODY JOHN P. 220 Essex [see adv. back colored]
PORTER M. A. 236 Essex [see adv. dept. p. 12]

Hotel.

ESSEX HOUSE, 176 Essex, J. S. Leavitt [see adv. inside back cover]

House Furnishing Goods.

SHAW & WINSON, 8 Lafayette [see adv. dept. p. 1]
SIMONDS S. C. & E. A. 82 Front [see adv. dept. p. 26]

Ice.

Haskell Jacob, 2 Lafayette

Ice Cream Saloons.

ROGERS S. F. 170 and 172 Essex [see adv. dept. p. 37]

Inner Soles, Heels, & Stiffenings.

COLLIER JOHN H. 16 Lafayette [see adv. dept. p. 16]
HENDERSON & CO. 150 Essex [see adv. dept. p. 18]

Insurance Agents.

ARCHER WM. jr. 34 Front and 18 Wash. [see adv. dept. p. 2]
Bly J. F. 248½ Essex
Derby John H. 214 Essex
Mackintire Samuel, 218 Essex
Mackintire S. A. 27 Washington
NICHOLS JOHN H. 42 Washington [see miscellaneous dept. p. 208]
Perkins N. B. Asiatic Building (*life*)

Intelligence Offices.

Bermingham C. 80 Norman
Byrne A. E. 77 Federal

Iron Foundries.

SMITH J. R. Union St. (S. Salem) [see adv. dept. p. 42]
SMITH S. South Prospect c. East Gardner [see adv. p. 48]

Jewellers.

APPLETON GEORGE B. 187 Essex [see adv. dept. p. 1]
FOGG JULIAN A. & Co. 237 Essex (*manuf.*) [see adv. front colored p.]
Luscomb John G. 143 Essex
Mackintire J. 10 Central (*manuf.*)
SKERRY HENRY F. 180 Essex [see adv. dept. p. 60]

SMITH & CHAMBERLAIN, 207 Essex [see adv. dept. p. 3] (*manuf.*)
SMITH JESSE, 262 Essex [see adv. opp. title page]

Junk.

Crafts George, 43 Derby
Eaton John D. 33 North

Jute Bagging Manufacturer.

Salem Jute Co. Skerry, n. Bridge

Kegs and Casks.

BATTIS JOHN, 147 Derby [see adv. dept. p. 35]
FLORANCE THOMAS T. 22 Cedar [see adv. dept. p. 35]
ROWELL EDWARD, Webb's Wharf [see adv. dept. p. 35]

Laces and Trimmings.

BROWNING & LONG, 177 Essex [see adv. dept. p. 13]
Davis H. L. 155 Essex
Pillsbury S. H. 264 Essex
PEABODY JOHN P. 220 Essex [see adv. back colored page]
REITH & Co. 188 Essex [see adv. inside back cover]
Twombly E. A. 242 Essex

Ladies' Furnishing Goods.

BROWNING & LONG, 177 Essex [see adv. dept. p. 13]
PEABODY JOHN P. 220 Essex [see adv. back colored page]

Lamps and Kerosene.

HALE HENRY, 223 Essex [see adv. dept. p. 4]
SIMONDS S. C. & E. A, 82 Front (*lamps*) [see adv. dept. p. 26]

Laundress.

Phippen Mary J. 170 Bridge

Lead Pipe and Sheet Lead.

ADAMS, RICHARDSON, & Co. 215 Essex [see adv. dept. p. 5]
HART WM. H. 13 Central [see adv. dept. p. 53]

Leather.

Ferguson Thos. B. 5 Washington

Libraries. (*Circulating.*)

PHILLIPS A. Mrs. 9 Central [see adv. dept. p. 9]
WHIPPLE G. M. & A. A. SMITH, 243 Essex [see adv. front colored]

Lime and Cement.

FLINT SIMEON, 221 Derby [see adv. dept. p. 49]

Lime and Twine.

CHISHOLM JOS. 68 Mill [see adv. dept. p. 18]
Gwinn James F. 38 Bridge

Livery Stables.

(*See Stables.*)

20

Lobsters.

TUCKER HENRY G. 4 Bridge [see adv. dept. p. 30]

Lumber.

Austin Eleazer, 16 Lafayette
Brown G. F. & S. 36 & 38 North
Buffum David, 9 Front
FAXON & LOCKE (*Hard Wood*) 72 Washington [see adv. dept. p. 49]
JEWETT D. H. 205 Derby [see adv. dept. p. 54]
LANGMAID J. P. 16 Lafayette [see adv. dept. p. 52]
Putnam Nathan, 157 Derby
Thayer Oliver & Co. 190 & 199 Derby
WIGGIN & CLARKE, 29 Peabody [see adv. dept. p. 52]

Machine Forging.

AGGE JACOB, 20 Peabody [see adv. dept. p. 42]

Machine Sewing.

MOORE S. 158 Essex (*button hole*) [see adv. dept. p. 6]
Phelps Chas. 17 St. Peter
Pitcher Sarah E. 42 Lafayette
Pray Isaac C. 9 Lafayette
Pray Isaac C. jr. 232 Derby
Swasey Wm. M., St. Peter Court
Waters T. S. 81 Endicott

Machinists.

Fairfield and Getchell, 41 Boston
Goodell Zina, 16 Lafayette
GRISWOLD D. L. 142 Essex (*Sewing Machines*) [see adv. front cover]
NEWCOMB GEORGE L. 18 Peabody [see adv. dept. p. 42]
SMITH STERRY, Prospect, cor. E. Gardner [see adv. dept. p. 43]
WESTON JOHN W. rear 11 Boston [see adv. dept. p. 42]

Maps, Charts, &c., for Mariners.

WHIPPLE HENRY, 243 Essex [see front colored adv.]

Manufacturing Companies.

(*See Miscellaneous.*)

Manufacturers of Inventors' Models.

GRANT JOHN C. 15½ Lafayette [see adv. dept. p. 42]
PERKINS WM. A., Union, S. Salem [see adv. dept. p. 43]
Russell T. B. 554 Essex

Marble Manufacturers.

LORD A. & D. Market wharf [see adv. dept. p. 41]
Lord Andrew H. 11 St. Peter
Morgan Thos. 14 Central

Marine Railway.

Salem Marine Railway Co., East Gardner street.

Masons and Colorers.

Bowditch George jr. 9 Bentley
Farmer & Harris, 72 Washington
FLINT SIMEON, 221 Derby [see adv. dept. p. 49]
Hayward Aaron, 82 Summer
Hayward Josiah, 120 Federal
Hurd Thomas, 24 Hathorne (*stone*)
Kehew William B. 24 North
MANSFIELD IRA, 57 Union [see adv. dept. p. 50]
Moulton Frederick, 105 Federal
Neal Jonathan, 12 Broad
Ricker Morrill, 56 Endicott
Roberts William P. 12 St. Peter
Stone Benjamin, 21 Williams
Stone James, 27 Warren
WHITE BENJ. R., St. Peter court [see adv. dept. p. 48]
Young Stephen, 10 Leach

Mechanical Engineer.

NEWCOMB G. L. 18 Peabody, [see adv. dept. p. 42]

Medicines. (*Patent.*)

CARTY JAS. H. Union st. Bridge [see adv. dept. p. 19]
FLINT & GOLDTHWAITE, 4 Cambridge [see adv. dept. p. 56]
PRICE C. H. & J. 226 Essex [see adv. inside front cover]
WEBB WM. jr. 169½ Essex [see adv. front colored page]

Merchants.

Bertram John, 22 Asiatic building
Bertram J. H. M. 22 Asiatic building
Curwen James B. 22 Asiatic building
Fabens Benjamin 211 Derby
Fabens Charles H. 211 Derby
GOODHUE WM. P. 44 Derby (*com.*) [see adv. dept. p. 25]
Hoffman Chas. 12 Derby wharf
Hunt Wm. & Co. 16 Asiatic building
JONES J. St & Co. Pierce's wharf [see adv. dept. p. 22]
Miller Chas. H. 172 Essex
Osgood John C. 25 Asiatic building
PHILLIPS W. P., Phillips' wharf [see adv. back colored page]
Pickman Wm. D. 14 Asiatic building
Pingree T. P. 8d, 172 Essex
Ropes George, 22 Asiatic building
Silsbee George Z. 14 Asiatic building
Silsbee B. H. 14 Asiatic building
Silsbee John B. 22 Asiatic building
Silsbee John H. 14 Asiatic building
Stone B. W. & Bro's. 12 Asiatic build.
Upton Edwin, 68 Union
Upton George, 68 Union
West Benjamin A. 218 Derby
West Samuel, 218 Derby

Milliners.

Crane Mary E. 168 Essex
Davis J. P. 110 Essex
Downie E. A. Mrs. 264 Essex
Draper A. Mrs. 260 Essex

DUDLEY SUSAN J. 224 Essex,
Brown's block [see adv. on back
cover]
Flaherty Mary, 291 Essex
Foster M. L. 174 Essex
Gray Elizabeth, 205 Essex
Gwinn Mary A. 294 Essex
HOLBROOK J. M. 238 Essex [see
adv. dept. p. 9]
Lake A. F. 256 Essex
PEABODY JOHN P. 220 Essex [see
adv. back colored page]
Pond Harriet, 276 Essex
REITH & Co. 2 West block, 188 Es-
sex [see adv. inside back cover]
Rowell S. B. Mrs. 31 Lafayette
Robinson Lucy T. 14 Crombie
Sanborn Caroline, 15 Buffum
Swan Miranda, 298 Essex
SYMONDS PAULINE, Miss, 184 Es-
sex [see adv. dept. p. 13]
Thompson W. S. Mrs. 3 North
Walker Mary M. 165 Essex
Ward Sarah A. 278 Essex
Walwork Sara E. 5 Central
Wilson Mary B. 250 Essex
Woodman M. E. 5 Central
Woodward E. S. 252½ Essex

Millinery Goods

PEABODY JOHN P. 220 Essex [see
adv. back colored page]
REITH & Co. 2 West block, 188 Essex [see adv. inside back cover]
Shatzwell J. A. 169 Essex
SYMONDS PAULINE, 184 Essex
[see adv. dept. p. 13]

Mineral Water.

WINN S. B. c. Front and Washington
[see adv. dept. p. 9]

Mineral Water and Beer.

WINN S. B. c. Front and Wash. [see
adv. dept. p. 9]

Morocco Dressers & Colorers.

Arnold Edward B. 8 Pope's court
Arnold Michael P. 8 Pope's court

Mouldings. (Wood.)

STRAW BENJ. 5 Front [see adv.
dept. p. 46]

Music Stores.

(See Piano Fortes.)

BROOKS D. B. & BRO. 6 Central &
201 Essex [see adv. front cover]
WHIPPLE G. M. & A. A. SMITH,
243 Essex [see adv. front colored]

Music. (Band.)

Upton's Quadrille Band, Henry O.
Upton, leader, 46 Washington

Nautical Inst. Maker.

Emery Samuel, 162 Derby

Notaries Public. (Salem.)

Cloutman Joseph
Endicott William C.
Fitz Daniel P.

Gillis James A.
Mansfield Micajah B.
Miller Ephraim F.
Osgood J. B. F.
Roberts David
Stimpson Thomas M.
Worcester Jona F.
Waters Joseph G.
Webb S. P.
Wheatland Stephen G.

Nurseries.

Manning Robert, 33 Dearborn

Nurses.

Allis Abigail, 22 Forrester
Armstrong Eliza J. 116 Derby
Arnold Mary E. 38 Derby
Barnes Nancy, 93 Bridge
Barron Phœbe H. 43 Charter
Begg Sarah A. 1 Hardy
Berg Nancy, 163 Boston
Berry Wm. H. 8 Cambridge
Bryant Lydia K. 87 Summer
Burrill Mary Mrs. 15 Becket
Bushby Mary, 6 Whittemore
Call M. A. Mrs. 14 Walnut
Cate Mary E. 19 Warren
Cheever Mary P. 25 North
Clark Elizabeth, 5 Orange
Cole Mary A. b. 69 Mill
Cook Mary, 28 Oliver
Crosby Sarah, 50 Mill
Cummings Susan S. 13 Ward
Dalton Sarah N. Mrs. 127 Essex
Dix Eliza A. 55 Derby
Dockham Elizabeth, 12 Essex
Dunham Margaret, b. 1 Perkins
Evans Eliza A. 25 Salem
Field Louisa, 14 Salem
Fisk R. P. 23 Pleasant
Francis Maria, 20 Pickman
Francis Mary Mrs. r. 19 Becket
Greenleaf Mary V. 28 Becket
Hart Hannah W. 48 Derby
Hitchings Abijah, jr. Mrs. r. 22 Derby
Hobbs James S. Mrs. 9 Rust
Isaackson Sarah A. 29 Norman
Littlefield Hannah, 6 River
Loflin Lydia A. 95 Essex
Matthews Sarah N. 2 Mason court
Maloon Lucy M. Union place
Morse Abigail H. 7 Lynn
Munroe J. 25 North
Newhall Rebecca, 39 St. Peter
Nourse Abigail, 80 North
Nowell Phœbe A. 21 Beckford
Nye Abbie P. r. 63 Essex
Odlin Mary, 25 Hardy
Peabody Sally, 30 St. Peter
Peterson Priscilla, 3 Hardy
Pope Rebecca S. 7 Herbert
Reed Mary, 406 Essex
Russell Susan, 5 Mall
Saunders Margaret, 65 North
Shaw Margaret A. 168 Boston
Smith Catharine, 18 Derby
Smith Lydia P. 24 Vale
Snelling John Mrs. Porter court
Southwick Eliza 40 Broad

Test Mary P. 5 Creek
Thompson, Matilda, 90 Federal
Townes Ann Mrs. 7 Federal
Tullock Clarissa A. 1 Aborn
Waldron Sarah A. 1 Harbor

Oil and Candles.

Reeves & Griffin [*fish oils*] 13 Front
Salem and S. Danvers Oil Co. Mason
[*resin oil*]
Secomb Oil Manufacturing Co. foot of
Harbor
WALTON TIMOTHY [*neatsfoot*] foot
of Ord [see adv. dept. p. 23]

Oysters and Refreshments.

(*See Dining Saloons.*)

Cook A. Eastern Railroad Depot
Covell T. N. 1 Phœnix building
Estes G. W. jr. 3 Newbury
Esty J. A. 17 Derby sq.
HOLBROOK J. 5 Derby sq. [see adv.
dept. p. 29]
Lewis Jessie W. 7 Franklin building
MORRIS JOSEPH B. 18 and 20 Der-
by sq. [see adv. dept. p. 30]
Newcomb D. B. & J. 24 Derby sq.
ROGERS S. F. 170 Essex [see adv.
dept. p. 87]

Painters.

(*House and Sign.*)

Abbott Philip, 9 Church
Ames Edward B. 3 Crombie
Averill James W. 18 Lafayette
BLANEY WM. 164 Main, South Dan-
vers [see adv. dept.]
BROWN C. E. 29 Liberty [see adv.
dept. p. 51]
BROWN R. L. Washington, c. Bridge
[see adv. dept. p. 50]
Calley Samuel, Bridge, near S. and L.
R. R. depot
Clark S. C. 112 Essex
Davis C. H. 85 North
DWINELL DAVID L. M. 87 North
[see adv. dept. p. 51]
FELT JOHN G. 27 Front [see adv.
dept. p. 49]
Ferguson J. B. Essex, cor. Beckford
FOLEY EDWARD, 32 Endicott [see
adv. dept. p. 51]
HENDERSON DANIEL, 8 Walnut
[see adv. dept. p. 51]
Lowd Mark & Son, 8 North
MANSFIELD B. S. 31 Endicott [see
adv. dept. p. 47]
Mansfield Joseph, 9 Lafayette
Meservey John, 36 Lafayette
POUSLAND GEORGE A. 17 Pea-
body [see adv. dept. p. 50]
PULSIFER C. H. 27 Front
PULSIFER D. & Co. 25 Front [see
adv. dept. p. 48]
Pulsifer Joseph, 230 Derby
Pulsifer N. [*carpet*] 11 Spring
ROWELL B. 4 Sewall [see adv. dept.
p. 48]
SIMONDS WM. H. Hardy, c. Derby
[see adv. dept. p. 70]

Swasey Joseph, 21 Dean
Tibbetts Henry H. 139 Derby

(*Carriage.*)

Burbank E. G. & E. A. West place
Davidson Moses & Co. 135 Boston
LATIONS JONATHAN P. Jeffrey ct.
[see adv. dept. p 44]
MOORE HIRAM W. r. 8 Cambridge
[see adv. dept. p. 45]
Rhodes John W. 23 Endicott

(*Portrait.*)

Osgood Charles, 14 Brown
Southward Geo. Bank bldg. Central

(*Ship Painters.*)

POUSLAND G. A. 17 Peabody [see
adv. dept p. 50]

(*Sign and Ornamental.*)

BROWN R. L. Washington, c. Bridge
[see adv. dept. p. 50]
FELT JOHN G. 27 Front [see adv.
dept. p. 49]
Luscomb Wm. H. 4 Hamilton
Mansfield J. 9 Lafayette
PULSIFER D. & Co. 25 Front [see
adv. dept. p. 48]

Paints, Oil, and Glass.

ADAMS, RICHARDSON & Co. 215
Essex [see adv. dept. p. 5]
DWINELL D. L. M. 87 North [see
adv. dept. p. 51]
FELT JOHN G. 27 Front [see adv.
dept. p. 49]
FOLEY EDWARD, 32 Endicott [see
adv. dept. p. 51]
MANSFIELD B. S. 31 Endicott [see
adv. dept. p. 47]
PULSIFER D. & Co. 25 Front [see
adv. dept. p. 48]
SIMONDS S. C. & E. A. 32 Front [see
adv. dept. p. 25]

Paper Box Manufacturer.

HENDERSON WM. C. 150 Essex [see
adv. dept. p. 18]

Paper Hangers.

BROWN C. E. 29 Liberty [see adv.
dept. p. 51]
DWINELL DAVID L. M. 87 North
[see adv. dept. p. 51]
FELT J. G. 27 Front [see adv. dept.
p. 49]
FOLEY EDWARD, 32 Endicott [see
adv. dept. p. 51]
HENDERSON D. 3 Walnut [see adv.
dept. p. 51]
Lowd Mark & Son, 8 North
Lyons Timothy, 3 Daniels
MANSFIELD B. S. 31 Endicott [see
adv. dept. p. 47]
Mansfield J. 9 Lafayette
POUSLAND GEO. A. 17 Peabody
[see adv. dept. p. 50]
PULSIFER D. & Co. 25 Front [see
adv. dept. p. 48]

ROWELL BENJ. 4 Sewall [see adv.
dept. p 48]
Simonds Wm. H. 76 Derby

Paper Hangings.

FOLEY EDWARD, 82 Endicott [see
adv. dept. p. 51]
Ives Henry P. 282 Essex
MANSFIELD B. S. 81 Endicott [see
adv., dept. p. 47]
WHIPPLE G. M. & A. A. SMITH 243
Essex [see adv. front colored]

Paper and Paper Stock.

Eaton John D. 88 North
Weston P. R. 166 Derby

Pattern and Model Makers.

GRANT JOHN C. 15½ Lafayette [see
adv. dept. p. 42]
PERKINS WM. A. Union, S. Salem
[see adv. dept. p. 43]

Perfumery, &c.

EMERTON JAMES, 119 Essex [see
adv. dept. p. 7]
PEABODY JOHN P. 220 Essex [see
adv. back colored page]
PRICE C. H. & J. 226 Essex [see adv.
front colored page]
WEBB WM. jr. 159½ Essex [see adv.
on front colored page]

Periodicals.

Chandler & Co. 4 Washington
Moody L. B. 24 Washington
PHILLIPS A. Mrs. 9 Central [see adv.
dept. p. 9]

Photograph Artists.

Bowdoin D. W. 175 Essex
Goss & Pepper 46 Washington
Moulton J. W. 214 Essex
Perkins E. R. 241 Essex
Proctor Geo. K. 208 Essex
Taylor George P. 188 Essex
White John, 224 Essex

Physicians.

Bryant H. K. 8 Carpenter
Buffum Joshua, jr. 8 Munroe
Cate S. M. 80 Washington
Choate David, 23 Norman
Choate George, 251 Essex
Cox Benjamin, jr. 182 Essex
DeGersdoff B. 257 Essex
Gove Hiram, 18 Washington
Holbrook S. H. 122 Bridge
Johnson Samuel, 2 Chestnut
Kemble Arthur, over 174 Essex
LaMont Daniel G. 243½ Essex
Mack Wm. 21 Chestnut
Morse Nathan R. 13 Washington
Neilson Wm. 49 Washington
Peirson E. B. 13 Barton square
Perkins George A. 129 Essex
Quimby Elisha, 48 Essex
Quimby E. Hervey, 46 Washington
Quimby S. F. 48 Federal

Stone H. Osgood, 19 Washington
Stone James, jr. 40 Broad
Wheatland H. 21 Chestnut

Piano Dealers.

Bray Ann R. 76 Federal
Brooks D. B. & Brother, 6 Central and
201 Essex
DOWNS M. S. 175 Essex [see adv.
dept. p. 7]
FENOLLOSA M. 286 Essex [see adv.
dept. p. 39]
Mackintire Samuel, 218 Essex

Piano Tuner.

DOWNS M. S. 175 Essex [see adv.
dept. p. 7]
FENOLLOSA M. 286 Essex [see adv.
dept. p. 39]

**Picture-Frame Makers and
Gilders.**

PHILLIPS A. Mrs. [see adv. dept.
p. 9]
Shaw X. H. & Son, 283 Essex

Pilots.

Plummer John F. rear 14 Barton
Perkins Joseph, 4 Allen
Perkins Joseph, jr. 4 Allen
Perry Ittai, 59 Derby

Plaster.

FLINT SIMEON, 221 Derby [see adv.
dept. p. 49]
GAYLE & Co. Phillips' wharf [see
adv. dept. p. 22]
GOODHUE W. P. 44 Derby [see adv.
dept. p. 25]
JONES J. S. & Co. Pierce's wharf
[see adv. dept. p. 22]

Plastering Hair.

GRIFFIN JAMES & Co. 20 Beaver
[see adv. dept. p. 50]

Plumbers.

Goss F. P. 7 St. Peter
HART WM. H. 13 Central [see adv.
dept. p. 53]

Pocket-Book Manufacturer.

CUTLER WILLIAM, 138 Boston [see
adv. dept. p. 8]

Printers.

CHAPMAN & PALFRAY, 193 Essex
[Salem Register] [see adv. dept.
p. 67]
FOOTE & HORTON, 199 Essex [Sa-
lem Gazette] [see adv. dept. p. 58]
Hutchinson T. J. 163 Essex
KIMBALL GEORGE, 224 Essex [Es-
sex Statesman] [see adv. dept. p. 55]
PEASE GEORGE W. 226½ Essex [Sa-
lem Observer] [see adv. dept. p. 59]
Swasey L. A. 241 Essex
THYNG & BABBRIDGE, 182 Essex
[Salem Witch] [see adv. dept. p. 56]

Produce.

GAYLE & Co. Phillips' wharf [see adv. dept. p. 22]
NELSON J. S. & Co. 26 Front [see adv. dept. p. 24]
Read John F. 7, 8, and 9 Market Ho.
Read W. A. 10 and 11 Market House [butter and cheese]
ROPES CHARLES A. 165 Derby [see adv. dept. p. 26]
White S. & B. R. 66 Washington

Provisions.

ALLEN WM. E. 50½ Derby [see adv. dept. p. 32]
Ballard B. 7½ Winter
Beckford A. N. 5 Boston
Bigelow Ira H. 12 and 13 Market
BROWN C. & SON, 22 Derby sq. [see adv. dept. p. 33]
Clark Albion J. 48 Harbor
Crocker William, Franklin Market, 9 Newbury
Danforth E. F. 33 Endicott
Daniels Stephen, 70 Federal
Davenport J. K. 46 Pleasant
Emerson D. P. 17 and 18 Market Ho.
Hancock & Morse, 39 Derby
Knight F. 48 North
MILLETT JOSEPH HENRY, 67 Derby [salt provisions] [see adv. dept. p. 24]
Plander John G. 116 Derby
Putnam J. H. 319 Essex
Roberts & Porter, 19 St. Peter
ROPES CHARLES A. [wholesale] 165 Derby [see adv. dept. p. 26]
SAWYER & TILTON, 9 Derby sq. [see adv. dept. p. 31]
Staples Lewis E. 69 Bridge
South Isaiah & Co. 33 Lafayette
Tuttle Henry G. 36 Boston
Upton Ezra, 2 Mill
Ward Alfred A. 566 City Market
WARD J. O. 15 and 16 Market House [see adv. dept. p. 31]
WELCH WM. E. 22 Central, c. Front [see adv. dept. p. 31]
WHEELER B. S. 1 and 2 Market Ho. [see adv. dept. p. 32]
WIGGIN & MUNROE, 111 Essex [see adv. dept. p. 32]
Winberry Thomas, 7½ Boston

Pump and Blockmakers.

Donaldson A. 141 Derby

Restorators.

(See Dining Saloons.)

Rigger.

Berry Charles H. 20 Derby wharf

Sailmakers.

Lane Edward B. 57 Union
Oakes Thomas, 7 Derby wharf
Whipple J. H. Phillips' wharf

Salt.

Bowker Brothers, 227 Derby

Salve Manufacturer.

CARTY JAMES H. Union st. bridge [see adv. dept. p. 19]

Sash, Blind, & Door Makers.

BLANEY WM. 164 Main, So. Danvers [see adv. dept. p.]
FOLEY EDWARD, 32 Endicott [see adv. dept. p. 51]
Hardy Temple jr. 26 Front
Newell Joseph, 7 Front
Phelps Wm. jr. & Co. 84 Federal

Saw Filer.

WILLISTON SAMUEL S. 60 Charter [see adv. dept. p. 30]

Sawing & Planing Mill.

Buffum David, Front, near Lafayette
Gifford Thomas J. & Co. rear 12 Carpenter

Scales and Balances.

ADAMS, RICHARDSON & Co. 215 Essex [see adv. dept. p. 5]

Seeds.

Ives J. S. 281 Essex

Sewing-Machines.

GRISWOLD B. L. 142 Essex [see adv. front cover]
MOORE SAMUEL (Union Button-Hole Machine), over 158 Essex [see adv. dept. p. 6]

Ship Builders.

Miller Edward F., E. Gardner

Ship Chandler.

GOODHUE WM. P. 44 Derby [see adv. dept. p. 25]

Shipsmith.

NICHOLS JOHN, 45 Union [see adv. dept. p. 42]

Shipwright and Calker.

Coffin Calvin, East Gardner

Shirt & Collar Manufacturer.

WALKER GEORGE S. 226 Essex [see outside back cover]

Shoes.

(See Boots and Shoes.)

Silver Ware.

APPLETON GEO. P. 187 Essex [see adv. dept. p. 1]
FOGG JULIAN A. & Co. 237 Essex [see adv. front colored page]
SKERRY HENRY F. 180 Essex [see adv. dept. p. 60]
SMITH & CHAMBERLAIN 207 Essex [see adv. dept. p. 3]
SMITH JESSE, 262 Essex [see adv. front colored page]

Skirts. (Watchspring.)

FOLLETTE L. B. 184 Essex [see adv. dept. p. 10]

PORTER M. A. 236 Essex [see adv. dept. p. 12]

Slaters.

FOWLER GEO. & Co. 2 St. Peter ct. [see adv. dept. p. 53]
Pinnock Thomas, 25 Peabody

Soap Manufacturer.

ROBERTSON S. W. r. 44 Boston [see adv. dept. p. 27]

Spectacles.

APPLETON GEO. B. 187 Essex [see adv. dept. p. 1]
FOGG JULIAN A. & Co. 287 Essex [see card on front colored]

Sporting Apparatus.

(*See Guns and Sporting.*)

Stables.

LEAVITT J. S. r. Essex House [see adv. inside back cover]
ROBBINS THOMAS A. r. 161 Essex & 167 Boston [see adv. dept. p. 21]
Smith & Manning, 212 Essex, 9 Hamilton, and 47 Washington
Tuttle John, 191 Federal

Stairbuilders.

Brown Geo. jr. 41 North, n. Bridge
FAXON & LOCKE, 72 Washington [see adv. dept. p. 49]
Kendall Alvah, 11 Hathorne

Stationery.

(*See Booksellers.*)

Steam and Gas Fitters.

SMALL WM. F. 273 Essex [see adv. dept. p. 20]
STATEN E. H. 147 Essex [see adv. front colored page]

Stencil Cutters.

FOGG JULIAN A. & Co. 287 Essex [see card on front colored page]

Stock Brokers.

NICHOLS JOHN H. 42 Washington [see adv. miscellaneous dept. p. 209]
PIERCE N. 161 Essex [see adv. dept. p. 60]

Stone Yards.

BLETHEN T. G. 25 Peabody [see adv. dept. p. 50]
BUTLER, DAVIS, & MERRILL, 18 Lafayette [see adv. dept. p. 48]
LORD A. & D. Market wharf [see adv. dept. p. 41]

Stoves, Tin Plate, & Sheet Iron Workers, &c.

Chipman Andrew A. 347 Essex
Clough D. E. & S. F. 4 Front
Eaton J. W. & Co. 84 North
Frothingham & Co. 31 Front
Fuller Wm. P. 17 St. Peter
Mooney & Wadlelgh, 40 and 42 North
Pease Samuel W. 126 Derby

Preston Jonathan, 12 Central
ROPES JOHN T. 17 and 19 Front [see adv. dept. p. 2]

Tailors and Drapers.

BROWN WM. P. 198 Essex [see adv. dept. p. 1]
BURBECK W. H. 249 Essex [see adv. dept. p. 2]
Cahill Thomas, 9 Herbert
Cornelius Alonzo G. 3 West's block, Essex
Dease Lawrence, 22 Central
Hannam Thos. 64 Boston
Hodgdon & Steadman 39 Washington
Jones S. G. 185 Essex
MACKENZIE RODERICK A. 287 Essex [see adv. dept. p. 3]
MOORE S. (*repairer and button-hole maker*) over 158 Essex [see adv. dept. p. 6]
Norris C. H. 189 Essex, c. Central
Perkins, Smith & Co. 44 Washington
Purbeck William A. 267 Essex
SIBLEY MOSES H. 41½ Washington (*garments cut for others to make*) [see adv. dept. p. 8]
Webb John K. 139 Essex

Tallow.

ROBERTSON S. W. r. 44 Boston [see adv. dept. p. 27]
WALTON TIMOTHY, foot of Ord. [see adv. dept. p. 28]

Tanners.

Bott James, rear 27 Boston
Braden James, 47 Boston
Carleton Edward F. 14 Franklin
Carleton H. W., 14 Franklin
Carleton Frazier, 14 Franklin
Conway John H. r. 68 Mason
Culliton John, r. 91 Mason
Egan Martin, foot of Buffum
Frye F. A. foot of Dean
Gibney John H. 11 Beach
Hadley Geo. S. Goodhue
Hamlin John, Goodhue
Harrington R. & W. H. 11 Franklin
Kenney William, r. Turnpike
Looby Thos. Grove n. Mildam
Lord James & Son, r. 180 Federal
McCarty M., Buffum, n. Mason
Muhlig Robert, foot of Buffum
Osgood N. W. Goodhue
Pope Eleazer & Son, r. 87 Boston
Putnam Jacob & Co. 17 Goodhue
Stimpson J. C. r. 48 Boston
Turner Calvin, 4 Goodhue
Tuttle Nathaniel, 21 Boston
Varney Henry, Goodhue, r. 88 Boston
Varney W. D. & S. r. 48 Boston
Weston Charles & Sons, May
Wilkins Albert, 50 Boston
Wilkins J. H. r. 48 Boston.

Tanners & Curriers' Machinery.

WESTON JOHN W. rear 11 Boston [see adv. dept. p. 42]

Teachers.

Arrington Augusta, 48 Lafayette
Bowland H. 1 Walnut, cor. Essex
Brooks Elizabeth, 8 Norman
Bunker Lizzie A. 5 Mason (music)
Carlton Mary, 8 Leach
Cutts Love P. 30 Beckford (music)
DOWNS M. S. 175 Essex (music), [see adv. dept. p. 7]
Emille E. 7 Central (music)
Euatis Nancy, 154 Boston (private)
FENOLLOSÁ MANUEL, 286 (music) Essex [see adv. dept. p. 39]
Francis A. B. 10 Pearl (French)
Gill Harriet P. Harbor st. school
Gomes Anna, 8 Cherry (private)
HANSON LIZZIE, (piano) 20 Union [see adv. dept. p. 8]
Hawkes Louisa M. 28 Broad
Honeycomb Sarah E. 7 Lemon
Kaula John A. 36 Charter (music)
LEAVITT W. 158 Essex (navigation) [see adv. inside back cover]
Lurd Emeline, 27 Pleasant
Luscomb Harriet A. 41 Lafayette
Munn Elizabeth N. 190 Federal
Orne John, jr. 4 Broad (private)
Pierce Elizabeth P. (private), 134 Essex
Quimby A. M. 48 Federal (music)
Read Geo. F. 42 Buffum
Safford Harriet M. 12 Laboratory
Smith Sarah, 8 Cambridge
Snow M. P. 13 Beckford
Stevens Ann P. Hamilton Hall
Upton Anna M. 59 Essex
Upton Francis, 31 Pleasant (music)
Very M. N. 78 Federal (private school)
Very Frances E. 95 Federal
Ward E. W. 34 Chestnut
Watson Lucy F. 412 Essex

Teamsters.

Cabeen John, 198 Derby
Evans James G. 41½ Derby
Pitts Darling, 2 Lafayette
Pitts Nathaniel, 5 Front
Smith Thomas, 194 Derby
SUMNER & CARTER, 130 Derby, [see adv. dept. p. 29]

Teas, &c.

CALEF JOHN, 80 Washington [see business card top front cover]
CHAMBERLAIN, HARRIS & Co. 24 Front [see adv. dept. p. 27]
FOSTER ISAAC P. 190 Derby [see adv. dept. p. 34]
NICHOLS DAVID A. 76 Derby, [see adv. dept. p. 33]
NOYES E. K. & Co. 6 and 8 Front [see adv. dept. p. 28]
REYNOLDS M. C. & Co. 20 Front [see adv. dept. p. 26]

Telegraph Offices.

American Telegraph, Eastern R. R. Depot
Independent Telegraph, Asiatic Build.

Thread.

PORTER M. A. 236 Essex [see adv.
Shillaber S. 268 Essex   [dept. p. 12.

Tobacconists.

BATTIS & BROWN, 30 Front [see adv. dept. p. 24]
ROWELL FREDERICK, jr. 130 Derby [see adv. dept. p. 23]
Skinner Richard, 62 and 64 Federal

Toys.

SKERRY HENRY F. 180 Essex [see adv. dept. p. 60]
ROGERS S. F. 170 and 172 Essex [see adv. dept. p. 37]

Turning and Sawing.

Clapp L. & A. 5. Front

Twine Factory.

CHISHOLM JOSEPH, 68 Mill [see adv. dept. p. 18]
Gwinn James F. 32 Bridge

Umbrella Makers.

Lynch P. 92 Derby
Servey Wm. T. 310 Essex
Tirnan Peter, 224 Essex

Undertakers.

BUFFUM CHARLES S. 48 Washington, and Central, S. Danvers [see adv. dept. p. 41]
HUBON HENRY G. 68 Washington [see adv. dept. p. 40]

Upholsterers.

Collier Perry, 12 Sewall
Mackie John, 8 Central
Shepard S. 298 Essex

Upholstery Goods.

GOLDTHWAITE WILLARD, 151 Essex [see adv. dept. p. 11]

Variety Store.

Beckford Thomas G. Mrs. 85 Bridge
Dermingham C. 30 Norman
Byrne Anna E. 17 Federal
Caraway C. S. 68 Derby
Carlton John, 158 Essex
Clark Sarah F. 18 Mill
Colby J. W. Mrs. 46 Peabody
Knight M. B. & M. 5 Pleasant
Lemon Helen W. 2 Walnut
Minor A. H. Mrs. 18 Beckford
Nichols Abigail, 68 Boston
Phillips George Mrs. 38 St. Peter
Plummer R. 248 Essex
Smith M. B. Miss, 48 Essex
Stephenson Elizabeth, 60 Essex
Story Francis B. 148 Essex
Symonds E. G. North, cor. School
Tibbets Elizabeth, 9 Winter
Wiihr L. W. 52 Endicott

Veterinary Surgeons.

SAUNDERS ROBERT J. 7 Buffum [see adv. dept. p. 38]
Saunders William, 5 Buffum

Watchmakers & Jewellers.

APPLETON G. B. 187 Essex see adv. dept. p. 1]

FOGG A. & Co. 237 Essex [see card on front colored page]
Kehew William H. 230 Essex
Lamson Charles, 234 Essex
Luscomb John G. 162 Essex
Nickorson A. W. 24 Washington
SKERRY HENRY F. 180 Essex [see adv. dept. p. 60]
SMITH JESSE, 282 Essex [see adv. opp. title page]
SMITH & CHAMBERLAIN, 207 Essex [see adv. dept. p. 8]

Water Pipes & Fixtures.

HART WM. H. 13 Central [see adv. dept. p. 58]
STATEN E. H. 147 Essex [see adv. front colored page]

Water for Shipping.

HATCH L. B. 113 Derby [see adv. dept. p. 54]
Parsons & Shackelford, 64 Union

Wharfingers.

HATCH L. B. 113 Derby [see adv. dept. p. 54]
Knight E. H., Phillips' wharf

Wheelwrights.

ADAMS PETER F. 23 Endicott [see adv. dept. p. 44]
ANDREWS GILMAN, 27 Beach [see adv. dept. p. 44]
Barker Joseph W. r. Essex house
Batchelder Joseph, 35 North
LATIONS JONATHAN P. Jeffery court [see adv. dept. p. 44]
Spiller John P. n. foot Perkins

Wines, &c.

Arvedson Wm. L. 25 Washington (city agent)
Cochran Thomas J. 14½ Derby sqr.
Hurley John, 8 High
Mudgett Samuel A., Higginson sqr. (ale depot)
Odell J. A. 23 Front
Perley R. M. & Co. 135 Derby
Remond John, 5 Higginson square

Wood and Bark.

(See Coal, &c.)

Brown G. F. & S. 36 and 38 North
Clark Patrick, 169 Derby
GAYLE & Co., Phillips' wharf [see adv. dept. p. 22]
HATCH L. B. 113 Derby [see adv. dept. p. 54]
JEWETT D. H. 205 Derby [see adv. dept. p. 54]
MANNING R. C. & Co. 169 Derby [see adv. dept. p. 55]
Pickering William, jr. 17 Peabody
Putnam Nathan, 157 Derby
Sanborn G. & F. T. 115 Derby
WIGGIN & CLARK, 29 Peabody [see adv. dept. p. 52]

Wood Moulding.

STRAW BENJAMIN, 5 Front [see adv. dept. p. 46]

Worsteds & Worsted Goods.

BROWNING & LONG, 177 Essex [see adv. dept.[
PEABODY JOHN F. 230 Essex [see adv. back colored page]

21

CITY GOVERNMENT, 1866.

City Election, first Monday in January; organization of the City Government, fourth Monday in January.

MAYOR. — DAVID ROBERTS. Salary, $1,000.

ALDERMEN. — William P. Goodhue, Francis W. Pickman, Thomas H. Prime, Thomas H. Frothingham, Nathaniel Brown, Jr., and Simon Stodder.

COMMON COUNCIL.

President, CHARLES S. OSGOOD.

WARD ONE. John H. Batchelder, Thomas Cousins, Jr., Joseph S. Cross, and James B. Nichols.

WARD TWO. Francis C. Butman, Josiah B. Osborn, Charles S. Osgood, and James O. Safford.

WARD THREE. William H. Burbeck, Stephen P. Driver, Edward A. Goldthwait, and Andrew Ober.

WARD FOUR. James M. Caller, William P. Martin, Thomas Nichols, Jr., and Joseph H. Webb.

WARD FIVE. James F. Almy, Charles S. Clark, George D. Glover, and A. Augustus Smith.

WARD SIX. William Maloon, William E. McIntire, James Dugan, and Nathaniel R. Treadwell.

The City Council meets regularly on the second and fourth Mondays of each month, in the evening, at the City Hall.

The Committee on Accounts meets on Thursday after the first Monday in each month, at 7½ o'clock, P. M., at the City Hall.

The meetings of all the Boards and Committees are held at the City Hall.

CITY OFFICERS.

City Clerk. — Stephen P. Webb.
Clerk of the Common Council. — Eben N. Walton.
Treasurer and Collector. — Henry J. Cross.
City Marshal. — Richard J. Skinner, Jr.
Assistant Marshal. — James Dalrymple (Police Office, Police Station, 11 Front).
Commissioner of Streets. — Joseph C. Foster.
City Messenger. — William Mansfield.
Clerk of Overseers of Poor. — Daniel P. Fitz.
Water Commissioners. — Stephen H. Phillips, Peter Silver, F. T. Sanborn.

WARD OFFICERS.

WARD 1. James Fairfield, Jr., *Warden;* J. Henry Nichols and Charles H. Felt, *Assistants;* N. Osgood Very, *Clerk.*
WARD 2. Israel H. Harris, *Warden;* Daniel Henderson and John P. Putnam, *Assistants;* John A. Currin, *Clerk.*
WARD 3. Parker D. Walker, *Warden;* Lewis D. Richards and Hezekiah Sleeper, *Assistants;* David R. Peabody, *Clerk.*
WARD 4. James F. Potter, *Warden;* John H. Dell and Charles H. Pulsifer, *Assistants;* Charles H. Daniels, *Clerk.*
WARD 5. Edward B. Phillips, *Warden;* Augustus H. Kimball and John Meservy, *Assistants;* Aaron Goldthwait, Jr., *Clerk.*
WARD 6. Benjamin S. Boardman, *Warden;* Thos. Ashby and Daniel W. Lord, *Assistants;* Samuel T. Goss, *Clerk.*

OVERSEERS OF THE POOR. — The Mayor and Aldermen and Messrs. Edward B. Lane, William P. Goodhue, John Jewett, William Chase, Oliver Thayer, John Preston, John Huse, William F. Nichols, Aaron Perkins, James Harris, Devereux Dennis, George F. Brown.
The Overseers of the Poor meet on the first Tuesday in each month at the Almshouse, and on Wednesday evening of each week at the City Hall.
Chaplain to the Almshouse, John Carlton.
Superintendent of Almshouse, Charles T. Dodge.
Almshouse Physician, W. Nielson.
Assessors. — Thomas S. Jewett, Allen Putnam, Jonathan Tucker. *Assistant Assessors.* Ward 1, Moses T. Upton, D. B. Hood; Ward 2, James M. Brown, Lemuel B. Hatch; Ward 3, Alvah Kendall, Joshua B. Grant; Ward 4, Eleazer Pope, Thomas Symonds, Jr.; Ward 5, Mark Kimball, Aaron Perkins; Ward 6, Nathaniel Horton, Dean C. Symonds.
The Assessors meet from 9 to 12, A. M., and 2 to 5, P. M., at City Hall every business day.
Board of Health. — Mayor and Aldermen, *ex officio.*
Board of Health Physician. — W. Nielson.
Superintendent of Burials. — Jeremiah S. Perkins. *Assistants,* Charles Creasy, Charles Staniford.
Surveyor-General of Lumber and Timber. — Ezra Woodbury. *Deputies.* — George A. Brown, Albert Day, Amos P. Day, William C. Hamond, Augustus Hutchings.
Superintendent of Bark brought into city on cars. — Edward Symonds.
Measurers of Wood and Bark. — Alfred R. Brooks, Thomas M. Dix, Rufus L. Gordon, Thomas W. Gwinn, John Waters, jr., Ed. Symonds, Thomas Symonds, jr.
Superintendent of Union Bridge. — Peter Ames.
    "   "   *South*   "   Wm. Moulton.
    "   "   *City Stables.* — D. P. Fitz.
City Weigher. — John McGuire.
City Crier. — William Newhall.

Fence Viewers. — Wm. F. Gardner, Henry L. Reed.
Pound Keepers. — Daniel Brown, Stephen O'Hare.
Field Drivers. — Daniel Brown, James Grover, John L. Hutchinson, Stephen O'Hare.

SCHOOL COMMITTEE.

David Roberts, Mayor, and Chas. S. Osgood, President of the Common Council, *ex officio.*
Ward 1. — James A. Farless, William P. Goodhue, George A. Perkins.
Ward 2. — Stephen B. Ives, jr., Charles R. Palmer, E. Hervey Quimby.
Ward 3. — Samuel P. Andrews, Edward S. Atwood, Edmund B. Willson.
Ward 4. — Robert C. Mills, Jacob Perley, Daniel Varney. Ward 5. —
Daniel ·D. Winn, Loranus Crowell, George F. Choate. Ward 6. — Chas.
E. Symonds, Charles A. Ropes, Henry J. Cross.
Stephen P. Webb, *Secretary.*

POLICE DEPARTMENT.

City Marshal. — Richard Skinner.
Assistant Marshals. — James Dalrymple and W. F. Chapple.
Patrolmen. — Joseph P. Allen, Benjamin Brown, John Chandler, Frederick H. Hunt, John W. Libbey, Joseph Peterson, Robert A. Phippen, Lewis D. Richards, Charles E. Skinner, Amos G. Teague.
Watchmen. — *Captain,* George E. Berry; *Clerk,* Moses A. Averill.
James Beaver, Eben Beckford, John M. Beckford, Thos. W. Brown, Charles E. Cloutman, John Innis, Payne Morse, William H. Odell, James Poor, jr., Norris Watson, John S. Wardwell, James Wells, William P. Wood.
Constables. — Joseph P. Allen, Moses A. Averill, Mark B. Avery, Oliver Adams, Benjamin Brown, George E. Berry, James Beaver, Eben Beckford, John M. Beckford, Thomas W. Brown, Thomas Bowen, Joseph S. Buxton, Jacob Berry, Bradford B. Burrill, Theodore Brown, Alfred R. Brooks, Wm. F. Chapple, John Chandler, Charles T. Conner, Robert P. Clough, Charles E. Cloutman, Aaron J. Cate, Charles Creasy, James H. Carty, Edward Collins, James Dalrymple, Thomas M. Dix, Wm. Dodge, Joseph E. Glover, Benjamin A. Gray, Andrew Gage, jr., Rufus L. Gordon, Frederick H. Hunt, Jacob S. Haskell, John Innis, Willis S. Knowlton, Joseph Kinsman, Alanson Kenney, John W. Libbey, Henry J. Lane, James A. Lord, jr. Lucius B. Morse, Payne Morse, George W. Moreland, Wm. Mansfield, Wm. H. Odell, Stephen O'Hare, Robert A. Phippen, Daniel Potter, James Poor, jr., Nathaniel W. Prince, Joseph Peterson, Frederick Parsons, Wm. R. Porter, Lewis D. Richards, Francis A. P. Rust, Richard Skinner, jr., Charles E. Skinner, Thomas Saul, Gorham Smith, Rolland Smalley, Irving Stone, Hezekiah Sleeper, Charles Staniford, George I. South, Amos G. Teague, Thomas Treadwell, Henry Upton, Samuel Very, John S. Wardwell, Wm. P. Wood, Norris Watson, James Wells, Aaron Welch, Wm. F. Warner, Eben N. Walton, James Westcott.

POLICE COURT.

Joseph G. Waters, *Justice.*
Stephen P. Webb, Jos. B. F. Osgood, *Associate Justices.*
Samuel P. Andrews, *Clerk.*
The Police Court is held in the Court Room in Police Station, 11 Front Street, for criminal business, every day at 9 o'clock, A. M.; and for civil business on 2d and 4th Wednesday in each month, at 10 o'clock, A. M.
William P. Upham, *Public Administrator.*

FIRE DEPARTMENT.

Chief Engineer. — George Sanborn.
Assistant Engineers. — James A. Lord, Wm. C. Hamond, Thomas J. Gifford, Augustus H. Kimball, Parker D. Walker.

Engine Companies.

Steamer, WM. CHASE, No. 1, Church Street. John B. Skinner, *Director*.
Steamer, SALEM, No. 2, Church Street. Joseph C. Foster, *Director*.
Steamer No. 3, Church Street. J. O. Chapman, *Director*.
Engine Co. No. 1, RELIANCE, Derby, c. Hardy Street. Andrew J. Tibbetts, *Director*.
No. 2, CONSTITUTION, Webb Street. W. D. Fernandez, *Director*.
No. 3, RELIEF, Mill, corner Lafayette. Justin Doust, *Director*.
No. 4, SUTTON, Boston Street. James L. Austin, *Director*.
No. 5, ACTIVE, North, c. Dearborn Sts. Thomas Ashby, *Director*.
No. 1, HOSE Co., William Penn, Forrester Street. John F. Staniford, *Director*.
No. 1, SAIL Co., Derby, c. Hardy. E. B. Lane, *Director*.
No. 2, SAIL Co., Boston Street. George S. Hadley, *Director*.
HOOK AND LADDER, Bridge, near new City Scales. Samuel Calley, *Director*.

PUBLIC SCHOOLS.

At the organization of the Board of School Committee, each elective member is appointed to one of the three visiting Committees that have the management of the respective divisions of schools, as regards the discipline, classification, and studies.

FIRST DIVISION. — *High School.*

Broad Street. A. H. Davis, *Master.* John Perkins, *Sub-Master.* Lois R. Wright, E. M. Fessenden, M. S. Merrill, *Assistants.*

SECOND DIVISION. — *Grammar Schools.*

BENTLEY, located between Essex and Forrester Streets; boundaries, that portion of the city between North and South Rivers east of the centre of St. Peter and Central Streets. Mary J. Fitz, *Principal;* Anna Whitmore, Mary A. Colman, Margaret A. Dunn, *Assistants.*
PHILLIPS, located between Essex and Forrester Streets; boundaries, that portion of the city between the North and South Rivers east of the centre of Washington Street. Silas Peabody, *Principal;* —— Brown, Aroline B. Meek, *Assistants.*
BROWNE, located on Ropes Street; boundaries, South Salem. Jacob F. Brown, *Principal;* Adeline Roberts, Ellen M. Pierce, Caroline Luscomb, Abby Baker, Harriet M. Gray, *Assistants.*
PICKERING, located on School, near North Street; boundaries, North Salem. William P. Hayward, *Principal;* Sarah E. Cross, Mary Ann Cross, and Eliza S. Symonds, *Assistants.*
HIGGINSON, located on Broad Street; boundaries, that portion of the city between North and South Rivers westward of a line through the centre of St. Peter and Central Streets, and below the Town Bridge, Boston St. M. L. Shepard, *Principal;* Anna M. Bates, *Sub-Principal;* P. Elizabeth Church, and Sarah A. Lynde, *Assistants.*
HACKER, located on Dean Street; boundaries, that portion of the city between North and South Rivers west of the centre of Washington Street, and below the Town Bridge, Boston Street. Henry F. Woodman, *Principal;* Harriet N. Felton and Margaret G. Stanley, *Assistants.*
EPES, located on Aborn Street; boundaries, that portion of the city north and west of the Town Bridge, Boston Street. Levi F. Warren, *Principal;* Ellen E. Wheeler, *Assistant.*

THIRD DIVISION. — *Intermediate and Primary Schools.*

Bridge Street. Caroline P. Laton, *Principal.* Frances A. Treadwell, *Assistant.*
Williams Street. R. A. Harris, *Principal.* Mary E. Davis, *Assistant.*
Bentley. Sarah A. Brown, *Principal.* Eliza G. Coggswell and S. E. Honeycomb, *Assistants.*

Phillips. Margaret E. Webb, *Principal.* L. A. Hill, Jeanette Gerald Helen White, *Assistants.*

Browne. Harriet N. Tyler, *Principal.* C. A. Arrington, Matilda Pollock, Harriet E. Lewis, Mary E. Stanley, *Assistants.*

Broad Street. Caroline Stevens, *Principal.* Emily Glover, L. F. Kehew, L. Boyce, *Assistants.*

North Street. Maria Cushing, *Principal.* E. R. Russell, Lucy A. Smith, and Caroline J. Symonds, *Assistants.*

Fowler Street. Hannah E. Morse, *Principal.* Mary E. Dockham and Eliza J. Phillips, *Assistants.*

Mason Street. L. L. A. Very, *Principal.* Emeline M. Littlefield, *Assistant.*

Epes. Abby F. Nichols, *Principal.* Sarah F. Daniels, *Assistant.*

Sisters of Notre Dame. School, 15 Walnut Street. Number of scholars, about 400. Tuition, free.

Boys' School. Old St. Mary's Church, Mall, corner Bridge. John Fitzgerald, *Principal.* Catherine Shaw and Mary Shaw, *Assistants.* Number of scholars, about 300.

Sisters' School of St. James. No. 160 Federal. Number of Scholars, 375. Tuition, free. Boys' School in Nonantum Hall, Warren Street. Patrick Kiernan, *Principal.* Number of scholars, about 300.

STATE NORMAL SCHOOL AT SALEM.

ESTABLISHED 1853.

Number of scholars, 124. Scholars are admitted twice a year, on the last Wednesday of February and first Wednesday of September. Tuition, free. Scholars are required to declare their intention to teach in the schools of the Commonwealth. This school is intended for females.

Daniel B. Hagar, *Principal.* Ellen M. Dodge, Mary E. Webb, Caroline J. Cole, Mary E. Godden, Mary N. Plumer, Ellen A. Chandler, Mary E. Nash, and Isabella C. Tenney, *Assistants.*

O. B. Brown, *Teacher of Music.*

CHURCHES.

First Church.

Unitarian Congregational. Organized, 1629. A brick edifice on Essex St., corner of Washington.

Rev. George W. Briggs, D. D., *Pastor ;* William A. Bowditch, *Treasurer ;* William P. Upham, *Clerk ;* J. F. Allen, Nathan Frye, Augustus J. Archer, William A. Bowditch, John T. Ropes, and A. C. Goodell, jr., *Committee ;* George W. Potter, *Sexton.*

East Church.

Unitarian Congregational. Gathered in 1717. A freestone edifice in Washington Square.

Rev. Samuel C. Beane, *Pastor ;* Gardner Barton, *Clerk and Treasurer ;* Benjamin H. Silsbee, Gardner Barton, Charles Millett, J. S. Kimball, Wm. Kimball, *Committee ;* N. Berry, *Sexton.*

North Church.

Unitarian Congregational. Organized, 1772. A stone edifice on Essex, near North Street.

Rev. Edmund B. Willson, *Pastor ;* Stephen G. Wheatland, *Clerk ;* Wm. S. Felton, *Treasurer ;* George Wheatland, Henry L. Williams, S. Endicott Peabody, James A. Farless, Ephraim A. Emerton, Emery S. Johnson, John R. Lakeman, *Committee ;* Benjamin Brown, *Sexton.*

Independent Church.

Unitarian Congregational. Organized, 1824. A brick edifice, Barton Sq. Rev. A. M. Haskell, *Pastor*; S. G. Jones, *Clerk*; Aaron Perkins, *Treasurer*; Willard P. Phillips, Nichols T. Snell, Enoch P. Fuller, James C. Stimpson, Benjamin M. Perkins, *Committee*; Jeremiah S. Perkins, *Collector*; Jacob S. Haskell, *Sexton*.

Independent Christian Church.

Organized, 1852. Place of worship, Union Street.

Rev. Rufus Wendell, *Pastor*; R. B. Reed, *Clerk*; Temple Hardy, jr., *Treasurer*; Temple Hardy, S. F. Rogers, *Deacons and Committee*; ——— *Sexton*. Vestry in Herbert Street. Sunday Schools held in the church.

First Universalist Society.

Formed 1805. A brick edifice on Rust Street.

Rev. Willard Spaulding, *Pastor*; Thomas H. Barnes, *Clerk and Treasurer*; T. H. Frothingham, Daniel Varney, Charles Harrington, T. H. Prime, J. P. Cook, N. R. Treadwell, E. A. Goldthwait, *Committee*; Hezekiah Sleeper, *Sexton*.

Tabernacle.

Orthodox Congregational. 1735. Place of worship, Washington, corner of Federal. A new edifice, erected 1854.

Rev. Charles Ray Palmer, *Pastor*; Richard C. Manning, *Clerk*; Joseph H. Phippen, *Treasurer*; Ezra Woodbury, *Collector*; Simeon Flint, Wm. H. Palmer, William Purbeck, George D. Phippen, Lyman Smith, *Committee*; Joseph Smith, *Sexton*.

Howard Street Church.

Orthodox Congregational. Formed as Congregational, December 29, 1803; became Presbyterian, 1815; returned to Congregational in 1828. Place of worship, Howard Street.

Rev. ——— ———, *Pastor*; Moses G. Farmer, *Clerk*; Henry Hale, Wm. H. Chapman, M. G. Farmer, J. Gillan, Stephen O'Hare, Francis M. Ashton, *Committee*; Stephen O'Hare, *Sexton*.

South Church.

Orthodox Congregational. Formed, 1735. Place of worship, Chestnut, corner of Cambridge Street.

Rev. Brown Emerson, D. D., and Rev. E. S. Atwood, *Pastors*; John Chapman, *Clerk*; George R. Chapman, *Treasurer*; William P. Goodhue, George R. Chapman, William L. Bowdoin, D. G. Batchelder, George T. Blake, *Committee*; Aaron J. Cate, *Sexton*.

Crombie Street Church.

Orthodox Congregational. Formed, 1832. Brick edifice on Crombie St.

Rev. ——— ———, *Pastor*; Henry J. Pratt, *Clerk*; John Barlow, *Treasurer*; Henry J. Pratt, James Trefren, Robert P. Clough, *Committee*; Chas. Staniford, *Sexton*.

New Jerusalem Church.

Organized, 1863. Place of Worship, Howard Street.

A. H. Hardy, *Pastor*; S. M. Cate, *Clerk and Treasurer*; A. H. Hardy and W. B. Pike, *Church Committee*.

First Baptist.

Organized, 1804. Brick edifice, 56 Federal Street.

Rev. Robert C. Mills, *Pastor*; N. Very, jr., *Clerk*; Joseph Price, *Treasurer*; James Upton, Alfred Peabody, George F. Brown, E. Seccomb, Josiah Beckford, *Committee*; Thomas Treadwell, *Sexton*.

Central Baptist.

Organized, 1826. Brick edifice, St. Peter Street.

Rev. Daniel D. Winn, *Pastor*; George Batchelder, *Clerk*; Daniel Potter, *Treasurer*; Levi Wiggin, William C. Hamond, Ed. H. Knight, Charles Creassy, Benjamin Edwards, *Committee*; W. S. Knowlton, *Sexton*.

Friends.

Organized, 1658. A brick edifice on Pine, corner of Warren Street.

William Chase, *Clerk*; Stephen A. Chase, *Treasurer*; William Chase, Sylvester C. Robinson, *Committee*; Jona. Buxton, William Chase, *Overseers of the Poor of the Society*.

Lafayette Street Methodist Episcopal Church.

Organized, March, 1841. Place of worship, corner Lafayette and Harbor Streets.

Rev. L. Crowell, *Pastor*; Matthew Robson, *Secretary*; James F. Almy, *Treasurer*; Abraham Bennett, Henry Brown, John Roberts, Matthew Robson, Charles H. Glazier, *Trustees*; George I. South, *Sexton*.

St. James Church.

Roman Catholic. Organized, 1859. Place of worship, No. 160 Federal Street.

Rev. William J. Daly, *Pastor*.

Church of the Immaculate Conception.

Roman Catholic. Organized, 1810. Place of worship, Walnut Street.

Rev. Michael Hartney, *Pastor*; Rev. James Quinlan, *Assistant*.

Grace Church.

Episcopalian. Organized, 1858. Gothic church, located on Essex Street, nearly opposite Monroe.

Rev. George D. Wildes, *Rector*; Benjamin Shreve, Charles S. Nichols, Henry R. Stone, *Wardens*; —— ——, *Clerk and Treasurer*; Samuel Pitman, jr., J. F. Tuckerman, Nathan A. Frye, *Vestrymen*; Royal M. Shorter, *Sexton*.

St. Peter's Church.

Episcopalian. Gathered in 1733. A stone edifice on St. Peter, corner of Brown Street.

Rev. James O. Scripture, *Rector*; John Kilburn, Gordon F. Bartlett, *Wardens*; Caleb Buffum, *Treasurer and Clerk*; James B. Curwen, James O. Safford, Francis Cox, William R. Gavett, S. B. Ives, *Vestrymen*; S. Berry, *Sexton*.

POST OFFICE.

Asiatic Building, 32 Washington Street.

John Chapman, *Postmaster;* Thomas H. Wiggin, *Assistant Postmaster;* William H. Flowers, Jr., John O. Chapman, *Clerks;* Richard P. Reed, John Henfield, Jr., Eben P. Trask, *Letter Carriers.*

THE MAILS FOR

Boston, close at 8 and 12½, A. M., and 6¼, P. M.; arrive at 8¼, A. M., and 1, 3¼, and 7, P. M.

Beverly Farms, close at 12½, P. M.; arrive at 11, A. M.

California, Isthmus, and Pacific Coast, close on the 10th, 20th, and last day of each month.

Danvers and Danversport, close at 9, A. M., and 1½, P. M.; arrive at 10, A. M., and 5, P. M.

Danvers Centre, close at 9, A. M., and 2, P. M.; arrive at 9¼, A. M., and 2¼, P. M.

Eastern, close at 7½, A. M., and 2¾, P. M.; arrive at 1 and 6¾, P. M.

Foreign, close day previous to sailing of Steamers — from Boston, 6¼, P. M.; from New York, 12½, P. M.

Gloucester, close at 7½, A. M., and 12½, P. M.; arrive at 11, A. M., and 4¾, P. M.

Lowell, close at 4, P. M.; arrives at 9, A. M.

Lynn, close at 12½, A. M., and 6¼, P. M.; arrives at 8¼, A. M., and 3¼, P. M.

Marblehead, close at 7½, A. M., and 12½, P. M.; arrives at 1, P. M.

New York, close at 8, A. M., and 12½ and 6¼, P. M.; arrives at 8¼, A. M., and 7, P. M.

South Danvers, close at 8½, A. M., and 1½, P. M.; arrives, 11½, A. M. and 5½, P. M.

Washington, D. C., close at 6¼, P. M.; arrive at 8¼, A. M.

FREE DELIVERY.

Letters delivered by the carriers throughout the city at 9, A. M., 1½ and 7, P. M.

RECEIVING BOXES.

Letter Boxes have been stationed at the places named below for the reception of all prepaid mail matters (*except valuable letters which must be deposited in the Post Office*).

☞ Letters deposited in these Boxes must be properly stamped before placing them therein.

Ward 1 — 44 Derby Street.
" " — 109 " "
Ward 2 — 69 Bridge Street.
" " — 9 Newbury Street.
Ward 3 — Eastern R. R. Station.
" " — 2 Flint Street.
Ward 4 — 106 Federal Street.
" " — 72 " "
" " — 36 Boston Street.
" " — South Reading Station.
Ward 5 — 33½ Lafayette Street.
Ward 6 — 48 North Street.

Collections will be made from these Boxes between 10 and 11 o'clock, A. M., and from 3 to 4 o'clock, P. M.

MONEY SENT WITHOUT DANGER OF LOSS.

Money orders for any amount not exceeding $30.00 on one order, will be issued on deposit at this office and payment of the following fees:

On order not exceeding $10.00 — 10 cents.
Over $10.00 and not exceeding $20.00 — 15 "
Over $20.00 and not exceeding $30.00 — 20 "

Lists of Money Order Offices may be seen at the Post Office.

CUSTOM HOUSE.

FOR THE DISTRICT OF SALEM AND BEVERLY,

No. 112 Derby Street, corner of Orange, Salem.

Robert S. Rantoul, *Collector.*
Charles S. Osgood, *Deputy Collector and Inspector.*
J. F. Dalton, *Clerk.*
Joseph Moseley, *Surveyor at Salem and Beverly.*
Simon O. Dalrymple, *Weigher and Gauger.*
William C. Waters, *Public Storekeeper.*
N. M. Hooper, William P. Buffum, Edward Hodges, Ephraim Felt, David Pulsifer, E. F. Miller, S. R. Hathaway, Salem; Gustavus Ober, Beverly; William Endicott, Danversport, *Inspectors.*
Ephraim Burr, *Aid to Revenue.*
William Lewis, *Porter.*
Stephen A. Powers, *Boatman.*

BRITISH CONSULAR AGENT.

Ephraim F. Miller, Custom House, 112 Derby Street.

U. S. INTERNAL REVENUE.

FIFTH COLLECTION DISTRICT OF MASS.

Office, No. 175 Essex Street, Salem.

J. Vincent Browne, *Collector;* Benjamin H. Ives, *Deputy Collector;* Amos Noyes, *Assessor, Newburyport;* Eleazer Austin, Edwin R. Bigelow, *Assistant Assessors in Salem.*

PROVOST MARSHAL'S OFFICE.

No. 46 Washington Street, Salem.

Capt. Daniel H. Johnson, jr., of Salem, *Provost Marshal;* Caleb H. Newcomb, *Chief Clerk.*

SALEM FIVE-CENT SAVINGS-BANK.

No. 175 Essex Street.

Henry L. Williams, *President;* J Vincent Brown, *Treasurer.*

ASIATIC NATIONAL BANK,

ASIATIC BUILDING,

NO. 32 WASHINGTON STREET.

Capital, ... $315,000
Par Value of Shares, ... $30.00

J. S. CABOT, President.   W. H. FOSTER, Cashier.

CHARLES S. REA, Teller.

WILLIAM J. FOSTER, Bookkeeper.

HENRY CURWEN, Clerk.

DIRECTORS.

GEORGE WHEATLAND,	N. A. FRYE,
LEONARD B. HARRINGTON,	JAMES B. CURWEN,
G. F. BROWN.	ROBERT BROOKHOUSE, JR.
JOHN C. OSGOOD.	

Discount, Mondays, Wednesdays, and Fridays.
Bank hours, 9 to quarter-past 1.

FIRST NATIONAL BANK,

NO. 7 CENTRAL STREET.

CAPITAL, ... $300,000
PAR VALUE OF SHARES, ... $100.00

Depositary and Financial Agent of the United States.

WILLIAM SUTTON, PRESIDENT.   E. H. PAYSON, CASHIER.

G. L. STREETER, TELLER,   WILLIAM AGGE, BOOKKEEPER,
CHARLES H. FLINT, CLERK.

DIRECTORS.

WILLIAM P. GOODHUE,	HARMON HALL,	M. W. SHEPARD,
JOHN JEWETT,	J. C. STIMPSON,	EBEN SUTTON,
GEO. W. KEENE,	WM. SUTTON, JR.	

Discount Daily. Directors Meetings, Mondays and Thursdays.
Bank hours, 8½ to 1½.
This Bank is prepared to furnish United States Securities of all kinds to all applicants free of expense.

MERCANTILE NATIONAL BANK.

NO. 7 CENTRAL STREET.

Capital, ... $200,000

Par Value of Shares,   .   .   . $100.00

JOHN DWYER, President.   J. HARDY PHIPPEN, Cashier.

GEO. PERKINS, Bookkeeper.   A. P. WEEKS, Clerk.

DIRECTORS.

John Dwyer,

WILLIAM F. NICHOLS,   JOHN HUSE,   AARON PERKINS,

OLIVER THAYER,   DAVID MOORE,   JOSIAH SPALDING.

Discount, Tuesdays and Fridays. Bank hours, 8¾ to 1½.

MERCHANTS NATIONAL BANK.

Asiatic Building, No. 32 Washington St.

CAPITAL, ... $200,000

Par value of Shares, ... $50.00

BENJAMIN H. SILSBEE, President.

NATHANIEL B. PERKINS, Cashier.

WILLIAM H. WHIPPLE, Bookkeeper.

HENRY O. FULLER, Clerk.

DIRECTORS.

BENJAMIN H. SILSBEE,

J. W. PERLE,   JAMES UPTON,   JAMES P. COOK,

WILLIAM VARNEY,   DANIEL C. HASKELL,   ANDREW B. ALMON.

Discount, Tuesdays and Fridays. Bank hours 8½ to 1½.

NATIONAL EXCHANGE BANK.

No. 231 ESSEX STREET.

CAPITAL, ... $200,000

Par value of Shares, ... $100.00

___

JOHN WEBSTER, President,   JOSEPH H. WEBB, Cashier,

S. G. SYMONDS, Bookkeeper,   CHAS. H. TUTTLE, Clerk.

___

DIRECTORS.

JOHN WEBSTER,

S. G. WHEATLAND,   NATHAN NICHOLS,   HENRY L. WILLIAMS

JOSEPH F. WALDEN,   JAS. S. KIMBALL, of Salem.

WILLIAM N. LORD, of South Danvers.

Discount Mondays and Thursdays. Bank hours from 8½ to 1½.

___

NAUMKEAG NATIONAL BANK.

No. 163 Essex Street.

CAPITAL, ... $500,000

PAR VALUE OF SHARES, . $100.00

___

CHARLES H. FABENS, President.

J. HARDY TOWNE, Cashier,   J. C TOWNE, Teller,

GEORGE R. FELT, Bookkeeper.

___

DIRECTORS.

W. B. PARKER,   CHARLES H. MILLER,   NATHANIEL WESTON,

JEREMIAH PAGE,   R. P. WATERS,   B. A. WEST,

FRANCIS COX,   EDW. D. KIMBALL,   CHAS. H. FABENS.

B. H. FABENS, Messenger.

Discount daily, 9½. Bank hours, 8½ A. M., to 1½ P. M.

SALEM NATIONAL BANK,

NO. 175 ESSEX STREET.

Capital, · · · · · · · · · · · · · · · $200,000

Par value of shares, · · · · · · · · · · · · $100.00

W. C. ENDICOTT, President.   GEO. D. PHIPPEN, Cashier.

BENJAMIN W. RUSSELL, Bookkeeper.

GEORGE G. CREAMER, Clerk.

DIRECTORS.

| W. C. Endicott, | James Chamberlain, | E. S. Poor, |
| Francis Brown, | Augustus Story, | George R. Chapman. |

Discount, Mondays and Thursdays. Bank hours, 9 to 1.

SALEM SAVINGS BANK,

ASIATIC BUILDING, NO. 32 WASHINGTON STREET.

Incorporated, 1818. Two and a half per cent. interest, half-yearly, is payable on the third Wednesday in April and October, which if not withdrawn, is added to the principal, and at the end of every five years all extra income is divided. The interest on long deposits has generally amounted to nearly 7 per cent.

October, 1865, the number of depositors were upwards of **11,000.** The amount deposited was **$2,580,000.**

JOSEPH H. CABOT, President.

CHAS. E. SYMONDS, Treasurer.

VICE PRESIDENTS.

| John C. Lee, | William B. Parker, | James Upton, |
| Leonard B. Harrington, | James B. Curwen, | Benj. H. Silsbee. |

TRUSTEES.

Alfred Peabody,	Peter Silver,	William H. Foster,
David Moore,	Nathan A. Frye,	J. Willard Peele,
Edward H. Payson,	John Dwyer,	William Sutton,
William C. Endicott,	Henry Gardiner,	John Webster,
Allen W. Dodge,	Chas. H. Fabens,	Geo. H. Chase,
	R. Brookhouse, Jr.	

FINANCE COMMITTEE.

| Joseph S. Cabot, | James Upton, | Benjamin H. Silsbee |
| Leonard B. Harrington, | William H. Foster, | William B. Parker. |

CHAS. H. TOWNE, Secretary.   WM. H. SIMONDS, Jr., Clerk.

SALEM MARINE INSURANCE CO.

CAPITAL, $100,000.

JEREMIAH PAGE, President.   WILLIAM NORTHEY, Sec'y.

Office, 32 Washington Street (Asiatic Building).

DIRECTORS,

WILLIAM B. PARKER,   B. H. SILSBEE,   WILLIAM HUNT,

JAMES B. CURWEN,   BENJAMIN A. WEST,   CHARLES H. FABENS.

ESSEX MUTUAL FIRE INSURANCE CO.

No. 42 Washington Street, Salem, Mass.

ANNUAL MEETING, THIRD SATURDAY IN SEPTEMBER.

JOHN H. NICHOLS, President.

CHARLES S. NICHOLS, Secretary

DIRECTORS,

DAVID PUTNAM,   GEORGE H. SMITH,   ROBERT PEELE,

JOHN PRATT,   LEONARD B. HARRINGTON,   JOHN JEWETT,

JEREMIAH PAGE,   WILLIAM P. GOODHUE,   STEPHEN B. IVES.

HOLYOKE MUTUAL
FIRE INSURANCE COMPANY.

SALEM, MASS.

AUGUSTUS STORY, . . . President and Treasurer.

THOMAS H. JOHNSON, Secretary.

Office, 27 Washington Street, (Holyoke Building).

Cash Assets, over . . . . . . **$175,000.00.**

AMOUNT INSURED, OVER $12,000,000.00.

DIRECTORS.

Asahel Huntington, Salem.	A. B. Almon, Salem.
Stephen Osborne, "	Charles H. Price, Salem.
Augustus Story, "	G. A. Tapley, Danvers.
James Chamberlain, "	F. Mitchell, Ipswich.
Aaron Perkins, "	Edward Todd, Rowley.

SALEM MUTUAL FIRE INSURANCE CO.

No. 42 WASHINGTON STREET.

ANNUAL MEETING, FOURTH MONDAY IN APRIL.

JOHN H NICHOLS, President.   CHARLES S. NICHOLS, Sec'y.

DIRECTORS.

Isaac P. Foster,	Samuel Chamberlain,
James Chamberlain,	Chas. M. Richardson,
George E. Brown,	Eben M. Price,
Francis Choate,	George Wheatland.

JOHN H. NICHOLS,

INSURANCE AGENT,

AUCTIONEER AND STOCK BROKER,

42 Washington Street, Salem,

—AGENT FOR—

National Ins. Co. of Boston,	Capital,	$300,000
Firemen Ins. Co. of Boston,	"	300,000
North American Ins. Co. of Boston,	"	200,000
Eliot Fire Ins. Co. of Boston,	"	200,000
Home Fire and Marine Ins. Co. of New York,		2,000,000
Croton Fire Ins. Co. of New York,	"	200,000
Columbian Marine Ins. Co.,	"	3,500,000
Ætna Fire Ins. Co. of Hartford, Ct.	"	2,250,000
New England Fire Ins. Co. of Hartford, Ct.,	"	200,000
Home Fire Ins. Co. of New Haven, Ct.,	"	500,000
Springfield Fire and Marine Ins. Co. of Springfield, Mass.,	"	300,000
Hampden Fire Ins. Co. of Springfield, Mass.,	"	150,000
Massasoit Ins. Co. of Springfield, Mass.,	"	200,000
Atlantic Fire and Marine Ins. Co. of Providence, R. I.,	"	200,000
Boot and Shoe Manufacturers' Mutual Ins. Co. of Lynn.		

23

SOCIETIES AND COMPANIES.

Plummer Hall.

This building is located at 134 Essex Street. It was erected, in 1856, from funds left by the late Miss Caroline Plummer to the Proprietors of the Salem Athenæum.

The first story is appropriated to the collections of the Essex Institute, and has two ante-rooms, — one of which contains the herbarium, the other the historical collections. A large hall in the rear has been finished expressly for the arrangement of the specimens in geology, mineralogy, and zoölogy.

The second story has a similar arrangement of rooms. The western ante-room is appropriated to the use of the librarian, and some of the principal works of reference, and the new books belonging to the Salem Athenæum ; the eastern, to bound volumes of newspapers belonging to the Essex Institute, and the library of the Essex South District Medical Society· The large library room is in the rear. The alcoves on the western side contain the library of the Salem Athenæum ; those on the eastern, that of the Essex Institute. The libraries of the two societies number about 35,000 volumes. The Library of the Essex Agricultural Society, containing about 10,000 volumes, is also deposited in this Hall.

Plummer Farm School of Reform for Boys.

This school was founded by the munificent bequest of Miss Caroline Plummer. It is a school for the instruction, employment, and reformation of juvenile offenders in the city of Salem, and is to be conducted on a plan similar to that of the State Reform School. The amount of the bequest is $25,000, present fund about $44,000, and the school will go into operation as soon as adequate means are obtained to carry it on successfully, in accordance with the will of the donor.

A Board of ten Trustees was chosen by the Mayor and Aldermen of the city of Salem, in May, 1855, and incorporated by an Act of the Legislature on the 21st of May, 1855. The first meeting of the Board of Trustees was held Nov. 26, 1855, at which time a code of By-Laws was adopted, and officers were elected. The Board of Trustees for 1865 is as follows : —

William I. Bowditch, *President* ; Henry M. Brooks, *Treasurer and Secretary;* William I. Bowditch, Joseph Andrews, James Kimball, James B. Curwen, John C. Lee, George W. Briggs, William Chase, James Upton, George R. Chapman, Samuel P. Andrews, *Trustees;* William I. Bowditch, Joseph Andrews, James B. Curwen, *Executive Committee.*

Salem Athenæum,

Incorporated in 1810, was formed by the union of the Social and Philosophical Libraries. The former was organized in 1760, the latter in 1781. Number of volumes, 13,000, which are deposited in Plummer Hall, 134 Essex Street.

Annual meeting for the choice of officers, last Wednesday but one in May. Library open every day between the hours of 9, A. M., and 1, P. M., and from 2 to 5, P. M.; in the summer months to 6, P. M.

Officers chosen in May, 1865. —Alpheus Crosby, *President* ; Henry Wheatland, *Clerk of the Corporation;* Henry Wheatland, *Treasurer;* Alpheus Crosby Wm. Mack, Henry Wheatland, John C. Lee, Jas. Chamberlain, William S. Messervy, John L. Russell, Nathaniel C. Robbins, Joseph G. Waters, *Trustees;* E. H. Roberts, *Librarian.*

Essex Southern District Medical Society,

Consists of all those members of the Massachusetts Medical Society who reside in Lynn, Swampscott, Nahant, Saugus, Marblehead, Salem, Danvers, Middleton, Beverly, Wenham, Topsfield, Ipswich, Hamilton, Essex, Rockport, Gloucester, and Manchester.

The Society was formed in 1805, in pursuance of a vote of the Massachusetts Medical Society, authorizing the establishment of district or subordinate associations. The Library is annually increased, and contains about 1000 volumes; it is deposited in Plummer Hall, where the regular quarterly meetings of the society are held.

Annual meeting on Tuesday of the week preceding the meeting of the Massachusetts Medical Society.

Officers elected, 1863. — Benjamin Cox, Jr., of Salem, *President;* E. Hunt, of Danvers, *Vice-President;* William Mack, of Salem, *Treasurer;* David Choate, of Salem, *Secretary;* William Neilson, of Salem, *Librarian.*

Essex Institute,

Incorporated in 1848, was formed by the Union of the Essex Historical Society and the Essex County Natural History Society.

The Library contains about 20,000 volumes; the cabinets are well filled with specimens of Natural History. The Institute have also portraits of several of the former Presidents of the Historical Society, and some of the early settlers of New England.

Exhibitions of Fruits and Flowers are held occasionally at their rooms, in Plummer Hall.

Annual Meeting on the second Wednesday in May.

Officers chosen in May, 1865. — Francis Peabody, *President;* J. Fiske Allen, A. C. Goodell, of Salem, S. P. Fowler, of Danvers, *Vice-Presidents;* Henry Wheatland, *Secretary and Treasurer;* Charles Davis, of Beverly, *Librarian;* F. W. Putnam, *Superintendent of Museum.*

Library open every day between the hours of 9, A. M., and 1, P. M., and 2 and 5, P. M.; in summer to 6, P. M.

Salem Lyceum,

Was formed the 18th of January, 1830, and organized as an Incorporated Association on the 2d of April, 1830. The introductory lecture was delivered in the Sewall Street Meeting House, by Hon. D. A. White.

The purchase of an annual ticket makes a person a member of the corporation; and the price of a ticket has never been more than ONE DOLLAR. Over six hundred lectures have been delivered in the annual courses.

The Legislature, on the 20th of April, 1852, passed an act, making Daniel A. White, Stephen C. Phillips, George Peabody, their associate petitioners and successors, and the male citizens of the city of Salem, of twenty-one years of age, purchasors of tickets to the twenty-third course of lectures, a corporation by the name of the Salem Lyceum. At a meeting of the corporation, held May, 1863, the following officers were elected : —

George W. Briggs, *President;* Albert G. Browne, *Vice-President;* Henry J. Cross, *Recording and Corresponding Secretary;* G. L. Streeter, *Treasurer;* James Kimball, S. P. Andrews, S. Johnson, Jr., Wm. L. Bowdoin, A. A. Smith, T. H. Frothingham, Alpheus Crosby, Geo. R. Chapman, *Managers.* George Peabody, Stephen H. Phillips, Caleb Foote, *Trustees.*

Young Mens' Union.

Organized, 1855.

For the benefit of the Young Men of all avocations *in this community.*

This association occupies convenient rooms (No. 224 Essex Street, Browne's block), and is in receipt of the leading daily and weekly journals, of all parts of the country; also the standard reviews and principal periodicals of the day. It has a library of reference, comprising the latest and most accurate maps.

No admission fee is required; and the assessments, payable in advance, are fixed at the low price of $2 per annum.

All gentlemen, wishing to sustain such an institution in our city, or avail themselves of its privileges, are cordially invited to join.
Officers for the year ending, April, 1865. — George M. Whipple, *President;* Joseph H. Webb, *Vice-President;* William O. Thayer, *Treasurer;* N. A. Horton, *Corresponding Secretary;* C. H. Buffum, *Recording Secretary;* R. C. Manning, W. J. Foster, Edward H. Knight, William P. Upham, *Directors.*

Young Men's Christian Association.

OFFICERS.

E. S. Atwood, *President;* John C. Osgood, Charles H. Price, William H. Whipple, *Vice-Presidents;* Levi F. Warren, *Corresponding Secretary;* George P. Daniels, *Recording Secretary;* S. S. D. Sheppard, *Treasurer.*

DIRECTORS.

Tabernacle. — D. Choate, Rev. C. R. Palmer, J. F. Smith.
South. — J. H. Collier, Irving Stone, D. B. Brooks, George R. Chapman.
First Baptist. — E. M. Walton, G. F. Jelly.
Central Baptist. — S. S. Skinner, H. F. Skerry, George E. Batchelder.
Crombie Street. — Jose Margati, James Trefren, W. T. Gaaett.
Methodist. — E. R. Bigelow, J. F. Almy, W. Robson.
Grace. — Rev. G. D. Wildes, Levi F. Warren.

Bible Society of Salem and Vicinity.

Instituted August 22, 1810. Annual Meeting, second Wednesday in June. Depository, No. 230 Essex Street.
Officers elected, June, 1865. — Rev. S. M. Worcester, D. D., *President;* Rev. Robert C. Mills, D. D., *Secretary;* Stephen B. Ives, *Treasurer;* R. P. Waters, James Upton, A. Huntington, J. H. Towne, *Trustees.*

Harmony Grove Cemetery Corporation.

Organized in 1839. Incorporated in 1840. Consecrated, June 14, 1840. Contains about 65 acres.
The cemetery was formerly situated within the town of Danvers. The Legislature of 1840 passed an act so altering the boundaries between Salem and Danvers, that the whole of the cemetery now lies within the limits of the city of Salem. The sale of lots is under the charge of W. H. Foster, to whom application can be made.
Annual Meeting for the choice of Trustees, first Wednesday in January.
Officers elected, January, 1860. Joseph S. Cabot, *President;* John C. Lee, J. W. Peele, Elijah A. Hanson, Francis Peabody, George Wheatland, Nathaniel Silsbee, William H. Foster, *Trustees;* William H. Foster, *Secretary and Treasurer;* Charles Creasy, *Keeper.*

Dorcas Society.

Mrs. A. L. Peirson, *Directress;* Mrs. Rebecca Grinnell, Miss Elizabeth J. Devereux, *Distributors;* Miss Mary C. Anderson, *Treasurer;* Miss Maria Chase, *Secretary.*

Salem Seamen's Orphan and Children's Friend Society.

The Salem Children's Friend Society was organized February 25, 1839, for the purpose of rescuing from evil, and improving the condition of, such children as are in indigent and suffering circumstances, and not otherwise provided for. Incorporated, March, 1841. In 1844, the house they now occupy No. 7 Carpenter Street, was purchased at an expense of $1,500, and presented to them by R. Brookhouse, Esq., of this city, when they took their present name.
Annual Meeting, 8th of May. Visitors admitted on Thursday.

Officers. — Mrs. Thorndike Proctor, *President;* Mrs. N. W. Osgood, *Vice-President;* Miss Ellen Brown, *Secretary;* Mrs. C. M. Richardson, *Treasurer;* Mrs. James Chamberlain, Mrs. B. R. Peabody, Mrs. A. J. Archer, Mrs. Joseph Winn, Mrs. J. H. Phippen, Mrs. N. H. Brooks, Mrs. Charles H. Miller, Mrs. N. B. Mansfield, Mrs. Henry I. Pratt, Mrs. James Braden, Miss Jane Nichols, Miss Elizabeth K. Whipple, *Managers;* Michael Carleton, A. Huntington, John Chapman, Charles Ropes, Robert Brookhouse, *Board of Advisers;* Miss Asconath Gage, *Teacher;* Mrs. Azuba Gillpatrick, *Matron.*

Seamen's Widow and Orphan Association.

Formed, 1833. Incorporated, 1844.

Annual Meeting on the first Thursday in May.

Officers, January, 1864-5. — Mrs. S. B. Ives, *President;* Mrs. John Barlow, *Vice-President;* Mrs. George D. Phippen, *Treasurer;* Miss M. E. W. Jocelyn, *Secretary;* Mrs. Joseph Webb, Mrs. E. K. Lakeman, Mrs. Thos. B. Russell, Mrs. Margaret W. Kimball, Mrs. Ephraim Burr, Mrs. Samuel Ropes, jr., Mrs. James Emerton, Mrs. W. H. Jelly, Miss English, Miss P. Carleton, Mrs. George A. Parker, *Managers.*

Ladies' Seamen's Friend Society.

Organized, January 22, 1844.

Present Officers. — Mrs. George H. Smith, *President;* Mrs. Samuel Benson, *Vice-President;* Miss Sarah Hobart, *Corresponding and Recording Secretary;* Mrs. Robert C. Mills, Mrs. Andrew Ward, Mrs. N. P. Rust, Mrs. Michael Carleton, Mrs. Robert Skerry, *Managers.*

Samaritan Society.

Annual Meeting on 2d Monday in December. Organized, December 10, 1832.

Board of Officers. — Mrs. E. N. Cheever, *President;* Mrs. J. M. Brown, 1st *Vice-President;* Mrs. L. Short, 2d *Vice-President;* Mrs. J. W. Walden, Mrs. E. Woods, Mrs. H. Pitman, Mrs. E. A. Goldthwait, Mrs. H. Luscomb, Mrs. S. R. Hathaway, *Trustees;* Mrs. Willard Goldthwaite, *Secretary and Treasurer;* Miss M. Kimball, *Assistant Treasurer.*

Salem Female Charitable Society.

This Society was one of the first of our charitable institutions, having been formed as early as 1801, and incorporated in 1804. Its objects were the support of female children, and to assist that unfortunate class, the aged and infirm widows.

Its first Board were Mrs. Sarah Fiske, *First Directress;* Mrs. Lucretia Osgood, *Second Directress;* Mrs. Lydia Nichols, *Treasurer;* Mrs. Abigail M. Dabney, *Secretary;* Mrs. Elizabeth White, Mrs. Deborah Hovey, Mrs. Hannah Robinson, Mrs. Hannah Ropes, Mrs. Eunice Richardson, Mrs. Sarah Crowninshield, Mrs. Hannah Hodges, Mrs. Sarah Dunlap, *Managers.* These ladies were succeeded by others, some long since deceased; the most recent, the late Mrs. Rebecca Dodge and Mrs. Richard S. Rogers.

The Society continued its operations, as above stated, until 1831 or 1832, when, by a vote of the Board, and by the authority granted them by the Legislature, it was decided to appropriate its income for the relief of indigent females. The Society meetings are held monthly.

The present Board consists of Mrs. R. Brookhouse, *First Directress;* Mrs. P. P. Pinel, *Second Directress;* Miss S. Frye, *Treasurer;* Miss H. O. Mack, *Secretary;* Mrs. S. P. Webb, Mrs. Emery Johnson, Mrs. G. B. Loring, Mrs. O. P. Lord, Miss Mary C. Anderson, Mrs. Maria Chase, Mrs. Eben Putnam, Miss Maria M. Neal, *Managers.*

Association for the Relief of Aged and Destitute Women.

Old Ladies' Home, 114 Derby, corner Orange Street.

Board of Government elected Nov. 1865. — B. H. Silsbee, *President;* James Upton, Stephen B. Ives,.Robt. Brookhouse, Jr., *Vice-Presidents;* J. Hardy Towne, *Treasurer;* Joseph H. Webb, *Secretary. Lady Managers,* Mrs. Robt. Brookhouse, Mrs. John Bertram, Miss Caroline Saltonstall, Mrs. John Webster, Mrs. Alfred Peabody, Mrs. Maria Chase, Mrs. George H. Chase, Mrs. Michael Carleton, Mrs. William F. Gardner, Miss Caroline Follansbee, Miss Lydia R. Nichols, Mrs. B. H. Silsbee. *Gentlemen Managers,* Charles A. Ropes, Henry F. Skerry, Richard C. Manning, Robert S. Rantoul, David Moore, Stephen G. Wheatland, Aaron Perkins, S. M. Cate, Oliver Thayer, Joseph H. Phippen, James O. Safford, John Webster. Mrs. Harriet Imperial, *Matron.*

Salem Employment Society.

Organized January, 16, 1861.

Objects: to give sewing to poor women, at a fair compensation, who cannot obtain employment elsewhere. The garments thus made, except those specially ordered, are sold at the stores of Miss Lydia Stone, 366 Essex Street, and R. Plummer, 248 Essex Street, and the proceeds are applied to extend the benefits of the Society.

Semi-annual sales in spring and autumn are also held under the direction of the Managers.

Annual meeting second Thursday in April.

Officers chosen in April, 1865. — Mrs. Samuel Johnson, *President;* Mrs. Thomas Cole, *Vice-President;* Miss Esther C. Mack, *Secretary;* Mrs. R. S. Rantoul, *Treasurer;* Miss Anna Johnson, *Purchaser.* Mrs. John Bertram, Mrs. Wm. S. Cleveland, Miss C. Archer, Miss S. Blanchard, Miss E. O. Williams, Miss Ellen Osgood, Mrs. Joseph Osgood, Miss Ellen M. Putnam, Miss Sarah H. Ropes, Miss Ellen D. Webb, Miss Martha G. Wheatland, *Managers.*

Salem East India Marine Society.

No. 163 Essex Street.

Instituted in 1799.   Incorporated in 1801.

The museum contains a fine collection of specimens in the various departments of Natural History, to which strangers have free access by first obtaining a pass from any of the members of the Society.

Annual meeting first Wednesday in November.

Officers elected, Nov. 1865. — Benjamin H. Silsbee, *President;* Charles Millett, Charles Mansfield, Charles Roundy, *Committee of Observation;* Nathaniel Griffin, *Treasurer;* Thomas Saul, *Rec. Sec. and Superintendent.*

Salem Marine Society.

Instituted, 1766.   Incorporated, 1771.

Annual meeting, last Thursday in October.   Meetings are likewise held on the evenings of the last Thursday of every month throughout the year.

Officers elected, Oct. 1865. — John Dwyer, *Master;* James Buffington, *Deputy Master;* Daniel H. Mansfield, *Treas.;* Robert W. Gould, *Clerk;* Augustine S. Perkins, James Gilbert, Peter Silver, Samuel R. Curwen, *Dis. Committee;* Allen Putnam, *Agent for the Franklin Building.*

Salem Charitable Mechanic Association.

Organized, Oct. 1, 1817. Incorporated, June 4, 1822.

Consists of regular apprenticed Mechanics, and of Manufacturers, citizens of the city of Salem and vicinity. Number of members about 300. Annual meeting for the choice of officers, first Wednesday in January.

In connection with this Association is a Library, containing 4000 volumes, for the use of members and their apprentices. The Library is open on Saturday evening of each week. The average weekly delivery is 150 volumes.

Officers elected, Jan. 1866. — Stephen B. Ives, *President;* Simeon Flint, *Vice-President;* John Chapman, *Treas.;* Thomas M. Dix, *Secretary;* E. H. Morse, Jonn. Davis, John Preston, William F. Gardner, Joseph Swasey, Andrew Elliot, Joseph, C. Chever, Wm. C. Hamond, Benj. S. Mansfield, Gilman A. Andrews, John A. Norfolk, Abraham Towle, John P. Phelps, Andrew Ober, Wm. H. Hurd, *Trustees.*

Salem Dispensary.

Organized, February, 1820. Incorporated, February, 1831.

Its object has been the relief of the poor by furnishing Medicines and Medical Advice gratuitously.

In 1859, it was reconstructed on the plan of similar institutions in larger cities, and a Central Office established at the Town Hall, where the Clerk is in attendance every day, Sundays excepted, from 3 to 5, P. M., to receive all applications for the privileges afforded by the institution. Any person approved by the Executive Committee, who shall pay the sum of five dollars per annum, or fifty cents per month, may be entitled to the benefit of the institution for himself and family. Those who may be unable to pay this small assessment, will be provided for gratuitously. The expenses to be paid by an annual subscription.

The city is divided into two districts, the Eastern and the Western, to each of which is assigned a Physician, and an Apothecary. The Eastern district includes all persons who may apply for relief, living Eastward of St. Peter and Central Streets, and in South Salem. The Western District includes those living Westward of the above streets, and in North Salem.

Annual meeting, first Thursday in January.

Board of Managers, elected January, 1864. — Asahel Huntington, *President;* John C. Towne, *Secretary and Treasurer;* George Peabody, Edward B. Peirson, Richard S. Rogers, Robert Brookhouse, John Bertram, William D. Pickman, Nathan A. Frye, Augustus Story, John Webster, James B. Curwen, R. C. Manning, David Choate.

Executive Committee. — E. B. Pierson, N. A. Frye, John Webster, William Neilson, Arthur Kemble, and the Dispensary Physicians.

Physicians. — Dr. Wm. Neilson, 49 Washington Street, for Eastern District; Dr. Arthur Kemble, 174 Essex Street, for Western District.

Apothecaries. — G. Barton, Eastern District; C. H. Pinkham, Western District.

Clerk. — Dr. William Neilson; office, south-west room in old Town Hall.

Salem Leg Company.

22 High Street.

Dr. E. B. Peterson, *President;* Joseph H. Webb, *Treasurer and Clerk;* John C. Osgood, George B. Jewett, A. Aug. Smith, Jas. O. Safford, Chas. H. Price, James A Gillis, *Directors.*

Salem Independent Protective Association.

Organized, August 26, 1847.

Edward A. Goldthwait, *President;* George Luscomb, *Vice-President;* H. Sleeper, *Secretary;* H. Luscomb, *Treasurer;* J. S. Henderson, Benjamin A. Gray, *Directors;* H. Luscomb, C. Warren Gardner, *Storekeepers.*

Salem Gaslight Company.

Office, 188 Essex Street. Organized, April 4, 1850.   Capital, $150,000.

Annual Meeting, second Monday in March.   The Company carries the branch-pipes into buildings to a distance of seventeen feet from the main pipe; beyond that, the pipe and the fixtures are at the expense of the consumer.   The Company also places the meter to measure the quantity of gas consumed by a self-registering process of wheel-work.   The price of gas is at the rate of $4.45 per 1000 cubic feet.

The stores were lighted with gas for the first time, on Tuesday evening, December 17, 1850; the street lamps, on Wednesday evening, December 25.

Stephen G. Wheatland, *President;* B. Frank Fabens, Stephen G. Wheatland, William Hunt, Salem; Francis Brown, Henry Gardner, *Directors;* David Moore, *Treasurer and Superintendent;* Richard Gardner, *Clerk.*

Salem Laboratory Company.

Office, 42 Washington Street.   Located on Laboratory Street, North Salem. Annual Meeting, last Wednesday in July.

William H. Foster, *President;* Charles S. Richardson, William H. Foster, George F. Brown, Edward B. Lane, Joseph C. Foster, John Jewett. Stephen Curran, *Directors;* Wm. H. Foster, *Secretary;* John H. Nichols, *Clerk and Agent;* Nathaniel A. Very, *Chemist.*

Salem and South Danvers (Horse) Railroad Company.

A. C. Goodell, jr., *President;* Wm. Mack, G. D. Phippen, W. R. L. Ward, Asa P. Robinson, *Directors;* James F. Foye, *Treasurer;* Moses H. Hale, *Superintendent.*

Commenced running to South Danvers, July 8, 1863; to Beverly, October 29, 1863; has carried between Salem and South Danvers about 42,000 passengers monthly, and run about 9000 miles in the same time.   It is estimated the Beverly travel will increase this nearly two-thirds.

Salem Car Company.

Office, 243½ Essex Street.   Works on Bridge Street.

Willard P. Phillips, *President;* J. Chamberlain, Thomas H. Frothingham, David Moore, Augustus Story, J. P. Phippen, Henry L. Williams, *Directors;* J. A. Gillis, *Treasurer and Clerk.*

Eastern Railroad.

Directors. — George M. Browne, *President;* G. M. Browne, of Boston; Samuel Hooper, of Boston; Franklin Haven of Boston; Benjamin E. Bates of Boston; Micajah Lunt, of Newburyport; Henry L. Williams, of Salem; Wm. L. Dwight, of Portsmouth.   J. Prescott, *Superintendent;* John B. Parker, *Treasurer.*

ESSEX RAILROAD.

From Salem to Lawrence.

This road is under the management of the Eastern Railroad.

SOUTH READING BRANCH RAILROAD.

From Danvers to the Boston and Maine R. R. at South Reading. Directors same as Eastern Railroad Company.

SALEM AND LOWELL RAILROAD.

This road is leased and operated by the Boston and Lowell R. R. Company.

DANVERS RAILROAD.

From Danvers to South Reading. This road is managed by the Boston and Maine Railroad Company.

Salem and Danvers Aqueduct Company.

Incorporated, 1797. Annual Meeting, first Thursday in May. Dividends in May and November, paid at Salem Bank. Office, No. 280½ Essex Street. William Sutton, *President;* Aaron Perkins, *Vice-President;* Robert Peele, Ebenezer Sutton, Aaron Perkins, John Lovejoy, Thos. P. Pingree, 3d, George D. Phippen, Joseph Leavitt, Otis P. Lord, Alfred A. Abbott, Benjamin H. White, Francis Brown, *Directors.*

Salem Water Commissioners.

Incorporated, 1865. Office, No. 4 Hubon Block.

Stephen H. Phillips, *Chairman;* Peter Silver and Franklin T. Sanborn, *Commissioners;* Daniel H. Johnson, jr., *Clerk of the Board;* James Slade, *Chief Engineer;* Charles H. Swan, *Assistant Engineer.*

Essex Marine Railway.

Incorporated, February, 1826. First vessel hauled up, ship, " Endeavor," September 21, 1826. Annual Meeting, third Monday in January. J. W. Getchell, *Superintendent:* Nathaniel B. Perkins, *Treasurer;* Benjamin Webb, Aaron Perkins, and W. P. Goodhue, *Directors.*

Salem Marine Railway Company.

Incorporated, 1823. First vessel hauled up, brig " Washington," September, 1823. Annual Meeting in January. J. W. Peele, George Dodge, Nathaniel Griffin, *Directors;* Nath. Griffin, *Treasurer;* Daniel C. Becket, *Superintendent.*

Salem Turnpike and Chelsea Bridge Corporation.

Officers chosen, September, 1863. — Stephen G. Wheatland, *President;* John H. Nichols, 1st, Herbert B. Newhall, 2d, *Vice-Presidents;* William S. Cleveland, *Clerk and Treasurer;* William Endicott, William C. Endicott, John Jewett, Robert Peele, John Lovejoy, James C. Stimpson, *Directors;* John Lovejoy, *Agent.*
Annual Meeting in September. Dividends first Wednesday in January, April, July, and October, paid at Commercial Bank.

East India Marine Hall Corporation.

Incorporated, 1824. Annual Meeting, second Wednesday in January.

Officers elected in January, 1863 — Benjamin H. Silsbury, *President;* William B. Parker, Charles Mansfield, Charles Millet, *Directors;* Nathaniel Griffin, *Clerk and Treasurer.*

Mechanic Hall Corporation.

Incorporated, 1839. Annual Meeting, first Thursday in January.

Directors. — Thomas Nichols, jr. *President ;* Aaron Perkins, Thomas Nichols, Daniel Potter, Josiah Crocker, John Jewett; T. M. Dix, *Clerk, Treasurer, and Agent.*

Forest River Lead Company.

Formed, 1843. Incorporated, 1846.

Officers, — E. D. Brigham, *President ;* William H. Chase, B. F. Fabens, George C. Chase, Elijah D. Brigham, *Directors ;* Geo. C. Chase, *General Agent ;* Henry M. Brooks, *Clerk and Treasurer.*

Mills at Forest River, on the road leading to Marblehead. Counting-room, 243½ Essex Street (upstairs.)   The Company manufacture White Lead, Sheet Lead, and Vinegar.

Great Pasture Company.

Annual Meeting, first Monday in April.

Officers elected, April, 1865. — John Archer, *President ;* John R. Andrews, Joseph S. Cabot, Henry L. Williams, *Directors ;* John P. Andrews, *Treasurer ;* H. Wheatland, *Secretary.*

Naumkeag Steam Cotton Company.

Annual Meeting, third Wednesday in January

Incorporated in 1839. Building erected in 1845, in Harbor Street, South Salem. Second building erected in 1860.

Asahel Huntington, *President ;* William Sutton, Asahel Huntington, Richard P. Waters, James Chamberlain, Stephen B. Ives, James S. Kimball, Francis Cox, E. F. Cutter of Boston, C. H. Miller, *Directors ;* Edward F. Brown, *Clerk ;* Edmund Dwight, *Treasurer.*

Seccomb Oil Manufacturing Company.

Amos Tufts, *President ;* E. Seccomb, *Treasurer ;* Edward S. Thayer, *Clerk ;* Amos Tufts, John Howarth, E. Seccomb, George L. Newcomb, N. H. Knapp, Benj. Beal, William B. Ashton, *Directors.*

MASONIC AND ODD FELLOW SOCIETIES.

Meetings are held at Masonic Hall, Downing's Block.

William L. Batchelder, General Superintendent of Hall.

Winslow Lewis Encampment Knights Templar.

William Sutton, *M. E. G. Comm.;* George H. Peirson, *G. ;* David S. Shattuck, *C. G.;* William C. Maxwell, *Prelate ;* Gamaliel Hodges, *S. W.;* Henry E. Jocelyn, *J. W.;* Thomas Hunt, *Treasurer:* John J. Coker, *Recorder ;* George Tapley, *Sw.'d B. ;* Dana T. Smith, *St.'d B. ;* Charles H. Norris, *W. ;* William H. Kimball, A. Lawrence Peirson, James Osborne, *Capt.'s G. ;* William L. Batchelder, *Sentinel.*

Washington Royal Arch Chapter.

Instituted, January 18, 1811. Reorganized, September 7, 1852.

Regular communications, 3d and 4th Thursday of each month. Officers elected annually, 3d Thursday in December.

Officers elected, Dec., 1865. — William C. Maxwell, *M. E. H. P. ;* Charles H. Nims, *E. K. ;* John J. Coker, *E. S. ;* James Kimball, *Chaplain ;* Alva

Kendall, *Treasurer;* William Archer, *Secretary;* John P. Browning, *C. of H.;* George W. S. Rollins, *P. S.;* Henry II. Blake, *R. A. C.;* George Tapley, *M. 3d V.;* Samuel C. Weston, *M. 2d V.;* Daniel H. Jewett, *M. 1st V.;* William L. Batchelder, *Tyler;* Israel P. Harris, *Organist.*

Essex Lodge of Free and Accepted Masons.

Chartered by the Grand Lodge of Massachusetts, June 6, 1791. Reorganized, June 11, 1845.

Regular communications on the first Tuesday evening in each month; other Tuesday evenings, meetings of the Lodge of Instruction.
Officers elected annually, on the first Tuesday evening in December.
Officers elected, Dec., 1865.—Israel S. Lee, *W. M.;* Thomas J. Hutchinson, *S. W.;* Charles H. Norris, *J. W.;* Alva Kendall, *Treasurer;* James Kimball, *Chaplain;* Thomas H. Lefavour, *Secretary;* George W. S. Rollins, *S. D.;* Joseph F. Full, *J. D.;* John P. Browning, *Marshal;* John W. Roberts, *S. S.;* George K. Proctor, *J. S.;* William L. Batchelder, *Tyler.*

Starr King Lodge of Free and Accepted Masons.

Dana Z. Smith, *W. M.;* Henry A. Brown, *S. W.;* George W. Williams, *J. W.;* Rev. Augustus M. Haskell, *Chaplain;* George Creamer, *Treasurer;* Jonathan Perley, *Secretary;* Henry E. Jocelyn, *S. D.;* Tristram Savary, *J. D.;* Henry R. Stone, *S. S.;* Nathaniel Peirce, *J. S.;* Samuel C. Weston, *J. S.;* William L. Batchelder, *Tyler;* Charles H. Towne, *Organist.*

Independent Order of Odd Fellows.

NAUMKEAG ENCAMPMENT, No. 13. I. O. OF O. F.

Instituted at Salem, June 26, 1845. The regular sessions are held on the second and fourth Thursday evenings in each month, in Asiatic Building. Officers chosen semi-annually, in the months of June and December.
Officers chosen, Dec., 1865.—J. E. Davis, *C. P.;* D. S. Holden, *H. P.;* Ezekiel Russell, *S. W.;* C. Prentiss, *J. W.;* E. B. Phillips, *Scribe;* Joseph Swasey, *Treasurer.*

ESSEX LODGE, NO. 26. I. O. OF O. F.

Instituted, November 6, 1843. Meetings every Monday evening in Asiatic Building. Officers chosen semi-annually, on the last Monday evening in June and December.
Officers elected, Dec., 1865.—John White, *N. G.;* William Holland, *V. G.;* E. B. Phillips, *Recording and Permanent Secretary;* J. P. Langmaid, *Treasurer.*

FRATERNITY LODGE, NO. 118. I. O. OF O. F.

Instituted, November 18, 1846. Meetings every Wednesday evening, at Asiatic Building. Officers chosen semi-annually, on the last Wednesday evenings in June and December.
Officers elected, Dec., 1865.—J. L. Lougee, *N. G.;* Charles H. Ingalls, *V. G.;* William M. Hill, *Secretary;* J. Farnum, *Treasurer;* James Kimball, *Chaplain.*

Sons of Temperance, Etc.

HENFIELD DIVISION, NO. 2.

Instituted, February 23, 1844.

Officers elected quarterly. Meetings in their Hall, No. 150 Essex Street, on every Thursday evening.

Officers for Term commencing January, 1866.—William E. Carey, *D. G. W. P.*; Abijah D. Scott, *W. P.*; Samuel Moore, *W. A.*; Willi m E. Carey, *R. S.*; Proctor Symonds, *A. R. S.*; Eben N. Walton, *F. S.*; Philip B. Ruee, *T.*; Charles Manning, *Chaplain*; Thomas W. Gwinn, *Con.*; Charles E. Legrand, *A. C.*; Joseph H. Walton, *I. S.*; Phillip Blaney, *O. S.*; Benjamin M. Kenney, *Organist*; Charles Manning, Andrew J. Tibbetts and Charles H. Mansfield, *Trustees.*

PHILLIPS DIVISION, NO. 84.

Instituted, February 15, 1859.

Meet Tuesday Evening, at Hall, 8 Lafayette Street.
Officers for Term commencing January, 1866.—Daniel P. Weir, *D. G. W. P.*; Daniel P. Weir, *W. P.*; Stover Grindal, *W. A.*; John O'Donnell, *R. S.*; James A. Evans, *A. R. S.*; Rufus L. Gordon, *F. S.*; Horace D. Eaton, *T.*; Edward B. Perkins, *Chap.*; Chas. F. Edgerly, *Cor.*; Geo. F. Melcher, *A. C.*; Geo. A. Chandler, *I. S.*; Ernest D. Lord, *O. S.*; Geo. W. Potter, *Chorister.*

MINNEHAHA LODGE, NO. 10, INDEPENDENT ORDER GOOD TEMPLARS.

Organized, February 22, 1862.

Meet at Henfield Hall, 150 Essex Street, Monday evenings.
Officers, Jan., 1866.—George B. Armstrong, *W. C. T.*; Elizabeth W. Peabody, *V. W. T.*; Robert Wilson, *W. S.*; James H. McCartney, *W. A. S.*; William Leonard, *W. F. S.*; Eleazer Pope, *W. T.*; Sarah Phillips, *W. C.*; Edward A. Daniels, *W. M.*; Sarah B. McCartney, *W. D. M.*; Mary M. Nimblet, *W. I. G.*; William Walker, *W. O. G.*; Lydia A. Farnham, *W. R. H. S.*; Margaret E. Wiggin, *W. L. H. S.*; Henry Morton, *P. W. C. T.*

YOUNG MEN'S CATHOLIC TEMPERANCE SOCIETY OF SALEM.

Room over 137 Essex. Entrance on Liberty Street.
Organized, October 19, 1857.

MILITARY.

13th Unattached Salem Light Infantry.

Armory, Franklin Building.

Robert W. Reeves, *Captain*. Geo. O. Stevens, *First Lieutenant*. Geo. H. Perkins, *Second Lieutenant.*

68th Unattached Salem Mechanic Light Infantry.

Armory, Phœnix Building.

Joseph H. Glidden, *Captain*. George M. Crowell, *First Lieutenant*. Robert P. Clough, *Second Lieutenant*.

2d Company Salem Independent Cadets.

Armory, Franklin Building.

———, *Major.* John P. Browning, *Adjutant.* Jona. A. Kenny, *Quartermaster.* ——— ———, *Captain.* Joseph C. Foster, A. Parker Brown, Edward A. Simonds, *First Lieutenants.* Phillip G. Skinner, Geo. D. Glover, John C. Dalton, Wm. Blaney, *Second Lieutenants.*

Salem Light Infantry Veteran Association.

Organized, Nov. 1862.

PAST CAPT. GEORGE PEABODY, PRESIDENT.

VICE PRESIDENTS. — *Past 'Captains,* Joseph Cloutman, George H. Devereux, Samuel A. Safford, Richard West, S. Endicott Peabody, William C. Endicott, James A. Farless, Arthur F. Devereux, George D. Putnam, Robert W. Reeves.

Finance Committee. — S. Endicott Peabody, Stephen G. Wheatland, James A. Farless, Jonathan F. Worcester, Benjamin A. West.

Secretary and Treasurer. — William Leavitt.

ESSEX AGRICULTURAL SOCIETY.

Incorporated, June 12, 1818.

Exhibitions held annually in the month of September. The Society is receiving from year to year large accessions to its list of members.

This society was the first in the State to publish in detail its transactions, — which have now extended to six large octavo volumes, containing much valuable information to the agriculturist.

A Library was commenced in the autumn of 1849, which now numbers about one thousand volumes, deposited in Plummer Hall, Salem.

In 1858, the Society came into possession of a valuable farm of 150 acres in Topsfield, bequeathed to it by the late Dr. Treadwell, of Salem for experimental purposes.

The following is the list of officers for 1865-6 : —

William Sutton, of South Danvers, *President;* Lewis Allen, of South Danvers, Jeremiah Colman, of Newburyport; David Choate, of Essex; *Vice Presidents;* E. H. Payson, *Treasurer;* Charles P. Preston, of Danvers, *Secretary.*

COURTS AND COUNTY OFFICERS.

Supreme Judicial Court.

Geo. T. Bigelow, Boston, *Chief Justice,* Salary,		$4,500
Associate Justices.		
Charles A. Dewey, Northampton,	"	4,000
Horace Gray, jr. Boston,	"	4,000
James D. Colt, Pittsfield, Boston,	"	4,000
Eben. R. Hoar, Concord,	"	4,000
Reuben A. Chapman, Springfield,	"	4,000

Charles Allen Boston, *Reporter.*

Chester I. Reed Taunton *Attorney General.*

Asahel Huntington, *Clerk of the Courts for the County of Essex.* (Office in the Court House, Salem.)

This Court is held at Salem, on the third Tuesday of April, and first Tuesday of November.

Superior Court.

Charles Allen, Worcester, *Chief Justice,* Salary, $3,700 ; Julius Rockwell, Pittsfield ; Otis P. Lord, Salem ; Marcus Morton, Jr., Andover ; Ezra Wilkinson, Dedham ; Henry Vose, Boston ; Seth Ames, Boston ; Thomas Russell, Boston ; John P. Putnam, Boston ; Lincoln F. Brigham, Boston, *Associate Justices,* $3,500.

This Court is held for civil business, at Salem, on the first Monday of June and December ; at Newburyport, on the first Monday of September ; at Lawrence, on the first Monday of March ; and for criminal business, at Salem, on the fourth Monday of January ; at Newburyport, on the second Monday of May ; and at Lawrence, on the second Monday of October.

A. A. Abbott, of South Danvers, *District Attorney for Essex County.*

Court of Probate and Insolvency for Essex County.

George F. Choate, of Salem, *Judge.*
A. C. Goodell, Salem, *Register.*
James Ropes, Salem, *Assistant Register.*
The records are kept at the office of the Register in the Granite Court House, in Salem.

The Probate Court sits as follows : —
Salem, first Tuesday in every month. Ipswich, third Tuesday in March and September. Newburyport, third Tuesday in January, February, April, June, July, October, and Dec.; Gloucester, second Tuesday in April and Oct.; Haverhill, third Tuesday in May and November; Lawrence second. Tuesday in January, February, March, June, September, November, and December.

The Court of Insolvency sits in the Insolvency Court room, in the Granite Court House in Salem, on the second and fourth Mondays of every month ; in Lawrence and Newburyport on the same days on which the Probate Court is held in those cities respectively.

County Commissioners. — Abram D. Wait, Ipswich, *Chairman.* James Kimball, Salem ; J: B. Swett, Haverhill.

Special Commissioners. — Moses T. Whittier, Nathaniel Rowley, N. H. Griffith of Groveland.

Clerk of County Commissioners. — Asahel Huntington, Salem.
Their meetings are held as follows : — At Ipswich, on the second Tuesday of April ; Salem, second Tuesday of July ; Newburyport, second Tuesday of October ; Lawrence, last Tuesday in August ; and on the fourth Tuesday of December, at Salem, Ipswich, or Newburyport, as may be determined at the preceding meeting.

County Treasurer. — A. W. Dodge, Hamilton. Office, Court House, Salem.

Register of Deeds. — Ephraim Brown, Salem. Office, Court House, Salem.

Sheriff of Essex County. — Horatio G. Herrick, of Lawrence.

Deputy Sheriffs. — John Rowell, Amesbury, W. F. M. Huntington, Amesbury ; E. Kendall Jenkins, Andover ; Charles H. Adams, Danvers ; Ezra Perkins, Essex ; Otis Thompson. Geo. W. Boynton, Georgetown ; Geo. Lane, Gloucester ; Phineas E. Davis. Haverhill, Yorick G. Hurd ; Joseph Spiller, Ipswich ; Alanson Briggs, James M. Currier, Lawrence ; Charles Merritt, Lynn ; Charles E. Goss, Methuen ; John Akerman, James W. Cheney, Newburyport ; Daniel Potter, John D. Cross, Salem ; John Rowell, Salisbury ; Stephen Upton, South Danvers.

John D. Cross, *Jail Keeper in Salem.*
John Akerman, *Jail keeper in Newburyport.*
Yorick G. Hurd, *Keeper of House of Correction in Ipswich.*
Horatio G. Herrick, *Keeper of Jail and House of Correction in Lawrence.*
Coroner in Salem. — Eben N. Walton.

Masters in Chancery for Essex County. — George F. Choate, D. E. Safford- [see Business Directory, page 181] Jonathan C. Perkins, 243½ Essex st. Salem ; N. W. Harmon, Lawrence.

Notaries Public in Salem. — Joseph Cloutman, William C. Endicott, James A. Gillis, Micajah B. Mansfield Ephraim F. Miller, J. B. F. Osgood, David Roberts, Thomas M. Stimpson, Jona. F. Worcester, Joseph G. Waters, S. P. Webb, Stephen G. Wheatland.

Commissioners for other States. — J. B. F. Osgood, for Iowa and New York. William C. Endicott, for Michigan. J. W. Perry, for Maine. David Roberts, for Maine, Rhode Island, and Louisiana. R. S. Rantoul, for Illinois, Iowa, New York, New Hampshire, Pennsylvania, and Ohio. S. P. Webb, for California, Illinois, Pennsylvania, Maine, Indiana, New York, Iowa, New Hampshire. Andrew B. Almon, Province of New Brunswick.

Commissioners to Qualify Civil Officers. — John Chapman, Asahel Huntington, Geo. R. Lord, Charles Kimball, Joseph B. F. Osgood, George Wheatland, Henry Whipple.

Justices throughout the Commonwealth. — Alfred A. Abbott, Albert G. Browne, John Chapman, George F. Choate, Caleb Foote, Asahel Huntington, Chas. Kimball, Otis P. Lord, Wm. D. Northend, Henry K. Oliver, J. B. F. Osgood, Jonathan C. Perkins, Stephen H. Phillips.

Justices of the Peace and Quorum. — Sam'l P. Andrews, Benj. F. Browne, Joseph S. Cabot, George H. Devereux, Stephen B. Ives, Jr., James Kimball, Nathan'l J. Lord, Ephraim F. Miller, Joseph B. F. Osgood, David Roberts, Augustus D. Rogers, Chas. W. Upham, Joseph G. Waters, Stephen P. Webb, George Wheatland, Henry Whipple.

Justices of the Peace. — Nathaniel K. Allen, Andrew B. Almon, Wm. Archer, Jr., Eleazer Austin, Sidney C. Bancroft, Geo. F. Brown, Ephraim Brown, J. Vincent Browne, John T. Burnham, Samuel B. Buttrick, John Carlton, Oliver Carlton, George F. Cheever, William S. Cleveland, Jos. Cloutman, Henry Cogswell, William Cogswell, Humphrey Cook, Francis Cox, John D. Cross, George R. Curwen, Wm. H. Dalrymple, Joseph A. Dalton, Henry Derby, John H. Derby, Humphrey Devereux, John F. Devereux, John Dwyer, John D. Eaton, William C. Endicott, John G. Felt, Daniel P. Fitz, Geo. F. Flint, Wm. H. Foster, Edw. F. W. Gale, Chas. B. Fowler, James A. Gillis, A. C. Goodell, Jr., Benjamin A. Gray, Henry B. Groves, Mark Haskell, Wm. P. Haywood, Moses Hill, Thorndike D. Hodges, Nath'l J. Holden, John Jewett, Thos. H. Johnson, Charles A. Kimball, David B. Kimball, John G. King, Edward H. Knight, Joseph S. Leavitt, Solomon Lincoln, Jr., Geo. R. Lord, George B. Loring, William Mack, Samuel Mackintire, William Maynes, James McGeary, John H. Nichols, Thos. Nichols, Jr., William Northey, Charles S. Osgood, Robert Osgood, Jeremiah Page, John Brooks Parker, William B. Parker, Ira J. Patch, Edward H. Payson, Francis Peabody, George Peabody, Robert Peele, Aaron Perkins, Dan'l Perkins, Jonathan Perley, Jairus W. Perry, Willard P. Phillips, Geo. D. Phippen, Chas. H. Price, Daniel Potter, Chas. A. Putnam, David Putnam, Robert S. Rantoul, Chas. M. Richardson, Joseph J. Rider, Stratton W. Robertson, James Ropes, D. E. Safford, Charles Sewall, James Shatswell, George H. Smith, Henry B. Smith, James C. Stimpson, Thomas M. Stimpson, Augustus Story, Gilbert L. Streeter, Charles E. Symonds, Nathaniel D. Symonds, Nath'l G. Symonds, J. Hardy Towne, William P. Upham, George Upton, Henry Upton, Abbott Walker, Eben N. Walton, Wm. D. Waters, Benjamin Webb, Nathaniel Weston, Henry Wheatland, Stephen G. Wheatland, John Whipple, Henry L. Williams, Jonathan F. Worcester, Isaac Wyman.

ALFRED A. ABBOTT,

ATTORNEY AND COUNSELLOR AT LAW,

And District Attorney for the Eastern District of Mass.

NO. 24 WASHINGTON ST.,

SALEM.

N. PEIRCE,
STOCK AND LOAN OFFICE,

— DEALER IN —

GOLD AND SILVER,

— AND —

UNITED STATES, STATE, AND CITY BONDS,

161 ESSEX STREET,

East India Marine }
Society Building. }

SALEM, MASS.

HENRY F. SKERRY,

— DEALER IN —

Watches, Clocks,

JEWELRY;

SILVER AND PLATED WARE, SPECTACLES,

FANCY GOODS,

Canton and Japanese Ware,

HAIR WORK,

BASKETS, TOYS, AND GAMES,

CHILDREN'S CARRIAGES, IN EVERY STYLE,

Watches, Jewelry, and Fancy Goods neatly repaired at

180 ESSEX STREET, - - - - - - - SALEM.

SOUTH DANVERS DIRECTORY.

The manufacturing and commercial business of South Danvers is again published in connection with the Salem Directory, in order to make the work as useful as possible. Grateful for previous patronage, the publishers hope the present edition will meet the wishes of all who may have occasion to use the work.

Location of Streets in South Danvers.

Aborn, from Washington to Boston, Salem
Andover, from Wilson's Corner to Felton's Corner
Central, from the square to Wilson's Corner
County, from Lynn to Lynnfield
Chestnut, from Lowell to Franklin
Elm, from Central to Wallis
English, from Walnut to Tremont
Foster, from the square to Washington
Franklin, from Foster to Lowell
Fulton, from Walnut to Tremont
Grove, from Main to Harmony Grove
Hardy from Central to Wallis
Harris, from Walnut to Tremont
High, from Walnut to Tremont
Holton, from Main to Aborn
Lowell, from the square, N. W. to Jonathan King's house
Liberty, from Wilson's Corner towards Danvers Port
Lynn, from Tapley's Brook to Lynn
Lynnfield, from Tapley's Brook to Lynnfield
Main, from the square to Salem
Mason, from Washington to Foster
Mill from the square to Wallis
Oak, from Foster to Washington
Park, from Main to Spring
Pleasant, from Washington to Holton
Pierpont, from Main to Aborn
Sewell, from Washington to Pierpont
Spring, from Foster to Park
Summer, from Park to Foster
Sutton, from Aborn, S. towards Swampscott
Tremont, from Central to Salem
Washington, from the Monument, Main Street, to Tapley's Brook
Wallis, from Main to Tremont
Walnut, from Wallis to Grove

TOWN OFFICERS . . . . . 1865.

SELECTMEN AND ASSESSORS — Joseph Poor, Dana Woodbury, George F. Sanger.

TOWN CLERK — Nathan H. Poor.

TREASURER — Francis Baker.

COLLECTOR — William Wolcott.

OVERSEERS OF THE POOR — Wingate Merrill, James P. King, Alphens W. Bancroft.

FENCE VIEWERS — Joseph Brown, Augustus H. Sanger, William H. Little, Abraham C. Osborn, Samuel Swett.

SURVEYORS OF LUMBER — Benjamin M. Hills, Mayhew S. Clark, Jas. B. Foster.

FIELD DRIVERS — Horatio Bodge, John Bagley, James B. Newhall, Leonard Cross, Daniel B. Southwick, Andrew Curtis, Enoch Bryant, jr. David W. Osborn, Mark M. Merrow, Hezekiah D. Twiss.

CONSTABLES — Moses A. Shackley, D. N. Stoddard, Samuel S. Parsons, Bowman Viles, William S. Osborn, Stephen Upton, D. S. Littlefield, Jas. B. Newhall, William H. Pingree, John Perkins, Samuel L. Abbott, Robert B. Bancroft.

TRUANT OFFICERS — Moses A. Shackley, Aaron F. Clark, William H. Little, William S. Osborn.

SURVEYORS OF HIGHWAYS — Jonathan E. Osborn, Philip L. Osborn, Joseph S. Hodgkins.

POUNDKEEPERS — John Bagley, Benjamin Taylor, Charles H. Richardson.

BOARD OF HEALTH — Alonzo P. Phillips, Dr. S. F. Bachelder, William Wolcott, Moses A. Shackley, Joseph Poor.

SCHOOL COMMITTEE — Amos Merrill, William M. Barbour, for three years; Fitch Poole, for two years; Thomas M. Stimpson, Francis Marsh, for 1 year.

ENGINEERS OF FIRE DEPARTMENT — William H. Little, D. S. Littlefield, James E. T. Bartlett, Gordon H. Wallis, Eleazer P. Barrett.

WEIGHER OF HAY AND COAL — Franklin Walker.

SEALER OF WEIGHTS AND MEASURES — Thomas Trask.

MEASURERS OF WOOD AND BARK — James B. Newhall, David Marston, William S. Osborn, Samuel Welch, Robert Morrill, James B. Foster.

LIQUOR AGENT — Thomas Trask.

BANKS.

SOUTH DANVERS NATIONAL BANK.

Main Street. Capital, $150,000. Par value Shares, 100.

Ebenezer Sutton, *President*; G. A. Osborn, *Cashier*; W. M. Jacobs, E. T. Osborn, A. A. Abbott, J. B. Elliot, Jno. King, Joseph Osgood, *Directors*.

Discount days, Tuesdays and Fridays. Bank hours from 9, A. M., to 12, M., and from 2 to 3, P. M.

WARREN NATIONAL BANK.

No. 11 Main Street. Capital, $250,000. Par value of Shares, $100.

Lewis Allen, *President*; Francis Baker, *Cashier*; Stephen Blaney, Benj. Wheeler, Rufus H. Brown, Franklin Osborne, George Osborne, Elijah W. Upton, C. Warren Osborne, Henry A. Hardy, *Directors.*

Discount days, Mondays and Thursdays. Bank hours, 9 to 12, A. M., 2 to 3, P. M.

WARREN FIVE CENTS SAVINGS BANK.

Warren Bank Rooms.

Incorporated, April, 27, 1854.

Deposits received from five cents to $1000.

George Osborne, *President*; Francis Baker, *Treasurer*.

DANVERS MUTUAL FIRE INSURANCE COMPANY.

Office at Danvers Bank. Annual Meeting 1st Monday in Oct.

Henry Cook, *President*; Benjamin Wheeler, George Osborne, Joseph Osgood, Henry Poor, John Whitney, John Safford, N. P. C. Patterson, W. M. Jacobs, *Directors*; G. A. Osborne, *Secretary*.

CHURCHES.

UNITARIAN.

D. H. Montgomery, *Pastor*.

FIRST CONGREGATIONAL.

William M. Barber, *Pastor*. George A. Osborne, *Clerk*.

BAPTIST.

N. M. Williams, *Pastor*. Edward Wilson, *Clerk*.

METHODIST.

S. B. Sweetser, *Pastor*.

UNIVERSALIST.

(Vacant), *Pastor*. Amos Merrill, *Clerk*.

POST OFFICE

10 Allen's Building.

Daniel Woodbury, *Postmaster*. Albert B. Woodbury, *Clerk*.

MASONIC.

JORDAN LODGE.

Chartered, 1808. Meetings Wednesday on, or preceding, full moon.

A. L. Pierson, *W. M.* Daniel P. Grosvenor, jr., *S. W.* Levi Preston, jr., *J. W.* B. F. Southwick, *S. D.* C. S. Nutter, *J. D.* N. P. C. Patterson, *Treasurer.* Albert B. Woodbury, *Secretary.* Rev. O. S. Butler, *Chaplain.* Joseph N. Burbeck, *S. S.* Daniel C. Brown, *J. S.* John W. Stevens, *Marshal.* David Potter, *Tyler.*

Nicholas Lodge of Good Templars, No. 34,

Sutton Hall, Main Street.

Joseph W. Merrill, *Secretary*.

SOUTH DANVERS
BUSINESS DIRECTORY.

Apothecaries.

Grosvenor D. P. jr. 88 Main
Meacom George E., 26 Main
Sweetser Thomas A. 87 Main, n. Park

Auctioneer.

TRASK THOMAS, 50 Main [see business card page 285]

Bakers.

Hathaway John, rear Main
Pratt Leonard, 162 Main
Stimpson Thomas, rear 50 Lowell

Bark Mills.

Hardy Isaac, Hardy, near Wallace
Jacobs J. Foster
Little William H., Foster
Lord J. A., Hardy, near Wallace

Blacksmiths.

Annable Nathaniel, 164 Main
Dodge C. H. 48 Central
Dole Wm. T. rear 11 Washington
Jones A. W. Wallace, near Hardy (edge tools)
Jones Thomas J. 82 Elm (edge tools and tanners' shovels)
Pike & Whipple, Andover, n. line
Smith Wm. rear Lowell depot

Bleachery and Dye Works.

Danvers Bleaching Co. Jonas Reed, supt. rear Foster, n. Washington

Booksellers.

Brooks D. B. & Bro. S. Danvers sq.

Boots and Shoes.

Dealers.

Bishop Benj. Grove, near Walnut
Colby Harris, Main, corner Foster
RADDIN ALONZO, 9 Main [see adv. dept p. 285.]
Trask Thos. S. 52 Main
Walton Wm. J. 94 Main

Makers.

Meacom E. between Depot of L. & E. R. R.
Walker Franklin, 88 Central

Manufacturers.

Dane Francis & Co. Foster, c. Lowell
Farwell C. C. & Co. Lowell, opposite Chestnut
Fuller Edward, rear 76 Main
Hardy & Osborn (shoes), Lowell, opp. Chestnut
Phillips A. P. & Son, 6 Main
Raddin Amos K. Lynnfield road
White & Fisk, Lowell, cor. Chestnut

Stiffenings.

Goldthwalt E. P. 159 Main
Flint H. & Co. rear S. Danvers sq.
Flint E. S. Mill, near Main (heels)
Osborn Jonathan E. Spring
PERKINS & MORRILL, Central, n. Lowell depot [see business card page 283]

Stitching.

Gallop D. B. 96 Main
Littlefield D. S. Lowell, opp. Chestnut
Pope O. E. Lowell, cor. Foster
Pray W. L. Lowell, opp. Chestnut
Trask & Knowlton, Lowell, opposite Chestnut

Box Makers.

Clark A. F. rear Main, near Grove

Butchers.

Cook James, Washington
Emerson Robert, Lowell (wholesale)
Sawyer Thomas H. Lowell
Thomas C. A. 21 Main
Thomas J. B. Oak (wholesale)
Tilton C. D. rear Lowell
Ward A. Elm
Ward A. A. Central
Wheeler Benj. S. Mason

Carpenters.

Beckett J. Sewell
Carr T. W. 52 Holton
CLARK & GIDDINGS, Wallace, n. Essex depot [see adv. dept. p. 285]
Folsom Charles, 74 Central
Grant John S. 54 Holten
Hills Benj. M. 88 Central
Parsons Samuel S. 54 Holten
Spalding Levi, 54 Holten

Carriage Builders.

Brine Chas. W. Foster
Dole William T. 11 Washington

Clothing and Furnishing Goods.

Bott S. R. 43 Main
Trask Thomas S. 52 Main

Coal and Wood.

Potter, Batchelder & Co. 6 Allen's building, and Danversport

Coffin Warerooms.

BUFFUM CHARLES S. Central, n. depot [see business card page 41 in Salem Directory)

Confectioner.

PEPPER GEO. W. 4 Elm. c. Central (manuf.) [see adv. dept. p. 282]

Cork Soles.

Peirce George C. 18 Aborn

Counsellors.

Perkins Benj. O. 10 Allen's building
Proctor John W. 9 Washington
Wiley H. O. 10 Allen's building

Crockery, Glass, and China Ware.

PEABODY GEORGE H. & CO. 15 Lowell [see business card page 286]

Curriers.

[See Tanners and Curriers.]

Dentists.

Crawford Aaron S. 4 Main

Dressmaker.

Brown L. Mrs. 34 Main

Expresses.

Gould's (Danvers), Foster, cor. Lowell
Grout & Monroe's (Boston), Freight depot, So. Danvers square
Littlefield's (So. D. and Salem), Post Office
Lummus (Wenham), Foster, corner Lowell
Townsend D. H. 45 Main

Fancy Goods and Trimmings.

Hyde Mary J. Mrs. 36 Main
Lord Mary, 58 Main

Fish.

Johnson B. F. Allen's building

Flour and Grain.

Batchelder W. O. 138 Main
Moulton John G. Central, r. L. R. R.
OSBORN HENRY M. 121 Central [see adv. dept. page 233]
PEABODY GEO. H. & Co. 15 Lowell [see business card, page 286]

Fruit and Confectionery.

Flint E. S. South Danvers square

Roche E. E. South Danvers square
Wilkinson R. W. 18 Main

Fruit and Vegetables.

Flint Eben S. 2 Main
Wilkinson Robert W. 18 Main

Furnishing Goods.

Trask Thomas S. 52 Main

Furniture.

Trask T. (spring bed bottom), 50 Main

Glue Manufacturers.

BROWN WM. H. r. Old Boston Road [see bus. card front colored, page
Essex Glue Co. (Upton & Walker), rear Foster
Sanger A. H. Lowell
Upton George, Washington

Grocers.

Arnold & Hutchinson, 1 Lowell, South Danvers st.
Batchelder W. O. 188 Main
Flint E. S. 2 Main
Howard Eben S. 81 Main
Humphrey B. B. 90 Washington
Mutual Union Store, Edw'd Kavanagh, agent, 76 Main
Newman & Symonds, Lowell, opposite Congregational Church
OSBORN H. M. 121 Central [see adv. dept. p. 288]
PEABODY GEO. H. & Co. 15 Lowell [see business card, page 286]
Stone Daniel jr. Old Boston Road, cor. Lynnfield Road

Hairdresser.

Heylingberg J. J. 26 Main

Harness Makers.

Cheever Samuel, 71 Central
Davis Charles, 11 Washington [depot
Simonds Edward, r. Central, n. Lowell

Hotels.

SIMONDS W. So. Danvers sq. [see adv. dept. p. 282]

Insurance Agent.

Poole Fitch, 10 Allen's building

Kerosene Oil and Lamps.

PEABODY GEO. H. & Co. 15 Lowell [see business card, page 286]

Last Manufacturers.

Brown & Stanley, Spring

Lightning Conductors.

Copper.

Trask Thomas, 46 Main

Lumber.

Clark A. F. rear Main, near Grove

Masons.

Bancroft Alpheus, 79 Washington
Manning John, Lowell
Trask Samuel, rear Lowell depot
Goodridge Zachariah, Mason
Gray Andrew W. Mason
Thurston Miller

Milk Dealers.

Linnehan John, Foster
Walker Wm. F. Main

Milliners.

Buxton Abby, 95 Main
Hyde M. J. Mrs. 36 Main

Millwrights.

Borner Caleb P. 7. Summer
Friend John P. Pleasant
Perkins James, 42 Washington
Whitney John, 16 Chestnut

Morocco Manufacturers.

Goodridge J. L. rear Foster
Clark & Co. 148 Main (bindings)
Egan & Nowell,. Walnut
Farrell John F. rear Essex R. R.
Hammond J. H. rear 102 Washington
Jacobs W. M. & Son, 148 Main (linings)
Peirce David Wallace, near Main
Pemberton F. K. & Son, 10 Central
Poole Joshua H. Pierpont
Roberts David, Walnut
Winchester & Blaney, rear Walnut
Woodbury Daniel, rear Walnut

News Room.

Exchange News Room, 11 Main

Oyster Saloon.

Merrill George, 7 Central

Painters.

BLANEY JOHN C. r. Lowell depot, in
Crowningshield building [see adv.
dept. page 234]
BLANEY WM. 164 Main, cor. Grove
(see adv. dept. page 234)
Price Edward, 84 Centre
WHIDDEN HENRY L. Cent'l, opp.
Cong. Church [see adv. dept. p. 234]

Paper Hangings.

BLANEY WM. 164 Main [see adv.
dept. p. 234]
WHIDDEN HENRY L., Cent'l, opp.
Cong. Church [see adv. dept. p. 234]

Periodicals, &c.

Wilkinson Robert W. 18 Main

Photographers.

Smith C. A. & J. W. 186 Main

Physicians.

Haley Geo. W. Union Bank building
Kittredge Floyer G. 54 Main
Osborn George, 19 Main
Osgood Joseph, Main, cor. Park

Potteries.

Reed J. W. 124 Central

Print Works.

Craig Print Works, James Craig, So.
Reading Road, near B. R. crossing

Printer.

HOWARD CHARLES D. Sutton
block, " The Wizard " [see adv. dept.
page 236]

Produce.

Flint E. S. 2 Main
Perkins P. D. Lowell (butter & eggs)

Provisions.

Batchelder W. O. 188 Main
Butman J. M. Lowell, S. Danvers sq.
FAIRFIELD JOSEPH, 5 Main, cor.
Foster [see adv. dept. p. 283]
Patterson N. P. C. 109 Main
PEABODY GEO. H. & Co. 15 Lowell
[see business card, p. 286]
Thomas C. A. 21 Main

Public Houses.

Naumkeag House, Wm. Southwick,
Wash. cor. High street court
SIMONDS HOTEL, Washington Simonds, So. Danvers sq. [see adv.
dept. p. 282]

Pumpmakers.

Peabody Stephen, Cent'l, n. school ho.

Sash, Doors, & Blinds.

BLANEY WILLIAM 164 Main [see
adv. dept. p. 234]

Sheepskin Mats.

Pierce George C. 18 Aborn

Soap and Candle Manufs.

BURBECK JOHN C. Grove, n. Main
[see adv. dept. p. 284]
Hildreth Paul, 142 Main
Winchester P. L. Grove, n. Main

Stables.

SIMONDS CHARLES S. South Danvers sq. [see adv. dept. p. 282]

Steam Sawing Planing.

Clark A. F. rear Main, near Grove

Stone Cutters.

Brown Samuel jr. n. Lynnfield road
Galencia Dan'l S. Old Boston road, n. Lynnfield Road
Larrabee Hersey, Old Boston road, n. Lynnfield Road
Newhall Henry H. Old Boston road, n. Lynnfield Road
Putnam David, O. B. road, n. Lynnfield Road
Shaw William, O. B. road, n. Lynnfield road

Stoves and Tin Ware.

Whitten James O. Lowell, opp. Chest.

Tanners and Curriers.

Adams O. F. Foster (currier) .
Brooks & Messer, Wallace, n. Walnut (curriers)
Cook Merritt, Foster (currier)
Elliot L. W. Foster
Fernald Luther & Co. Foster (currier)
Frost John, rear Main
Giddings Joshua, Spring (currier)
Hardy Isaac jr. Hardy, n. Wallace
Harris Samuel, r. Main, n. Wallace
Jacobs Joseph, Foster (tanner & miller)
Jacobs Joseph jr. Central, cor. Hardy (currier)
Kimball Obadiah, Mason
Little William H. Foster
Lord J. A. Hardy, n. Wallace (currier)
Lord W. N. Foster, cor. Spring
Mahone & Relihan, Wallace, corner Walnut
Munroe Isaac, Lowell
Nelson & Merrill, Foster
Osborn Calvin P. r. Washington
Osborn C. W. Lowell
Osborn D. W. Walnut, n. Grove
Osborn Franklin jr. & Co. Foster

Osborn Miles, & Co. Lowell
Pierce William, Foster
Pinder & Brown, Walnut, r. Main
Poor Henry C. 86 Central
Poor Joseph, Hardy
Porter Andrew, Hardy (currier)
Proctor Abel, r. Main, n. Wallace
Richardson & Coolidge, rear Foster (curriers)
Smith R. Foster
Southwark S. A. Grove, n. Main
Stevens & Bacon, Wallace, c. Walnut (curriers)
Stevens John V. Central, n. Hardy
Symonds R. S. D. Spring (currier)
Symonds Samuel jr. 150 Main
Torr Andrew, Foster
Upton Franklin & Co. Foster
Wheeler A. F. Foster (currier)
Wilson Warren, Foster
Woodbury Dana, Wallace, cor. Upton (currier)

Tanners' Shovels.

Jones Thomas J. Elm, c. Wallace

Undertakers.

BUFFUM CHARLES S. Central, rear depot [see business card, p. 41 Salem Directory!

Watchmaker and Jeweller.

Stevens Benjamin F. 16 Main

Wheelwrights.

Berry William, 46 Central
Dole Wm. T. rear 11 Washington
Pike & Whipple, Andover, n. line

Wool Dealers and Pullers.

Blaney Stephen, Foster
Sutton William jr. Pierpont
Tufts Joseph W. Foster, c. Franklin

PERKINS & MORRILL,

Manufacturers of

Boot & Shoe Stiffenings, Inner Soles,

HALF SOLES, HEEL STOCK, Etc.

CENTRAL STREET,

NEAR LOWELL DEPOT.

ALONZO RADDIN,

Manufacturer and Retailer of

BOOTS & SHOES,

No. 9

Warren Bank Build'g,

SOUTH DANVERS.

Repairing neatly executed

HENRY M. OSBORN,

WEST INDIA GOODS

AND

GROCERIES.

ALSO,

FLOUR AND GRAIN OF ALL KINDS.

121 Central Street, --- SOUTH DANVERS.

☞ Goods delivered in any part of the town free of expense.

JOSEPH FAIRFIELD,

MEAT MARKET,

AND

PROVISION DEALER.

Constantly on hand the best variety of Meat and Vegetables that the market affords.

No. 5 MAIN STREET,

SOUTH DANVERS, MASS.

I very respecifully take this method of informing the citizens of Salem, that, having purchased a

BUTTON-HOLE MACHINE

of the UNION BUTTON-HOLE MACHINE CO., and secured the services of an experienced operator, who will devote her whole attention to this branch of business, I am ready to receive and make all the BUTTON-HOLES in garments that the citizens will send to me, at the low price of three cents per Button-Hole.

This is the *only* Machine sewing a Button-Hole with the same stitch as hand work; introducing the "bar" or cord so essential to make firm and substantial work, in precisely the same manner as always found necessary in Button-Holes made by hand.

The stitch is formed with two threads instead of one, thereby imparting *double* strength and durability over hand work; at the same time the materials may be closely matched if desired by two shades or colors of silk.

Button-Hole Machines heretofore invented have failed from the want of some of the important features introduced in this Machine, and they are therefore found impracticable. I have been to considerable expense in getting this machine; and, by giving particular attention to the work sent me, I hope to merit the confidence and patronage of a liberal public, promising that their orders shall be promptly attended to.

I wish also to extend an invitation to the ladies and gentlemen who would like to see the Machine in operation to call at rear of

No. 158 ESSEX STREET.

Very respectfully, yours,   **SAMUEL MOORE.**

Any person wishing to purchase a machine can receive all necessary information by applying as above

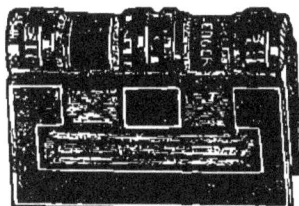

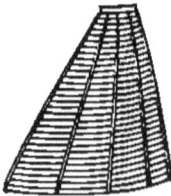

J. B. & S. D. SHEPARD,

DEALERS IN

DRY GOODS,

CLOAKS, SHAWLS, &c.

No. 173 ESSEX ST., SALEM.

WILLARD GOLDTHWAITE,

DEALER IN

Carpets and Upholstery Goods,

No. 151 ESSEX ST., SALEM.

☞ *UPHOLSTERY WORK DONE AT SHORT NOTICE.* ☜

SALEM DYE-HOUSE,

No. 7 Franklin Street, North Salem, Mass.

Ladies' and Gent's Garments, of all descriptions, dyed all colors, at short notice. Particular attention paid to dyeing articles of MOURNING. Bonnets and Hats bleached, colored, and pressed for Milliners, in the latest fashion. Gents' Clothing colored or cleansed without being ripped. Carpets, Rugs, Blankets, and Shawls cleansed, and colors much improved. ☞ All orders left with the Agents punctually attended to. Goods taken from and returned to any part of the city.

SAMUEL ROLES, Jr., Proprietor.

Agents for Receiving Goods: F. M. Ward, Pleasant St., Gloucester; M. D. Brackett, Swampscott; J. Bulfinch, Chestnut St., Lynn; B. Chase, Broad St., Lynn; W. T. Webster, 19 Exchange St., Lynn; J. W. Proctor, 76 Market St., Lynn; C. B. Holmes, 8 Market St., Lynn; Wm. Chase, 4 Taylor's Building, Lynn; A. E. Woodley, Broad St., Lynn; T. Evans & Co., Marblehead; J. L. Morse, Beverly; J. F. Clothey & Co., Ipswich; Perley & Currier, North Danvers; E. G. Collins, 3 Water St., Haverhill.

Office, 236 Essex St., Salem. . . . M. A. PORTER, Agent.

DRY GOODS.

A. J. ARCHER & CO.,

181 ESSEX STREET, SALEM.

WOOLLEN CLOTHS, of English, French, German, and American manufacture. A fine and large assortment constantly on hand. Also,

FOREIGN & AMERICAN DRESS GOODS.

Our stock is large, and we offer a choice selection in every branch of the business, well worth the attention of buyers.

M. A. PORTER,

Watch Spring Skirt Maker,

236 ESSEX STREET,

SALEM, MASS.

DEALER IN

BUTTONS, BRAIDS, THREAD STORE GOODS,

Hosiery, Gloves, Corsets,

HANDKERCHIEFS, SMALL WARES, &c.

JOSEPH CHISHOLM,

Manufacturer of

LINES, TWINE, CORDS,

ENGINE PACKING, WINDOW LINES, &c.

68 Mill St. (opp. Harbor St.) *Salem, Mass.*

WM. C. HENDERSON,

Manufacturer of

PLAIN & FANCY

PAPER BOXES,

Including Cartoons, Wedding Cake, &c.

150 ESSEX STREET,

BOWKER BLOCK,

SALEM, MASS.

HENDERSON & CO.,

Manufacturers of

INNER SOLES

AND

HEEL STIFFENINGS.

150 ESSEX ST.,

SALEM, MASS.

AARON T. LOW,

DEALER IN

BOOTS, SHOES,

AND

RUBBERS,

NO. 76 BOSTON STREET, SALEM.

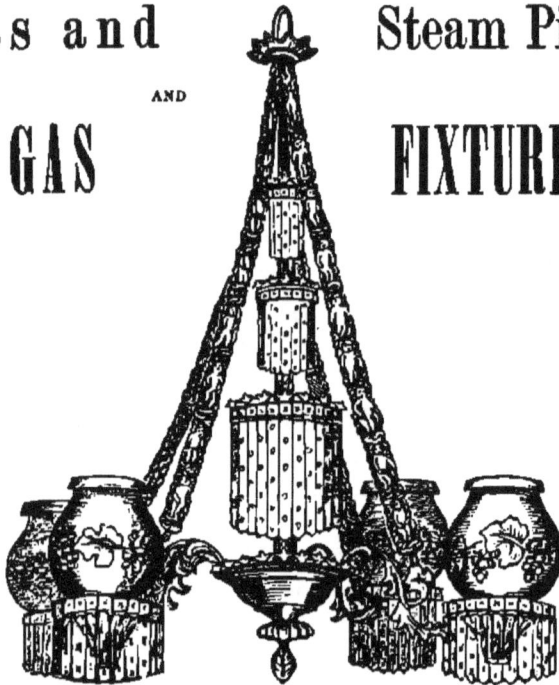

THOMAS A. ROBBINS',

LIVERY & SALE STABLES,

No. 161 ESSEX STREET,

(REAR EAST-INDIA MARINE MUSEUM.)

Mr. Robbins has recently fitted up the " Old Stand " formerly occu-
pied by E. L. Littlefield, Esq., rear 161 Essex Street, where he intends
keeping at Livery (in addition to the Boston-street Stable) as choice a
selection of

Horses, Buggies, Carryalls, & Carriages

Of every description as can be found in Essex County.

———◆———

ALSO

CARRIAGE, SLEIGH & HARNESS

REPOSITORY.

Mr. Robbins keeps constantly on hand all styles of Carriages, Sleighs,
and Harness, from the best manufactories in the country. Persons
desiring a " Livery Fit-out," in whole or in part, will find it to their
advantage to call as above before purchasing elsewhere.

S. C. & E. A. SIMONDS,

DEALERS IN

Crockery

AND

HARDWARE,

KEROSENE

Lamps & Lanterns,

PAINTS, OILS,

AND

WINDOW GLASS.

32 FRONT ST.,

LAWRENCE PLACE.

WM. P. GOODHUE,

Wholesale and Retail Dealer in

SHIP CHANDLERY,

SHIP AND FAMILY STORES,

LIME, CEMENT, AND PLASTER,

No. 44 Derby Street, Salem, Mass.

Freight obtained for Vessels, and Produce received on Commission.

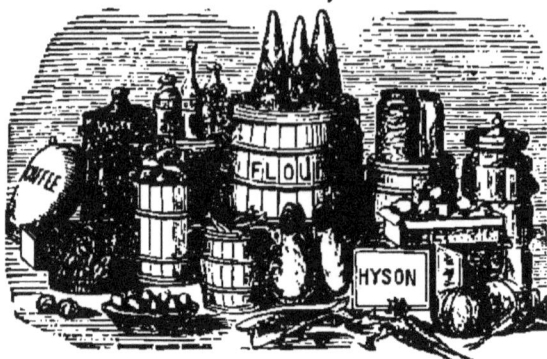

CHAMBERLAIN, HARRIS & CO.,

DEALERS IN

WEST-INDIA GOODS,

Choice Teas, Coffees, &c.

WHOLESALE & RETAIL.

No. 24 Front Street, Corner of Derby Square.

I. J. WEBBER,

CASH DEALER IN

BEST FAMILY GROCERIES,

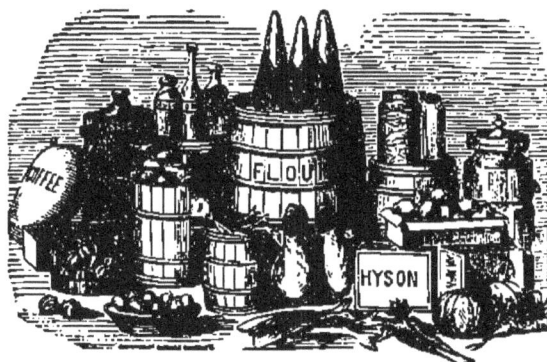

At Lowest Prices,

STORE, NO. 58 WASHINGTON STREET, SALEM.

PLEASE CALL AND EXAMINE.

S. W. ROBERTSON,

Manufacturer of and Dealer in

SOAP, CANDLES,

TALLOW, &c.,

Rear 44 Boston Street,

SALEM.

CHARLES H. COLLINS,
DEALER IN ALL KINDS OF

PICKLED, SMOKED,

AND

FRESH FISH,

Also Lobsters, Oysters, and Clams.

NO. 80 DERBY STREET, SALEM.

HENRY G. TUCKER,

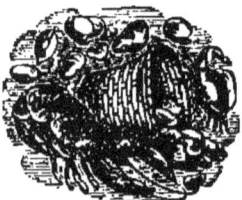

Wholesale and Retail Dealer

— IN —

LOBSTERS,

No. 4 Bridge Street,

NEAR BEVERLY BRIDGE, SALEM.

ALL ORDERS FILLED WITH PROMPTNESS.

Saws Re-Cut, Set, and Filed.

KNIVES, SCISSORS, AND OTHER CUTLERY,
Ground and put into the best order.

BROWN'S PATENT WINDOW SPRINGS,

Stove Shovels, Fish Turners, Skimmers, &c.,

CURRIERS' PLATES AND SCRAPERS,
Made and for sale by

S. S. WILLISTON,

NO. 60 CHARTER STREET . . . . SALEM.

MORRIS' RESTAURANT,

Nos. 18 and 20

DERBY SQUARE,

SALEM, MASS.

OYSTERS, CLAMS, STEAK, POULTRY,

GAME, FISH, &c.,

Served to order, at short notice.

PICKLED OYSTERS, LOBSTERS, AND CLAMS.

THE
SALEM REGISTER

WAS ESTABLISHED IN THE YEAR 1800,

AND IS PUBLISHED ON

MONDAYS AND THURSDAYS

AT

No. 193 ESSEX, COR. OF CENTRAL ST.,

BY

JOHN CHAPMAN and CHAS. W. PALFRAY.

Terms, $4.00 per year; $3.50 if paid in advance.

TERMS OF ADVERTISING.

Advertisements of more than half a square, $1.50 for three insertions, once a week, or in three papers in succession, at the option of the advertiser; 16¢ cts. for every additional insertion.

Advertisements not exceeding half a square, $1.00 for three insertions as above; 12½ cts. for every additional insertion.

Probate Notices of every kind, not exceeding a square, $1.50 for three insertions.

Sixteen lines of Nonpareil type are equal to a square.

When advertisements are ordered to be continued on the INSIDE, ten per cent. extra must be paid for each insertion.

6¼ cents a line must be paid for notices for meetings for political, civic, and religious purposes, notices of societies, cards of acknowledgment from individuals, companies, &c., for one insertion. All leaded notices, 8 cents per line.

The privilege of Annual Advertisers is limited to their own immediate business; and all advertisements for the benefit of other persons, as well as all legal advertisements, and advertisements of real estate, or auction sales, sent in by them, must be paid for at the usual rates.

☞ All advertisements intended for this paper must be marked on the margin of the copy the number of insertions desired, otherwise they will be published till ordered out, and charged accordingly.

*** No paper will be discontinued until all arrearages are paid, except at the option of the publishers; and any person wishing his paper discontinued must give notice thereof *at the expiration of the term, whether previous notice has been given or not.*

BOOK, JOB, AND FANCY

PRINTING

EXECUTED AT THE OFFICE OF THE

SALEM GAZETTE, AND ESSEX-COUNTY MERCURY,

In the best style, and on favorable terms.

The Salem Gazette,

Established Weekly, 1768; Semi-Weekly, 1796,

Is printed on TUESDAY and FRIDAY mornings, at $3.50 per year when paid in advance — $4 when not in advance. The length of time which it has been before the public, and the extensive circulation it has obtained for the larger part of a century, render it unnecessary here to enter into a formal exposition of its character. The intention is that it shall always contain the most important foreign and domestic intelligence, political, moral, and literary; original communications upon all subjects connected with the public welfare; a full and correct shipping list; business advertisements; and, in short, everything that is usually found and expected in a Family Newspaper.

   The large country circulation of the Gazette (including the Mercury, in which all new advertisements of the Gazette are published) renders it particularly valuable as a medium for the publication of Probate advertisements, sales of Real Estate, and other notices of interest to the farming population.

The Essex County Mercury,

OR WEEKLY SALEM GAZETTE,

ESTABLISHED A.D. 1832,

Is made up from the reading matter of the Salem Gazette, and is one of the largest and cheapest papers in New England. The subscription price is $2.00 a year, when paid in advance. The quantity of reading afforded is much greater than is usually found in a Newspaper; and, as it circulates extensively in all parts of the County of Essex, particular pains are taken to present all the local matters of the County. The Mercury is published every Wednesday morning; the price, when not paid in advance, is $2.50 per year, payable semi-annually.

No. 199 ESSEX STREET.

INDEX TO BOSTON ADVERTISEMENTS

IN

SALEM DIRECTORY.

FOSTER & ROBY,

AGENTS NEW-HAVEN COPPER CO.

Also Manufacturers and Dealers in every description of

SHIPS' FASTENINGS

AND TRIMMINGS,

COPPER, BRASS, COMPOSITION, AND LEAD WORK.

Copper, Composition, and Yellow-Metal Nails and Spikes of every variety. Copper, Composition, and Yellow-Metal Bolts and Clinch Rings. Sheet Copper, and Copper and Yellow-Metal Sheathing ; Copper, Composition, Yellow-Metal, Zinc, and Galvanized Iron Sheathing, and Slating Nails.

BELLS,

Pumps, Water-Closets, Sidelights, and Steering Apparatus for Vessels and Steamships ; Ship and Boat Trimmings of every description. Castings in Copper, Brass, Composition, German Silver, Zinc, and Lead.

Old metal bought and sold at the market rates for cash.

178 and 180 Commercial Street,

BOSTON.

HUNT, LYON & CO.,

MANUFACTURERS OF

Best Oak-Tanned Leather Belting.

DEALERS IN

Rubber Machine Belting, Steam Packing, Engine Hose,

And all other articles of Vulcanized India Rubber. Also constantly on hand,

LACE LEATHER, BELT RIVETS AND BURRS, BELT CEMENT, ETC.

26 Devonshire Street, Boston.

BILLIARD TABLE MANUFACTURER,

865 Washington Street, Boston,

BETWEEN DOVER AND CHAPMAN STS.

The undersigned manufactures Billiard Tables of various kinds of wood, with all the latest improvements, at the lowest prices that they can be obtained in the city or elsewhere. These tables are in use in this city, throughout the country, the British Provinces, East Indies, and California, and are well recommended wherever they are used.

Also Small Tables for Parlors, and Second-hand Tables. Tables taken down and set up, and repairing done at short notice. All the appurtenances belonging to the business constantly on hand.

H. HEIMS.

N. U. LYON,

GENERAL AGENT FOR

Davis's Inflammatory Extirpator,

THE BEST MEDICINE THAT EVER WAS KNOWN.

IT WILL CURE MORE DISEASES than any other medicine. During the first six years more than *Seven Hundred Thousand Bottles* were sold. I have cured more than *30,000* persons, out in the open air, of Toothache, Headache, Sprains, Sore Throat, Colds, Coughs, Dysentery, Diarrhœa, Kidney and Spinal Diseases, &c. Call or send for a circular that tells the truth. Also the only Agent for

SANFORD'S GREAT SPANISH REMEDY,

A medicine that has been used in private practice more than forty years, and never was known to fail of giving perfect satisfaction, when used according to directions.

ALSO MANUFACTURER OF

It polishes much easier, and is much cheaper to use.

It is free from all injurious matter.

Age never spoils it, and it is the best article of Blacking known.

N. U. LYON, Proprietor,

To whom all orders for the above should be addressed.

N. B.—CASTOR-OIL; GODFREY'S CORDIAL; PAREGORIC; TINCT. RHUBARB, &c., &c., *all of standard quality*, made and put up by

N. U. LYON,

No. 109 BAY STREET, (formerly Turnpike,

FALL RIVER, MASS.

Sold by GEO. C. GOODWIN & CO., 38 Hanover St., Boston.

CAMPBELL, WHITTIER & C?

MANUFACTURERS OF

STEAM ENGINES & MACHINERY.

WORKS CORNER ORANGE AND RUGGLES STS.

ROXBURY, MASS.

WILLARD P. PHILLIPS,

Forwarding and Commission Merchant,

AND DEALER IN

COALS,

AT WHOLESALE AND RETAIL.

RAILROAD FREIGHT STATION,

PHILLIPS' WHARF,

SALEM.

WILLIAM MILLS,

PLUMBER,

DEALER IN

Iron and Stone Ware, Drain

Pipe, and all kinds of

Plumbing Materials,

28 Devonshire Street,

BOSTON.

Estimates prepared and Contracts faithfully executed.

HUNT, LYON, & CO.,

(Established by N. Hunt in 1847,)

— MANUFACTURERS OF —

Best Oak Tanned Leather Belting.

— DEALERS IN —

Rubber Machine Belting, Steam Packing, Engine Hose,

And all other articles of Vulcanized India Rubber. Also constantly on hand

LACE LEATHER, BELT RIVETS AND BURRS, BELT CEMENT, ETC.

26 DEVONSHIRE ST., BOSTON.

LOMBARD & CO.,

NO. 14 LEWIS AND 9 T WHARVES,

IMPORTERS AND DEALERS IN THE BEST

Nova Scotia, English, and Scotch

GRINDSTONES,

For Farmers, Machinists, and Glass Cutters.

A LARGE ASSORTMENT CONSTANTLY ON HAND.